Triumph Tiger 800
Service and Repair Manual

by Matthew Coombs

Models covered (5752 - 272)

Tiger 800. 2010-on
Tiger 800XC. 2010-on
ABS versions included

© Haynes Publishing 2015

ABCDE
FGHIJ
KLMNO
PQRST

A book in the **Haynes Service and Repair Manual Series**

All rights reserved. No part of this book may be reproduced or transmitted in any form or by any means, electronic or mechanical, including photocopying, recording or by any information storage or retrieval system, without permission in writing from the copyright holder.

ISBN 978 0 85733 752 8

British Library Cataloguing in Publication Data
A catalogue record for this book is available from the British Library

Library of Congress Control Number 2014952987

Printed in the USA

Haynes Publishing
Sparkford, Yeovil, Somerset BA22 7JJ, England

Haynes North America, Inc
861 Lawrence Drive, Newbury Park, California 91320, USA

Haynes Publishing Nordiska AB
Box 1504, 751 45 Uppsala, Sweden

Printed using 33-lb Resolute Book 65 4.0 from Resolute Forest Products Calhoun, TN mill. Resolute is a member of World Wildlife Fund's Climate Savers programme committed to significantly reducing GHG emissions. This paper uses 50% less wood fibre than traditional offset. The Calhoun Mill is certified to the following sustainable forest management and chain of custody standards: SFI, PEFC and FSC Controlled Wood.

Contents

LIVING WITH YOUR TRIUMPH

Introduction

A Phoenix from the ashes	Page	0•4
Acknowledgements	Page	0•8
About this Manual	Page	0•8
Safety first!	Page	0•9
Bike spec	Page	0•10
Model development	Page	0•11
Identification numbers	Page	0•12
Buying spare parts	Page	0•12

Pre-ride checks

Engine oil level	Page	0•13
Suspension, steering and final drive	Page	0•13
Brake fluid levels	Page	0•14
Coolant level	Page	0•15
Tyres	Page	0•16
Legal and safety	Page	0•16

MAINTENANCE

Routine maintenance and servicing

Specifications	Page	1•2
Lubricants and fluids	Page	1•2
Maintenance schedule	Page	1•3
Component locations	Page	1•4
Maintenance procedures	Page	1•6

Contents

REPAIRS AND OVERHAUL

Engine, transmission and associated systems

Engine, clutch and transmission	Page	**2•1**
Cooling system	Page	**3•1**
Engine management system (fuel and ignition)	Page	**4•1**

Chassis components

Frame and suspension	Page	**5•1**
Brakes, wheels and final drive	Page	**6•1**
Bodywork	Page	**7•1**

Electrical system

Page **8•1**

Wiring diagrams

Page **8•22**

REFERENCE

Tools and Workshop Tips	Page	**REF•1**
Security	Page	**REF•20**
Lubricants and fluids	Page	**REF•23**
MOT Test Checks	Page	**REF•26**
Storage	Page	**REF•31**
Conversion Factors	Page	**REF•34**
Fault Finding	Page	**REF•35**
Technical Terms Explained	Page	**REF•47**

Index

Page **REF•51**

A Phoenix from the ashes

by Julian Ryder

Where is the most modern motorcycle factory in the World? Tokyo? Berlin? Turin, maybe? No, it's in Hinckley, Leicestershire. Unlikely as it may seem, the Triumph factory in the Midlands of England is a more advanced production facility than anything the mighty Japanese industry, German efficiency or Italian flair can boast. Since the marque was reborn in 1991, Triumph has grown into a big player on the world stage and is now the only volume manufacturer of automotive transport that can call itself truly British.

It's important to realise that the new Triumph company has very little to do with the company that was a giant on the world stage in the post-war years when British motorcycle makers dominated the global markets. It is true that new owner John Bloor bought the patents, manufacturing rights and, most importantly, trademarks when the old factory's assets were sold in 1983, but the products of the old and new companies bear no relation at all to one another. Apart, of course, from the name on the tanks. Bloor's research-and-development team started work in Collier Street, Coventry and in 1985 work started on the ten-acre green-field factory site, which was occupied for the first time the following year.

The reborn Triumphs

The R & D team soon dispensed with the old Meriden factory's project for a modern DOHC, eight-valve twin known within the factory as the Diana project (after Princess Di) but shown at the NEC International Bike Show in 1982 as the Phoenix. The world got to see the real new Triumphs for the first time at the Cologne Show in late 1990. The company was obviously anxious to distance itself from the old, leaky, unreliable image of the British motorcycle, but it was equally anxious not to engage in a head-on technology war with the big four Japanese factories. The watchword was 'proven technology', the new engines were in-line triples and housed in a universal steel chassis with a large-diameter tubular backbone. Seemingly contrary to the company's desire to distance itself from the past, the new bikes would all carry famous model names from Triumph's past.

But if Triumph's technology wasn't exactly path-breaking it was certainly very clever. The key concept was the modular design of the motor based around long and short-throw crankshafts in three and four-cylinder configurations. Every engine used the common 76 mm bore with either 55 or 65 mm throw cranks so that the short-stroke engine would be 750 cc in three-cylinder form and 1000 cc as a four. Put the long-stroke crank in and you get a 900 cc triple and a 1200 cc four. The first bike to hit the shops was the 1200 Trophy, a four-cylinder sports tourer which was immediately competitive in a very strong class. There was also a 900 cc, three-cylinder Trophy. The 750 and 1000 Daytonas used the short-stroke motor in three and four-cylinder forms in what were intended to be the sportsters of the range. The other two models, 750 and 900 cc three-cylinder Tridents, cashed in on the early-'90s fad for naked retro bikes that followed the world-wide success of the Kawasaki Zephyr.

The reborn Triumphs were received with acclaim from the motorcycle press – tinged with not a little surprise. They really were very good motorcycles, the big Trophy was a match for the Japanese opposition in a class full of very accomplished machinery. The fact it could live with a modern day classic like the Yamaha FJ1200 straight off the drawing board was a tribute to John Bloor's designers and production engineers. The bike was big, fast, heavy and quite high, but it worked and worked well. And it didn't leak oil or break down, it was obvious that whatever else people were going to say about Triumphs they weren't going to able to resurrect the old jokes about British bangers leaving puddles of lubricant under them. As the rest of the range arrived and tests of them got into print, the star of the show emerged; it was the long-stroke, three-cylinder, 900 cc motor. It didn't matter how it was dressed up, the big triple had that

The original 1200 Trophy

indefinable quality – character. It was the motor the Japanese would never have made, very torquey but with a hint of vibration that endears rather than annoys. Somewhere among the modern, water-cooled, multi-valve technology, the 900-triple had the genes of the old air-cooled OHV Triumph Tridents that appeared in 1969 and stayed in production until '75.

Model development

The range stayed basically unchanged until the Cologne Show of '92. Looking back at the first range it is now easy to see – hindsight again – that the identity of all the models was far too close. The sports tourer Trophy models were reckoned to be a little too sporting, the basic Tridents still had the handlebar and footrest positions of faired bikes. Triumph management later agreed that the first range evinced a certain lack of confidence; that was certainly not the case with the revamped 1993 range.

Visitors to the Cologne Show in September '92 agreed that the Triumphs were the stars, any lack of confidence there may have been two years earlier was completely gone. Any shyness the management may have felt about the Triumph name's past was shaken off as the new Tridents went retro style. Overall, the identities of the original bikes became more individual and more obviously separated; the Trophy models became more touring oriented, the Daytona more sporty looking and the Trident models more traditional. The factory even had the confidence to put small Union Flag emblems on the side panels of each model, no more apologising for the imagined shortcomings of British engineering. Despite this spreading of the range's appeal, all these bikes were still built on the original modular concept.

There was, however, an exception to this rule of uniformity in the shape of a brand new bike, the Tiger 900. This model was in the enduro/desert-racer style much favoured in Continental Europe but not at all popular at home in the UK. Here was a Triumph with a 19-inch front tyre, wire wheels and a lower power output than the other 900s. Both the chassis and engine parts were slightly different from the rest of the range. Judging their market as cleverly as ever, the factory held back another new model for the International Bike Show at the Birmingham NEC. This was the Daytona 1200, an out and out speed machine with a hidden political agenda. Its high-compression, 147 PS engine gave it brutal straight-line performance in much the same way as the big Kawasakis of the mid-'80s, and like them it wasn't too clever in the corners because of its weight and length. The bike was built as much to show that Triumph could do it as to sell in big numbers, it also had the secondary function of thumbing the corporate nose at the UK importers' gentlemen's agreement not to bring in bikes of over 125 PS.

The first Hinckley Tiger with 855cc engine

Next year's NEC show saw two more new Triumphs, both reworkings of what was now regarded as a modern classic, the 900 triple. The Speed Triple was a clever reincarnation of the British cafe racer style, complete with clip-on handlebars and rear-set footrests. The big three-cylinder engine in standard tune got an all-black finish with black chrome pipes and silencers for the appropriately mean look. Black wheel rims and new bodywork completed a superbly styled bike available with black or yellow bodywork, the Speed Triple was the star of the show, a bike with an attitude.

The other newcomer was a more radical project, the Daytona Super III. Externally the motor looked like the usual 900 cc three, but a lot of work by Cosworth Engineering was

The Thunderbird led the way to a range of Triumph retros

Introduction

hidden under the cases. The result was 115 PS as opposed to the standard 900 Daytona's 98 PS.

Triumphs in America

Triumph's next big step was into the US market, where the old company was so strong in the post-war years when the only competition was Harley-Davidson and where there is considerable affection for the marque. The name Triumph chose to spearhead this new challenge was Thunderbird, a trademark sourced in Native American mythology. This time the famous name adorned yet another version of the 900 triple but this time heavily restyled and in a retro package. Dummy cooling fins give it the look of an air-cooled motor, the logo was cast into the clutch cover, and there were soft edges and large expanses of polished alloy. Inside those restyled cases, the motor was retuned even more than the Tiger's for a very user-friendly dose of low-down punch and mid-range power. The cycle parts were given an equally radical redesign, although the retro style stopped short of giving the Thunderbird twin rear shock absorbers. But everything else, the shape of the tank, the chrome headlight and countless other details, harks back to the original Thunderbird and nothing does so as shamelessly as the 'mouth-organ' tank badge, a classic icon if ever there was one.

The first Thunderbird derivative, the Adventurer, appeared for 1996 with a different rear subframe and rear-end styling including a sissy bar and single seat. That same year, the short-stroke 750 cc motor bowed out of the range, but it went with a bang not a whimper not in a final batch of Tridents but in a limited-edition run of 750 Speed Triples. The bigger Speed Triple's motor was inserted in the Sprint and the result called the Sprint Sport. The reason for using up all those motors was the advent of the new range of fuel-injected and heavily revised three-cylinder engines that first powered the T509 Speed Triple and T595 Daytona of 1997.

Fuel Injection

The first fuel-injected Triumph, the Daytona T595, was a major milestone for the Factory. It represented a change of policy, the first time Triumph would venture to confront their opposition on the cutting edge of technology. In early 1997, the Honda FireBlade and Ducati 916 ruled. The T595 was able to play in the same ball park. Only on a race track could the Japanese and Italian machines be shown to be better. In the real world the T595 was at least as good a bike. The old long stroke of 65 mm was retained but everything else was new, it was a radical departure from the modular concept that had dominated production until now. You could see how the new motor was a lightened version of the old triple, but fuel injection was new and the frame was a radical departure from previous practice. Serpentine tubing ran from steering head to swingarm pivot and it was aluminium. Bodywork looked tasty too. Despite what Triumph had said about not taking on the Japanese back in 1991, the T595 came out of comparative tests with the 'Blade and 916 on equal terms. The new bike was also given the Speed Triple treatment and adorned with bug-eyed twin headlights in the fashionable 'streetfighter' style.

The trouble with the Supersports end of the market is that the goal posts keep moving, so Triumph hedged their bets by softening the 955i's nominal 128 PS to 108, housing it in a simpler twin-beam frame and calling the result the Sprint ST. This continuation of the original Sprint concept was one of the hits of 1999. As a sports tourer, the fuel-injected Sprint ST was right up there with Honda's classic class leader, the VFR. Some magazines even preferred the British bike. High praise. The Tiger got the fuel-injected 855 cc motor in '99. The result was a much more svelte machine than the original carburetted model, but Britain still refused to fall in love with the concept. Not that development of the carburetted bikes was neglected. Triumph got a Thunderbird derivative right in 1998 with the Thunderbird Sport.

Up to 1999 Triumph concentrated on big bikes but then they took another giant step towards the big time by taking on the Japanese in the most competitive market sector of them all, Supersports 600, with the TT600. For 2001 the most famous name of all was bought out of retirement: Bonneville. And it was an air-cooled twin! From a standing start in 1991, the Hinckley factory was competing in all the major motorcycle market sectors. Much bigger production volumes meant the original modular concept was no longer a necessity. By the dawn of the 21st Century Triumph had sold over 100,000 motorcycles.

Then the factory was struck by one of the biggest fires ever at a British industrial site. In March 2002 the production line, moulding shop and stores were destroyed and many other parts of the plant severely damaged. Just six months later the rebuilt factory was running at full capacity. The first new product out of the doors was the Daytona 600, a replacement for the TT600. Where the first Supersports 600 Triumph had failed to compete with the Japanese this one was good enough to win a TT in the hands of Kiwi Isle of Man hero Bruce Anstey.

With an eye on America Triumph then unleashed their most audacious bike yet: the Rocket III. (Whisper it, but Rocket III was actually a BSA model name back in the 1970s.) They call it a cruiser but behemoth would be a better description, it's the first production bike to boast a capacity of over two litres and the only thing on the roads that can make a Harley V-Rod look shy and retiring.

The twin cylinder Bonneville T100

The 2011 Tiger 800

In total contrast to the Rocket III, Triumph got serious about the supersports sector in 2006 with the 675cc Daytona triple. Use of the hallmark three-cylinder layout allowed the bike to race against 600cc fours in Supersport competition despite its capacity advantage. It has had success on the track at national level and has been far from disgraced in the World Supersport Championship. However, the Daytona has dominated its sector in the annual Masterbike test that brings journalists from all over the world to test the leading sports bikes from every manufacturer. It is by common consent one of the best middleweights on the market.

The twins first went from 790 to 865cc before getting fuel injection in 2008. The Thunderbird name came back (for the second time) in 2009 for a 1600cc twin as the range's Cruisers were aimed more and more at the American market. The Modern Classics, as Triumph call the Bonneville and its derivatives, cater more for the British and European traditions, with the Thruxton being a modern take on the classic café racer so beloved of the rockers of the 1960s.

Triumph use the label Urban Sports for the triples, but that phrase covers a range of applications. For 2007 Triumph's signature triple motor was stroked to up capacity to 1050cc and the engine powers Triumph's top-of-the-range trio: the Sprint ST, now with touring equipment as standard, is as good a sports tourer as you can buy; the Tiger, now with aluminium frame, is right up there with the GS BMW as an all-rounder/go-anywhere machine, and the Speed Triple is – well, it's the Speed Triple!

Big pussy cat

Most successes in motorcycle sales are the result of years of careful planning, observation of market trends, economic forces, legal restrictions, focus groups, and all the other tools of modern marketing. With one major exception, and that is the adventure bike. The boom in go-anywhere motorcycles can trace its origin to a TV series, specifically The Long Way Round first aired in 2004 in which Ewan McGregor and Charley Borman rode from London to New York via big chunks of Russia and Mongolia. It was a major success and all of a sudden you couldn't buy a GS BMW for love nor money.

In a market already out of love with sports bikes, the adventure bike was the answer for the rider looking for something out of the mainstream with a good dash of credibility. And one thing the big BMW wasn't lacking was presence or street cred. Every manufacturer hurried to produce what were now known as 'Adventure Bikes,' with varying degrees of off-road capability. They are now an essential part of any manufacturer's range.

Even before the LWR-induced boom, there was a niche market. Continental Europe was obsessed with the Paris-Dakar Rally in the early and mid 1980s and the first Yamaha Tenere,

Introduction

The 2012 Tiger 800 XC

Acknowledgements

Our thanks are due to Fowlers Motorcycles of Bristol who supplied the machine featured in the illustrations throughout this manual. We would also like to thank NGK Spark Plugs (UK) Ltd for supplying the colour spark plug condition photographs, the Avon Rubber Company for supplying information on tyre fitting, and Draper Tools for supplying many of the tools shown in the photographs.

Thanks are also due to Julian Ryder for providing the introductory copy – A Phoenix from the ashes. We would also like to extend thanks to Triumph Motorcycles, Hinckley, for permission to use pictures of the Triumph models. Triumph Motorcycles Limited bears no responsibility for the content of this book, having had no part in its origination or preparation.

About this manual

The aim of this manual is to help you get the best value from your motorcycle. It can do so in several ways. It can help you decide what work must be done, even if you choose to have it done by a dealer; it provides information and procedures for routine maintenance and servicing; and it offers diagnostic and repair procedures to follow when trouble occurs.

We hope you use the manual to tackle the work yourself. For many simpler jobs, doing it yourself may be quicker than arranging an appointment to get the motorcycle into a dealer and making the trips to leave it and pick it up. More importantly, a lot of money can be saved by avoiding the expense the shop must pass on to you to cover its labour and overhead costs. An added benefit is the sense of satisfaction and accomplishment that you feel after doing the job yourself.

References to the left or right side of the motorcycle assume you are sitting on the seat, facing forward.

We take great pride in the accuracy of information given in this manual, but motorcycle manufacturers make alterations and design changes during the production run of a particular motorcycle of which they do not inform us. No liability can be accepted by the authors or publishers for loss, damage or injury caused by any errors in, or omissions from, the information given.

Illegal Copying

It is the policy of Haynes Publishing to actively protect its Copyrights and Trade Marks. Legal action will be taken against anyone who unlawfully copies the cover or contents of this Manual. This includes all forms of unauthorised copying including digital, mechanical, and electronic in any form. Authorisation from Haynes Publishing will only be provided expressly and in writing. Illegal copying will also be reported to the appropriate statutory authorities.

an XT600 in a party frock, was a massive sales success, helped by licensing categories in some big markets. Even the old, pre-Bloor Triumph company had a go with the Tiger Trail in 1981. It was based on the conventional Tiger, the factory's designation for single-carburetor twins, and hastily designed to offer an alternative to BMW's first GS. The Tiger model name was first used pre-War but the Tiger Trail was the first time it was applied to a bike with off-road pretensions. After the Bloor revolution and the birth of the new company, which first sold bikes in 1991, the Tiger designation was first used on a 1993 bike using the now established 885cc three-cylinder engine.

It wasn't a major sales success, and as time went on revisions to the Tiger made it much more road-orientated – a street bike with high bars. Capacity went up first to 955 then to 1050 and finally to 1215cc with the launch of the Tiger Explorer.

As the Explorer name was tagged on the new, biggest ever Triumph Adventure bike, a new middleweight Tiger arrived. Personally, I think the factory bought in the Explorer name to avoid having to use the old Tiger Cub name as applied to a 200cc single back in the '50s. The litre bike will be the Explorer, the new 800cc versions will be Tigers. The plural is there because both Tigers now came in two versions, standard and XC, which presumably stands for Cross Country. But whereas the bigger bike could be seen as another version of an older model, the new middleweight was just that – new.

The 799cc motor is not a transplant from the 675 Street Triple, it has the same bore but a longer stroke making it easier to produce the more easy-going power characteristics needed for a dual-purpose bike. So the 800cc Tigers are brand new motorcycles. The standard model is very much in the tradition of all the Bloor-era Tigers, a road bike that is capable of dealing happily with dirt roads but the XC takes it a step further. It has a couple of inches more suspension travel (nine as opposed to seven), bigger forks and a 21-inch front wheel as opposed to the stocker's 19-inch hoop and a longer wheelbase, all giving slightly different steering geometry. The XC also has wider bars as befits a more dirt-capable machine, and the wire wheels and GS-like beak front mudguard are giveaways. The profile is striking and reminiscent of the BeeEm but with enough of its own character; the lattice-like rear subframe plus the Speed Triple-like dual-tube side members of the main frame ensure that.

The GS – which stands for Gelande/Strasse or Open Country/Road (yes, for pedants the very first models did have the oblique indicating alternatives) may have started the Adventure Bike trend, but the Tigers are genuine competition in a class that continues to produce interesting motorcycles that are also happily fun to ride.

Safety First! 0•9

Professional mechanics are trained in safe working procedures. However enthusiastic you may be about getting on with the job at hand, take the time to ensure that your safety is not put at risk. A moment's lack of attention can result in an accident, as can failure to observe simple precautions.

There will always be new ways of having accidents, and the following is not a comprehensive list of all dangers; it is intended rather to make you aware of the risks and to encourage a safe approach to all work you carry out on your bike.

Asbestos

● Certain friction, insulating, sealing and other products - such as brake pads, clutch linings, gaskets, etc. - contain asbestos. Extreme care must be taken to avoid inhalation of dust from such products since it is hazardous to health. If in doubt, assume that they do contain asbestos.

Fire

● Remember at all times that petrol is highly flammable. Never smoke or have any kind of naked flame around, when working on the vehicle. But the risk does not end there - a spark caused by an electrical short-circuit, by two metal surfaces contacting each other, by careless use of tools, or even by static electricity built up in your body under certain conditions, can ignite petrol vapour, which in a confined space is highly explosive. Never use petrol as a cleaning solvent. Use an approved safety solvent.

● Always disconnect the battery earth terminal before working on any part of the fuel or electrical system, and never risk spilling fuel on to a hot engine or exhaust.
● It is recommended that a fire extinguisher of a type suitable for fuel and electrical fires is kept handy in the garage or workplace at all times. Never try to extinguish a fuel or electrical fire with water.

Fumes

● Certain fumes are highly toxic and can quickly cause unconsciousness and even death if inhaled to any extent. Petrol vapour comes into this category, as do the vapours from certain solvents such as trichloro-ethylene. Any draining or pouring of such volatile fluids should be done in a well ventilated area.
● When using cleaning fluids and solvents, read the instructions carefully. Never use materials from unmarked containers - they may give off poisonous vapours.
● Never run the engine of a motor vehicle in an enclosed space such as a garage. Exhaust fumes contain carbon monoxide which is extremely poisonous; if you need to run the engine, always do so in the open air or at least have the rear of the vehicle outside the workplace.

The battery

● Never cause a spark, or allow a naked light near the vehicle's battery. It will normally be giving off a certain amount of hydrogen gas, which is highly explosive.

● Always disconnect the battery ground (earth) terminal before working on the fuel or electrical systems (except where noted).
● If possible, loosen the filler plugs or cover when charging the battery from an external source. Do not charge at an excessive rate or the battery may burst.
● Take care when topping up, cleaning or carrying the battery. The acid electrolyte, evenwhen diluted, is very corrosive and should not be allowed to contact the eyes or skin. Always wear rubber gloves and goggles or a face shield. If you ever need to prepare electrolyte yourself, always add the acid slowly to the water; never add the water to the acid.

Electricity

● When using an electric power tool, inspection light etc., always ensure that the appliance is correctly connected to its plug and that, where necessary, it is properly grounded (earthed). Do not use such appliances in damp conditions and, again, beware of creating a spark or applying excessive heat in the vicinity of fuel or fuel vapour. Also ensure that the appliances meet national safety standards.
● A severe electric shock can result from touching certain parts of the electrical system, such as the spark plug wires (HT leads), when the engine is running or being cranked, particularly if components are damp or the insulation is defective. Where an electronic ignition system is used, the secondary (HT) voltage is much higher and could prove fatal.

Remember...

✗ **Don't** start the engine without first ascertaining that the transmission is in neutral.
✗ **Don't** suddenly remove the pressure cap from a hot cooling system - cover it with a cloth and release the pressure gradually first, or you may get scalded by escaping coolant.
✗ **Don't** attempt to drain oil until you are sure it has cooled sufficiently to avoid scalding you.
✗ **Don't** grasp any part of the engine or exhaust system without first ascertaining that it is cool enough not to burn you.
✗ **Don't** allow brake fluid or antifreeze to contact the machine's paintwork or plastic components.
✗ **Don't** siphon toxic liquids such as fuel, hydraulic fluid or antifreeze by mouth, or allow them to remain on your skin.
✗ **Don't** inhale dust - it may be injurious to health (see Asbestos heading).
✗ **Don't** allow any spilled oil or grease to remain on the floor - wipe it up right away, before someone slips on it.
✗ **Don't** use ill-fitting spanners or other tools which may slip and cause injury.

✗ **Don't** lift a heavy component which may be beyond your capability - get assistance.
✗ **Don't** rush to finish a job or take unverified short cuts.
✗ **Don't** allow children or animals in or around an unattended vehicle.
✗ **Don't** inflate a tyre above the recommended pressure. Apart from overstressing the carcass, in extreme cases the tyre may blow off forcibly.
✔ **Do** ensure that the machine is supported securely at all times. This is especially important when the machine is blocked up to aid wheel or fork removal.
✔ **Do** take care when attempting to loosen a stubborn nut or bolt. It is generally better to pull on a spanner, rather than push, so that if you slip, you fall away from the machine rather than onto it.
✔ **Do** wear eye protection when using power tools such as drill, sander, bench grinder etc.
✔ **Do** use a barrier cream on your hands prior to undertaking dirty jobs - it will protect your skin from infection as well as making the dirt easier to remove afterwards; but make sure your hands aren't left slippery. Note that long-term contact with used engine oil can be a health hazard.
✔ **Do** keep loose clothing (cuffs, ties etc. and long hair) well out of the way of moving mechanical parts.
✔ **Do** remove rings, wristwatch etc., before working on the vehicle - especially the electrical system.
✔ **Do** keep your work area tidy - it is only too easy to fall over articles left lying around.
✔ **Do** exercise caution when compressing springs for removal or installation. Ensure that the tension is applied and released in a controlled manner, using suitable tools which preclude the possibility of the spring escaping violently.
✔ **Do** ensure that any lifting tackle used has a safe working load rating adequate for the job.
✔ **Do** get someone to check periodically that all is well, when working alone on the vehicle.
✔ **Do** carry out work in a logical sequence and check that everything is correctly assembled and tightened afterwards.
✔ **Do** remember that your vehicle's safety affects that of yourself and others. If in doubt on any point, get professional advice.
● If in spite of following these precautions, you are unfortunate enough to injure yourself, seek medical attention as soon as possible.

0•10 Bike spec

Weights and dimensions

Tiger 800
Overall length	2215 mm
Overall width	795 mm
Overall height	1350 mm
Wheelbase	1530 mm
Seat height	813 mm
Wet weight	210 kg
Max. payload (rider, passenger, luggage, accessories)	225 kg

Tiger 800XC
Overall length	2215 mm
Overall width	865 mm
Overall height	1390 mm
Wheelbase	1545 mm
Seat height	847 mm
Wet weight	215 kg
Max. payload (rider, passenger, luggage, accessories)	223 kg

Bike spec

Engine

Type	Liquid-cooled, 12 valve in-line three cylinder
Capacity (bore x stroke)	799 cc (74 x 61.94 mm)
Compression ratio	11.1 to 1
Camshafts	DOHC, chain-driven from the right-hand end of the crankshaft
Engine management system	Multipoint sequential fuel injection, digital inductive ignition
Clutch	Wet multi-plate, cable-operated
Gearbox	6-speed constant mesh
Final drive	Chain and sprockets

Chassis

Frame type ... Steel trellis
Rake and trail
  Tiger 800 ... 23.9°, 92.4 mm
  Tiger 800XC ... 24.3°, 95.3 mm
Front suspension
  Tiger 800 ... 43 mm upside-down cartridge forks, non-adjustable
  Tiger 800XC ... 45 mm upside-down cartridge forks, non-adjustable
Rear suspension
  Tiger 800 ... Twin-sided swingarm, single shock with rising-rate linkage, spring pre-load adjustment
  Tiger 800XC ... Twin-sided swingarm, single shock with rising-rate linkage, spring pre-load and rebound damping adjustment
Wheels
  Tiger 800 ... 10-spoke cast alloy – Front 19 x 2.5, Rear 17 x 4.25
  Tiger 800XC ... Steel multi-spoke, steel rim – Front 21 x 2.5, Rear 17 x 4.25
Tyres*
  Tiger 800 ... Front – 100/90-19, Rear – 150/70-17
  Tiger 800XC ... Front – 90/90-21, Rear – 150/70-17
*Refer to the owners handbook, the tyre information label on the swingarm, or your Triumph dealer or a tyre specialist for approved tyre brands and ratings.
Front brake ... 2 x 305 mm discs with 2-piston sliding calipers
Rear brake ... 1 x 255 mm disc with single piston sliding caliper

Model development

Tiger 800

The Tiger 800 was introduced in 2010.

The engine is a liquid-cooled in-line three cylinder unit based on the 675 engine used in the Daytona and Street Triple models, with larger bores and modifications to the clutch release mechanism, gearchange mechanism and sump. Drive to the double overhead camshafts is by chain off the right-hand end of the crankshaft. Drive to the rear wheel is via a wet multi-plate clutch, a six-speed constant mesh gearbox, and chain and sprockets.

It has a one-piece steel trellis frame, with adjustable seat and handlebars. Front suspension is by 43 mm non-adjustable upside forks with cartridge dampers. Rear suspension is by a single shock absorber with spring pre-load damping via a rising rate linkage and double-sided swingarm.

The front brake system has two twin-piston sliding calipers, and the rear has a single piston sliding caliper. Non-ABS and ABS versions were available up to 2012 and from 2013 the model was fitted with ABS as standard.

Tiger 800XC

The XC uses the same engine, frame and brakes as the standard model, but has revised suspension for longer travel, with 45 mm front forks, and a different rear shock absorber with both spring pre-load and rebound damping adjustment and a remote reservoir. It also has wire-spoke wheels, with a larger diameter front wheel, giving it more off-road capability.

Identification numbers

Frame and engine numbers

The engine number is stamped into the top of the crankcase on the right-hand side of the engine. The VIN (vehicle identification number) is stamped into the right-hand side of the steering head and is duplicated on a plate either on the left-hand side of the steering head or on the frame cross-piece under the seat. These numbers should be recorded and kept in a safe place so they can be furnished to law enforcement officials in the event of a theft.

The VIN, engine number, and model code should be recorded and kept in a handy place (such as with your driver's licence) so that they are always available when purchasing or ordering parts for your machine.

The procedures in this manual distinguish between the bikes by model name. If a model has been modified during its production life, then either the VIN or engine number is used to differentiate between the versions, as appropriate.

Buying spare parts

Once you have found the identification numbers, record them for reference when buying parts. Since the manufacturers change specifications, parts and vendors (companies that manufacture various components on the machine), providing the ID numbers is the only way to be reasonably sure that you are buying the correct parts.

Whenever possible, take the worn part to the dealer so direct comparison with the new component can be made. Along the trail from the manufacturer to the parts shelf, there are numerous places that the part can end up with the wrong number or be listed incorrectly.

The two places to purchase new parts for your motorcycle – the accessory store and the franchised dealer – differ in the type of parts they carry. While dealers can obtain virtually every part for your motorcycle, the accessory dealer is usually limited to spark plugs, chain and sprocket kits, lubes and fluids.

Used parts can be obtained for roughly half the price of new ones, but you can't always be sure of what you're getting. Once again, take your worn part to the breaker's yard for direct comparison.

Whether buying new, used or rebuilt parts, the best course is to deal directly with someone who specialises in parts for your particular make.

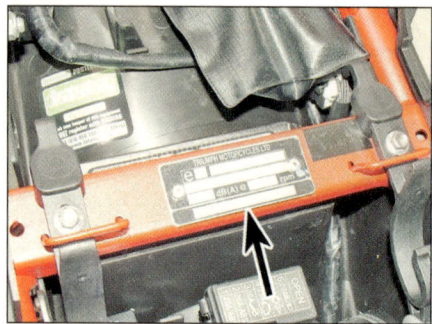

The VIN is duplicated on an information plate (arrowed), on this model under the seat

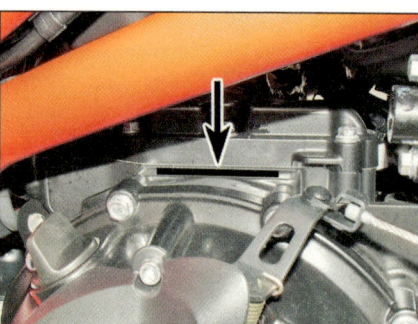

The engine number (arrowed) is stamped into the crankcase on the right-hand side of the engine

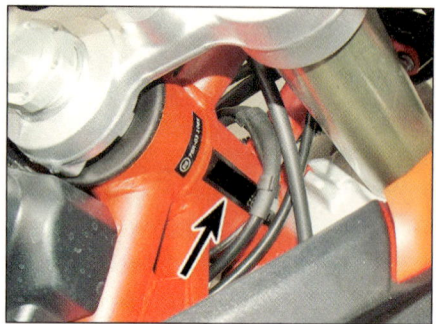

The VIN (arrowed) is stamped into the right-hand side of the steering head

Pre-ride checks

Engine oil level

Before you start:
✔ Support the motorcycle in an upright position on level ground – have an assistant support the bike, or use an auxiliary stand. Don't check the oil level with the bike on its sidestand.
✔ Start the engine and let it idle for several minutes to allow it to reach normal operating temperature.
Caution: Do not run the engine in an enclosed space such as a garage or workshop.
✔ Stop the engine and leave the motorcycle undisturbed for a few minutes to allow the oil level to stabilise.

Bike care:
● If you have to add oil frequently, you should check whether you have any oil leaks. If there is no sign of oil leakage from the joints and gaskets the engine could be burning oil, in which case there will be white smoke coming out of the exhaust (see *Fault Finding*).

The correct oil
● Modern, high-revving engines place great demands on their oil. It is very important that the correct oil for your bike is used.
● I Always top up with a good quality oil of the specified type and viscosity and do not overfill the engine. Triumph recommend using Castrol Power 1 Racing 4T oil.
Caution: Do not mix any chemical additives with the oil, however good they may sound, as they could cause clutch slip. Never use 100% mineral, vegetable, non-detergent or castor based oils.

Oil type	Semi or fully synthetic motorcycle engine oil, API grade SH or higher and JASO MA
Oil viscosity	SAE 10W/40 or 10W/50

1 The oil level inspection window is located on the right-hand side of the engine. If necessary wipe the window so that it is clean. With the motorcycle vertical, the oil level should lie between the upper and lower level lines (arrowed).

2 If the level is near, on or below the lower line, unscrew the oil filler cap.

3 Top up the engine with the recommended grade and type of oil to bring the level almost up to the upper line on the inspection window. Do not overfill.

4 Make sure the O-ring (arrowed) on the underside of the cap is in good condition and properly seated. Fit a new one if necessary. Wipe it clean and smear new oil onto it. Fit the cap, making sure it is secure in the cover.

Suspension, steering and final drive

Suspension and Steering
● Check that the front and rear suspension operates smoothly without binding. Check that there are no fluid leaks from the front fork seals or rear shock absorber.
● Check that the suspension is adjusted as required, where applicable (see Chapter 5).
● Check that the steering moves smoothly from lock-to-lock.

Final drive
● Check that the chain slack isn't excessive, and adjust it if necessary (see Chapter 1).
● If the chain looks dry, lubricate it (see Chapter 1).

0•14 Pre-ride checks

Brake fluid levels

 Warning: *Brake hydraulic fluid can harm your eyes and damage painted surfaces, so use extreme caution when handling and pouring it and cover surrounding surfaces with rag. Do not use fluid that has been standing open for some time, as it absorbs moisture from the air which can cause a dangerous loss of braking effectiveness.*

Before you start:

✔ Make sure you have the correct hydraulic fluid. DOT 4 is recommended.
✔ Support the motorcycle in an upright position, using an auxiliary stand if required.
✔ The front master cylinder reservoir is on the right handlebar - turn the handlebars until reservoir is as level as possible.
✔ The rear master cylinder reservoir is located on the right-hand side towards the rear.
✔ Wrap a rag around the reservoir being worked on to ensure that any spillage does not come into contact with painted surfaces.

Bike care:

● The fluid in the front and rear brake master cylinder reservoirs will drop very gradually as the brake pads wear down. If the fluid level is low check the brake pads for wear (see Chapter 1), and replace them with new ones if necessary (see Chapter 6).
● If either fluid reservoir requires repeated topping-up there could be a leak somewhere in the system, which should be investigated immediately.
● Check for signs of fluid leakage from the hydraulic hoses and brake system components – if found, rectify immediately (see Chapter 6).
● Check the operation of both brakes before taking the machine on the road; if there is evidence of air in the system (spongy feel to lever or pedal), it must be bled as described in Chapter 6.

FRONT BRAKE FLUID LEVEL

1 The front brake fluid level is visible through the window in the reservoir body – it must be above the LOWER level line (arrowed).

2 To top up, undo the reservoir cover screws (arrowed) and remove the cover and diaphragm.

3 Top up with DOT 4 hydraulic fluid until the level is up to the UPPER level line (arrowed) cast into the inside of the reservoir – do not overfill. Take care to avoid spills (see **Warning** above).

4 Wipe any moisture off the diaphragm, opening it out to access the folds.

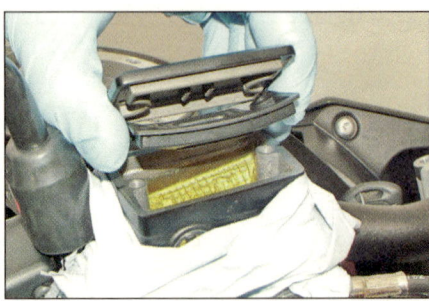

5 Make sure the diaphragm is correctly seated before fitting the cover.

Pre-ride checks

REAR BRAKE FLUID LEVEL

1 The rear brake fluid level is visible through the reservoir body – it must be between the UPPER and LOWER level lines (arrowed).

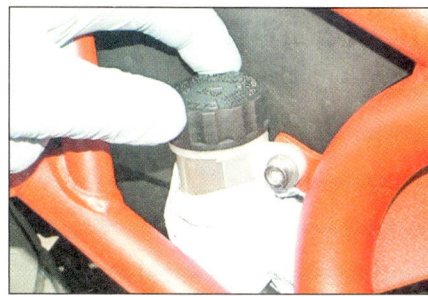

2 To top up, undo the reservoir cap and remove the plate and diaphragm.

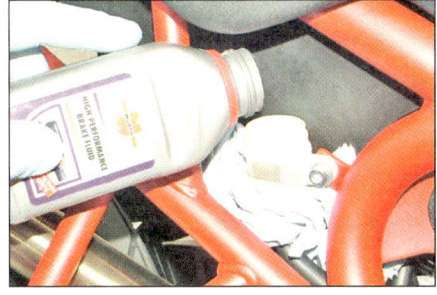

3 Top up with DOT 4 hydraulic fluid, until the level is between the LOWER and UPPER level lines – do not overfill. Take care to avoid spills (see **Warning** on page 0•14).

4 Wipe any moisture off the diaphragm, opening it out to access the folds.

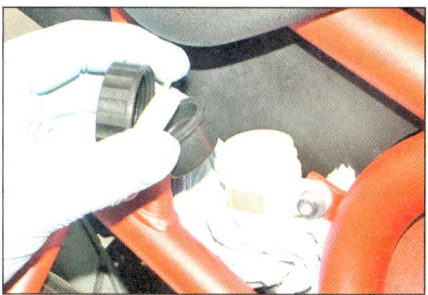

5 Ensure that the diaphragm is correctly seated before fitting the plate and cap.

Coolant level

Bike care:
- Use only the specified coolant mixture. It is important that anti-freeze is used in the system all year round, and not just in the winter. Do not top the system up using only water, as the system will become too diluted.
- Do not overfill the reservoir. If the coolant is significantly above the MAX level line at any time, the surplus should be siphoned or drained off to prevent the possibility of it being expelled out of the overflow hose.
- If the coolant level falls steadily, check the system for leaks (see Chapter 1). If no leaks are found and the level continues to fall, fit a new pressure cap to the radiator (see Chapter 1). If this does not cure the problem take the bike to a Triumph dealer for a pressure test.

Before you start:
✔ Make sure you have a supply of coolant available – a mixture of 50% distilled water and 50% corrosion inhibited ethylene glycol anti-freeze is needed. Triumph specify their HD4X Hybrid OAT coolant.
✔ Always check the coolant level when the engine is cold.
✔ Support the motorcycle in an upright position on level ground, using an auxiliary stand if required.

1 The reservoir is mounted behind the right-hand fairing sidepanel. The coolant level is visible via the aperture in the panel and should be between the MAX and MIN level lines (arrowed) marked on the reservoir.

2 If the coolant level does not lie between the MAX and MIN level lines open the reservoir filler cap.

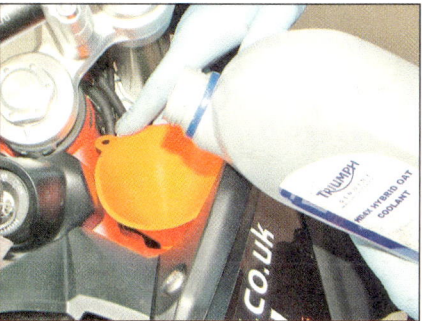

3 Top the coolant level up with the recommended coolant mixture using a suitable funnel. Fit the cap.

Pre-ride checks

Tyres

The correct pressures

Caution: On models fitted with the tyre pressure monitoring system (TPMS) refer also to Section 18 in Chapter 6.

● The tyres must be checked when cold, not immediately after riding. Note that low tyre pressures will cause abnormal tread wear and unsafe handling, and may cause the tyre to slip on the rim or come off. High tyre pressures will also cause abnormal tread wear and unsafe handling.

● Use an accurate pressure gauge. Many garage forecourt gauges are wildly inaccurate. If you buy your own, spend as much as you can justify on a quality gauge.
● Correct air pressure will increase tyre life and provide maximum stability, handling capability and ride comfort.
● On XC models, for off-road use the tyre pressure should be reduced (see table below), but do not ride on the road until the pressures have been increased again to the specified pressures.

Tyre care

● Check the tyres carefully for cuts, tears, embedded nails or other sharp objects and excessive wear. Operation of the motorcycle with excessively worn tyres is extremely hazardous, as traction and handling are directly affected. Also check the wheels for signs of damage and distortion.
● Check the condition of the tyre valve and make sure a dust cap is fitted.

● Pick out any stones or nails which may have become embedded in the tyre tread. If left, they will eventually penetrate through the casing and cause a puncture.
● If tyre damage is apparent, or unexplained loss of pressure is experienced, seek the advice of a tyre fitting specialist without delay.

Tyre tread depth

● At the time of writing UK law requires that tread depth must be at least 1 mm over 3/4 of the tread breadth all the way around the tyre, with no bald patches. Many riders, however, consider 2 mm tread depth minimum to be a safer limit. Triumph recommend a minimum of 2 mm for normal riding, or 3 mm on the rear tyre for high speed riding (over 80 mph, 130 km/h).
● Many tyres now incorporate wear indicators in the tread. Identify the triangular pointer or TWI mark on the tyre sidewall to locate the indicator bar. Fit a new tyre if the tread has worn down to the bar.

1 Remove the cap (arrowed) from the valve – if it is missing fit a new one.

	Front	Rear
Tiger	36 psi (2.5 Bar)	42 psi (2.9 Bar)
Tiger XC – on road	36 psi (2.5 Bar)	42 psi (2.9 Bar)
Tiger XC – off road	22 psi (1.5 Bar)	22 psi (1.5 Bar)

2 Check the tyre pressures when the tyres are **cold**.

3 Measure tread depth at the centre of the tyre using a tread depth gauge.

4 Tyre tread wear indicator bars (A) and their location marking – the marking could be either an arrow, a triangle or the letters TWI, either on the edge of the tread or on the top of the sidewall.

Legal and safety

Lighting and signalling

● Take a minute to check that the headlight, tail light, brake light, instrument lights and turn signals all work correctly.
● Check that the horn sounds when the button is pushed.
● A working speedometer graduated in mph is a statutory requirement in the UK.

Safety

● Check that the throttle grip rotates smoothly and snaps shut when released, in all steering positions. Also check for the correct amount of freeplay (see Chapter 1).
● Check that the clutch cable is working smoothly and with the correct freeplay (see Chapter 1).
● Check that the brake lever and pedal, the clutch lever and the gearchange lever operate smoothly. Lubricate them at the specified intervals or when necessary (see Chapter 1).
● Check that the engine shuts off when the kill switch is operated.
● Check the starter safety circuit (see Chapter 1).
● Check that sidestand return springs, and where fitted the centrestand return springs, holds the stand securely up when retracted.
● Check for any nuts and bolts that may have worked loose.

Fuel

● This may seem obvious, but check that you have enough fuel to complete your journey. Check for signs of fuel leakage – if any are found, rectify the cause immediately.
● Ensure you use the correct grade fuel – see Chapter 4 Specifications.

Chapter 1
Routine maintenance and Servicing

Contents

	Section number
Air filter	17
Battery	20
Brake fluid level check	see *Pre-ride checks*
Brake pad wear check	9
Brake system	10
Clutch	13
Coolant level check	see *Pre-ride checks*
Cooling system	5
Drive chain and sprockets	1
Engine management system	3
Engine oil and filter change	2
Engine oil level check	see *Pre-ride checks*
Engine wear assessment	see Chapter 2
Fuel system	6

	Section number
Headlight aim	see Chapter 8
Idle speed	15
Nuts and bolts tightness check	11
Spark plugs	14
Sidestand and starter safety circuit	8
Stand, lever pivot and cable lubrication	19
Steering head bearings	16
Suspension	7
Throttle body synchronisation	15
Throttle cables	4
Tyre pressures and tread depth	see *Pre-ride checks*
Valve clearances	18
Wheels, wheel bearings and tyres	12

Degrees of difficulty

| **Easy,** suitable for novice with little experience | **Fairly easy,** suitable for beginner with some experience | **Fairly difficult,** suitable for competent DIY mechanic | **Difficult,** suitable for experienced DIY mechanic | **Very difficult,** suitable for expert DIY or professional |

1•2 Servicing specifications

Engine
Spark plugs
    Type .... NGK CR9EK
    Electrode gap .... 0.7 mm
Engine idle speed .... 1100 rpm
Cylinder identification .... numbered 1 to 3 from left to right
Valve clearances (COLD engine)
    Intake valves .... 0.10 to 0.20 mm
    Exhaust valves .... 0.325 to 0.375 mm

Cycle parts
Brake pad minimum thickness .... 1.5 mm
Drive chain slack .... 20 to 30 mm
Chain stretch limit (see Section 1) .... 319 mm
Throttle opening cable freeplay (at twistgrip flange) ..... 2 to 3 mm
Throttle closing cable freeplay .... 2 to 3 mm
Clutch cable freeplay (at lever stock) .... 2 to 3 mm
Tyre pressures (cold) .... see Pre-ride checks

Lubricants and fluids
Engine oil type .... Semi or fully synthetic motorcycle engine oil, SAE 10W/40 or 10W/50, API grade SH or higher with JASO MA – Triumph recommend Castrol Power 1 Racing 4T oil

Engine oil capacity (see Text)
    Dry engine, new filter .... 3.75 litres
    Wet fill with new filter .... 3.6 litres
    Wet fill without new filter .... 3.4 litres
Coolant type .... Triumph HD4X Hybrid OAT pre-mixed coolant
Coolant capacity .... 2.4 litres
Brake fluid .... DOT 4
Drive chain .... Chain spray lubricant suitable for O-ring chains
Steering head bearings .... Lithium-based multi-purpose grease to NLGI 2 specification
Swingarm pivot and bearings, suspension linkage bearings .... Lithium-based multi-purpose grease to NLGI 2 specification
Wheel bearings and seal lips .... Lithium-based multi-purpose grease to NLGI 2 specification
Gearchange lever/clutch lever/front brake lever/
    rear brake pedal/sidestand pivots .... Lithium-based multi-purpose grease to NLGI 2 specification
Cables .... Aerosol cable lubricant
Throttle grip .... Multi-purpose grease or dry film lubricant

Torque wrench settings
Fork clamp bolts (top yoke) .... 20 Nm
Fuel pump mounting plate bolts .... 9 Nm
Oil drain plug .... 25 Nm
Oil filter .... 10 Nm
Rear axle nut .... 110 Nm
Spark plugs .... 12 Nm
Steering head bearing adjuster nut
    Initial (pre-load) setting .... 40 Nm
    Final setting .... 10 Nm
Steering head bearing adjuster locknut .... 40 Nm
Steering stem nut .... 90 Nm

Maintenance schedule 1•3

Pre-ride
☐ See *Pre-ride checks* at the beginning of this manual.

After the initial 500 miles (800 km)
Note: *This check is usually performed by a Triumph dealer after the first 500 miles (800 km) from new. Thereafter, maintenance is carried out according to the following intervals of the schedule.*

Every 200 miles (300 km)
☐ Check, adjust, clean and lubricate the drive chain (Section 1)

Every 500 miles (800 km)
☐ Check the drive chain for wear and stretch and the sprockets for wear (Section 1)

Every 6000 miles (10,000 km) or 12 months
☐ Check the drive chain slider (Section 1)
☐ Change the engine oil and filter and check the oil cooler (Section 2)
☐ Check the engine management system (Section 3)
☐ Check and adjust the throttle cables (Section 4)
☐ Check the cooling system (Section 5)
☐ Check the fuel system (Section 6)
☐ Check the suspension (Section 7)
☐ Check the sidestand and starter safety circuit (Section 8)
☐ Check the brake pads (Section 9)
☐ Check the brake system and brake light switch operation (Section 10)
☐ Check the tightness of all nuts, bolts and fasteners (Section 11)
☐ Check the condition of the wheels, wheel bearings and tyres (Section 12)
☐ Check the clutch (Section 13)
☐ Check the spark plugs (Section 14)

Every 6000 miles (10,000 km) or 12 months (continued)
☐ Check/adjust engine idle speed and throttle body synchronisation (Section 15)
☐ Check and adjust the steering head bearings (Section 16)

Every 12,000 miles (20,000 km) or two years
Carry out all the items under the 6000 mile (10,000 km) check, plus the following
☐ Change the coolant (Section 5)
☐ Lubricate the swingarm and suspension linkage bearings (Section 7)
☐ Change the brake fluid (Section 10)
☐ Fit new spark plugs (Section 14)
☐ Lubricate the steering head bearings (Section 16)
☐ Fit a new air filter element (Section 17)
☐ Check and adjust the valve clearances (Section 18)
☐ Lubricate the clutch and brake levers, gearchange lever linkage, brake pedal pivot and sidestand pivots and the throttle and clutch cables (Section 19)

Every 24,000 miles (40,000 km) or four years
Carry out all the items under the 12,000 mile (20,000 km) check, plus the following
☐ Fit new fuel system hoses (Section 6)
☐ Fit new EVAP system hoses – California models only (see Chapter 4)
☐ Change the front fork oil (Section 7)

Non-scheduled maintenance
☐ Fit new brake hoses (Section 10)
☐ Fit new brake master cylinder and caliper seals (see Section 10)
☐ Check the battery (Section 20)
☐ Check and adjust the headlight aim (Chapter 8)

1•4 Component locations

1 Toolkit
2 VIN plate (alternative location)
3 Rear brake fluid reservoir
4 Rear shock pre-load adjuster
5 Oil filler cap
6 Engine number
7 Clutch cable lower adjuster
8 Coolant reservoir level marks
9 Front brake fluid reservoir
10 Throttle cable upper adjuster
11 Front fork seal
12 VIN (frame number)
13 Coolant reservoir filler cap
14 Engine oil level window
15 Rear shock damping adjuster
16 Drive chain adjuster

Component locations 1•5

1 VIN plate (alternative location)
2 Clutch cable upper adjuster
3 Steering head bearing adjuster
4 Air filter
5 Battery
6 Fuseboxes
7 Drive chain adjuster
8 Drive chain slider
9 Hose disconnection point for coolant drain
10 Oil drain plug
11 Oil filter
12 Cooling system pressure cap
13 Fork seal

1•6 Introduction

1 This Chapter is designed to help the home mechanic maintain his/her motorcycle for safety, economy, long life and peak performance.

2 Deciding where to start or plug into the routine maintenance schedule depends on several factors. If the warranty period on your motorcycle has just expired, and if it has been maintained according to the warranty standards, you may want to pick up routine maintenance as it coincides with the next mileage or calendar interval. If you have owned the machine for some time but have never performed any maintenance on it, then you may want to start at the beginning and include all frequent procedures to ensure that nothing important is overlooked. If you have just had a major engine overhaul, then you should start the engine maintenance routines from the beginning. If you have a used machine and have no knowledge of its history or maintenance record, you should combine all the checks into one large initial service and then settle into the maintenance schedule prescribed.

3 Before beginning any maintenance or repair, the machine should be cleaned thoroughly, especially around the oil filter, valve cover, side panels, etc. Cleaning will help ensure that dirt does not contaminate the engine and will allow you to detect wear and damage that could otherwise easily go unnoticed.

4 Many of the bolts used in the building of the engine are of the Torx type. Unless you are already equipped with a good range of Torx bits, you are advised to obtain a set. Make sure you get bits that can be used in conjunction with a socket set so that a torque wrench can be applied – a Torx key set will not be adequate on its own, though will be useful in addition to the bits.

5 Certain maintenance information is sometimes printed on decals attached to the motorcycle. If any information on the decals differs from that included here, use the information on the decal.

6 Note that in many cases, Triumph use the machine's VIN number as a means of identification rather than the year of manufacture. Always check the VIN number against the details given in this manual to ensure you follow the correct procedure.

1 Drive chain and sprockets

Check

1 As the chain stretches with wear, adjustment is necessary. A neglected drive chain won't last long and can quickly damage the sprockets. Routine chain adjustment and lubrication isn't difficult and will ensure maximum chain and sprocket life.

2 To check the chain slack the bike should be supported upright (off the stand) with no extra weight on it. Make sure the transmission is in neutral.

3 Push up on the bottom run of the chain and measure the slack midway between the two sprockets (see illustration). Compare your measurement to that listed in the Specifications at the beginning of the Chapter. Since the chain will rarely wear evenly, resulting in a tight spot, move the bike so that another section of chain can be checked – do this several times to check the entire length of chain. Any adjustment should be based upon the measurement taken at the tightest point.

4 In some cases where lubrication has been neglected, corrosion and galling may cause the links to bind and kink, which effectively shortens the chain's length (see illustration). Any such links should be thoroughly cleaned and worked free. If they are rusty or the links have seized together and cannot be freed replace the chain with a new one. If you find a tight area, clean off the oil and dirt, mark it with felt pen or paint, and repeat the measurement after the bike has been ridden. If the chain's still tight or kinked in the same area it can damage the transmission output shaft bearing, so replace it with a new one (see Chapter 6).

Adjustment

5 Make sure the transmission is in neutral. Position the bike so the tightest point of the chain is at the centre of its bottom run.

6 Slacken the axle nut (see illustration).

7 Slacken the adjuster locknut on each side of the swingarm (see illustration). Turn the adjusters evenly, anti-clockwise to reduce freeplay and clockwise to increase it, until the amount of freeplay specified at the beginning of the Chapter is obtained at the centre of the bottom run of the chain. Push the wheel forwards to eliminate any clearance between the head of each adjuster and the front of each adjustment marker, then check that the back edge of each chain adjustment marker is in the same position in relation to the marks on the swingarm (see illustration). It is important each adjuster aligns with the same mark; if not, the rear wheel will be out of alignment with the front.

1.3 Push up on the chain and measure the slack

1.4 Neglect has caused the links in this chain to kink

1.6 Slacken the rear axle nut (arrowed)

1.7a Slacken the locknut (A) and turn the adjuster (B) as required

1.7b Check the relative position of the back edge of each adjustment marker with the marks on the swingarm

Routine maintenance and Servicing

1.10 Specially shaped chain cleaning brushes are available from good suppliers

1.11 Apply the lubricant to the overlap between the sideplates

 Refer to Chapter 6 for information on checking wheel alignment.

8 If there is a difference in the chain adjuster positions, adjust one of them so that its position is exactly the same as the other. Check the chain freeplay as described above and readjust if necessary.

9 Check again that there is no clearance between the head of each adjuster and the front of each adjustment marker. Push the wheel forwards and tighten the axle nut to the torque setting specified at the beginning of the Chapter. Tighten the adjuster locknuts **(see illustration 1.7a)**. Recheck the adjustment.

Cleaning and lubrication

10 If required, using a dedicated aerosol cleaner, or in paraffin (kerosene) or a suitable non-flammable or high flash-point solvent that will not damage the O-rings, using a soft brush to work any dirt out if necessary **(see illustration)**. Wipe the cleaner off the chain and allow it to dry. If the chain is excessively dirty remove it from the bike and allow it to soak in the paraffin or solvent (see Chapter 6). **Caution: Don't use petrol (gasoline), solvent or other cleaning fluids that might damage the internal sealing properties of the chain. Don't use high-pressure water. The entire process shouldn't take longer than ten minutes – if it does, the O-rings in the chain rollers could be damaged.**

11 The best time to lubricate the chain is after the motorcycle has been ridden – when the chain is warm, the lubricant will penetrate the joints between the side plates better than when cold. Use a dedicated spraychain lubricant suitable for O-ring chains; other types may contain solvents that could damage the O-rings. Apply the lubricant to the area where the side plates overlap, not to the middle of the rollers, making sure the entire chain gets an even coating, but not too much as it will be wasted – little and often is best **(see illustration)**. Triumph recommend that the bike should not be ridden for 8 hours after applying lubricant to allow the solvent to evaporate so the lubricant sticks to the chain and has time to penetrate – if you ride the bike too soon much of the lubricant will simply be flung off. Before riding the bike wipe off any excess lubricant.

 Apply the lubricant to the top of the lower chain run, so centrifugal force will work it into the chain when the bike is moving.

Drive chain wear and stretch check

12 Make sure the transmission is in neutral. Support the bike on its sidestand, or on the centrestand if fitted.

13 Check the entire length of the chain for damaged rollers, loose links and pins, and missing O-rings. Fit a new chain if damage is found (see Chapter 6). **Note:** *Never fit a new chain onto old sprockets, and never use the old chain if you fit new sprockets – replace the chain and sprockets as a set.*

14 To check the amount of chain stretch, hang a 10 to 20 kg (20 to 40 lb) weight from the middle of the bottom run of the chain. Measure along the top run the length of 20 links (from the centre of the 1st pin to the centre of the 21st pin) and compare the result with the service limit specified at the beginning of the Chapter. Rotate the wheel so that several sections of the chain are measured, then calculate the average. If the chain exceeds the service limit it must be replaced with a new one (see Chapter 6).

Sprocket check

15 Remove the front sprocket cover (see Chapter 6). Check the teeth on the front and rear sprockets for wear **(see illustration)**.

Drive chain slider check

16 Create maximum slack in the chain (see Section 'Adjustment').

1.15 Check the sprockets in the areas indicated to see if they are worn excessively

Routine maintenance and Servicing

1.17 Lift the chain and check the slider for wear and damage

1.18a Undo the screws (arrowed) and remove the heel guard

1.18b Chainguard screws (arrowed)

1.18c Unscrew the bolt (arrowed)...

1.18d ...and remove the slider...

1.18e ...noting the collar

Routine maintenance and Servicing

1.19 Seat the front mount between the slider and the lug

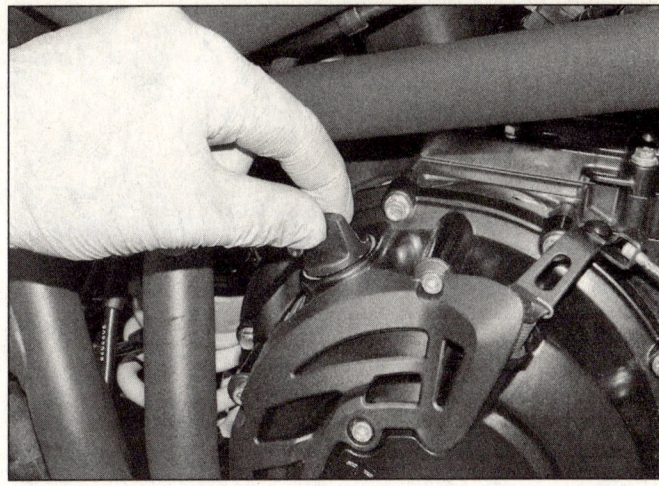

2.3 Remove the oil filler cap

17 Clean the chain slider with a suitable solvent to remove all traces of grease and road dirt. Inspect the surface of the slider – if it is deeply grooved or damaged it must be replaced with a new one **(see illustration)**.

18 To remove the slider first remove the heel guard and the chain guard **(see illustrations)**. Remove the rear wheel (see Chapter 6). Unscrew the bolt securing the slider and draw it back off the swingarm **(see illustrations)** – note there is a collar for the bolt that fits into the inner side of the slider **(see illustration)**.

19 Installation is the reverse of removal. Make sure the slider bolt collar is fitted **(see illustration 1.18e)**. Make sure the front mount of the chain guard seats correctly between the slider and the mounting lug on the swingarm **(see illustration)**.

2 Engine oil and filter change

⚠️ **Warning: Be careful when draining the oil, as the exhaust pipes, the engine, and the oil itself can cause severe burns.**

1 Consistent routine oil and filter changes are the single most important maintenance procedure you can perform on a motorcycle. The oil not only lubricates the internal parts of the engine, transmission and clutch, but it also acts as a coolant, a cleaner, a sealant, and a protector. Because of these demands, the oil takes a terrific amount of abuse and should be changed often with new oil of the recommended grade and type. Saving a little money on the difference in cost between good oil and cheap oil won't pay off if the engine is damaged. The oil filter should be changed with every oil change.

2 Warm up the engine so the oil will drain easily. Place the motorcycle on its sidestand, making sure it is on level ground. For best visual access remove the sump guard (see Chapter 7). Position a clean drain tray under the front of the engine.

3 Unscrew the oil filler cap from the clutch cover to vent it and to act as a reminder that there is no oil in the engine **(see illustration)**.

4 Unscrew the oil drain plug and allow the oil to flow into the drain tray **(see illustrations)**. Discard the sealing washer – a new one must be fitted.

5 Unscrew the filter using a filter removal socket or a strap wrench and tip any residual

2.4a Unscrew the oil drain plug (arrowed)...

2.4b ...and allow the oil to drain

1•10 Routine maintenance and Servicing

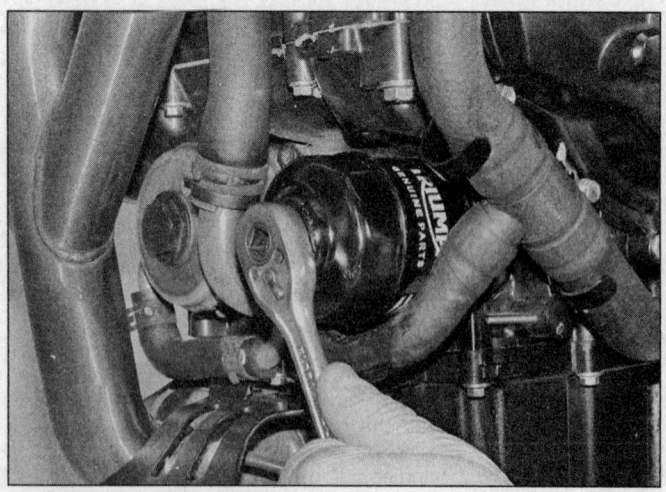

2.5a Unscrew the filter using a filter removal socket or strap...

2.5b ...and drain its oil into the tray

oil into the drain tray **(see illustrations)**. Triumph dealers can supply an oil filter tool (Part No. T3880313).

6 When the oil has completely drained, fit a new sealing washer onto the drain plug, then fit the plug into the sump and tighten it to the torque setting specified at the beginning of the Chapter **(see illustration)**. Avoid overtightening, as you will damage the sump.

7 Smear some new engine oil onto the rubber seal on the filter, then screw the filter onto the engine until the seal just seats **(see illustrations)**. If a filter socket is available, tighten the filter to the torque setting specified at the beginning of the Chapter. Otherwise, tighten the filter as tight as possible by hand, or by the number of turns specified on the filter or its packaging. **Note:** *Do not use a strap or chain type removal tool to tighten the filter – you will damage the body.*

8 Refill the engine to the upper level lines on the inspection window using the recommended type of oil (see Specifications) **(see illustrations)**. Fit the filler cap, using

2.6 Fit the drain plug using a new sealing washer and tighten it to the specified torque

2.7a Smear some clean oil onto the seal...

2.7b ...then thread the filter onto the engine and tighten it as described

2.8a Add the specified oil...

2.8b ...so the level is at the upper lines

Routine maintenance and Servicing

2.8c Check the O-ring (arrowed)

a new O-ring if the old one is damaged, deformed or deteriorated **(see illustration)**. Start the engine and let it run for two or three minutes. Stop the engine, wait a few minutes, then check the oil level. If necessary, add more oil to bring the level up to the upper level line. Check that there are no leaks around the filter and drain plug. If the filter is leaking tighten it some more. If the drain plug is leaking make sure it is tightened to the correct torque, and if it is you will need to drain the oil again and replace the sealing washer with a new one.

9 Refer to Chapter 2, Section 6, and check the oil cooler and its hoses for damage and leaks. Replace any components as necessary with new ones.

10 The old oil drained from the engine cannot be re-used and should be disposed of properly. Check with your local refuse disposal company, disposal facility or environmental agency to see whether they will accept the used oil for recycling. Don't pour used oil into drains or onto the ground as this is likely to pollute your local environment. Remember to drain all the old oil from the filter (you can punch a hole in the filter to ensure it drains fully) into the drain pan. Note that the old filter should be taken to the oil disposal facility rather than disposed of with the household rubbish.

> **HAYNES HiNT** Check the old oil carefully – if it is very metallic coloured, then the engine is experiencing wear from break-in (new engine) or from insufficient lubrication. If there are flakes or chips of metal in the oil, then something is drastically wrong internally and the engine will have to be disassembled for inspection and repair. If there are pieces of fibre-like material in the oil, the clutch is experiencing excessive wear and should be checked.

Note: It is illegal and anti-social to dump oil down the drain. To find the location of your local oil recycling bank in the UK, call 03708 506 506 or visit www.oilbankline.org.uk

3 Engine management system

Note: *The idle speed is controlled by the idle air control valve, which in turn is controlled by the electronic control module (ECM). Idle speed cannot be manually adjusted – it can only be done using the diagnostic tool.*

1 The engine management system should be checked for any stored diagnostic fault codes. To do this, either the Triumph diagnostic tool or an EOBD (OBD2) fault code reader is essential – both of these plug into the socket under the passenger seat **(see illustration)**. If you don't have an after-market reader take your bike to a dealer and have them check the system – it should not take them long. Note that the Triumph diagnostic tool requires an authorisation code to operate it and these are only available to Triumph dealers.

2 If any problems with the system occur during use, the malfunction indicator light (MIL) in the instrument cluster will illuminate. If this happens, the management system switches itself into 'limp home' mode, so that in theory you should not be left stranded. Depending on the problem, it is possible that you will notice no difference in the running of the motorcycle. In order to diagnose the fault and to turn the MIL off, the diagnostic tool is essential, so again the machine must be taken to a Triumph dealer.

3 Further information on the system, including all tests and checks that can be performed, is contained in Chapter 4.

3.1 After-market EOBD (OBD2) fault code reader plugged into the socket (arrowed)

4 Throttle cables

1 Make sure the throttle twistgrip rotates easily from fully closed to fully open with the front wheel turned at various angles. The twistgrip should return automatically from fully open to fully closed when released.

2 If the throttle sticks, this is probably due to a cable fault. Remove the cables (see Chapter 4) and lubricate them (see Section 19). If the inner cables still do not run smoothly in the outer cables, fit new cables. With the cables removed, check that the twistgrip runs smoothly and freely around the handlebar – dirt and debris combined with a lack of lubrication can cause the action to be stiff. If necessary remove the end-weight from the handlebar, slide the twistgrip off and clean and lubricate it. Inspect the area around the cable sockets in the twistgrip for cracks – some have been known to break when there has been too little or no cable freeplay.

3 Install the lubricated or new cables, making sure they are correctly routed (see Chapter 4). If this fails to improve the operation of the throttle, the fault could lie in the throttle bodies. Remove the airbox and clean, check and lubricate the throttle linkage and idle air control valve linkage (see Chapter 4).

> **HAYNES HiNT** *If the motorcycle is constantly used in wet, dirty or dusty conditions, clean the throttle linkage and the idle air control valve linkage regularly, and lubricate them with a light spray lubricant.*

4 With the throttle operating smoothly, check for a small amount of freeplay in the opening cable. This is measured in terms of the amount of twistgrip rotation before the throttle opens **(see illustration)**. Compare the amount to that listed in this Chapter's Specifications.

4.4 Check for the specified amount of free rotation in the twistgrip

1•12 Routine maintenance and Servicing

4.5 Pull back the rubber boots to expose the opening throttle cable adjuster locknut (A) and adjuster (B)

4.8 Throttle opening cable locknut (A) and adjuster nut (B). Throttle closing cable deflection measurement point (C)

If it's incorrect, adjust the cables as follows.

5 An adjuster is incorporated at the twistgrip end of the opening cable – slide the rubber boot back to expose it (see illustration). Slacken the locknut on the adjuster, then turn the adjuster until the specified amount of freeplay is obtained (see this Chapter's Specifications), then retighten the locknut. Turn the adjuster in to increase freeplay and out to reduce it.

6 If the opening cable adjuster has reached its limit of adjustment, reset it so that it is halfway along its adjustment limit, then adjust both cables at the throttle body end as follows.

7 Remove the airbox (see Chapter 4).

8 Fully slacken the locknut holding the opening (upper) cable in the bracket to free the adjuster nut from its holding tabs (see illustration). Thread the adjuster nut up the cable to increase freeplay, and down to decrease it, then draw it up against the bracket and check the freeplay, readjusting as required until the specified amount of freeplay is obtained. Tighten the locknut onto the bracket on completion. With the throttle fully closed, check that there is the specified amount of freeplay (measured as total deflection of the inner cable wire) in the closing (lower) cable and adjust it at the bracket in the same way.

9 Further adjustments can now be made at the twistgrip end. If the cables cannot be adjusted as specified, replace them with new ones (see Chapter 4).

10 Check that the throttle twistgrip operates smoothly and snaps shut quickly when released. Install the airbox and fuel tank (see Chapter 4).

Warning: *Turn the handlebars all the way through their travel with the engine idling. Idle speed should not change. If it does, the cable may be routed incorrectly. Correct this condition before riding the bike.*

5 Cooling system

Warning: *The engine must be cool before beginning this procedure.*

Check

1 Check the coolant level in the reservoir (see *Pre-ride checks*).

2 Remove the side panels (see Chapter 7).

3 Check the entire cooling system for evidence of leaks. Examine each rubber coolant hose along its entire length. Look for cracks, abrasions and other damage. Squeeze each hose at various points (see illustration). They should feel firm, yet pliable, and return to their original shape when released. If they are dried out or hard, replace them with new ones.

4 Check for evidence of leaks at each cooling system joint. If necessary, tighten the hose clips carefully to prevent future leaks.

5 To prevent leakage of water from the cooling system to the lubrication system and vice versa, two seals are fitted on the water pump shaft. There is a drain hole between the seals in the seal housing section of the pump. If either seal fails, the drain allows the coolant or oil to escape via a tube through a hole in the bottom of the sump and prevents them mixing (see illustration). The seal on the water pump side is the mechanical type and bears on the rear face of the impeller. The second seal, mounted behind the mechanical seal, is of the normal feathered lip type. If on inspection the drain hole shows signs of coolant leakage, remove the pump and replace it with a new one (see Chapter 3) – the seals are not available separately.

6 Check the radiator for leaks and other damage. Leaks in the radiator leave tell-tale scale deposits or coolant stains on the outside of the core below the leak. If leaks are noted, remove the radiator (see Chapter 3) and either have it repaired by a professional or replace it with a new one.

Caution: *Do not use a liquid leak stopping compound to try to repair leaks.*

7 Check the radiator fins for mud, dirt and insects, which may impede the flow of air through the radiator – if a radiator guard is fitted remove one of the radiator panels and the grille for best visual access (see Chapter 7). If the fins are dirty, clean the radiator using

5.3 Squeeze the hoses to check for cracks, deterioration and hardening

5.5 Check the drainage tube (arrowed) in the sump for signs of leakage – shown with sump guard removed

Routine maintenance and Servicing 1•13

5.8a Clamp the hose (arrowed)...

5.8b ...otherwise the reservoir will drain itself when you remove the cap

water or low pressure compressed air directed through the fins from the rear face of the radiator – remove the radiator if necessary. If the fins are bent or distorted, straighten them carefully with a screwdriver. If airflow is restricted by bent or damaged fins over more than 30% of the radiator's surface area, fit a new radiator.

8 Clamp the hose from the reservoir close to its union on the radiator filler neck **(see illustration)** – this is because the coolant reservoir is mounted higher than the radiator, so it will start to empty itself via the hose into the filler neck, which will then overflow (assuming the radiator is full) as soon as you remove the pressure cap. Remove the pressure cap from the filler neck in the radiator by turning it anti-clockwise until it reaches a stop **(see illustration)**. If you hear a hissing sound (indicating there is still pressure in the system), wait until it stops. Now press down on the cap and continue turning it until it can be removed.

9 Check the condition of the coolant in the system. If it is rust-coloured or if accumulations of scale are visible, drain, flush and refill the system with new coolant (see below). Check the antifreeze content of the coolant with an antifreeze hydrometer – a 50% content should give a reading of 1.084 at 5°C to 1.074 at 25°C, varying accordingly in between. The system must have the correct coolant mixture (see Specifications) – if the coolant is too weak (i.e. too little anti-freeze giving a low reading – anything below 1.07 when cold and 1.06 when hot) there will not be adequate protection against freezing and corrosion, and if it is too strong the ability to cool the engine is reduced. If the hydrometer indicates an incorrect mixture, drain and refill the system (see below).

10 The function of the pressure cap is crucial to the correct running of the cooling system. Check the cap seal for cracks and other damage. If the coolant level consistently drops and/or the bike overheats, and no evidence of leaks can be found, fit a new pressure cap – the expense is minimal. If a new cap does not cure the problem have the entire system pressure checked by a dealer.

11 Fit the cap by turning it clockwise until it reaches the first stop, then push down on it and continue turning until it reaches the main stop. Remove the clamp from the reservoir hose.

12 Start the engine and let it reach normal operating temperature, then check for leaks again. As the coolant temperature increases beyond normal, the fan should come on automatically and the temperature should begin to drop. If it doesn't, refer to Chapter 3 and check the fan motor, relay and fan circuit carefully, then if the fan still does not work, refer to Chapter 4 and check the ECT sensor and the EMS relay, which controls the fan. Note that if the engine is switched off while the fan is running, the fan should continue to run until the coolant temperature has dropped to a normal level.

Coolant change

 Warning: Allow the engine to cool completely before performing this maintenance operation. Also, don't allow antifreeze to come into contact with your skin or the painted surfaces of the motorcycle. Rinse off spills immediately with plenty of water. Antifreeze is highly toxic if ingested. Never leave antifreeze lying around in an open container or in puddles on the floor; children and pets are attracted by its sweet smell and may drink it. Check with local authorities (councils) about disposing of antifreeze. Many communities have collection centres which will see that antifreeze is disposed of safely. Antifreeze is also combustible, so don't store it near open flames.

Draining

Note: *Car type hose clamps are used on the large bore coolant hoses. To release the clamps squeeze the ends together using large pliers, or use a dedicated automotive clamp tool, available from good tool suppliers* **(see illustrations 5.17a and b)**.

13 Remove the side panels (see Chapter 7).
14 Open the reservoir cap **(see illustration)**. Position a suitable container beneath the reservoir. Release the clamp and detach the hose from the bottom of the reservoir and allow it to drain **(see illustration)**.
15 Remove the pressure cap from the filler neck in the radiator by turning it anti-clockwise until it reaches a stop **(see illustration 5.8b)**.

5.14a Open the cap...

5.14b ...then detach the hose and drain the reservoir

1•14 Routine maintenance and Servicing

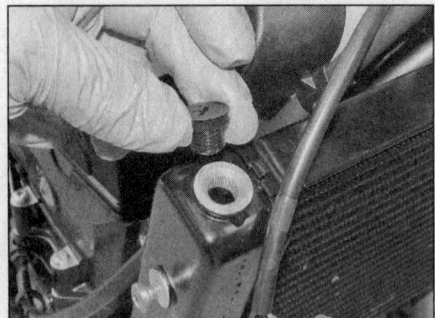

5.16 Remove the bleed-hole cap

If you hear a hissing sound (indicating there is still pressure in the system), wait until it stops. Now press down on the cap and continue turning it until it can be removed.

16 Unscrew the bleed-hole cap on the right-hand end of the radiator **(see illustration)**. Where fitted also remove the bleed-hole screw from the top hose coming from the radiator, noting the rubber sealing washer.

17 Position a suitable container beneath the pipe on the left-hand side of the engine. Release the clamp securing the bottom hose to the pipe and slide it along the hose, then detach the hose and allow the coolant to completely drain from both the radiator and the engine **(see illustrations)**.

Flushing

18 Run the radiator through with clean tap water by inserting a garden hose in the filler neck until the water flows out clear. If the radiator is extremely corroded, remove it (see Chapter 3) and have it cleaned professionally. Reconnect the hose and position the clamp as it was before – there should be 3 to 7 mm of hose exposed between the clamp and the end of the hose. Also flush the reservoir. Reconnect the hose to the reservoir and secure it with the clamp.

Refilling

19 Fill the system via the filler neck with the proper coolant mixture (see this Chapter's Specifications) **(see illustration)**. **Note:** *Pour the coolant in slowly to minimise the amount of air entering the system.* When the system appears full, squeeze the large-bore hoses to dislodge air bubbles, then take the bike off its stand and shake it and lean it to dissipate the coolant, then place the bike back on the stand and top the system up. Check that there is coolant visible in the bleed-hole(s). If there isn't, but the filler neck appears full, there is an air-lock somewhere. Try squeezing the pipes and shaking and leaning the bike again to disperse it. If that doesn't work you will need to siphon the coolant through the radiator using a vacuum pump – these are commercially available. Alternatively you may be able to form a sufficient seal using a piece of clear flexible tubing that fits tightly into the bleed hole, then sucking on the end of the

5.17a Release the clamp using long-nose pliers...

5.17b ...or a purpose-made tool...

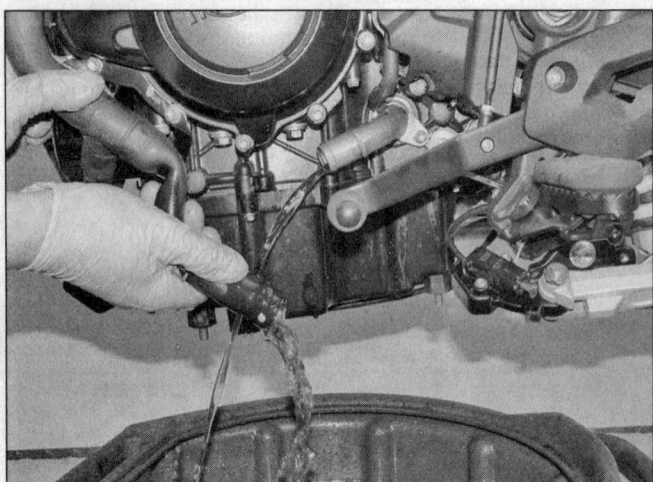

5.17c ...and allow the system to drain

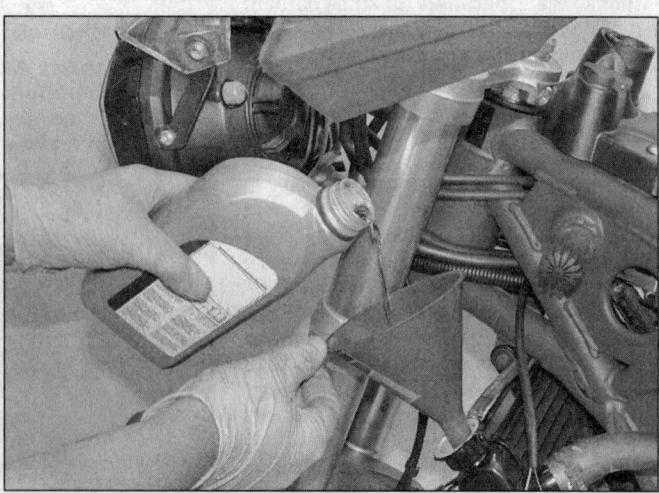

5.19 Fill the system as described

Routine maintenance and Servicing

tube – the reason the tube must be clear is so you can see the coolant when it exits the bleed hole and enters the tube, at which point stop sucking. DO NOT use tubing you can't see through – see **Warning**. If you cannot get coolant through to the bleed hole it is possible the radiator is blocked, and if so must be replaced with a new one.

20 Fit the bleed-hole screw(s), using a new rubber sealing washer with the screw for the top hose where fitted **(see illustration 5.16)**. Fit the pressure cap by turning it clockwise until it reaches the first stop, then push down on it and continue turning until it reaches the main stop.

21 Fill the coolant reservoir to the MAX level line.

22 Start the engine and allow it to idle for 2 to 3 minutes. Flick the throttle twistgrip part open 3 or 4 times, so that the engine speed rises to approximately 4000 – 5000 rpm, then stop the engine. Take the bike off its stand and shake it and lean it to dissipate the coolant, then place the bike back on the stand. Any air trapped in the system should have bled back to the filler neck.

23 Let the engine cool then remove the pressure cap as described in Step 8. Check that the coolant level is still up to the top of the filler neck – if it's low, add the specified mixture until it reaches the top, then refit the pressure cap and repeat Steps 22 and 23.

24 Check the coolant level in the reservoir and top up if necessary.

25 Run the engine until the cooling fan comes on. Check the system for leaks. Repeat Steps 23 and 24.

26 Do not dispose of the old coolant by pouring it down the drain. Instead pour it into a heavy plastic container, cap it tightly and take it into an authorised disposal site or service station – see **Warning** at the beginning of this Section.

27 Install the side panels (see Chapter 7).

6 Fuel system

Warning: Petrol (gasoline) is extremely flammable, so take extra precautions when you work on any part of the fuel system. Don't smoke or allow open flames or bare light bulbs near the work area, and don't work in a garage where a natural gas-type appliance is present. If you spill any fuel on your skin, rinse it off immediately with soap and water. When you perform any kind of work on the fuel system, wear safety glasses and have a fire extinguisher suitable for a Class B type fire (flammable liquids) on hand.

General checks

1 Raise and support the fuel tank (see Chapter 4). Check for signs of leaks, deterioration or damage; in particular check that there are no leaks from the fuel feed hose and its connector and from the fuel pump assembly sealing ring on the underside of the fuel tank **(see illustration)**. Also check the condition of the fuel tank drain and breather hoses.

2 Remove the airbox (see Chapter 4). Check the fuel supply hose connection to the fuel rail and the joints between the rail, the injectors and the throttle bodies **(see illustration)**. Refer to Chapter 4 for removal of the fuel rail if fuel leakage is evident.

3 If the tank has been leaking from the fuel pump seal, tightening the mounting plate bolts may help – remove the tank (see Chapter 4), then rest it upside down on some rag to do this. To ensure the plate is evenly seated, slacken the bolts a little first, then tighten them evenly and a little at a time in a criss-cross pattern to the torque setting specified at the beginning of the Chapter. If leakage persists,

6.1 Check the fuel hose and connector (A) and the pump seal (B)

remove the pump assembly and replace the seal with a new one (see Chapter 4).

4 Check the MAP sensor hoses for loose connections, cracks and deterioration, and replace them with new ones if necessary **(see illustration)**.

5 On California models, check the EVAP system hoses for loose connections, cracks and deterioration and replace them with new ones if necessary. At the specified service interval new hoses should be fitted whatever the apparent condition of the existing ones (see Chapter 4).

Fuel filter

6 A fuel filter is incorporated in the fuel pump assembly inside the tank.

7 If fuel starvation occurs and no other fault can be found it is possible the filter is blocked. The filter is part of the fuel pump assembly and is not available separately, so a new pump must be fitted (see Chapter 4).

Hose renewal

8 At the specified service interval new hoses should be fitted whatever the apparent condition of the existing ones. Remove the fuel tank, and if necessary the airbox, as required for access

6.2 Check the fuel hose connector on the fuel rail (arrowed), the fuel rail and injector joints, and the vacuum hoses

6.4 MAP sensor vacuum hose arrangement – throttle bodies shown removed and upside down for clarity

1•16 Routine maintenance and Servicing

7.2 Pump the forks to check their action

7.3 Check the fork inner tube (arrowed) below the dust seal for leaks, pitting and corrosion

to the hose(s) being replaced (see Chapter 4). Refer to the procedure in the relevant Section of Chapter 4 and detach the hose at each end, noting how it is secured and its routing. When fitting the new hose make sure it is correctly routed and secured as before.

9 Run the engine and check that there are no leaks before taking the machine out on the road.

7 Suspension

1 The suspension components must be maintained in top operating condition to ensure rider safety. Loose, worn or damaged suspension parts decrease the motorcycle's stability and control.

Front suspension

2 Stand alongside the motorcycle, apply the front brake and push on the handlebars to compress the forks several times (see illustration). Check they move up-and-down smoothly without binding. If binding is felt, the forks should be disassembled and inspected (see Chapter 5).

3 Inspect each fork inner tube for scratches, corrosion and pitting in the area of travel through the seals, which will cause premature seal failure (see illustration) – if the damage is excessive, new inner tubes should be fitted (see Chapter 5), or the inner tubes must be re-chromed using hard chrome.

4 Also check the inner tubes for signs of oil leakage. Carefully lever the dust seal out using a flat-bladed screwdriver and inspect the area around the oil seal. If leakage is evident, the seals must be replaced with new ones (see Chapter 5). If there is evidence of corrosion between the oil seal retaining ring and its groove in the fork tube, spray the area with a penetrative lubricant, otherwise the ring will be difficult to remove if needed. Press the dust seal back into the outer tube on completion.

5 Check the tightness of the fork clamp bolts to be sure none have worked loose, referring to the torque settings specified at the beginning of Chapter 5.

Rear suspension

6 Check the rear shock absorber for fluid leaks. If leaks are found, a new shock must be installed (see Chapter 5).

7 With the aid of an assistant to support the bike, compress the rear suspension several times (see illustration). It should move up and down freely without binding or rough spots or noises. If necessary the worn or faulty component must be identified and replaced with a new one. The problem could be due to the shock absorber, the suspension linkage components or the swingarm.

8 Support the bike on its centrestand if fitted, or on an auxiliary stand (but not a paddock stand under the swingarm!) so that the rear wheel is off the ground. Grab the swingarm and rock it from side-to-side – there should be no discernible movement at the rear (see illustration).

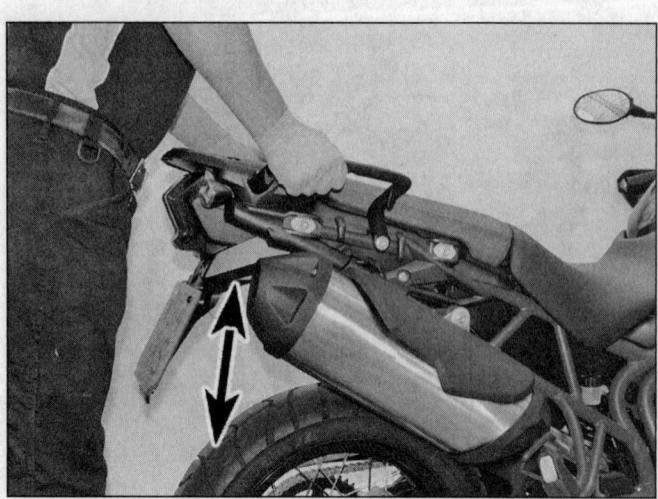

7.7 Pump the rear suspension to check its action

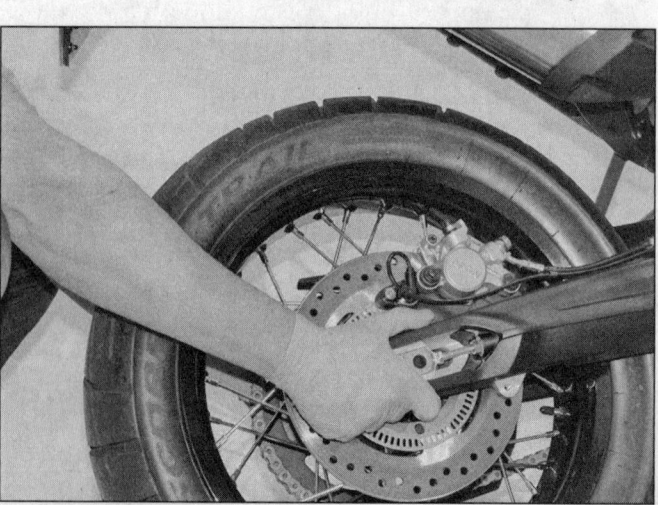

7.8 Checking for play in the swingarm bearings

Routine maintenance and Servicing

9 Next, grasp the top of the rear wheel and pull it upwards – there should be no discernible freeplay before the shock absorber begins to compress **(see illustration)**.

10 If there's a little movement or a slight clicking can be heard, check the tightness of the swingarm pivot nut, the shock absorber mounting bolts/nuts, and the suspension linkage mounting bolts/nuts,then re-check for movement. If there is still some noise or freeplay after everything has been correctly tightened then there is a worn bearing or bearings in the shock absorber, swingarm or linkage. The worn components must be identified and replaced with new ones (see Chapter 5).

11 You can make a more accurate assessment by isolating the swingarm and shock absorber from the linkage – remove the rear wheel (see Chapter 6) and the bolts securing the linkage to the shock absorber and swingarm (see Chapter 5).

12 Grasp the rear of the swingarm with one hand and place your other hand at the junction of the swingarm and the frame. Try to move the rear of the swingarm from side-to-side. Any wear (play) in the bearings should be felt as movement between the swingarm and the frame at the front. If there is any play, the swingarm will be felt to move forward and backward at the front (not from side-to-side). Next, move the swingarm up and down through its full travel. It should move freely, without any binding or rough spots. If there is any play in the swingarm or if it does not move freely, remove the bearings for inspection (see Chapter 5).

13 With the shock absorber and linkage detached check the bearings or bush in each component for corrosion and wear and failure of the seals, referring to Chapter 5 for details, and clean and re-grease or replace components as required.

Front fork oil change

14 Fork oil degrades over a period of time and loses its damping qualities.

15 At the prescribed interval change the oil as described in Chapter 5.

16 Fork oil quantity, level and oil type are given in the Specifications at the beginning of Chapter 5.

Swingarm and suspension linkage bearing lubrication

17 Over a period of time the seals are likely to fail and the grease in the bearings will be washed out, or it will harden and allow dirt and water to penetrate.

18 The rear suspension components are not equipped with grease nipples. Remove the swingarm and the suspension linkage as described in Chapter 5 for re-greasing of the bearings.

8 Sidestand and starter safety circuit

1 The sidestand return springs must be capable of retracting the stand fully, and holding the stand retracted when the motorcycle is in use **(see illustration)**. If a spring is sagged or broken it must be replaced with a new one. If a centrestand is fitted check it in the same way.

2 Lubricate the stand pivot regularly (see Section 19).

3 The sidestand switch prevents the motorcycle being started if it is in gear and the stand is down, and cuts the engine if the stand is put down while it is running and in gear. Check its operation by shifting the transmission into neutral, retracting the stand, pulling the clutch lever in and starting the engine. Pull in the clutch lever again and select a gear. Extend the sidestand. The engine should stop as the sidestand is extended. If the sidestand switch does not operate as described, check its circuit (see Chapter 8).

4 The neutral and clutch switches are also part of the same circuit – to check them, make sure the engine can be started with the sidestand in either position, as long as the transmission is in neutral and the clutch is pulled in, and cannot be started with the transmission in gear, even with the stand up and the clutch pulled in. If any of the situations are not as stated, check the circuit (see Chapter 8).

7.9 Checking for play in the suspension linkage bearings and shock mounts

9 Brake pad wear check

1 Each brake pad has one or more wear indicators that can be viewed without removing the pads from the caliper.

2 On the front brake pads when the friction material has worn to the bottom of the grooves (i.e. the grooves are only just or no longer visible), the pads must be replaced with new ones **(see illustration)**. Also check for uneven wear across the brake pads, which is indicative of a sticking or seized piston. If found, the calipers must be overhauled (see Chapter 6).

3 On the rear brake pads when the friction material has worn to the start of the groove in the rear edge of the friction material the

8.1 Check the stand springs (arrowed) with the sidestand up

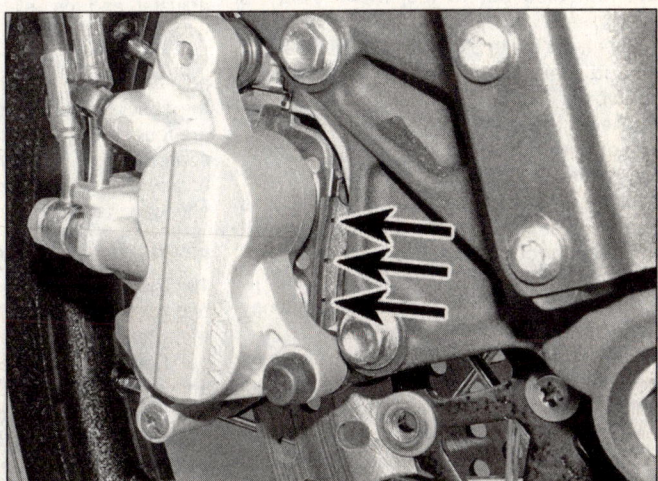

9.2 Front brake pad wear indicators (arrowed)

1•18 Routine maintenance and Servicing

9.3 Rear brake pad wear indicator (arrowed)

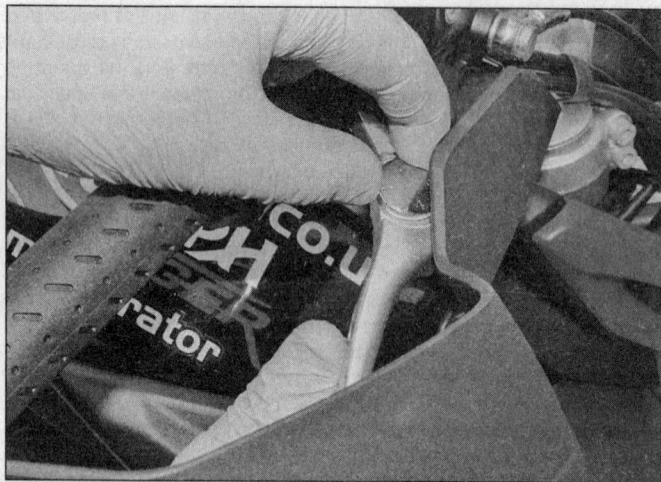

10.9 Adjusting the front brake lever span

pads must be replaced with new ones **(see illustration)**.

4 If the pads are dirty, or you are in doubt as to the amount of friction material remaining, remove them (see Chapter 6), clean them using brake system cleaner, and measure the amount of friction material remaining – the minimum specified by Triumph is 1.5 mm.

Caution: Do not allow the pads to wear beyond the wear limit indicator or minimum thickness.

5 Always renew brake pads in pairs, and renew the pads in both front brake calipers at the same time.

10 Brake system

General check

1 A routine general check of the brake system will ensure that any problems are discovered and remedied before the rider's safety is jeopardised.

2 Check the brake pads for wear (see Section 9), and make sure the fluid level in each reservoir is correct (see *Pre-ride checks*).

3 Check the brake lever and pedal for looseness, improper or rough action, excessive play, bends, and other damage. Replace any damaged parts with new ones (see Chapter 5). Clean and lubricate the lever and pedal pivots if their action is stiff or rough (see Section 19).

4 If the lever or pedal action feels spongy bleed the brakes (see Chapter 6).

5 Make sure all brake component fasteners are tight. Check that there is no sign of fluid leakage at the hose connections and that the hoses between the calipers and master cylinders are not cracked or damaged. On models with ABS also check the brake pipes to and from the modulator, and the hose/pipe joints – refer to Chapter 6 for details.

6 Inspect the master cylinders and calipers for any sign of fluid leakage due to failed seals. Leakage from the master cylinders is unlikely, but the caliper pistons can become corroded over a period of time, especially due to road salt over the winter, and this can lead to seal damage. Seal kits are available for the master cylinders and calipers – refer to Chapter 6.

7 Make sure the brake light comes on when the front brake lever is pulled in. The front brake light switch, mounted on the underside of the lever bracket, is not adjustable. If it fails to operate properly, check it (see Chapter 8).

8 Make sure the brake light comes on just before the rear brake takes effect. The switch is on the top of the master cylinder, securing the brake hose, and is actuated hydraulically and cannot be adjusted. If the brake light fails to operate properly check the switch (see Chapter 8).

9 The front brake lever has a span adjuster that alters the distance of the lever from the handlebar to suit different hand sizes. Each setting is identified by a number on the adjuster, and the selected number must align with the arrow on the lever bracket. Pull the lever away from the handlebar and turn the adjuster ring until the setting which best suits the rider is obtained **(see illustration)**. There are four settings – setting 1 gives the largest span, 4 the smallest. When making adjustment ensure that the pin set in the lever bracket is engaged in its detent in the adjuster.

Brake fluid change

10 The brake fluid should be changed every two years (or every 12,000 miles) or whenever a master cylinder or caliper overhaul is carried out. Refer to Chapter 6, Section 10 for details. Ensure that all the old fluid is pumped from the hydraulic system and that the level in the fluid reservoir is checked and the brakes tested before riding the motorcycle.

Brake hoses

11 The hoses will deteriorate with age and should be replaced with new ones if they show signs of cracking or deterioration. No interval is specified by Triumph, although generally every four years is advisable for the flexible hoses (see Chapter 6).

12 Always replace the banjo union sealing washers with new ones when fitting new hoses. Refill the system with new brake fluid and bleed the system as described in Chapter 6.

Brake caliper and master cylinder seals

13 Brake system seals will deteriorate with age and lose their effectiveness, leading to sticky operation of the brake master cylinders or the pistons in the brake calipers, or fluid loss. They should be replaced with new ones as soon as any loss in performance or fluid is noticed.

14 Replace all the seals in each caliper and master cylinder as a set; master cylinder seals are supplied as a kit along with a new piston and spring – see Chapter 6 for details.

11 Nuts and bolts tightness check

1 Since vibration of the machine tends to loosen fasteners, all nuts, bolts, screws, etc. should be periodically checked for proper tightness. If you feel the engine vibrating more than usual, check all engine mountings before assuming there are extensive internal problems.

2 Pay particular attention to the following:
Spark plugs
Engine oil drain plug
Gearchange lever and linkage, brake and clutch lever, and brake pedal
Sidestand nut/bolt
Engine mounting nuts/bolts
Shock absorber and suspension linkage nuts/bolts and swingarm pivot nut

Routine maintenance and Servicing

12.2 Adjusting the tension of a spoke

12.6 Checking for play in the wheel bearings

Handlebar clamp bolts
Front axle and axle clamp bolts
Front fork clamp bolts (top and bottom yoke)
Rear axle nut and chain adjuster locknuts
Brake caliper mounting bolts
Brake hose banjo bolts and caliper bleed valves
Brake disc bolts
Exhaust system nuts/bolts

3 If a torque wrench is available, use it along with the torque specifications at the beginning of this and other Chapters.

12 Wheels, wheel bearings and tyres

Wheels

Tiger 800

1 Cast wheels are virtually maintenance free, but they should be kept clean and checked periodically for cracks and other damage. Never attempt to repair cast wheels – if damaged they must be replaced with new ones. Also check wheel run-out and alignment (see Chapter 6). Check that the wheel balance weights are fixed firmly to the wheel rim. If you suspect that a weight has fallen off, have the wheel rebalanced by a motorcycle tyre specialist.

Tiger 800XC

2 Visually check the spokes for damage and corrosion. A broken or bent spoke must be replaced with a new one immediately because the load taken by it will be transferred to adjacent spokes which may in turn fail. Check the tension in each spoke by tapping each one lightly with a screwdriver and noting the sound produced – each should make the same sound of the correct pitch – properly tensioned spokes will make a sharp pinging sound, loose ones will produce a lower pitch dull sound, and tight ones will be higher pitched. If a spoke needs adjustment turn the adjuster at the rim using a spoke adjustment tool or a 6 mm open-ended spanner **(see illustration)**.

3 Unevenly tensioned spokes will promote rim misalignment – refer to information on wheel runout in Chapter 6 and seek the advice of a Triumph dealer or wheel building specialist if the wheel needs realigning, which it may well do if many spokes are unevenly tensioned. Check front and rear wheel alignment as described in Chapter 6. Check that any wheel balance weights are fixed firmly to the wheel rim. If you suspect that a weight has fallen off, have the wheel rebalanced by a motorcycle tyre specialist.

Wheel bearings

4 Wheel bearings will wear over a considerable mileage and should be checked periodically to avoid handling problems.

5 Support the motorcycle upright using an auxiliary stand so that the wheel being examined is off the ground.

6 Check for any play in the bearings by pushing and pulling the wheel against the hub **(see illustration)**. When checking the front wheel turn the handlebars to full lock on one side and hold the wheel against the lock. Also rotate the wheel and check that it turns smoothly and without any grating noises (bearing in mind that the brakes and final drive make some noise – do not confuse them).

7 If any play is detected in the hub, or if the wheel does not rotate smoothly (and this is not due to brake or transmission drag), the wheel should be removed and the bearings inspected for wear or damage (see Chapter 6).

Tyres

Note: *On models fitted with the tyre pressure monitoring system (TPMS) refer to Section 18 in Chapter 6.*

8 Check the tyre condition and tread depth thoroughly – see *Pre-ride checks*.

9 Make sure the valve cap is in place and tight. Check the valve for signs of damage. If tyre deflation occurs and it is not due to a slow puncture the valve core may be loose or it could be leaking past the seal – remove the cap and make sure the core is tight; if it is tight then it could be leaking – unscrew the core from the valve housing using a core removal tool (sometimes incorporated in the valve cap) and thread a new one in its place. A tool can be made quite easily by cutting a slot into the threaded end of a bolt using a hacksaw – the bolt must fit inside the valve housing and the slot must be the correct thickness to fit over the top of the core.

13 Clutch check

1 Check that the clutch lever operates smoothly and easily.

2 If the clutch lever operation is heavy or stiff, detach the cable at each end so it hangs down, and lubricate it (see Section 19). If the cable is still stiff, replace it with a new one. With the cable detached check the action of the clutch lever. If the lever is stiff or rough remove it and check for damage or distortion, or any other cause, and remedy as necessary. Clean and lubricate the pivot and contact areas (see Section 19). If the lever is good, refer to Chapter 2 and check the release mechanism in the cover, and if necessary the clutch itself.

3 With the cable operating smoothly, check that it is correctly adjusted with the correct amount of freeplay. Periodic adjustment is necessary to compensate for wear in the clutch plates and stretch of the cable. Take up the freeplay in the lever end until resistance is felt and check that the gap between the inner end of the lever and its bracket is within the range specified at the beginning of the Chapter

1•20 Routine maintenance and Servicing

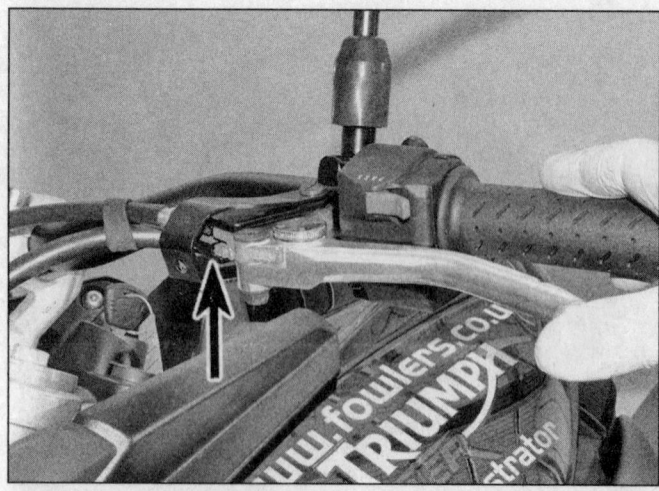

13.3 Clutch cable freeplay is measured at the gap between lever stock and bracket (arrowed)

13.4 Slacken the lockring (A) and turn the adjuster (B) to set the correct freeplay

(see illustration). On XC models remove the hand guard for better visual access if required (see Chapter 7).

4 If adjustment is required, slacken the lockring and turn the adjuster in or out until the required amount of freeplay is obtained **(see illustration)**. To increase freeplay, turn the adjuster clockwise (into the lever bracket). To reduce freeplay, turn the adjuster anti-clockwise (out of the lever bracket). Tighten the lockring on completion.

5 If all the adjustment has been taken up at the lever, reset the adjuster to give the maximum amount of freeplay by screwing it fully into the bracket (make sure the cable release slot in the adjuster does not align with that in the bracket), then set freeplay using the adjuster nuts on each end of the threaded section in the cable bracket on the right-hand side of the engine. To increase freeplay, slacken the front nut, then thread the rear nut up the cable until the freeplay is correct **(see illustration)**. To decrease freeplay, slacken the rear nut, then thread the front nut down the cable towards the bracket until the freeplay is correct. Now use the adjuster at the clutch lever bracket to set the specified clearance between the clutch lever and its bracket.

Caution: The specified clearance is very small and care must be taken to ensure that there is actually some freeplay in the cable, albeit a small amount, otherwise the clutch may slip.

6 The clutch lever has a span adjuster that alters the distance of the lever from the handlebar to suit different hand sizes. Each setting is identified by a number on the adjuster, and the selected number must align with the arrow on the lever bracket. Pull the lever away from the handlebar and turn the adjuster ring until the setting which best suits the rider is obtained **(see illustration)**. There are four settings – setting 1 gives the largest span, 4 the smallest. When making adjustment ensure that the pin set in the lever bracket is engaged in its detent in the adjuster.

14 Spark plugs

Check and adjustment

1 To remove the spark plugs you need a 16 mm plug socket. Make sure the ignition is switched OFF.

2 Remove the fuel tank (see Chapter 4).

3 The ignition coils, one for each cylinder, are integral with the spark plug caps. Clean the area around each coil to prevent any dirt falling into the spark plug channels.

4 Disconnect the wiring connector from each ignition coil **(see illustration)**. Pull the coils off the spark plugs **(see illustration)**.

5 Using compressed air if available, clean the area around the base of the spark plugs to prevent any dirt falling into the engine when they are removed.

6 Using either the plug removing tool supplied

13.5 Front nut (A), rear nut (B)

13.6 Adjusting the clutch lever span

Routine maintenance and Servicing

14.4a Disconnect the wiring connector from the coil...

14.4b ...then pull the coil off the spark plug

in the bike's toolkit or a deep socket type wrench, unscrew the plugs from the cylinder head and remove them **(see illustration)**. Lay each plug out in relation to its cylinder – if any plug shows up a problem it will then be easy to identify the troublesome cylinder.

7 Inspect the electrodes for wear. Both the centre and side electrodes should have square edges and the side electrodes should be of uniform thickness. Look for excessive deposits and evidence of a cracked or chipped insulator around the centre electrode. Compare your spark plugs to the colour spark plug reading chart on the inside rear cover of this manual. Check the threads, the washer and the ceramic insulator body for cracks and other damage.

8 If the electrodes are not excessively worn, and if the deposits can be easily removed with a wire brush, and there are no cracks or chips visible in the insulator, the plugs can be re-gapped and re-used. If in doubt concerning the condition of the plugs, replace them with new ones, as the expense is minimal.

9 Cleaning spark plugs by sandblasting is permitted, provided you clean the plugs with a high flash-point solvent afterwards.

10 Before installing the plugs, make sure they are the correct type and heat range and check the gap between the electrodes **(see illustrations)**. Compare the gap to that specified and adjust as necessary. If the gap must be adjusted, bend the side electrodes carefully and be very careful not to chip or crack the insulator nose **(see illustration)**. Make sure the sealing washer is in place on the plug before installing it.

11 Since the cylinder head is made of aluminium, which is soft and easily damaged, thread the plugs into the head turning the tool by hand **(see illustration 14.6)**. Once the plugs have seated and are finger-tight, tighten them to the torque setting specified at the beginning of the Chapter using a torque wrench if available, or by 1/4 to 1/2 turn more using the tool supplied or a socket drive if not. Do not over-tighten them.

14.6 Unscrew and remove the plug

connectors, making sure each goes to its correct cylinder **(see illustration 14.4a)**.
13 Install the fuel tank (see Chapter 4).

HAYNES HiNT As the plugs are quite deeply recessed, you can slip a short length of hose over the end of the plug to use as a tool to thread it into place. The hose will grip the plug well enough to turn it, but will start to slip if the plug begins to cross-thread in the hole – this will prevent damaged threads.

12 Fit the coils onto the spark plugs **(see illustration 14.4b)**. Connect the coil wiring

HAYNES HiNT Stripped plug threads in the cylinder head can be repaired with a Heli-Coil thread insert – see 'Tools and Workshop Tips' in the Reference section.

Renewal

14 Remove the old spark plugs as described above and install new ones.

14.10a Using a feeler gauge to measure the spark plug electrode gap

14.10b Using a wire type gauge to measure the spark plug electrode gap

14.10c Adjust the electrode gap by bending the side electrode only

1•22 Routine maintenance and Servicing

15 Idle speed and throttle body synchronisation

Idle speed

1 The engine idle speed cannot be adjusted in the conventional way. It can only be adjusted using the Triumph engine management system diagnostic tool (see Section 3). If the idle speed is incorrect (see Specifications at the beginning of the Chapter), first refer to Section 4 to clean and check the throttle cables and the throttle and idle air control valve linkages, then if necessary check the idle air control valve itself (see Chapter 4). If that is good take the bike to a Triumph dealer.

Throttle body synchronisation

⚠️ **Warning:** Petrol (gasoline) is extremely flammable, so take extra precautions when you work on any part of the fuel system. Don't smoke or allow open flames or bare light bulbs near the work area, and don't work in a garage where a natural gas-type appliance is present. If you spill any fuel on your skin, rinse it off immediately with soap and water. When you perform any kind of work on the fuel system, wear safety glasses and have a fire extinguisher suitable for a Class B type fire (flammable liquids) on hand.

⚠️ **Warning:** Do not allow exhaust gases to build up in the work area; either perform the check outside or use an exhaust gas extraction system.

2 Throttle body synchronisation is the process of adjusting the throttle bodies so they pass the same amount of fuel/air mixture to each cylinder. Throttle bodies that are out of synchronisation will result in a rough tick-over, less than ideal throttle response and may increase vibration levels.

Using the Triumph engine management system diagnostic tool

3 The most accurate way to synchronise the throttle bodies is with the Triumph engine management system diagnostic tool – take the bike to a Triumph dealer for this. The tool reads the three signals generated during each engine cycle by the MAP sensor, and by knowing which cylinder is on its intake stroke is able to distinguish which signal applies to which cylinder. The ECU sends the signals to the tool and this converts each one into a vacuum reading that is displayed on the screen. If the readings vary by more than a pre-determined amount and adjustment is required, this is done manually using the adjustment screws on the throttle bodies.

4 The throttle bodies can also be synchronised in the same way using some after-market diagnostic and tuning tools such as TuneECU, which is a software tool that can be downloaded to a Windows PC or laptop. A lead will then be needed to connect the PC or laptop to the bike via the diagnostic connector under the seat. Follow the on-screen instructions, and if adjustment is required do so in the same way as described in Step 5 for conventional gauges – you need to remove the airbox for access to the adjusters, and run the engine with the airbox removed but with the IAT and MAP sensors reconnected as described, but obviously you don't need to connect any vacuum hoses.

Using a set of vacuum gauges or a manometer

5 The throttle bodies can be adjusted in the conventional way by measuring the vacuum present in each throttle body using a set of vacuum gauges or a manometer. Note that the accuracy of the readings you will get depends entirely on the quality of the gauges you are using – there are budget DIY versions, such as the Morgan Carbtune Pro4 manometer, and there are expensive digital gauges more suited to a professional mechanic who is using them regularly. Follow the instructions supplied with your chosen tool.

6 First run the engine until it is warm. Remove the airbox (see Chapter 4). Disconnect the

15.6 Disconnect the No. 2 injector wiring

No. 2 fuel injector wiring connector (see illustration).

7 Carefully ease the blanking plug off each vacuum take-off point on each throttle body (see illustration) – on California models the unions have the EVAP system vacuum hoses instead of caps, so pull these off instead, and make sure you are disconnecting the EVAP hoses and not the MAP sensor hoses. Connect the gauge hoses in their place, No. 1 gauge to the No. 1 (left-hand) cylinder and so on (see illustrations). Make sure the hoses are in good condition and are fully pushed onto the unions on the gauges as well as on the throttle bodies – any air leak will result in false readings.

8 Reconnect the No. 2 injector wiring connector (see illustration 15.6). Remove the IAT and MAP sensors from the airbox cover and airbox respectively and reconnect the IAT sensor wiring and the MAP sensor wiring and vacuum hose (see Chapter 4). Fit the fuel tank back onto the bike in its raised position (see Chapter 4) – do not fit the airbox.

9 Run the engine at tick-over and check the readings on the gauges – the Nos. 1 and 3 cylinder readings should be the same as, or within 10 mmHg of, the No. 2 reading, which is the base (non-adjustable) throttle body (see illustrations). If there is a difference, adjust the relevant throttle body by turning the adjuster screw situated between it and the middle one

15.7a No. 1 throttle body vacuum point blanking plug (arrowed)

15.7b No. 2 throttle body vacuum point blanking plug (arrowed)

Routine maintenance and Servicing 1•23

15.7c No. 3 throttle body vacuum point blanking plug (arrowed)

15.7d Connect the gauge hoses to the take-off points as described

until it is the same as the No. 2 reading **(see illustration)** – turn the screw a small amount at a time and allow the reading to stabilise before making further adjustment. As the synchronisation improves the tick-over will sound smoother. Flick the throttle open and closed a couple of times then let it settle to idle speed again, and recheck the gauge readings, making further adjustments as required.

10 On completion disconnect the No. 2 fuel injector wiring connector and remove the gauge hoses, then refit the blanking caps (or EVAP hoses on California models) to the take-off points, and reconnect the injector. Install the airbox and fuel tank (see Chapter 4).

15.9a Using a Carbtune Pro 4

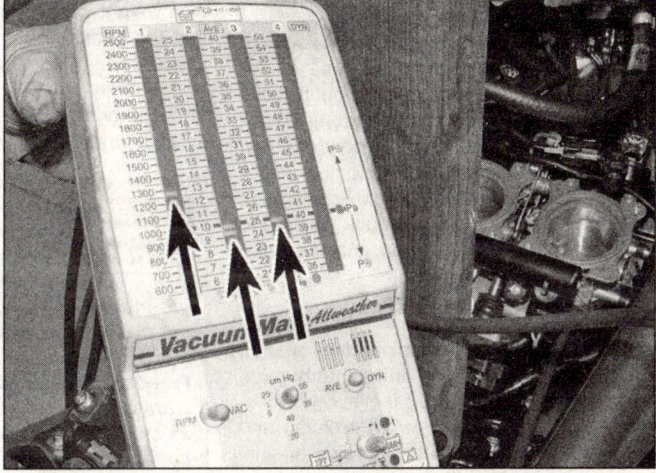

15.9b Using a professional digital gauge – this shows No. 1 reading to be higher than Nos. 2 and 3

15.9c Synchronisation screws (arrowed)

15.9d Adjusting No. 1 to bring it in line with No. 2

Routine maintenance and Servicing

16.4 Checking for play in the steering head bearings

16.6 Rest the handlebars as shown

16 Steering head bearings

1 Steering head bearings can become dented, rough or loose during normal use of the machine – wear or damage will be noticeable in the way the bike handles. In extreme cases, worn or loose steering head bearings can cause steering wobble – a condition that is potentially dangerous. It is good practice to check the bearings on a regular basis and adjust them if necessary as described below.

Check

2 Using the centrestand if fitted, and/or an auxiliary stand (not a front paddock stand), support the motorcycle in an upright position so that the front wheel is off the ground.
3 Point the front wheel straight-ahead and slowly move the handlebars from side-to-side. Any dents or roughness in the bearing races will be felt and the bars will not move smoothly and freely. Again point the wheel straight-ahead, and tap the front of the wheel to one side. The wheel should 'fall' under its own weight to the limit of its lock, indicating that the bearings are not too tight (take into account the restriction that the cables, hose and wiring have). Check for similar movement to the other side.
4 Next, grasp the forks and try to pull and

 Haynes Hint Make sure you are not mistaking any movement between the bike and stand, or between the stand and the ground, for freeplay in the bearings. Do not pull and push the forks too hard – a gentle movement is all that is needed. Freeplay between the fork tubes due to worn bushes can also be misinterpreted as steering head bearing play – do not confuse the two.

push them forward and backward **(see illustration)**. Any looseness in the steering head bearings will be felt as front-to-rear movement of the forks. If play is felt in the bearings, adjust the steering head as follows.

Adjustment

Caution: Take great care not to apply excessive pressure when adjusting the bearings because this will cause premature bearing failure.
5 Remove the cockpit trim panel (see Chapter 7). Remove the fuel tank to avoid the possibility of damage should a tool slip (see Chapter 4).
6 Displace the handlebars from the top yoke (see Chapter 5) – rest them behind the ignition switch on some rag **(see illustration)**.
7 Slacken the fork clamp bolts in the top yoke **(see illustration)**.
8 Wrap some masking tap around the steering stem nut to protect its finish **(see illustration)**. Unscrew the nut, and where fitted remove the

16.7 Slacken the clamp bolts (arrowed)

16.8a Wrap some tape around the steering stem nut...

Routine maintenance and Servicing

16.8b ...then unscrew it...

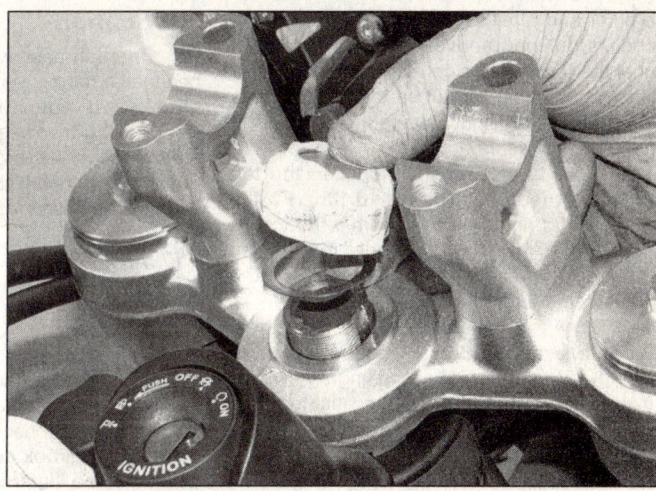

16.8c ...and remove the washer if fitted

washer **(see illustration). Note:** *The washer is fitted on models from VIN 515213-on, and Triumph specify that a new washer should be used each time it is removed. On models up to VIN 515212 Triumph specify to use a new nut each time it is removed, but will supply you with the new nut/washer arrangement, so that in the future you only have to replace the washer.*

9 Ease the top yoke up off the forks **(see illustration)**.
10 Using either the Triumph service tool (Part No. T3880023) or a C-spanner, unscrew the locknut, then lift off the tabbed washer **(see illustrations)**.
11 Triumph specify a torque setting for the adjuster nut, which can only be applied using their service tool (Part No. T3880023), or a suitable peg spanner, either bought commercially or fabricated by cutting castellations into an old 36 mm deep socket to fit the adjuster nut slots – two castellations opposite each other should be sufficient.

16.9 Lift the top yoke up and rest it on some rag

16.10a Unscrew the locknut using a C-spanner...

Slacken the adjuster nut slightly, then with the tool fitted to a torque wrench, apply a torque of 40 Nm to the adjuster nut – this will preload the bearings. Now slacken the nut and tighten it to the final torque setting of 10 Nm.
12 If a tool isn't available slacken the adjuster nut slightly using a C-spanner until pressure is just released, then tighten it until all freeplay is removed, then tighten it a little more **(see illustration)**. This pre-loads the bearings. Now slacken the nut, then tighten it again, setting it so that all freeplay is just removed yet the steering is able to move freely from side to side. To do this tighten the nut only a little at

16.10b ...and remove the tabbed washer

16.12 Using a C-spanner to adjust the steering head bearings

1•26 Routine maintenance and Servicing

a time, and after each tightening repeat the checks outlined above (see Steps 3 and 4) until the bearings are correctly set. The object is to set the adjuster nut so that the bearings are under a very light loading, just enough to remove any freeplay.

13 Fit the tabbed washer, locating the tab in the slot **(see illustration 16.10b)**. Fit the locknut and tighten it to 40 Nm if the tool is available, or using a C-spanner if not – the tabbed lockwasher is there to prevent the adjuster nut turning with it.

14 Fit the top yoke onto the steering stem **(see illustration 16.9)**. Fit the new washer and the steering stem nut (using a new one if necessary – see Step 8) and tighten it to 90 Nm **(see illustration 16.8b)**. Now tighten the fork clamp bolts to 20 Nm **(see illustration 16.7)**.

15 Install the handlebars (see Chapter 5).

16 Install the fuel tank (see Chapters 4 and 7).

Lubrication

17 Triumph specify that the steering head bearings must be re-greased at every second check and adjustment service interval. Re-greasing involves removing the steering stem – follow the procedure in Chapter 5 to remove and install the stem and adjust the bearings as described above on reassembly.

17 Air filter

1 Remove the fuel tank (see Chapter 4).
2 Disconnect the intake air temperature (IAT) sensor wiring connector **(see illustration)**.
3 Undo the airbox cover screws then lift the cover off **(see illustration)**.
4 Undo the filter element screws then lift the filter out **(see illustrations)**.
5 Clean the inside of the airbox. Remove

17.2 Disconnect the IAT sensor wiring connector (arrowed)

the crankcase breather mesh and clean it if necessary **(see illustration 17.4b)**. Check the condition of the crankcase breather hose and replace it with a new one if it is cracked or split **(see illustration)**. Check the condition of the cover sealing ring and replace it with

17.3 Airbox cover screws (arrowed)

17.4a Undo the screws (arrowed)...

17.4b ...and lift the filter out. Crankcase breather mesh (arrowed)

17.5a Crankcase breather hose (arrowed)

Routine maintenance and Servicing

17.5b Cover sealing ring (arrowed)

18.6 With the cam lobe pointing up use a feeler gauge to check the clearance

a new one if it is damaged or deformed **(see illustration)**. Make sure it is correctly seated.
6 Fit the new filter element into the airbox and secure it with its screws **(see illustration 17.4b and a)**. Fit the cover and secure it with the screws **(see illustration 17.3)**.
7 Connect the IAT sensor wiring connector **(see illustration 17.2)**.
8 Install the fuel tank (see Chapter 4).

> **HAYNES HiNT** If the motorcycle is constantly used in wet, dirty or dusty conditions, it is worth cleaning the element between renewal intervals. Remove it as described above, and tap it on a hard surface to dislodge any large particles of dirt, and check between the folds for any that are stuck. If compressed air is available, use it to clean the element, directing the air in the opposite direction of normal flow. If the element is torn or cannot be cleaned, or is obviously beyond further use, replace it with a new one.

18 Valve clearances

Check

1 The engine must be completely cold for this maintenance procedure.
2 Remove the spark plugs (see Section 14).
3 Remove the valve cover (see Chapter 2). The cylinders are numbered 1 to 3 from left to right. Make a chart or sketch of all valve positions so that a note of each clearance can be made against the relevant valve.
4 The clearance for a particular valve can be measured when the cam lobe for that valve is pointing away from it, and there is one point during the engine cycle when all the lobes above the valves for a particular cylinder are pointing up – this is when the piston in that cylinder is at top dead centre (TDC) on the compression stroke, and all its valves are closed. To turn the camshafts, place the motorcycle on its centrestand if fitted, or on an auxiliary stand or stands so that the rear wheel is off the ground – a rear paddock stand is ideal, but axle stands can be used with care, using rag to cushion and protect components and prevent scratches. Tie the front brake lever on so the bike can't roll forwards. Select a high gear, and rotate the rear wheel by hand in its normal direction of rotation.
5 Turn the rear wheel until all the camshaft lobes above the No. 1 cylinder are pointing away from the valves. The No. 1 cylinder is now at TDC on the compression stroke. Insert a feeler gauge of the same thickness as the correct valve clearance (see Specifications at the beginning of the Chapter) between the base of the camshaft lobe and the cam follower of each valve in turn and check that it is a firm sliding fit – you should feel a slight drag when the you pull the gauge out **(see illustration 18.6)**. If not, use the feeler gauges to obtain the exact clearance. Record the measured clearance on the chart. Note that there is a difference in the clearance between the intake valves (across the back of the cylinder head) and the exhaust valves (across the front).

6 Now turn the rear wheel until the camshaft lobes for the No. 2 cylinder are facing away from the valves. The No. 2 cylinder is now at TDC on the compression stroke. Measure the clearances of the valves using the method described in Step 5 **(see illustration)**.
7 Now turn the rear wheel until the camshaft lobes for the No. 3 cylinder are facing away from the valves. The No. 3 cylinder is now at TDC on the compression stroke **(see illustration 18.6)**. Measure the clearances of the valves using the method described in Step 5.
8 When all clearances have been measured and charted, identify whether the clearance on any valve falls outside the ranges specified. If it does, the valve shim on that particular valve must be replaced with one of a thickness that will restore the correct clearance – see Step 9-on). If all clearances are good install the valve cover (see Chapter 2) and spark plugs (Section 14).

Shim adjustment

9 Remove the camshafts (see Chapter 2). Place rags over the spark plug holes and the cam chain tunnel to prevent a shim dropping into the engine on removal.
10 Remove the cam follower of the valve in question, using a suction tool or magnet if needed **(see illustration)**. Retrieve the shim from inside the follower **(see illustration)** – if it

18.10a Lift out the cam follower...

18.10b ...and retrieve the shim (arrowed)

1•28 Routine maintenance and Servicing

18.11 Measure the shim using a micrometer to confirm its size

18.16a Fit the shim into its recess...

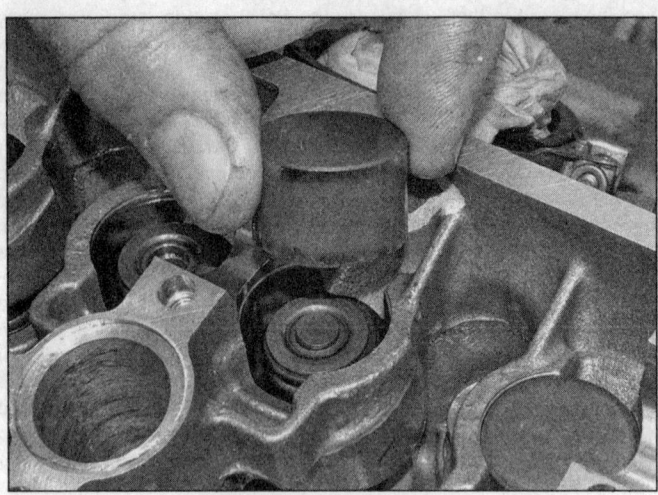

18.16b ...then fit the follower

19.3a Fit the cable into the adapter...

19.3b ...and tighten the screw to seal it in...

19.3c ...then apply the lubricant using the nozzle provided inserted in the hole in the adapter

is not there pick it out of the top of the valve using a magnet or a small screwdriver with a dab of grease on it (the shim will stick to the grease) **(see illustration 18.16a)**. Do not allow the shim to fall into the engine.

11 The shim size may be marked on one face, but ignore this as the shim may be worn, and any wear must be taken into account when calculating the valve clearance. Measure the thickness of the shim with a micrometer **(see illustration)**.

12 The required new shim size can be calculated as follows – always aim to get the clearance at the mid-point of the specified range.

13 If the valve clearance is less than specified, subtract the measured clearance from the specified clearance, then deduct the result from the original shim thickness to obtain the required thickness of the new shim. For example:

Sample calculation – intake valve clearance too small

Specified clearance: 0.15 mm
(0.10 to 0.20 mm)
Measured clearance: 0.08 mm
Difference: 0.07 mm
Shim thickness fitted: 2.575 mm
Correct shim thickness required is
2.575 – 0.07 = 2.505 mm

14 If the valve clearance is greater than specified, subtract the specified clearance from the measured clearance, and add the result to the thickness of the original shim to obtain the required thickness of the new shim. For example:

Sample calculation – exhaust valve clearance too large

Specified clearance: 0.35 mm
(0.325 to 0.375 mm)
Measured clearance: 0.42 mm
Difference: 0.07 mm
Shim thickness fitted: 1.975 mm
Correct shim thickness required is
1.975 + 0.07 = 2.045 mm

15 Obtain the correct thickness shim(s) from a Triumph dealer. Where the required thickness is not equal to the available shim thickness, round off the measurement to the nearest available size. Shims are available in 0.025 mm increments from 1.70 mm to 3.00 mm. **Note:** *If the required replacement shim is greater than 3.00 mm (the largest available), the valve is probably not seating correctly due to a build-up of carbon deposits or valve damage. Remove the valve for checking (see Chapter 2).*

16 Lubricate the new shim with molybdenum disulphide oil (a 50/50 mixture of molybdenum disulphide grease and engine oil) and fit it into its recess in the top of the valve **(see illustration)**. Check that the shim is correctly seated, then lubricate the follower with molybdenum disulphide oil and fit it onto the valve **(see illustration)**. Repeat the procedure for any other valves as required, then install the camshafts (see Chapter 2).

17 Rotate the rear wheel several turns to seat the new shim(s), then check the clearances again.

18 Install the valve cover and spark plugs.

19 Stand, lever pivots and cable lubrication

1 Since the controls, cables and various other components of a motorcycle are exposed to the elements, they should be lubricated periodically to ensure safe and trouble-free operation.

2 The footrests, clutch and brake levers, brake pedal, gearchange lever and linkage, and stand pivot(s) should be lubricated frequently. In order for the lubricant to be applied where it will do the most good, the component should be disassembled (see Chapter 5), cleaned, and the recommended lubricant applied (see Specifications). However, if an aerosol spray lubricant is used, it can be applied to the pivot joint gaps and will usually work its way into the areas where friction occurs.

3 To lubricate the throttle and clutch cables, disconnect the relevant cable at its upper end, then lubricate the cable with a pressure adapter **(see illustrations)**. See Chapter 4 for the throttle cable removal procedures, and Chapter 2 for the clutch cable.

20 Battery

1 All models are fitted with a maintenance-free (sealed) battery, which requires no maintenance. **Note:** *Do not attempt to remove the battery caps to check the electrolyte level or battery specific gravity. Removal will damage the caps, resulting in electrolyte leakage and battery damage.* All that should be done is to check that the terminals are clean and tight and that the casing is not damaged or leaking. See Chapter 8 for further details.

2 If the machine is not in regular use, disconnect the battery and give it a refresher charge every month to six weeks (see Chapter 8).

Notes

Chapter 2
Engine, clutch and transmission

Contents

	Section number
Alternator	see Chapter 8
Balancer shaft	26
Cam chain and tensioner/guide blades	10
Cam chain tensioner	8
Camshafts and followers	9
Clutch	16
Clutch cable	17
Clutch check	see Chapter 1
Component access	2
Connecting rods and big-end bearings	24
Crankcase inspection	22
Crankcase separation and reassembly	21
Crankshaft and main bearings	25
Cylinder head and valve overhaul	13
Cylinder head removal and installation	12
Cylinder liners	14
Engine overhaul information	5
Engine removal and installation	4

	Section number
Engine wear assessment	3
Gearchange mechanism	20
General information	1
Main and connecting rod bearing information	23
Oil and filter change	see Chapter 1
Oil cooler	6
Oil level check	see *Pre-ride checks*
Oil and water pump	19
Pistons and piston rings	15
Running-in procedure	30
Selector drum and forks	29
Starter clutch and gears	11
Starter motor	see Chapter 8
Sump, oil strainer and oil pressure relief valve	18
Transmission shaft overhaul	28
Transmission shaft removal and installation	27
Valve clearance check	see Chapter 1
Valve cover	7

Degrees of difficulty

Easy, suitable for novice with little experience	**Fairly easy,** suitable for beginner with some experience	**Fairly difficult,** suitable for competent DIY mechanic	**Difficult,** suitable for experienced DIY mechanic	**Very difficult,** suitable for expert DIY or professional

Specifications

General
Capacity	799 cc
Bore	74.0 mm
Stroke	61.94 mm
Compression ratio	11.11 to 1
Cylinder numbering (from left side to right side of the bike)	1-2-3
Firing order	1-2-3

2•2 Engine, clutch and transmission

Camshafts and cam chain
Camshaft runout	0.015 mm max.
Camshaft end-float	
Standard	0.23 to 0.33 mm
Maximum	0.4 mm
Camshaft bearing oil clearance	
Standard	0.040 to 0.081 mm
Service limit (max)	0.13 mm
Camshaft journal diameter	23.940 to 23.960 mm
Camshaft bearing bore diameter	24.000 to 24.021 mm
Cam chain stretch limit	149.48 mm
Cam follower diameter	
Standard	25.380 to 25.406 mm
Service limit (min)	25.368 mm
Cam follower bore diameter	
Standard	25.415 to 25.435 mm
Service limit (max)	25.449 mm

Valves, guides and springs
Valve clearances	see Chapter 1
Valve head diameter	
Intake valve	30.5 mm
Exhaust valve	25.5 mm
Intake valve stem diameter	
Standard	3.975 to 3.990 mm
Service limit	3.965 mm
Exhaust valve stem diameter	
Standard	3.955 to 3.970 mm
Service limit	3.945 mm
Intake and exhaust valve guide bore diameter	
Standard	4.000 to 4.015 mm
Service limit	4.043 mm
Intake valve stem-to-guide clearance	
Standard	0.01 to 0.04 mm
Service limit	0.078 mm
Exhaust valve stem-to-guide clearance	
Standard	0.03 to 0.06 mm
Service limit	0.098 mm
Intake valve seat width (in head)	
Standard	0.8 to 1.2 mm
Service limit	1.5 mm
Exhaust valve seat width (in head)	
Standard	1.0 to 1.4 mm
Service limit	1.7 mm
Valve seat width (on valve)	
Intake valve	0.99 to 1.86 mm
Exhaust valve	1.06 to 1.93 mm
Valve spring load at length	483 to 533 N at 27.5 mm

Cylinder liners
Cylinder liner ID	
Standard	74.040 to 74.060 mm
Service limit	74.150 mm
Cylinder compression	150 to 180 psi (10 to 12.5 Bars)

Pistons
Piston OD (measured 8 mm up from skirt, at 90° to piston pin axis)	
Standard	73.974 to 73.990 mm
Service limit	73.930 mm
Piston pin bore diameter in piston	
Standard	16.004 to 16.012 mm
Service limit	16.040 mm
Piston pin diameter	
Standard	15.995 to 16.000 mm
Service limit	15.985 mm
Connecting rod small-end diameter	
Standard	16.016 to 16.029 mm
Service limit	16.039 mm

Piston rings
Ring-to-groove clearance – top and second rings
  Standard.. 0.02 to 0.06 mm
  Service limit.. 0.075 mm
End gap (installed)
  Top ring
    Standard.. 0.15 to 0.3 mm
    Service limit.. 0.6 mm
  Second ring
    Standard.. 0.30 to 0.45 mm
    Service limit.. 0.75 mm
  Oil control ring side rails................................ 0.20 to 0.70 mm

Clutch
Friction plates
  Quantity... 9
  Thickness
    Standard.. 3.0 mm
    Service limit.. 2.8 mm
Plain plates
  Quantity... 8
  Warpage (service limit)................................. 0.20 mm
Clutch cable freeplay...................................... see Chapter 1
Clutch pack height.. 41.54 to 42.54 mm

Lubrication system
Oil pressure @ 5000 rpm.................................. 49 psi (3.4 Bars) @ 5000 rpm, oil at 80°C
Oil pump rotor tip-to-outer rotor clearance
  Standard... 0.15 mm
  Service limit.. 0.20 mm
Oil pump outer rotor-to-body clearance
  Standard... 0.15 to 0.22 mm
  Service limit.. 0.35 mm
Oil pump rotor end-float
  Standard... 0.04 to 0.09 mm
  Service limit.. 0.17 mm

Connecting rods and bearings
Connecting rod big-end side clearance
  Standard... 0.15 to 0.30 mm
  Service limit.. 0.50 mm
Connecting rod big-end bearing oil clearance
  Standard... 0.035 to 0.065 mm
  Service limit.. 0.07 mm

Crankshaft and main bearings
Main bearing oil clearance
  Standard... 0.020 to 0.044 mm
  Service limit.. 0.07 mm
Main bearing journal diameter
  Standard... 32.984 to 33.000 mm
  Service limit.. 32.960 mm
Crankpin journal diameter
  Standard... 32.984 to 33.000 mm
  Service limit.. 32.960 mm
Crankshaft end-float.. 0.15 to 0.30 mm
Crankshaft run-out
  Standard... 0.02 mm or less
  Service limit.. 0.05 mm

Transmission
Primary reduction ratio..................................... 1.667 to 1 (85/51)
Gear ratios (No. of teeth)
  First gear... 2.313 to 1 (37/16)
  Second gear.. 1.857 to 1 (39/21)
  Third gear.. 1.500 to 1 (36/24)
  Fourth gear.. 1.285 to 1 (27/21)
  Fifth gear... 1.136 to 1 (25/22)
  Sixth gear.. 1.043 to 1 (24/23)
Final reduction ratio... 3.125 to 1 (50/16)

Selector drum and forks

Selector fork end width
   Standard .... 5.9 to 6.0 mm
   Service limit .... 5.8 mm
Selector fork groove width in gears
   Standard .... 6.10 to 6.17 mm
   Service limit .... 6.27 mm
Selector fork-to-groove clearance .... 0.47 mm maximum

Torque settings

Balancer shaft cover bolts .... 12 Nm
Cam chain guide blade pivot bolt .... 9 Nm
Cam chain support bolt .... 12 Nm
Cam chain tensioner mounting bolts .... 9 Nm
Camshaft holder bolts
   Initial setting .... 5 Nm
   Final setting .... 10 Nm
Camshaft sprocket bolts
   Up to engine No .602077 .... 10 Nm
   From engine No. 602078 .... 22 Nm
Clutch centre nut .... 98 Nm
Clutch cover bolts .... 12 Nm
Clutch pressure plate bolts .... 10 Nm
Connecting rod cap bolts .... see Section 24
Coolant inlet and outlet pipe bolts .... 12 Nm
Crankcase 6 mm bolts (see text) .... 12 Nm
Crankcase 8 mm bolts (see text) .... 22 Nm
Crankcase breather tube screw .... 9 Nm
Cylinder head bolts
   Stage 1 .... 15 Nm
   Stage 2 .... 20 Nm
   Stage 3 .... Angle-tighten 120°
Cylinder head-to-crankcase screws .... 10 Nm
Engine mounting bolts
   Rear mounting adjuster (where fitted) .... 3 Nm
   Front mounting bolt nuts .... 48 Nm
   Centre mounting bolts .... 48 Nm
   Rear mounting bolt nut .... 48 Nm
Internal oil pipe bolts .... 12 Nm
Gearchange mechanism centralising spring locating pin .... 15 Nm
Oil cooler bolt .... 59 Nm
Oil pressure relief valve .... 15 Nm
Oil pump body bolts .... 12 Nm
Oil pump drive chain guide bolts .... 9 Nm
Oil pump driven sprocket bolt .... 12 Nm
Oil pump mounting bolts .... 12 Nm
Oil strainer bolts .... 12 Nm
Right-hand crankcase cover bolts .... 12 Nm
Selector fork shaft and drum bearing retainer bolts .... 12 Nm
Selector drum camplate bolt .... 12 Nm
Starter clutch bolts .... 16 Nm
Sump bolts .... 12 Nm
Transmission input shaft bearing housing bolts .... 12 Nm
Valve cover bolts .... 10 Nm

Engine, clutch and transmission

1 General information

The engine/transmission is a water-cooled, in-line three-cylinder design, fitted across the frame. The twelve valves are operated by double overhead camshafts, chain driven off the right-hand end of the crankshaft. The pistons run in removable liners, surrounded by a water jacket. A single balancer shaft is gear driven directly off the crankshaft.

The engine/transmission unit is constructed in aluminium alloy with the crankcase divided horizontally. The crankcase incorporates a wet sump, pressure fed lubrication system. The oil pump, which comes as an integrated assembly with the water pump, is chain driven off the back of the clutch housing.

The clutch is the wet, multi-plate type and is gear driven off the crankshaft. The alternator is mounted on the left-hand end of the crankshaft.

The transmission is six-speed constant mesh. Final drive to the rear wheel is by chain and sprockets.

Some of the bolts used on Triumph motorcycles are of the Torx type. Unless you are already equipped with a good range of Torx bits, you are advised to purchase a set before attempting work on the engine. Make sure you get bits that can be used in conjunction with a socket set so that a torque wrench can be applied – a Torx key set will not be adequate on its own, though will be a useful addition to the bits.

2 Component access

Operations possible with the engine in the frame

The components and assemblies listed below can be removed without having to remove the engine/transmission assembly from the frame. However if a number of areas require attention at the same time, removal of the engine is recommended.

Valve cover
Cam chain tensioner
Camshafts and followers
Cam chain, tensioner blade and guide blade
Starter motor
Alternator and starter clutch
Clutch
Gearchange mechanism (selector arm/shaft, stopper arm and detent camplate)
Oil pump/water pump
Oil cooler
Sump, oil strainer and pressure relief valve

Operations requiring engine removal

It is necessary to remove the engine/transmission assembly from the frame to gain access to the following components.
Cylinder head
Cylinder liners and pistons
Connecting rods and bearings
Crankshaft and bearings
Balancer shaft
Transmission shafts
Selector drum and forks

3 Engine wear assessment

1 Poor engine performance may be caused by leaking valves, incorrect valve clearances, a leaking head gasket, or worn pistons, piston rings or cylinders. A cylinder compression check will highlight these conditions and can also indicate the presence of excessive carbon deposits in the cylinder head, and a leakdown test (for which special equipment is needed – consult a Triumph dealer) will pinpoint the actual cause(s) of the problem.

Cylinder compression check

Special tool: *A compression gauge is needed – use one with a threaded hose and adaptor to fit the spark plug holes. Depending on the outcome of the initial test, a squirt-type oil can may also be needed.*
Note: *Turning the engine over with the ignition coils removed could generate a fault code in the engine management system – to clear this you will need to see a Triumph dealer equipped with the Diagnostic tool. See Chapter 4 for more information.*

2 Make sure the valve clearances are correctly set (see Chapter 1).
3 Run the engine until it is at normal operating temperature.
4 Remove the spark plugs (see Chapter 1).
5 Select the adapter that matches the spark plug threads (10mm diameter x 1.0mm pitch) and fit it onto the gauge **(see illustration)**. Fit the gauge into the No. 1 cylinder spark plug hole **(see illustration)**.
6 With the ignition switch ON, the kill switch set to RUN, the clutch lever pulled in and the throttle held fully open, turn the engine over on the starter motor until the gauge reading has built up and stabilised **(see illustration)**.
7 Record the reading, then repeat for the other two cylinders.
8 Triumph give no specification for cylinder compression, but generally a range of 150 to 180 psi (10 to 12.5 Bar) is normal, while much above or below this can be considered high or low and should be investigated. Also, there should be no more than about 25 psi (1.7 Bar) difference between any of the cylinders, even if the figures for all cylinders are within the general limits.
9 If the reading is low, it could be due to a worn cylinder bore, piston or rings, failure of the head gasket, or worn valve seats. To determine which is the cause, pour a small quantity of engine oil into the spark plug hole to seal the rings, then repeat the compression test. If the figures are noticeably higher the cause is worn cylinder, piston or rings. If there is no change the cause is a leaking head gasket or worn valve seats.
10 If the reading is high there could be a build-up of carbon deposits in the combustion chamber. Remove the cylinder head and scrape all deposits off the piston and the cylinder head.

Leak-down (cylinder leakage) test

11 A leak down or 'cylinder leakage' test is similar to a compression test in that it tells you how well a cylinder is sealing, but it does so by testing how much pressure is lost through leakage, as opposed to how much pressure is created through compression.

3.5a Make sure the adapter matches the plug...

3.5b ...then thread it into the plug hole

3.6 Checking cylinder compression

2•6 Engine, clutch and transmission

Many professionals prefer a leak test to a compression test as it more accurately pin-points the cause of the problem before any disassembly is done, as it is easy to tell where the leakage is occurring. Generally however the required equipment is more expensive than for a compression test and a source of compressed air is essential. If you think a test is needed take the bike to a suitably equipped dealer or workshop. If you decide to purchase your own equipment follow the manufacturer's instructions.

12 A leakage test can also be used in conjunction with a compression test to diagnose other kinds of problems, such as a faulty valve train component, incorrect valve timing, faulty ignition or fuel delivery problems.

Oil pressure check

Special Tool: *An oil pressure gauge and adapter that screws into the oil pressure switch are needed. Triumph do not list an adapter as a spare part, but it is worth checking with a dealer as to availability. Otherwise, remove the pressure switch (see Chapter 8), and take it to an accessory dealer to match it up – if you are buying a pressure gauge, it may well come with a range of adapters.*

13 Warm the engine up to normal operating temperature then stop it.
14 Remove the oil pressure switch (see Chapter 8). Select the adapter that matches the switch threads and fit it onto the gauge. Screw the gauge adapter into the switch hole. Connect the gauge to the adapter. Install all parts essential for running the engine that were removed to access the oil pressure switch (i.e. throttle bodies, airbox and fuel tank – see Chapter 4).
15 Start the engine and increase the engine Street to 5000 rpm whilst watching the gauge reading. The oil pressure should be similar to that given in the Specifications at the start of this Chapter.
16 If the pressure is significantly lower than the standard, either the relief valve is stuck open, the oil pump is faulty, the oil pump pick-up strainer is blocked or there is other engine damage. Begin diagnosis by checking the oil pump pick-up strainer (see Section 18), then the oil pump. If those items check out okay, chances are the bearing oil clearances are excessive and the engine needs to be overhauled.
17 If the pressure is too high, the relief valve is stuck closed. To check it, see Section 18.
18 Stop the engine. Unscrew the gauge and adapter from the crankcase. Install the oil pressure switch (see Chapter 8).

4 Engine removal and installation

Caution: *The engine is very heavy. Engine removal and installation should be carried out with the aid of at least one assistant.*

4.10a Note the alignment of the punch mark (arrowed)...

Personal injury or damage could occur if the engine falls or is dropped. An hydraulic or mechanical floor jack should be used to support and lower or raise the engine if possible.

Note: *If you are removing the engine for an overhaul it is best to remove the alternator and clutch with the engine still in the frame – refer to Section 16 for the clutch and Chapter 8 for the alternator.*

Note: *Triumph specifies that new nuts should be used on the engine mounting bolts on installation of the engine.*

Removal

1 Position the bike on the centrestand if fitted, or on an auxiliary stand or stands, so that it is supported in an upright position and is secure – as the swingarm has to be removed it is best supported as described at the beginning of Section 13 in Chapter 5. Lock the front brake on by fitting a cable-tie around the handlebar and brake lever. Work can be made easier by raising the machine to a suitable height on an hydraulic ramp.
2 Remove the sump guard, and where fitted the engine protection bars (see Chapter 7). If the engine is dirty, particularly around its mountings, wash it thoroughly before starting any major dismantling. This will make work much easier and rule out the possibility of caked-on lumps of dirt falling into some vital component.
3 Remove the battery (see Chapter 8).

4.15 Disconnect the sub-loom wiring connector (arrowed)

4.10b ...then unscrew the bolt and slide the arm off

4 Remove the fuel tank, the airbox and the throttle bodies (see Chapter 4).
5 Remove the ignition coils (see Chapter 4).
6 Drain the engine oil (see Chapter 1). If required remove the oil filter (see Chapter 1).
7 Drain the coolant (see Chapter 1).
8 Remove the radiator along with all the coolant hoses (i.e. detaching them from the engine rather than the radiator), noting their routing (see Chapter 3). It is advisable to tag the end of each hose using masking tape, then write the location of the hose on the tape. If required remove the oil cooler (see Section 6).
9 Remove the exhaust system (Chapter 4).
10 Note the alignment of the punch mark on the gearchange shaft end with the slit in the linkage arm clamp **(see illustration)**. Unscrew the pinch bolt and slide the arm off the shaft **(see illustration)**.
11 Remove the front sprocket (see Chapter 6).
12 Remove the rear brake pedal and the swingarm (see Chapter 5).
13 Unscrew the clutch cable bracket bolt then detach the cable end from the release mechanism arm **(see illustrations 16.2a and b)**.
14 Remove the starter motor (see Chapter 8).
15 Disconnect the sub-loom wiring connector for the ECT (engine coolant temperature) sensor, CKP (crankshaft position) sensor and oil pressure switch **(see illustration)**.
16 Displace the ignition switch wiring connector from its bracket **(see illustration)**.

4.16a Displace the ignition switch connector (arrowed)...

Engine, clutch and transmission 2•7

4.16b ...and where fitted the ABS sensor connector (arrowed)...

4.16c ...then unscrew the bolt (arrowed)

4.16d Disconnect the grey connector (arrowed)...

4.16e ...then draw the connector through

4.17 Speed sensor location (arrowed) – this actually shows the blanking plate fitted in place of the sensor on ABS models

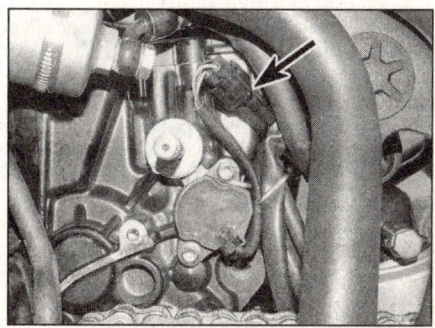
4.18 GP sensor wiring connector (arrowed)

On models with ABS also displace the front wheel speed sensor connector **(see illustration)**. Unscrew the left-hand bolt securing the immobiliser ECM **(see illustration)**. Disconnect the grey wiring connector from the regulator/rectifier **(see illustration)**. Feed the connector down to the alternator cover, releasing it from any ties and guides and noting the routing **(see illustration)**.

17 On models without ABS trace the wiring from the speed sensor, which is in the top of the crankcase, and disconnect it at the connector **(see illustration)**.
18 Disconnect the gear position sensor wiring connector **(see illustration)**.
19 Detach the earth leads from the engine **(see illustration)**.
20 At this point, position an hydraulic jack under the engine with a block of wood between the jack head and sump. Make sure the jack is centrally positioned so the engine will not topple in any direction when the last mounting bolt is removed. Take the weight of the engine on the jack, but make sure the jack is not trying to raise the whole bike.
21 Check that all wiring, cables and hoses are disconnected from and clear of the engine.
22 After removing the engine mounting bolts, fit all nuts, washers and spacers from the mountings back on the bolts in their correct order for safekeeping, noting carefully where each fits. On models up to VIN 520718 the rear mounting bolt is fitted either with a shim or with an adjustable sleeve on the left-hand side – the only way to tell what is fitted to your bike is by having a look. On models from VIN 520719 the rear mounting bolt is fitted with an adjustable sleeve on each side. A special tool (Part No. T3880166), which is similar to a very large flat-bladed screwdriver tip, or a suitable equivalent such as a flat-bladed socket bit (or a large screwdriver will do, but you will be unable to apply the correct torque when refitting the engine), is required to undo and tighten the adjustable sleeve(s) where fitted – see Step 25 or 26.
23 Unscrew the nut on the left-hand end of the rear mounting bolt and remove the washer **(see illustration)**. Withdraw the bolt, noting the washer, where fitted **(see illustration)**.
24 On models up to VIN 520718 fitted with a shim adjustment for the rear bolt retrieve the shim from between the engine and frame.
25 On models up to VIN 520718 fitted with an adjustable sleeve for the rear bolt unscrew the sleeve until it no longer protrudes from

4.19 Unscrew the bolt (arrowed) and detach the leads, then refit the bolt

4.23a Unscrew the nut, remove the washer...

4.23b ...and withdraw the bolt

2•8 Engine, clutch and transmission

4.26a A socket bit like this, or a suitable equivalent...

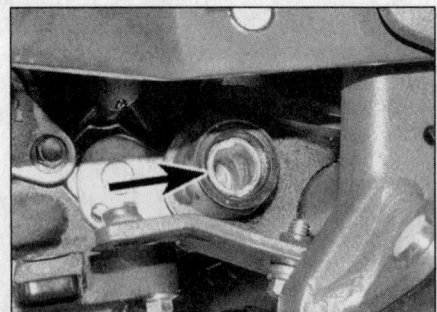

4.26b ...is required for the left-hand adjuster sleeve (arrowed)...

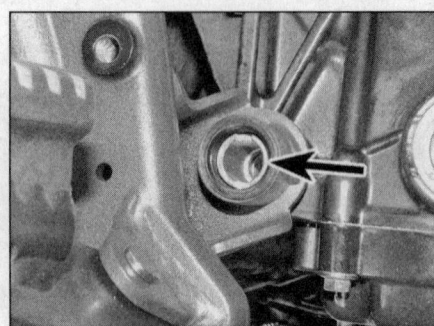

4.26c ...and the right-hand adjuster sleeve

4.27a Left-hand centre mounting bolt (A) and its spacer (B)

4.27b Right-hand centre mounting bolt (arrowed)

the inside of the frame **(see illustration 4.26a and b)**.

26 On models from VIN 520719 unscrew the adjustable sleeves until they no longer protrude from the inside of the frame **(see illustrations)**.

27 Unscrew the centre mounting bolt on each side and remove the spacer from between the engine and frame on the left-hand side **(see illustrations)**.

28 Have an assistant hold the engine steady on the jack.

29 Unscrew the nut from each front mounting bolt **(see illustrations)**. Remove the bolts, noting the washer with the right-hand bolt, and remove the spacer from between the engine and frame on the left-hand side.

30 Lower the engine on the jack and slip the drive chain off the output shaft. Remove the jack from under the engine and lower the

engine until it rests, then manoeuvre the engine clear of the frame and onto the work surface.

 Warning: The engine is heavy and may cause injury if it falls.

31 Discard the nuts for the front and rear mounting bolts – new ones must be used when installing the engine.

Installation
Models up to VIN 520718

32 Where fitted make sure the engine mounting adjuster in the left-hand side of the lower mount does not protrude from the inside of the frame.

33 With the aid of an assistant place the engine under the frame and carefully lift it onto the jack. Raise the engine, slipping the drive chain around the output shaft as you do, until all the mounting holes align. Make sure

no wires, cables or hoses become trapped between the engine and the frame. Now follow the correct procedure to install and tighten the mounting bolts as detailed below.

Caution: The engine mounting bolts must be tightened in the correct sequence. Failure to do so could leave the engine incorrectly aligned in the frame, placing undue stress on it, which could lead to severe damage.

34 Fit the right-hand centre mounting bolt and tighten it finger-tight **(see illustration 4.27b)**.

35 Fit the left-hand centre mounting spacer, then fit the bolt and tighten it finger-tight **(see illustration 4.27a)**.

36 Insert the rear mounting bolt from the **right**-hand side, with its washer where fitted **(see illustration 4.23b)**.

37 Fit the left-hand front mounting spacer, insert the bolt, then fit a new nut and tighten it finger-tight **(see illustration 4.29a)**.

38 Fit the right-hand front mounting bolt with its washer, then fit a new nut and tighten it finger-tight **(see illustration 4.29b)**.

39 On models fitted with an adjustable sleeve for the rear bolt, partially withdraw the bolt until the slot in the sleeve is exposed, then tighten the sleeve to a torque of 3 Nm using the Triumph tool or suitable equivalent **(see illustrations 4.26a and b)**.

40 On models fitted with a shim adjustment for the rear bolt, partially withdraw the bolt until it is clear of the frame and fit the shim between the engine and frame on the left-hand side. Note that different shim sizes are available in 0.5 mm increments from 0.5 mm to 3.5 mm. The shim that was originally fitted should be the correct size, which is a firm, but not tight, sliding fit between the engine and frame, but if it is loose or over-tight, replace the shim with a different size that gives the correct fit – basically use the largest possible shim that does not require force to fit.

41 Slide the rear bolt fully back in, then fit the washer and a new nut and tighten it finger-tight **(see illustration 4.23a)**.

42 Tighten the centre mounting bolt on the right-hand side to 48 Nm **(see illustration 4.27b)**.

43 Tighten the front mounting bolt nut on the right-hand side to 48 Nm **(see illustration 4.29b)**.

4.29a Left-hand front mounting bolt nut (A), bolt (B) and its spacer (C)

4.29b Right-hand front mounting bolt nut (A) and bolt (B)

44 Tighten the centre mounting bolt on the left-hand side to 48 Nm **(see illustration 4.27a)**.
45 Tighten the front mounting bolt nut on the left-hand side to 48 Nm **(see illustration 4.29a)**.
46 Tighten the rear mounting bolt nut to 48 Nm.
47 Lower the jack and remove it.
48 Install the swingarm (see Chapter 5).

Models from VIN 520719

49 Where fitted make sure the engine mounting adjuster in each side of the lower mount does not protrude from the inside of the frame.
50 With the aid of an assistant place the engine under the frame and carefully lift it onto the jack. Raise the engine, slipping the drive chain around the output shaft as you do, until all the mounting holes align. Make sure no wires, cables or hoses become trapped between the engine and the frame. Now follow the correct procedure to install and tighten the mounting bolts as detailed below.
Caution: The engine mounting bolts must be tightened in the correct sequence. Failure to do so could leave the engine incorrectly aligned in the frame, placing undue stress on it, which could lead to severe damage.
51 Fit the right-hand centre mounting bolt and tighten it finger-tight **(see illustration 4.27b)**.
52 Fit the left-hand centre mounting spacer, then fit the bolt and tighten it finger-tight **(see illustration 4.27a)**.
53 Insert the rear mounting bolt from the **right**-hand side, with its washer where fitted **(see illustration 4.23b)**.
54 Fit the left-hand front mounting spacer, insert the bolt, then fit a new nut and tighten it finger-tight **(see illustration 4.29a)**.
55 Fit the right-hand front mounting bolt with its washer, then fit a new nut and tighten it finger-tight **(see illustration 4.29b)**.
56 Install the swingarm (see Chapter 5).
57 Tighten the centre mounting bolt on the right-hand side to a torque of 48 Nm **(see illustration 4.27b)**.
58 Tighten the front mounting bolt nut on the right-hand side to 48 Nm **(see illustration 4.29b)**.
59 Tighten the centre mounting bolt on the left-hand side to 48 Nm **(see illustration 4.27a)**.
60 Tighten the front mounting bolt nut on the left-hand side to 48 Nm **(see illustration 4.29a)**.
61 Withdraw the rear bolt **(see illustration 4.23b)**. Tighten the adjuster sleeve on the left-hand side to 3 Nm using the Triumph tool or suitable equivalent, then repeat for the adjuster on the right-hand side **(see illustrations 4.26a, b and c)**.
62 Slide the rear bolt fully back in, then fit the washer and a new nut and tighten it to 48 Nm **(see illustrations 4.23b and a)**.
63 Lower the jack and remove it.

All models

64 The remainder of the installation procedure is a direct reversal of the removal sequence, referring to the relevant Chapters where directed, and noting the following points.
- Tighten all nuts and bolts to the specified torque settings where directed.
- Align the slit in the gearchange linkage arm with the mark on the gearchange shaft end **(see illustration 4.10a)**.
- Make sure all wires, cables and hoses are correctly routed and connected, and secured by any clips or ties.
- Use new gaskets on the exhaust pipe connections.
- Refill the engine with oil and coolant (see Chapter 1).
- Adjust the throttle and clutch cable freeplay (see Chapter 1).
- Adjust the drive chain slack (see Chapter 1).
- Start the engine and check that there are no oil or coolant leaks.

5 Engine overhaul information

1 Before beginning the engine overhaul, read through the related procedures to familiarise yourself with the scope and requirements of the job. Overhauling an engine is not all that difficult, but it is time consuming. Check on the availability of parts and make sure that any necessary special tools are obtained in advance.
2 Most work can be done with a decent set of typical workshop hand tools, although a number of precision measuring tools are required for inspecting parts to determine if they are worn.
3 To ensure maximum life and minimum trouble from a rebuilt engine, everything must be assembled with care in a spotlessly clean environment.

Disassembly

4 Before disassembling the engine, thoroughly clean and degrease its external surfaces. This will prevent contamination of the engine internals, and will also make the job a lot easier and cleaner. A high flash-point solvent, such as paraffin (kerosene) can be used, or better still, a proprietary engine degreaser such as Gunk. Use old paintbrushes and toothbrushes to work the solvent into the various recesses of the casings. Take care to exclude solvent or water from the electrical components and intake and exhaust ports.

 Warning: The use of petrol (gasoline) as a cleaning agent should be avoided because of the risk of fire.

5 When clean and dry, position the engine on the workbench, leaving suitable clear area for working. Gather a selection of small containers, plastic bags and some labels so that parts can be grouped together in an easily identifiable manner. Also get some paper and a pen so that notes can be taken. You will also need a supply of clean rag, which should be as absorbent as possible.
6 Before commencing work, read through the appropriate section so that some idea of the necessary procedure can be gained. When removing components note that great force is seldom required, unless specified (checking the specified torque setting of the particular bolt being removed will indicate how tight it is, and therefore how much force should be needed). In many cases, a component's reluctance to be removed is indicative of an incorrect approach or removal method – if in any doubt, re-check with the text.
7 When disassembling the engine, keep 'mated' parts that have been in contact with each other during engine operation together – i.e. cylinder liners, pistons and rings, connecting rods, valves, etc). These 'mated' parts must not be mixed up and must be installed in their original location.
8 Engine/transmission disassembly should be done in the following general order with reference to the appropriate Sections.
  Remove the camshafts
  Remove the cam chain and blades
  Remove the cylinder head
  Remove the cylinder liners and pistons
  Remove the clutch
  Remove the gearchange mechanism
  Remove the alternator (see Chapter 8)
  Remove the starter motor (see Chapter 8)
  Remove the sump
  Remove the oil/water pump
  Separate the crankcase halves
  Remove the crankshaft/connecting rods
  Remove the balancer shaft
  Remove the transmission shafts
  Remove the selector drum and forks

Reassembly

9 Reassembly is accomplished by reversing the general disassembly sequence.

6 Oil cooler

Removal

Note: Car type hose clamps are used on the coolant hoses. To release the clamps squeeze the ends together using large pliers, or use a dedicated automotive clamp tool, available from good tool suppliers (see illustrations 5.17a and b in Chapter 1).

1 Drain the engine oil (see Chapter 1). Keep the container below the sump to catch any residual oil in the cooler.
2 Either drain the coolant (see Chapter 1), or fit clamps to the hoses close to the unions on the cooler **(see illustration 6.3)**. Whichever method you choose, be prepared to catch any residual coolant in the hoses and cooler.

2•10 Engine, clutch and transmission

6.3 Release the clamps (arrowed) and detach the hoses

6.4 Unscrew the bolt and remove the cooler, noting how the tabs locate around the lug (arrowed)

6.6a Fit a new O-ring into the groove

6.6b Fit a new sealing washer onto the bolt

3 Release the hose clamps and slide them along the hoses, then detach the hoses from the cooler **(see illustration)**.
4 Unscrew the cooler bolt and remove the cooler, noting how it locates **(see illustration)**. Remove the sealing washer from the bolt and the O-ring from the cooler – new ones must be used **(see illustrations 6.6b and a)**.
5 Check the cooler for leaks and other damage.

Installation

6 Installation is a reverse of the removal procedure, noting the following:
- Use a new O-ring and sealing washer **(see illustrations 6.6a and b)**.
- Make sure the cooler unions are correctly positioned and locate the tabs on each side of the lug on the crankcase **(see illustration 6.4)**.
- Tighten the cooler bolt to the torque setting specified at the beginning of the Chapter.
- Refill the engine with oil (see Chapter 1). Refill or top up the cooling system as required (see Chapter 1). Make sure there are no leaks from the cooler when the engine is run.

7 Valve cover

Removal

1 Disconnect the battery negative lead (see Chapter 8).
2 Remove the fuel tank and the airbox (see Chapter 4).
3 Remove the ignition coils (see Chapter 4).
4 Displace the throttle bodies from the cylinder head and lay them over the frame on some rag (see Chapter 4) – there is no need to disconnect the throttle cables, but you do need to disconnect the wiring **(see illustration)**.
5 Undo the valve cover bolts evenly and in the order shown, noting which fit where **(see illustration)**. Remove the bolts with their seals, then lift the valve cover off the cylinder

7.4 Displace the throttle bodies and hang them over the frame

7.5a Unscrew the bolts in the order shown...

Engine, clutch and transmission 2•11

7.5b ...and remove the cover

7.7 Remove the old washers if new ones are needed

7.8 Make sure the seals are the correct way up and lubricate them with oil

head and remove from the right-hand side **(see illustration)**. *Note: If the cover is stuck, do not try to lever it off with a screwdriver. Tap it gently around the sides with a rubber hammer or block of wood to dislodge it.*

6 Remove the dowels if they are loose **(see illustration 7.9)** – they may remain in the head or come off with the cover.

7 Examine the valve cover gasket for signs of damage or deterioration – remove the gasket and replace it with a new one if necessary **(see illustration 7.10)**. Check the bolt seals in the cover for cracks, hardening and deterioration and replace them with new ones if necessary **(see illustration)**.

Installation

8 Clean the mating surfaces of the cylinder head and the valve cover with a suitable solvent. If the original gasket is being used, remove any traces of old glue or sealant. Lubricate the bolts seals with oil, using new ones if necessary **(see illustration)**.

9 Fit the dowels if removed **(see illustration)**.

10 Fit the gasket onto the cylinder head, flat side up, making sure it locates correctly around the rim, the plug bores and the dowels **(see illustration)**.

11 Position the valve cover on the cylinder head, locating it on the dowels and making sure the gasket stays in place **(see illustration 7.5b)**.

7.9 Fit the dowels (arrowed) if removed

Fit the bolts, with the two shorter bolts at the cam chain end. Tighten the bolts evenly in the same order as on removal, to the torque setting specified at the beginning of the Chapter **(see illustration 7.5a)**.

12 Install the remaining components in the reverse order of removal.

8 Cam chain tensioner

Removal

1 Remove the valve cover (see Section 7). Remove the spark plugs (see Chapter 1).

7.10 Fit the gasket, making sure it locates correctly all round

2 Unscrew the right-hand crankcase cover bolts, noting the positions of the two longer ones **(see illustration)**. Remove the cover. Remove the gasket – a new one must be used. Remove the dowels if loose **(see illustration 8.15)**.

3 On models up to engine No. 602077 rotate the crankshaft clockwise using a socket on the nut **(see illustration 8.4a)**, until the punch mark on the primary drive gear is aligned with the index mark on the crankcase **(see illustration 8.4b)**, and the lines marked with an 8 on the camshaft sprockets face inwards towards each other, parallel with the top of the cylinder head **(see illustration)**. In this position, the No. 1 cylinder is at TDC. If the lines marked 8 face away from each

8.2 Unscrew the bolts (arrowed) and remove the cover – bolt tightening sequence shown

8.3 Camshaft sprocket mark positions for models up to engine No. 602077

2•12 Engine, clutch and transmission

8.4a Turn the engine clockwise...

8.4b ...until the mark (A) aligns with the index mark (B)...

8.4c ...and the line (arrowed) on each camshaft points in and is parallel with the head mating surface

8.4d Using a punch as a locking pin

8.5 Cable-tie the chain to each sprocket to prevent the possibility of it jumping a tooth

8.6 Unscrew the bolts (arrowed) and withdraw the tensioner from the head

Engine, clutch and transmission 2•13

other when the punch mark aligns, turn the crankshaft clockwise one full turn so that the punch mark again aligns with the index mark – the lines on the camshaft sprockets will now be facing towards each other.
4 On models from engine No. 602078 rotate the crankshaft clockwise using a socket on the nut, until the punch mark (highlighted with paint) on the primary drive gear is aligned with the index mark (also highlighted) on the crankcase, and the lines (highlighted) on the camshaft ends face inwards towards each other, parallel with the top of the cylinder head **(see illustrations)**. In this position, the No. 1 cylinder is at TDC. If the lines face away from each other when the punch mark aligns, turn the crankshaft clockwise one full turn so that the punch mark again aligns with the index mark – the lines on the camshaft ends will now be facing towards each other. Fit a locking pin (Triumph part No. T3880601 or a suitable equivalent, such as a punch of the correct diameter) through the holes in the crankcase and crankshaft web to lock the crankshaft in position **(see illustration)**.
5 When the tensioner is withdrawn from the cylinder head, the cam chain will be un-tensioned, and could jump a tooth on the intake camshaft sprocket. To prevent this, fit a suitable wedge between the tensioner blade and the crankcase to keep the blade pressed against the chain, and as a back-up also fit a cable-tie through a hole and around the chain on each sprocket as shown **(see illustration)**.
6 Unscrew the two mounting bolts, evenly and a little at a time, and withdraw the tensioner, noting that the plunger will be pushed out under spring pressure **(see illustration)**. Remove the gasket and O-ring – new ones must be used.

Inspection

7 Examine the tensioner components for signs of wear or damage.
8 Examine the tensioner for signs of wear or damage **(see illustration)**. Hold the ends of the resister spring together and withdraw the plunger and spring **(see illustration)**. Drain

1 Tensioner body
2 O-ring
3 Resister ring
4 Snap ring
5 Spring
6 Plunger
7 Snap ring groove

8.8a Cam chain tensioner assembly

the oil out of the body. Clean all components. Make sure the resister ring and snap ring are correctly located in their grooves **(see illustration)**. Fit the spring back into the tensioner. Hold the ends of the resister ring together to expand it and push the plunger through it and all the way in **(see illustration 8.8b)** – when the snap ring aligns with the outer groove in the plunger keep it held there, release the resister ring, then move one end of the snap ring into the groove and hold it there, then slowly release the plunger so the snap ring holds it in the retracted position **(see illustration)**.

Installation

Note: *If a new tensioner is being fitted it will come with the plunger compressed into the body ready for installation – do not release the plunger before fitting.*

9 If the original tensioner is being refitted, and if not already done, refer to Step 8 and drain and clean the tensioner, then reset the plunger in the retracted position as described.
10 Fit a new O-ring and gasket on the tensioner body. Fit the tensioner and tighten the bolts to the torque setting specified at the beginning of the Chapter **(see illustration 8.6)**.
11 Remove the wedge holding the tensioner blade and the cable-ties from around the sprockets **(see illustration 8.5)**.
12 On models from engine No. 602078 remove the crankshaft locking pin **(see illustration 8.4d)**.
13 To release the tensioner plunger rotate the engine anti-clockwise a quarter turn, then turn it clockwise until the timing marks align as in Step 3 or 4, according to engine number. Check that the tensioner plunger is correctly located against the tensioner blade when viewed from above, and that the chain is tensioned. Rotate the crankshaft clockwise through four full turns, then reset it to TDC on number 1 as described in Step 3 or 4. Check again that the tensioner plunger is correctly located against the tensioner blade when viewed from above, and that the chain is tensioned.
14 Install the spark plugs (see Chapter 1) and valve cover (see Section 7).
15 Fit the crankcase cover dowels if removed,

8.8b Hold the resister spring ends (1) together and withdraw the plunger (2) and spring

8.8c Make sure the resister ring (1) and snap ring (2) are correctly located

8.8d Locate the snap ring (2) in the groove (1) then release the plunger, which should lock in place

2•14 Engine, clutch and transmission

8.15 Fit the new gasket onto the dowels (arrowed)

9.2 Slacken the bolts in the order shown

then fit a new gasket over the dowels **(see illustration)**. Clean the threads of the two longer bolts for the crankcase cover then apply some fresh threadlock. Fit the cover onto the dowels, then fit the bolts finger-tight – the two longer bolts go where the dowels are fitted. Tighten the bolts in the sequence shown to the specified torque, then go round the bolts again to the same torque **(see illustration 8.2)**.

9 Camshafts and followers

Removal

1 Remove the cam chain tensioner (see Section 8). Note that it is not necessary to fit the wedge or cable-tie the cam chain to the sprockets.
2 Undo the camshaft holder bolts evenly and a little at a time in the order shown **(see illustration)**.
Caution: A camshaft could break if the holder bolts are not slackened as described and the pressure from a depressed valve causes the shaft to bend. Also, if the holder does not come squarely away from the head, the holder is likely to break. If this happens the cylinder head must be replaced with a new one; the holders are matched to the head and cannot be obtained separately.
3 Remove the bolts and the cam chain upper guide, then lift the holder off **(see illustrations)**. The two bolts that secure the guide are slightly longer than the rest. Remove the spark plug bore O-rings, and remove the dowels for safekeeping if they are loose **(see illustration)**. If the O-rings are damaged or deformed they must be replaced with new ones.

4 Lift the cam chain off the intake camshaft sprocket and remove the camshaft **(see illustration 9.24b)**.
5 Repeat the procedure for the exhaust camshaft **(see illustration 9.24a)**.
6 The cam chain can be left to rest on its support bolt in the tunnel. Note that for identification the exhaust camshaft is marked with an 'E' on the right-hand end and the intake camshaft is marked with an 'I'. Also the exhaust camshaft has a rib near its centre, which on the intake camshaft has been machined off **(see illustration)**.
7 If the followers and shims are being removed from the cylinder head, obtain a container that is divided into twelve compartments. Label each compartment with the location of a valve, i.e. cylinder identity (i.e. 1, 2 or 3), intake or exhaust valve (I or E), left or right valve (L or R). If a container is not available, use labelled plastic bags (egg cartons also work very well!).
8 Remove the cam follower of the first valve,

9.3a Remove the upper guide...

9.3b ...then lift the holder off

9.3c Remove the O-rings from plug bores; dowel locations (arrowed)

9.6 Exhaust camshaft rib (A), intake camshaft machined section (B)

Engine, clutch and transmission 2•15

9.8a Remove the cam follower...

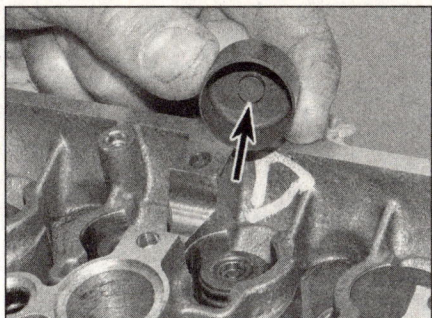

9.8b ...and retrieve the shim (arrowed)

9.14 Measure the cam bearing journals with a micrometer

using a suction tool or magnet if needed **(see illustration)**. Retrieve the shim from inside the follower **(see illustration)** – if it is not there pick it out of the top of the valve using a magnet or a small screwdriver with a dab of grease on it (the shim will stick to the grease) **(see illustration 9.21a)**. Do not allow the shim to fall into the engine. Repeat for all the valves.

Inspection

9 Inspect the bearing surfaces on the camshafts and in the cylinder head and camshaft holder. Look for score marks, deep scratches and evidence of spalling (a pitted appearance). Check the camshaft lobes for heat discoloration (blue appearance), score marks, chipped areas, flat spots and spalling.
10 Next, check the camshaft bearing oil clearances, using a product called Plastigauge. Check each camshaft in turn rather than both at the same time.
11 Clean the camshaft journals, the bearing surfaces in the cylinder head and the camshaft holder with a clean, lint-free cloth, then lay the camshaft in place in the cylinder head – there is no need to engage the chain on the sprocket. Ensure the crankshaft and camshaft are positioned as for removal (see Section 8, Step 3 or 4). Apply a thin smear of grease to each journal and silicone release agent to each bearing surface in the holder.
12 Cut strips of Plastigauge and lay one piece on each camshaft journal, parallel with the camshaft centreline. Fit the dowels if removed, then fit the camshaft holder **(see illustration 9.3b)**. Fit the holder bolts and the cam chain upper guide and tighten the bolts finger-tight – the longer bolts go with the guide **(see illustration 9.3a)**. Making sure the camshaft does not rotate, tighten the bolts evenly and a little at a time in the correct tightening sequence **(see illustration 9.27)**, to the torque setting specified at the beginning of the Chapter.
13 Now unscrew the bolts evenly and a little at a time in the removal sequence **(see illustration 9.2)** and carefully lift off the holder, again making sure the camshaft does rotate.
14 To determine the oil clearance, compare the crushed Plastigauge (at its widest point) on each journal to the scale printed on the Plastigauge container. Compare the results

to this Chapter's Specifications. If the oil clearance is greater than specified, measure the diameter of the camshaft journal with a micrometer **(see illustration)**. If the journal diameter is less than the specified limit, replace the camshaft with a new one and recheck the clearance. If the clearance is still too great, or if the camshaft journal is within its limit, replace the cylinder head and holder as a set with new ones – individual components are not available. Note that if specialist measuring tools are available, the camshaft bearing bore inside diameter can be compared with the nominal specification.

 HAYNES HiNT *Before renewing the camshafts, cylinder head/caps because of damage, check with local machine shops specialising in motorcycle engine work. In the case of the camshafts, it may be possible for cam lobes to be welded, reground and hardened, at a cost far lower than that of a new camshaft. If the bearing surfaces in the head or holder are damaged, it may be possible for them to be bored out to accept bearing inserts. Due to the cost of new components it is recommended that all options are explored!*

15 Repeat the oil clearance check on the other camshaft.
16 Check the amount of camshaft runout by supporting each end of the camshaft on V-blocks, and measuring any runout using a dial gauge. If the runout exceeds the specified limit the camshaft must be replaced with a new one.

 HAYNES HiNT *Refer to Tools and Workshop Tips (Section 3) in the Reference section for details of how to read a micrometer and dial gauge.*

17 On models up to engine No. 602077 check the camshaft sprockets for wear, cracks and other damage, replacing them with new ones if necessary by unscrewing the bolts and removing the sprockets from the ends of the camshaft. The same design sprocket is used for each camshaft, but different bolt hole positions are provided for fitting to the intake or exhaust camshaft. When fitting the sprocket to the intake camshaft, the hole nearest to the IN marking and its corresponding opposite must be used; for the exhaust camshaft sprocket, the hole nearest to the EX marking and its opposite must be used **(see illustration 8.3)**. Clean the sprocket bolt threads then fit the sprockets as described, apply non-permanent thread locking compound to the bolts and tighten them to the specified torque setting. Follow the installation procedure below under the heading 'Models up to engine No. 602077, and models from engine No. 602078 if the sprocket bolts have not been loosened'.
18 On models from engine No. 602078 check the camshaft sprockets for wear, cracks and other damage, replacing them with new ones if necessary – on these models the holes for the bolts are elongated, allowing adjustment of the position of the sprocket on the camshaft for fine tuning the valve timing, but this makes the set-up procedure complicated (see below). Unscrew the bolts and remove the sprockets only if absolutely necessary. The same design sprocket is used for each camshaft. Clean the sprocket bolt threads then fit the sprockets with the bolts in the elongated holes, but tighten the bolts finger-tight only at this stage so the sprocket can turn slightly within the restrictions of the holes. Make sure you follow the installation procedure below under the heading 'Models from engine No. 602078 if the sprocket bolts have been loosened'. If the sprocket bolts on these models are not loosened at all, so the position of the sprocket on the camshaft has not changed since removal of the camshaft, follow the installation procedure below under the heading 'Models up to engine No. 602077, and models from engine No. 602078 if the sprocket bolts have not been loosened'.
19 If the sprockets are worn, it is likely the cam chain and sprocket on the crankshaft will be worn as well. Refer to Section 10 for details of how to check the cam chain for wear.
20 Inspect the outer surfaces of the followers and surfaces of the bores they run in for evidence of scoring, wear or other damage **(see illustration 9.8a)**. If necessary the followers and cylinder head must be replaced with new ones.

2•16 Engine, clutch and transmission

9.21a Fit each shim into the recess on the top of the valve assembly...

9.21b ...then fit the follower

9.24a Keeping the front run of the chain taut, fit the exhaust camshaft as described

9.24b Fit the intake camshaft as described, making sure the chain is taut between the sprockets

Installation

Note: *It is important that the followers and shims are returned to their original valves otherwise the valve clearances will be inaccurate.*

21 If removed, lubricate each shim with molybdenum disulphide oil and fit it into its recess in the top of the valve **(see illustration)**. Check that the shims are correctly seated, then lubricate and fit the followers **(see illustration)**.
22 Make sure the bearing surfaces in the cylinder head, on the camshafts and in the holder are clean, then liberally apply molybdenum disulphide oil (a 50/50 mixture of molybdenum disulphide grease and engine oil) to each of them. Also apply the oil to the camshaft lobes.

Models up to engine No. 602077, and models from engine No. 602078 if the sprocket bolts have not been loosened

23 Check that the crankshaft is positioned as described in Section 8, Step 3 or 4, according to engine number.
24 On models up to engine No. 602077, lift the cam chain off the support bolt, and make sure that it is engaged around the drive sprocket on the crankshaft. Keeping the front run of the chain taut, lay the exhaust camshaft (marked with an 'E' and a rib) in position so that the line marked 8 on its sprocket faces rearwards and is parallel with the top mating surface of the cylinder head, then engage the chain on the sprocket teeth **(see illustration and 8.3)**. Slip the intake camshaft (marked with an 'I') through the cam chain so that the line marked 8 on its sprocket faces forwards and is parallel with the head **(see illustration and 8.3)**. Engage the chain fully on the sprocket teeth, making sure that the chain is tight between the camshafts, with any slack lying in the rear run where it will be taken up by the tensioner. Check that the punch mark on the primary drive gear is still aligned with the index mark on the crankcase.
25 On models from engine No. 602078, lift the cam chain off the support bolt, and make sure that it is engaged around the drive sprocket on the crankshaft. Keeping the front run of the chain taut, lay the exhaust camshaft (marked with an 'E' and a rib) in position so that the line on its end faces rearwards and is parallel with the top mating surface of the cylinder head, then engage the chain on the sprocket teeth **(see illustrations 9.24a and 8.4c)**. Slip the intake camshaft (marked with an 'I') through the cam chain so that the line on its end faces forwards and is parallel with the head **(see illustration 9.24b and 8.4c)**. Engage the chain fully on the sprocket teeth, making sure that the chain is tight between the camshafts, with any slack lying in the rear run where it will be taken up by the tensioner.
26 Fit the spark plug bore O-rings, and the dowels if removed **(see illustration 9.3c)** – use new O-rings if necessary. Fit the holder onto the camshafts **(see illustration 9.3b)** – make sure it locates correctly over the raised section on each shaft **(see illustration)**. Clean and lightly oil the camshaft holder bolt threads. Fit the bolts, not forgetting the cam chain upper guide (which is secured by the two longer bolts) and tighten them finger-tight **(see illustration 9.3a)**.
27 Tighten the holder bolts evenly and a little at a time in the sequence shown to an initial torque setting of 5 Nm **(see illustration)**. Now

9.26 Make sure the camshaft holder locates correctly

9.27 Camshaft holder bolt tightening sequence

Engine, clutch and transmission 2•17

9.33 Fit the tool or piece of bar into the slots (arrowed) to align and lock the camshafts

tighten them in the same sequence to the final torque of 10 Nm.

28 With all bolts tightened down, check that the timing marks still align (see Section 8, Step 3 or 4). If they don't, remove the cam chain upper guide, then slip the cam chain off the sprockets (there should be enough slack in the rear run to do this easily without having to displace the camshafts). Turn the camshaft(s), and on models up to engine No. 602077 the crankshaft, as required until their alignment is correct. Refit the upper guide and tighten the bolts to 10 Nm.

29 Install the cam chain tensioner (Section 8).

30 Check the valve clearances (see Chapter 1).

Models from engine No. 602078 if the sprocket bolts have been loosened

31 Check that the crankshaft is positioned as described in Section 8, Step 4. Make sure each sprocket is positioned so the bolts are central in their holes, and that the bolts are tight enough to hold them in that position, but not so tight that they can't be moved by hand.

32 Lift the cam chain off the support bolt, and make sure that it is engaged around the drive sprocket on the crankshaft. Keeping the front run of the chain taut, lay the exhaust camshaft (marked with an 'E' and a rib) in position so that the line on its end faces rearwards and is parallel with the top mating surface of the cylinder head, then engage the chain on the sprocket teeth (see illustration 9.24a and 8.4c). Slip the intake camshaft (marked with an 'I') through the cam chain so that the line

10.6 Unscrew and remove the support bolt...

on its end faces forwards and is parallel with the head (see illustration 9.24b and 8.4c). Engage the chain fully on the sprocket teeth, making sure that the chain is tight between the camshafts, with any slack lying in the rear run where it will be taken up by the tensioner.

33 On the left-hand end of the camshafts there are slots for aligning and locking the camshafts in the correct positions using either the Triumph tool, part No. T3880640, or a suitable piece of steel bar of the correct thickness to fit in the slots. Fit the tool or bar into the slots in both camshafts so they are locked in the correct position (see illustration).

34 Fit the spark plug bore O-rings, and the dowels if removed (see illustration 9.3c) – use new O-rings if necessary. Fit the holder onto the camshafts (see illustration 9.3b) – make sure it locates correctly over the raised section on each shaft (see illustration 9.26). Clean and lightly oil the camshaft holder bolt threads. Fit the bolts, not forgetting the cam chain upper guide (which is secured by the two longer bolts) and tighten them finger-tight (see illustration 9.3a).

35 Tighten the holder bolts evenly and a little at a time in the sequence shown to an initial torque setting of 5 Nm (see illustration 9.27). Now tighten them in the same sequence to the final torque of 10 Nm.

36 With the camshafts and crankshaft locked with the bar tool and the pin respectively, the positions of the sprockets can now be set by pushing in on the back of the cam chain tensioner blade via the tensioner hole so the slack is taken up – again Triumph have a special tool for this, part No. T3880607, which fits in the place of the cam chain tensioner, and when the centre stud is tightened (a 6mm hex key is supplied with the tool to do this) to 0.6 Nm it sets the chain at exactly the correct tension so the sprockets are in exactly the right position. If you are not using the tool then just take up all the slack in the chain by pushing on the tensioner blade via the tensioner hole using a suitable tool so it is under some tension, but you do not have to push hard. With the chain tensioned remove the exposed camshaft sprocket bolt from each sprocket and apply some thread locking compound, then refit the bolts and tighten them to the specified torque.

10.7 ...then remove the chain

37 Remove the camshaft locking bar and the crankshaft locking pin. Keeping the chain tensioned turn the crankshaft clockwise as before until the two other sprocket bolts are exposed. Remove the bolts and apply some thread locking compound, then refit the bolts and tighten them to the specified torque. Remove the tensioning tool.

38 Install the cam chain tensioner (Section 8).

39 Check the valve clearances (see Chapter 1).

10 Cam chain and tensioner/guide blades

Cam chain upper guide

1 Remove the valve cover (see Section 7).

2 Unscrew the bolts securing the upper guide and lift off (see illustration 9.3a).

3 Installation is the reverse of removal. Tighten the bolts to the torque setting specified at the beginning of the Chapter for the camshaft holder bolts.

Cam chain

Removal

4 Remove the camshafts (see Section 9).

5 Remove the guide blade (Step 17).

6 Mark the outer face of the chain with a dab of paint so it can be re-fitted the same way round. Hold the cam chain and remove the support bolt from the centre of the right-hand side of the cylinder head (see illustration). Remove the seal from the bolt – a new one should be used.

7 Disengage the cam chain from the crankshaft sprocket and draw it out of the tunnel (see illustration).

Inspection

8 Check the cam chain for binding, loose pins and worn or damaged plates and replace it with a new one if necessary.

9 Inspect the crankshaft and camshaft sprockets for worn, chipped or missing teeth. If the chain and sprockets show signs of extensive wear renew them as a complete set.

10 If the chain appears to be in good condition, check it for stretch as follows. Hang the chain from a hook and attach a 13 kg (28 lb) weight to its lower end. Measure the length of 24 pins (from the outer edge of the 1st pin to the outer edge of the 24th pin) and compare the result to the service limit specified at the beginning of the Chapter. If the chain exceeds the service limit replace it with a new one.

Installation

11 Installation is a reverse of removal. If the original chain is being refitted make sure the mark made on removal faces out. Make sure the chain is correctly engaged around the drive sprocket on the crankshaft. Fit the cam chain support bolt using a new sealing washer and tighten to the torque setting specified at the beginning of the chapter. Refer to Step 19 to fit the guide blade.

2•18 Engine, clutch and transmission

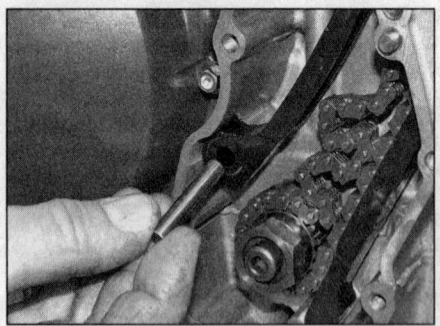
10.13a Withdraw the pivot pin...

10.13b ...and lift the blade out

10.17 Guide blade pivot bolt (arrowed)

Cam chain tensioner blade
Removal
12 Remove the camshafts (see Section 9).
13 Withdraw the tensioner blade pivot pin and lift the blade out of the cam chain tunnel **(see illustrations)**.
14 Check the tensioner blade for wear, cracking and other damage, and replace it with a new one if necessary – the blade consists of three separate components – the tensioner plunger contact pad, the main aluminium body of the blade, and the facing blade that the chain runs on – all of which are available separately.

Installation
15 Installation is the reverse of removal. Lubricate the pivot pin.

Cam chain guide blade
Removal
16 Remove the camshafts (see Section 9).
17 Unscrew the guide blade pivot bolt and lift the blade out of the front of the cam chain tunnel, noting how it locates **(see illustration)**. Note the collar for the pivot bolt and remove it if required.
18 Check the guide blade for wear, cracking and other damage, and replace it with a new one if necessary.

Installation
19 Make sure the collar is in place. Fit the guide blade into the front of the tunnel and locate it correctly in its cut-out in the top of the cylinder head. Clean the threads of the pivot bolt, then apply some fresh threadlock and tighten the bolt to the torque setting specified at the beginning of the Chapter.
20 Install the camshafts (see Section 9).

11 Starter clutch and gears

Starter clutch check
1 If you suspect the starter clutch of being faulty, a simple check can be performed as follows.
2 Remove the starter motor (see Chapter 8).
3 Using your finger, check that the starter idle/reduction gear turns clockwise, and locks when turned anti-clockwise, when looked at via the starter motor aperture. If not, remove the starter clutch for further investigation.

Removal
4 Remove the alternator rotor (see Chapter 8) – the starter clutch is bolted to the back of it. If the starter driven gear does not come away with the rotor slide it off the crankshaft.

Inspection
5 With the alternator face down on a workbench, check that the starter driven gear rotates freely anti-clockwise and locks against the rotor clockwise **(see illustration)**. If it doesn't, the starter clutch should be dismantled for further investigation.
6 Withdraw the starter driven gear from the starter clutch, rotating it anti-clockwise as you do **(see illustration)**.

11.5 Starter clutch gear should turn freely anti-clockwise

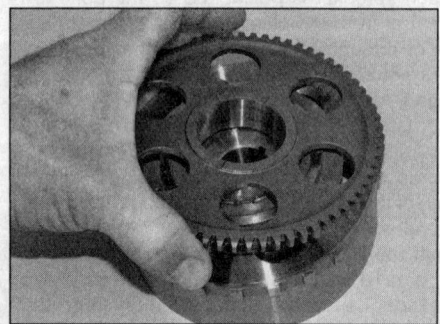
11.6 Lift the gear out of the starter clutch body

7 Examine the outer bearing surface of the gear hub and the condition of the sprags inside the housing **(see illustration)**. If the hub or sprags show signs of excessive wear or are damaged, replace them with new parts. To remove the starter clutch assembly, hold the alternator rotor using a holding strap and unscrew the six bolts inside the rotor **(see illustration)**. The sprag housing and sprag assembly are available separately. Lift the sprag assembly out of the housing, noting which way round it fits. Install the new assembly in a reverse sequence – the sprag assembly fits into the lipped side of the housing, and the lipped side faces the alternator rotor. Press the sprag assembly in until seated in the lip. Tighten the bolts evenly and a little at a time in the sequence shown in illustration 11.7b to the torque setting specified at the beginning of the Chapter. Go round all the bolts two more times in

11.7a Check the surface of the hub (A) and the sprags (B) for wear and damage

11.7b Starter clutch bolts (arrowed)

Engine, clutch and transmission 2•19

11.8 Check the bearing (arrowed)

12.5 Release the clamp (arrowed) and detach the hose

12.6 Remove the two screws (arrowed) from the right-hand end of the head

sequence checking that all remain tightened to the correct torque.

8 Check the condition of the needle bearing on the crankshaft and fit a new bearing if necessary **(see illustration)** – refer to *Tools and Workshop Tips* in the Reference Section for details of bearing checks and removal and installation methods. Also check the inner bearing surface in the starter driven gear hub.

9 Examine the teeth of the idle/reduction gear and the corresponding teeth of the starter driven gear and starter motor driveshaft. Replace the gears and/or starter motor with new ones if worn or chipped teeth are discovered on related gears. Also check the idle/reduction gear shaft for damage.

Installation

10 Lubricate the outside of the starter driven gear hub, the needle bearing and the clutch sprags with molybdenum disulphide oil (a 50/50 mixture of molybdenum disulphide grease and engine oil).

11 Fit the gear into the clutch, rotating it clockwise as you do so to spread the sprags and allow the hub to enter **(see illustration 11.6)**.

12 Install the alternator rotor (see Chapter 8).

12 Cylinder head removal and installation

Removal

1 Remove the engine from the frame (see Section 4).
2 Remove the camshafts, followers and shims (see Section 9).
3 Remove the cam chain blades (see Section 10).
4 Remove the cam chain support bolt from the right-hand side of the cylinder head **(see illustration 10.6)**. Remove the seal from the bolt – a new one should be used. Either remove the cam chain, or let it drop down the tunnel.
5 Release the coolant bypass hose clamp and detach the hose from the back of the head **(see illustration)**.
6 Undo the two screws from the right-hand end of the cylinder head **(see illustration)**.
7 Slacken the eight cylinder head bolts evenly and a little at a time at a time in the sequence shown **(see illustration)**. When all are loose, remove the bolts and their washers. Triumph

specify to use new bolts and washers on installation.
8 Tap around the joint of the cylinder head and the crankcase with a soft-faced mallet to free the head. Don't attempt to free it by inserting a screwdriver in the joint – you'll damage the sealing surfaces.
9 Carefully lift the head off and remove it **(see illustration)**. Remove the head gasket, and the two dowels if they are loose **(see illustrations 12.15)**.
10 If the crankshaft is rotated with the head off it is possible that the liners may move and the seal between them and the crankcase broken, causing coolant from the cylinder block water jacket to seep into the crankcase. If this happens the cylinder liners must be removed and resealed. Refer to Section 14 for liner removal and installation details. Alternatively clamp them in place using the bolt, nut and washer arrangement described and shown in Section 14 **(see illustration 14.10b)**.
11 Clean the mating surfaces of the cylinder head and crankcase with a suitable solvent to remove all traces of old gasket. If a scraper is used, take care not to scratch or gouge the soft aluminium. Ensure none of the old gasket material falls into the cylinders or water jacket.

12.7 Sequence for loosening the cylinder head bolts

12.9 Carefully lift the cylinder head up off the engine

2•20 Engine, clutch and transmission

 HAYNES HiNT *Refer to Tools and Workshop Tips for details of gasket removal methods.*

12 Inspect the cylinder head gasket and the mating surfaces for signs of leakage, which could indicate that the head is distorted. If necessary, check the cylinder head for warpage using a straight-edge (see Section 13, Step 14). Discard the old head gasket as a new one must be fitted on reassembly.

Installation

13 If removed fit and seal the liners in the cylinder block (see Section 14). Remove the clamping bolts once the sealant has set.

14 Check that the bolt holes in the crankcase are clean and dry. Clean the threads and under the heads of the new head bolts.

15 If removed, fit the two dowels into the crankcase **(see illustration)**. Fit the new head gasket over the dowels – it should be obvious which way round it fits, but check that all the holes are correctly aligned.

16 Carefully fit the cylinder head, locating it on the dowels **(see illustration 12.9)**.

17 Fit the cylinder head bolts with their washers and tighten them finger-tight only at this stage **(see illustration)**.

18 Tighten the cylinder head bolts in the correct numerical sequence to the stage 1 torque setting **(see illustration)**. Repeat to the stage 2 torque setting. Finally, attach a degree disc to the torque wrench and angle-tighten each bolt 120° following the same sequence **(see illustration)**.

19 Fit the screws into the right-hand end of the cylinder head and tighten them to the specified torque setting **(see illustration 12.6)**.

20 Fit the coolant by-pass hose and tighten the clamp hose **(see illustration 12.5)**.

21 Install the cam chain if removed, or lift it out of the tunnel if not – in each case make sure it is correctly engaged around the drive sprocket on the crankshaft. Fit the cam chain support bolt using a new sealing washer and tighten to the torque setting specified at the beginning of the chapter **(see illustration 10.6)**.

22 Install the remaining components in the reverse order of removal.

13 Cylinder head and valve overhaul

Note: *The valve guides are an integral part of the cylinder head and are not available separately. If the guides are worn the cylinder head must be replaced with a new one.*

1 Because of the complex nature of this job and the special tools and equipment required, most owners leave servicing of the valves and valve seats to a specialist. However, you can make an initial assessment of whether the valves are seating correctly, and therefore

12.15 Fit the dowels (arrowed) then lay the head gasket on

12.17 Fit the bolts with their washers...

12.18a ...then tighten them in the sequence shown and in stages as described...

12.18b ...using a degree disc for the final stage

Engine, clutch and transmission 2•21

sealing, by pouring a small amount of solvent into each of the valve ports. If the solvent leaks past any valve into the combustion chamber area the valve is not seating correctly and sealing.

2 With the correct tools (a valve spring compressor is essential – make sure it is suitable for motorcycle work), you can also remove the valves and associated components from the cylinder head, clean them and check them for wear to assess the extent of the work needed, and, unless seat cutting is required, reassemble them in the head.

3 A dealer service department or specialist can re-cut the valve seats.

4 After the valve service has been performed, be sure to clean it very thoroughly before installation on the engine to remove any metal particles or abrasive grit that may still be present from the valve service operations. Use compressed air, if available, to blow out all the holes and passages.

Disassembly

5 Remove the followers and their shims if you haven't already done so (see Section 9, Steps 7 and 8). Store them as specified to ensure they are returned to their original locations without getting mixed up. Arrange to label and store the valves and their related components in the same way as the followers and shims (or with them if there is room) so they can be reinstalled in the same valve guides they are removed from **(see illustration)**.

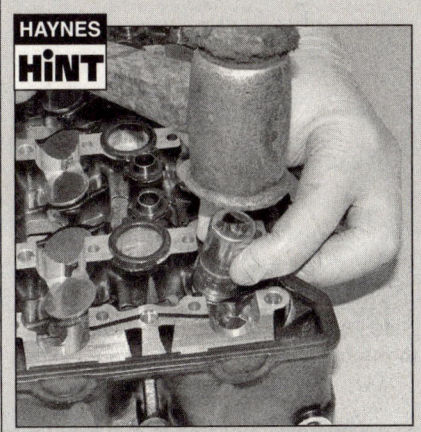

There is a quick way of removing valve components that avoids having to use a spring compressor: select a socket that seats on the valve retainer and give it a sharp tap with a soft hammer – this compresses the spring without moving the valve itself and unseats the collets. Note that a valve spring compressor has to be used when refitting the valve assembly.

6 Compress the valve spring on the first valve with a spring compressor, making sure it is correctly located onto each end of the valve assembly **(see illustration)**. On the top of the valve the adaptor needs to be about the same

13.5 Valve components

1 Collets
2 Spring retainer
3 Valve spring
4 Spring seat
5 Valve stem oil seal
6 Valve

size as the spring retainer – if it is too big it will contact the follower bore and mark it, and if it is too small it will be difficult to remove and install the collets **(see illustration)**. On the underside of the head make sure the plate on the compressor only contacts the valve and not the soft aluminium of the head **(see illustration)** – if the plate is too big for the valve, use a spacer between them. Do not compress the springs more than is necessary to release the collets.

Caution: Take great care not to mark the cam follower bore with the spring compressor.

7 Remove the collets, using a magnet or a screwdriver with a dab of grease on it **(see illustration)**. Carefully release the valve spring compressor and remove the spring retainer, noting which way up it fits, the spring and the valve **(see illustrations)**. If the valve binds in

13.6a Compressing the valve springs using a valve spring compressor

13.6b Make sure the compressor is a good fit both on the top...

13.6c ...and the bottom of the valve assembly

13.7a Remove the collets with needle-nose pliers, tweezers, a magnet or a screwdriver with a dab of grease on it

13.7b Remove the spring retainer and the spring...

2•22 Engine, clutch and transmission

13.7c ...then push the valve down and draw it out

13.7d If the valve stem (2) won't pull through the guide, deburr the area above the collet groove (1)

the guide and won't pull through, push it back into the head and deburr the area around the collet groove with a very fine file or whetstone **(see illustration)**.

8 Pull the valve stem seal off the top of the valve guide with pliers and discard it (the old seals should never be re-used), then remove the spring seat noting which way up, it fits – using a magnet is the easiest way to remove the seat from the head **(see illustrations)**.

9 Repeat the procedure for the remaining valves. Remember to keep the parts for each valve together so they can be reinstalled in the same location.

10 Clean the cylinder head with solvent and dry it thoroughly. Compressed air will speed the drying process and ensure that all holes and recessed areas are clean. **Note:** *Do not use a wire brush mounted in a drill motor to clean the combustion chambers as the head material is soft and may be scratched or eroded away by the wire brush.*

11 Clean all of the valve springs, collets, retainers and spring seats with solvent and dry them thoroughly. Do the parts from one valve at a time so that no mixing of parts between valves occurs.

12 Scrape off any deposits that may have formed on the valves. Again, make sure the valves do not get mixed up.

Inspection

13 Inspect the head very carefully for cracks and other damage. If cracks are found, a new head will be required. Check the cam bearing surfaces for wear and evidence of seizure. Check the camshafts for wear as well (see Section 9).

14 Using a precision straight-edge and a feeler gauge, check the head gasket mating surface for warpage. Refer to *Tools and Workshop Tips* (Section 3) in the Reference section for details of how to use the straight-edge. If the head is warped, but not excessively so, a specialist repair shop may be able to resurface it. If the head is excessively warped, replace it with a new one.

15 Examine the valve seats in the combustion chamber. If they are pitted, cracked or burned, the head will require work beyond the scope of the home mechanic. Measure the valve seat width and compare it to this Chapter's Specifications **(see illustration)**. If it exceeds the service limit, or if it varies around its circumference, valve seat overhaul is required.

16 Working on one valve and guide at a time, measure the valve stem diameter **(see illustration)**. Clean the valve's guide to remove any carbon build-up, then measure the inside diameter of the guide (at both ends and the centre of the guide) with a small hole gauge and micrometer **(see illustration)**. Measure the guide at the ends and at the centre to determine if it is worn in a bell-mouth pattern (more wear at the ends). Subtract the stem diameter from the valve guide diameter to obtain the valve stem-to-guide clearance. If the stem-to-guide clearance is greater than listed in this Chapter's Specifications, and fitting new valves will restore the clearance, fit new valves. If the guides are excessively worn, or worn unevenly, a new head will have to be fitted.

> **HAYNES HiNT** *Refer to Tools and Workshop Tips in the Reference Section for details on how to use a micrometer.*

17 Carefully inspect each valve face, stem and collet groove area for cracks, pits and burned spots.

18 Rotate the valve and check for any

13.8a Pull the seal off the top of the guide...

13.8b ...then remove the spring seat

13.15 Measure the valve seat width with a ruler (or for greater precision use a Vernier caliper)

13.16a Measure the valve stem diameter with a micrometer

13.16b Insert a small bore gauge into the valve guide and expand it so there's a slight drag when it's pulled out, then measure the gauge with a micrometer

13.18 Check the valve stem for runout using V-blocks and a dial gauge

13.23a Fit the valve stem seal...

13.23b ...and carefully push it on until it clicks into place

obvious indication that it is bent. Use V-blocks and a dial gauge if available **(see illustration)**. If the valve is bent, it must be replaced with a new one. Check the end of the stem for pitting and excessive wear. The presence of any of the above conditions indicates the need for valve servicing. The stem end can be ground down, provided that the amount of stem above the collet groove after grinding is sufficient.

19 Check the end of each valve spring for wear and pitting. Measure the spring length with the specified load on it (see Specifications) and compare it to that listed. If any spring compresses further than specified it has sagged and must be replaced with a new one – it is a good policy to replace the springs on all valves at the same time. Also place the spring upright on a flat surface and check it for bend by placing a ruler against it. If the bend in any spring is excessive, it must be replaced with a new one.

20 Check the spring retainers and collets for obvious wear and cracks. Any questionable parts should not be reused, as extensive damage will occur in the event of failure during engine operation.

21 If the inspection indicates that no overhaul work is required, the valve components can be reinstalled in the head.

Reassembly

22 Working on one valve at a time, lay the spring seat in place in the cylinder head with its shouldered side facing up **(see illustration 13.8b)**.

23 Fit a new valve stem seal onto the guide, using finger pressure, a stem seal fitting tool or an appropriate size deep socket, to push the seal squarely onto the end of the valve guide until it is felt to clip into place **(see illustrations)**. Make sure the seal does not get cocked sideways as it could be damaged – using a rod as a guide as for the seat helps.

24 Coat the valve stem with molybdenum disulphide oil (a 50/50 mixture of molybdenum disulphide grease and engine oil), then fit it into its guide **(see illustration)**. Check that the valve moves up and down freely.

25 Fit the spring with its closer-wound coils facing down into the cylinder head **(see illustration)**. Now fit the spring retainer, with its shouldered side facing down so that it fits into the top of the spring **(see illustration)**.

26 Apply a small amount of grease to the inside of the collets – this will help to help hold them in place as the pressure is released from the spring. Compress the spring with the valve spring compressor, making sure it is correctly located onto each end of the valve assembly (see Step 6) and fit the collets **(see illustration)**. Do not compress the spring any more than is necessary to slip the collets into place. Locate each collet in turn into the groove in the valve stem using a screwdriver with a dab of grease on it **(see illustration)**. Carefully release the compressor, making sure the collets seat and lock in the retaining groove.

13.24 Lubricate the stem and slide the valve into its guide

13.25a Fit the valve spring with the closer-wound coils facing down...

13.25b ...then fit the spring retainer

13.26a Compress the spring and install the collets, making sure they locate in the groove

13.26b Make sure the collets lock as you remove the compressor...

2•24 Engine, clutch and transmission

13.27 ...then tap the valve stem to make sure

27 Support the cylinder head on blocks so the valves can't contact the workbench top, then very gently tap the top of the valve stem to help seat the collets in the groove **(see illustration)**.

28 Repeat the procedure for the remaining valves. Remember to keep the parts for each valve together and separate from the other valves so they can be reinstalled in the same location.

29 After the cylinder head and camshafts have been installed, check the valve clearances and adjust as required (see Chapter 1).

Components of the home-made drawbolt tool; steel strap (A), drawbolt and bottom plate (B) and top nut and washer (C). The drawbolt tool can be made using a section of steel plate, accurately cut and chamfered so that it bears on the bottom edge of the liner, just inside the outside diameter of the liner. You will also need a length of flat steel bar of a suitable thickness, a length of threaded rod (15 mm diameter x 200 mm length), some washers and two nuts, and two pieces of wood (see illustration 14.4b). The thickness of the pieces of wood will determine by how much the liners can be extracted before they contact the flat steel bar, so make sure they are thick enough to allow the seal on the liner to be broken, and thus enable the liners to be removed by hand. Assemble the tool as described in Step 4.

14 Cylinder liners

Note: *The cylinder liners can be removed with the pistons in situ, following removal of the cylinder head. However to do this requires the use of Triumph special tools, Part Nos. T3880315 and 3880101, to extract the liners. It may be possible to purchase a universal liner extractor from a good automotive tool supplier, but first make sure it is suitable for the size of the engine. A suitable home-made tool can be used to release the liners, but as it uses the drawbolt principle it is necessary to separate the crankcase halves and remove the crankshaft, connecting rods and pistons before it can be applied. If the liners are being removed as part of a complete engine overhaul anyway, then no extra work is involved, apart from making up the tool.*

Removal

1 If the Triumph special tool or a liner extractor is being used, just remove the cylinder head (see Section 12). Otherwise, separate the crankcase halves, then remove the crankshaft and connecting rods and pistons, referring to the relevant Sections of this Chapter.

2 Before removing the liners, mark the top edge of each liner at the front with a felt marker pen or similar, which will not damage the gasket surfaces. Indicate the cylinder number (1 to 3 from left to right) and the front face of each liner.

3 If the Triumph tool or a liner extractor is being used, turn the engine so that the piston in the liner being removed is at bottom dead centre (i.e. the bottom of its stroke). Gently draw each liner out of the cylinder block **(see illustration)**. The purpose of the extractor is to break the seal between the liner and the crankcase; once this has been achieved, the liner can be lifted out by hand – support the piston and rod so they do not fall against the crankcase. Do not attempt to lever the liners out because the gasket surfaces will be damaged. As each liner is removed, stuff the crankcase aperture with clean rag to cushion the piston and prevent anything falling into the crankcase.

14.4a Make sure the bottom plate is accurately cut and fitted

14.3 Extracting a liner using the Triumph tool

4 If the home-made drawbolt tool is being used (see **Tool Tip**), assemble the tool as shown. The bottom plate must be accurately fitted so that is bears on the bottom edge of the liner only – there must be no danger of it cocking sideways or slipping off the edge and scratching the inner surface of the liner **(see illustration)**. Also note that the bottom plate must locate inside the crankcase bore for the liner and have no sharp edges that will score the crankcase as the liner is drawn out. Tighten the top nut and gently draw the liner out of the cylinder block **(see illustration)**. Do not attempt to lever the liners out.

Inspection

5 Check the liner walls carefully for scratches and score marks. Using telescoping gauges and a micrometer (see Section 3 of *Tools and Workshop Tips*), check the internal diameter of each liner to assess the amount of wear. Measure near the top (but below the level of the top piston ring at TDC), centre and bottom (but above the level of the oil ring at BDC) of the bore, both parallel to and across the crankshaft axis **(see illustration)**. Compare the results to the specifications at the beginning of the Chapter. If the precision measuring tools are not available, take the liners to a Triumph dealer or specialist motorcycle repair shop for assessment and advice. If the liners are worn beyond the service limit, or badly scratched,

14.4b Turn the top nut clockwise and draw the liner up until the seal is broken

Engine, clutch and transmission 2•25

14.5 Measure the cylinder bore in the directions shown with a telescoping gauge, then measure the gauge with a micrometer

14.10a Carefully fit the liner down over the piston, making sure the rings enter correctly

14.10b Assemble a bolt, nut and washers as shown to clamp the liners

scuffed or scored, replace them with new ones. The liners cannot be re-bored.

6 Note that the cylinder liners must not be honed.

Installation

Note: *If the crankcases were separated and the piston/connecting rod assemblies removed in order to remove the liners, you can either fit the piston/connecting rod assemblies into the liners before the liners are installed, then install them as an assembly (method 2) – or you can install the liners, then fit the piston/connecting rod assemblies into them afterwards (method 3).*

7 Remove all traces of old sealant from the mating surfaces of the liners and the crankcase. If the connecting rods and pistons are still in situ, this will be tricky because you must avoid old sealant dropping into the sump. Remove any rag from the crankcase and make sure the mating surfaces of the liner and crankcase are clean, oil-free and dry. Check that the piston rings are correctly positioned in relation to the front of the engine **(see illustration 15.28)**.

Method 1 – piston/connecting rod assemblies in situ

8 Apply a continuous bead of a suitable silicone sealant (Triumph use ThreeBond 1215) to the liner mating surface as shown, following any instructions on the sealant package regarding use **(see illustration 14.14)**.

9 Lubricate the bore surface of the liner with engine oil. Make sure that the No. 1 liner is matched with the No. 1 piston/connecting rod assembly and so on, and that it is installed with the previously made mark at the front (see Step 2). Make sure that the piston is at top dead centre (i.e. at the top of its stroke).

10 Slip the liner over the piston, compressing each ring with your fingers as it enters the liner, and use a gentle rocking motion as the liner is pushed downwards **(see illustration)**. The liner has a chamfered lead-in to enable the piston to be installed without the use of ring compressors. Press the liner fully down until it is felt to seat. Clamp the liner in place using suitable bolts, nuts and soft washers threaded into the head bolt holes as shown to prevent it lifting **(see illustration)** – do not overtighten the clamps and do not use steel washers as the mating surface of the head could be indented, causing leakage and compression problems.

11 Turn the crankshaft to position the next piston at TDC, then install the other liners in the same way, with No. 2 in the middle and No. 3 on the right. As the crankshaft is rotated, make sure that the installed liner does not lift off its seating. If this happens, the liner must be removed, cleaned and fresh sealant applied. After fitting the second and third liners make sure that there is an even gap between the flat side of the centre liner and each outer liner – you should be able to fit a 0.1mm feeler gauge blade into the gap and slide it all the way along.

Method 2 – piston/connecting rod assemblies removed

12 Lubricate the bore surface of the liner with engine oil. Make sure that the No. 1 piston/connecting rod assembly is matched with the No. 1 liner and so on, and that they are installed the correct way round – the dot on the piston crown must point to the front of the liner and the front of the engine.

13 Slip the piston into the bottom of the liner, compressing each ring with your fingers as it enters, and use a gentle rocking motion as the liner is pushed downwards **(see illustration)**. The liner has a chamfered lead-in to enable the piston to be installed without the use of ring compressors. Position the piston near the top of the liner.

14 Apply a continuous bead of a suitable silicone sealant (Triumph use ThreeBond 1215) to the liner mating surface as shown, following any instructions on the sealant package regarding use **(see illustration)**.

15 Fit the No. 1 liner into the left-hand side of the crankcase, with the previously made mark at the front (see Step 2), and press it down until it is felt to seat **(see illustration)**. Clamp the liner in place using suitable bolts, nuts and soft washers threaded into the head bolt holes as shown to prevent it lifting **(see illustration 14.10b)** – do not overtighten the

14.13 Carefully feed the piston into the liner, making sure the rings enter correctly

14.14 Apply the silicone sealant as shown...

14.15 ...then fit the liner into the crankcase

2•26 Engine, clutch and transmission

14.20a Carefully lower the connecting rod and piston into the liner...

14.20b ...feeding each ring in as you do

14.21 Check that the liners are all flush using a straight-edge

clamps and do not use steel washers as the mating surface of the head could be indented, causing leakage and compression problems.

16 Install the other liners in the same way, with No. 2 in the middle and No. 3 on the right. Note that if the cylinder head is being installed immediately, there is no need to clamp the individual liners in place. After fitting the second and third liners make sure that there is an even gap between the flat side of the centre liner and each outer liner – you should be able to fit a 0.1mm feeler gauge blade into the gap and slide it all the way along.

Method 3 – piston/connecting rod assemblies removed

17 Apply a continuous bead of a suitable silicone sealant (Triumph use ThreeBond 1215) to the liner mating surface as shown, following any instructions on the sealant package regarding use **(see illustration 14.14)**.
18 Fit the No. 1 liner into the left-hand side of the crankcase, with the previously made mark at the front (see Step 2), and press it down until it is felt to seat. Fit the No. 2 liner into the middle, then the No. 3 into the right-hand side, again with the marks at the front. After fitting the second and third liners make sure that there is an even gap between the flat side of the centre liner and each outer liner – you should be able to fit a 0.1mm feeler gauge blade into the gap and slide it all the way along. Clamp the liners in place using suitable bolts, nuts and soft washers threaded into the head bolt holes as shown to prevent them lifting **(see illustration 14.10b)** – do not overtighten the clamps and do not use steel washers as the mating surface of the head could be indented, causing leakage and compression problems.
19 Lubricate the bore surface of each liner with engine oil. Make sure that the No. 1 piston/connecting rod assembly is matched with the No. 1 liner and so on, and that they are installed the correct way round – the dot on the piston crown must point to the front of the liner and the front of the engine.
20 Slip the piston into the liner, making sure the connecting rod does not scratch the surface, then carefully compress and feed each piston ring into the liner until the piston crown is flush with the top **(see illustrations)**.

If available, a piston ring compressor makes installation a lot easier.

All methods

21 When all liners are installed, check that their top surfaces are all exactly level with the cylinder block using a precision straight-edge as shown **(see illustration)**.
22 Install the cylinder head soon after installing the liners to avoid crankshaft movement accidentally breaking the seals.
23 Install the remaining components in the reverse order of removal, referring to the relevant Sections of the Chapter.

15 Pistons and piston rings

Removal

1 Remove the cylinder head (see Section 12).
2 If the crankcases are not being separated and a cylinder liner extractor is available, remove the cylinder liners (see Section 14). Make sure that all apertures into the crankcase are well blocked with clean rag. Rotate the crankshaft so that the best access is obtained for each piston, and on the outer pistons extract the pins inwards.
3 If the crankcases are being separated, do so now (see Section 21), then follow the procedure in Section 24 and separate the connecting rods from the crankshaft, and remove the rods with the pistons from the tops of the liners. Now remove the liners (see Section 14).
4 Before removing the pistons, mark the cylinder number on the crown of each piston. Also note the dot on each crown which points to the front of the engine – if the mark is not visible, make your own as the piston must be installed the correct way round. If the connecting rods have been removed, the marks you made across the front are the same way as the piston mark.
5 Carefully prise out the circlip on one side of the piston using needle-nose pliers or a small flat-bladed screwdriver inserted into the notch **(see illustration)**. Push the piston pin out from the other side to free the piston from the connecting rod **(see illustration)**. Remove the other circlip and discard them as new ones must be used. When the piston has been removed, fit its pin back into its bore so that related parts do not get mixed up. Remember the importance of the rag in preventing dropped circlips from falling into the crankcase.

> **HAYNES HiNT** *To prevent the circlip from pinging away, pass a rod or screwdriver, which has a diameter greater than the gap between the circlip ends, through the piston pin. This will trap the circlip if it springs out.*

15.5a Use a small screwdriver or pointed instrument inserted in the notch to lever out the circlip

15.5b Withdraw the pin and remove the piston

Engine, clutch and transmission 2•27

  If a piston pin is a tight fit in the piston bosses, use a heat gun to expand the alloy piston sufficiently to release its grip of the pin. Alternatively purchase (or make up) a piston pin drawbolt tool – see 'Tools and Workshop Tips' in the Reference section.

Inspection

Pistons

6 Before the inspection process can be carried out, remove the piston rings and clean the pistons as follows.

7 Using your thumbs or a piston ring removal and installation tool, carefully remove the rings from the pistons **(see illustrations 15.27, 15.26a, 15.24c, b and a)**. Do not nick or gouge the pistons in the process. Carefully note which way up each ring fits and in which groove as they must be installed in their original positions and the same way up if being re-used. The upper surface of the top and second rings should be marked N1 and N2 respectively – if the mark on each ring is different, note which mark is for the top ring and which is for the second. The rings can also be distinguished by their different profiles.

8 Scrape all traces of carbon from the tops of the pistons. A hand-held wire brush or a piece of fine emery cloth can be used once most of the deposits have been scraped away. Do not, under any circumstances, use a wire brush mounted in a drill motor to remove deposits from the pistons; the piston material is soft and will be eroded away by the wire brush.

9 Use a piston ring groove cleaning tool to remove any carbon deposits from the ring grooves. If a tool is not available, a piece broken off an old ring will do the job. Be very careful to remove only the carbon deposits. Do not remove any metal and do not nick or gouge the sides of the ring grooves.

10 Once the deposits have been removed, clean the pistons with solvent and dry them thoroughly. Make sure the oil return holes below the oil ring groove are clear.

11 Carefully inspect each piston for cracks around the skirt, at the pin bosses and at the

15.13 Measure the piston ring-to-groove clearance with a feeler gauge

ring lands. Normal piston wear appears as even, vertical wear on the thrust surfaces of the piston and slight looseness of the top ring in its groove. If the skirt is scored or scuffed, the engine may have been suffering from overheating and/or abnormal combustion, which caused excessively high operating temperatures. The oil pump and cooling systems should be checked thoroughly.

12 A hole in the piston crown, an extreme to be sure, is an indication that abnormal combustion (pre-ignition) was occurring. Burned areas at the edge of the piston crown are usually evidence of spark knock (detonation). If any of the above problems exist, the causes must be corrected or the damage will occur again.

13 Measure the piston ring-to-groove clearance by laying the ring in its groove and slipping a feeler blade in beside it **(see illustration)**. **Note:** *Make sure you have the correct ring for the groove – the two compression rings can be identified by their markings (see Step 7).* Check the clearance at three or four locations around the groove. If the clearance is greater than that specified, replace the pistons and rings as a set.

14 Measure the piston diameter 8 mm up from the bottom of the skirt and at 90° to the piston pin axis **(see illustration)**. If outside of the specified figure, the piston must be replaced with a new one.

15 If the necessary measuring equipment is available, measure the connecting rod

15.14 Measure the piston diameter with a micrometer at the specified distance from the bottom of the skirt

small-end bore diameter, the piston pin outside diameter and the inside diameter of the pin bores in the piston **(see illustrations)**. Replace any component that has worn beyond the specified limits with a new one.

Piston rings

16 It is good practice to use new piston rings when an engine is being overhauled. Before fitting the piston rings, the ring end gaps must be checked.

17 Lay out the pistons and the new ring sets so the rings will be matched with the same piston and cylinder during the end gap measurement procedure and engine assembly.

18 Fit the top ring into the top of the first liner and square it up with the cylinder walls by pushing it in with the top of the piston until the third ring on the piston is level with and parallel all the way round to the top of the liner. To measure the end gap, slip a feeler blade between the ends of the ring and compare the measurement to the Specification **(see illustration)**.

19 If the gap is larger or smaller than specified, double check to make sure that you have the correct rings before proceeding.

20 If the gap is too small, check the liner for distortion (see Section 14). If the liner is good get another set of rings from your dealer, who should exchange them if you explain the circumstances, as they should fit correctly.

21 If the end gap exceeds the service limit

15.15a Measure the internal diameter of the small-end bore, the external diameter of the pin…

15.15b …and the internal diameter of the bore in the piston

15.18 Measuring piston ring installed end gap

2•28 Engine, clutch and transmission

15.24a Fit the oil ring expander in its groove...

15.24b ...then fit the lower side rail...

15.24c ...and the upper side rail each side of it

15.26a Fit the second ring into the middle groove

15.26b Old pieces of feeler gauge blade can be used to guide the ring over the piston

15.27 Fit the top ring into the top groove

specified with the old rings, fit new rings and check again. If it is still excessive check the liner for wear (see Section 14).

22 Repeat the procedure for each ring that will be installed in the first cylinder and for each ring in the remaining cylinders. Remember to keep the rings, pistons and cylinders matched up.

23 Once the ring end gaps have been checked/corrected, the rings can be fitted onto the pistons.

24 The oil control ring (lowest on the piston) is installed first. It is composed of three separate components, the expander and the upper and lower side rails. First slip the expander into the groove, making sure the ends butt against each other and do not overlap. Next fit the lower side rail, then the upper (see illustrations). New side rails can be fitted either way up, but if the removed ones are being reused they must be installed the same way up as they were removed. Do not use a piston ring installation tool on the side rails as they may be damaged. Instead, place one end of the side rail into the groove between the expander and the ring land. Hold it firmly in place and slide a finger around the piston while pushing the rail into the groove.

25 After the three oil ring components have been installed, check to make sure that both the upper and lower side rails can be turned smoothly in the ring groove.

26 Fit the second (middle) ring next – it should be marked N2 at one end, and this mark must face up. If no mark is visible the second ring and top rings can be distinguished by their different profiles, the top ring having a chamfered inner top edge, the second ring having square edges – make sure you have the correct ring. **Note:** *From new the top ring has a blue mark on its outer edge, and the second ring has a yellow mark and an overall bronze appearance.* Fit the ring into the middle groove on the piston (see illustration). Either use your thumbs to hold the ring ends apart when installing the ring over the piston, or slip sections of old feeler gauge blades between the ring and piston to guide it into its groove (see illustration), or use a ring removal/installation tool.

Caution: *Do not expand the ring any more than is necessary to slide it into place – the ring material is brittle and is easily broken if overstressed.*

27 Finally, fit the top ring into the top groove in the same manner. Make sure the N1 mark near the end gap is facing up (see illustration).

28 Position the ring end gaps around the piston as shown (see illustration).

15.28 Stagger the ring end gaps as shown

1 Top ring end gap
2 Second (middle) ring end gap
3 Top oil ring side rail end gap
4 Oil ring expander ends
5 Bottom oil ring side rail end gap

Engine, clutch and transmission 2•29

15.30a Slide the pin through the piston and rod...

15.30b ...and secure it with a new circlip

16 Clutch

Removal

Note: *If you are just fitting a new set of clutch plates follow Steps 1 to 7 to remove the old set, and Steps 21 and 26 to 36 to fit the new set.*

1 If required remove the guard from the clutch cover (see illustration) – you will need to do this if you are removing the release mechanism shaft from the cover (see Step 19).
2 Unscrew the clutch cable bracket bolt then detach the cable end from the release mechanism arm (see illustrations).
3 Working in a criss-cross pattern, unscrew the clutch cover bolts, noting the positions of the two longer ones (see illustration).
4 Remove the cover, being prepared to catch any residual oil.
5 Remove the gasket and discard it. Note the two locating dowels and remove them for safe-keeping if loose (see illustration 16.33a).
6 Working in a criss-cross pattern, gradually and evenly slacken the clutch spring bolts until spring pressure is released, then remove the bolts and springs (see illustration).

Installation

29 If the connecting rods have not been removed from the engine, stuff clean rag into the crankcase mouth to prevent any dropped circlips falling in. Lubricate the connecting rod small-end bore with engine oil.
30 Fit a new circlip into the groove in one side of the piston bore (the outer side for the outer pistons if the connecting rods have not been removed). Locate the piston on its rod so that the dot marking on its crown is facing forwards, the same way as the mark you made on the rod if removed. Push the piston pin fully into the piston and secure with a second new circlip – make sure the circlip is fully seated in its groove (see illustrations).
31 Install the other pistons in the same way. If the connecting rods have not been removed from the engine, rotate the crankshaft to gain the best access.
32 Check that the piston rings are still correctly positioned in relation to the front of the engine (see illustration 15.28).
33 Install all components and assemblies according to your removal procedure, referring to the relevant Sections of the Chapter.

16.1 Clutch cover guard screws (arrowed)

16.2a Unscrew the bolt (arrowed)...

16.2b ...and detach the cable end

16.3 Clutch cover bolts (arrowed)

16.6 Unscrew the bolts (arrowed) as described and remove the springs

2•30 Engine, clutch and transmission

16.7a Draw the clutch plates out...

16.7b ...using a magnet or hook on the inner ones

16.8 Using a commercially available tool to hold the clutch centre while unscrewing the nut

16.10a Fit the pin to keep the gear teeth aligned

Remove the pressure plate and the pull-rod **(see illustrations 16.30b and a)**.

7 Grasp as many of the clutch plates as you can and remove them as a pack, then draw the remaining plates out using a magnet or a piece of wire as a hook **(see illustrations)**. Unless the plates are being replaced with new ones, keep them in their original order. Note that the outer friction plate is slightly darker in colour, and that the inner friction plate is also slightly darker and has a larger internal diameter. Also note there are two different thicknesses of plain plate, with the thinner one(s) fitting outermost. Remove the anti-judder spring and spring seat, noting how they fit **(see illustrations 16.28b and a)**.

8 The clutch centre must be held to enable the clutch nut to be slackened. A Triumph service tool (Part No. T3880306) is available from dealers, or a commercially available (and not expensive) clutch holding tool along with a suitable block of wood can be used as shown (do not fit it too tightly) **(see illustration)**. Remove the heel guard if using the after-market tool and block of wood. Unscrew the nut and remove the Belleville washer and plain washer from the input shaft **(see illustrations 16.25b and a)**. A new nut and Belleville washer must be used on installation.

9 Slide the clutch centre off the input shaft, followed by the large thrust washer **(see illustrations 16.24b and a)**.

10 Get a suitable steel pin to fit into the holes in the primary driven gear and its sprung sub-gear to keep them in alignment **(see illustration)**. Jiggle the clutch housing backwards and forwards and draw out the sleeve, using a magnet or a pair of pliers to help, then support the housing and slide the bearing off the shaft **(see illustrations)**.

16.10b Draw the sleeve out as described...

16.10c ...then remove the bearing...

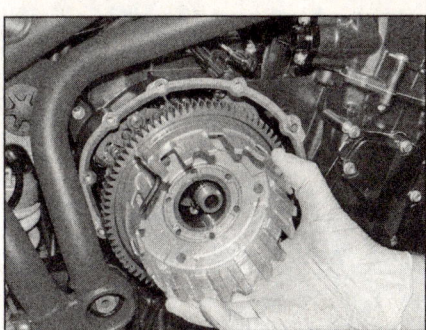

16.11 ...and the clutch housing

16.12 Measuring clutch friction plate thickness

16.14 Check the plain plates for warpage

11 Remove the housing **(see illustration)**. Note how the oil pump drive pegs locate in the holes in the back of the clutch housing.

Inspection

12 After an extended period of service the clutch friction plates will wear and promote clutch slip. Measure the thickness of each friction plate using a Vernier caliper **(see illustration)**. If any plate has worn to or beyond the service limit given in the Specifications, the friction plates must be replaced with a new set.

13 If the plates are good, but the clutch has been slipping, it could be that the springs have sagged. As no specification is available for the spring free length, the only way to check them is to compare them with new ones. If the springs have sagged, replace them as a set.

14 The plain plates should not show any signs of excess heating (bluing). Check for warpage using a flat surface and feeler blades **(see illustration)**. If any plate exceeds the maximum permissible amount of warpage, or shows signs of bluing, all plain plates must be renewed as a set.

15 Inspect the clutch assembly for burrs and indentations on the edges of the protruding tangs of the friction plates and/or the slots in the edge of the outer drum with which they

16.15a Check for wear of the friction plate tabs and the clutch housing slots...

engage **(see illustration)**. Similarly check for wear between the inner tongues of the plain plates and the slots in the clutch centre **(see illustration)**. Wear of this nature will cause clutch drag and slow disengagement during gear changes, as the plates will snag when the pressure plate is lifted. With care a small amount of wear can be corrected by dressing with a fine file, but if this is excessive the worn components should be replaced with new ones.

16 Inspect the clutch housing needle bearing and the bearing surfaces of the sleeve and housing **(see illustration)**. Check the springs in the back of the clutch housing and check

16.15b ...and of the plain plate tongues and clutch centre slots

the teeth on the primary driven gear. If any components are worn of damaged, replace them with new ones. If any damage is evident on the gear teeth, check the teeth on the primary drive gear on the crankshaft.

17 Inspect the anti-judder spring and spring seat for wear. If the spring is flattened, replace the spring and seat as a set.

18 Check the pressure plate and the bearing for signs of damage and wear **(see illustration)**. Check that the inner race of the bearing spins freely without any sign of notchiness. Push the bearing out of the pressure plate if a new one is needed.

16.16 Inspect the needle bearing, the sleeve and the bearing surface in the housing

16.18 Check the pressure plate and bearing for wear

16.19a Withdraw the shaft...

16.19b ...and check the seal and the bearings (arrowed) for wear

16.19c Lever the seal out...

16.19d ...and press the new one in with your fingers or a socket

16.19e Correct positioning of shaft return spring ends (arrowed)

16.20 Check for wear and damage where the pull-rod and shaft engage

19 Check the clutch release mechanism in the clutch cover for smooth operation. Note how the return spring ends locate, then withdraw the shaft from the cover, noting the washer **(see illustration)**. Check the shaft, oil seal and bearings for wear **(see illustration)**. If necessary, lever the old seal out **(see illustration)**. Refer to the Reference Section for bearing removal methods. Press the new seal in with your fingers or a socket **(see illustration)**. Lubricate the seal and bearings with grease. Make sure the shaft return spring ends locate correctly **(see illustration)**.

20 Check the pull-rod end and its locating cut-out in the shaft for signs of wear and damage, and replace them with new ones if necessary **(see illustration)**.

Installation

21 Remove all traces of gasket material from the crankcase and clutch cover mating surfaces.

22 Lubricate the clutch housing needle bearing and sleeve with clean engine oil **(see illustration 16.16)**.

23 Slide the clutch housing over the input shaft and manoeuvre it into the crankcase so that the primary driven gear engages with the primary drive gear on the crankshaft, then push the housing on so that the holes in the back of the housing engage with the pegs on the oil pump drive sprocket – if necessary, turn the oil pump driven sprocket until the holes align and clutch housing is felt to engage with the pegs **(see illustration)**. Fit the bearing and the sleeve into the housing, with the grooved face of the sleeve outwards **(see illustrations)**. When correctly fitted the bearing sleeve should be flush with the outer face of the clutch housing. With everything correctly aligned withdraw the rod from the hole in the gear **(see illustration 16.10a)**.

24 Slide the large thrust washer over the input shaft, then slide the clutch centre onto the input shaft splines **(see illustrations)**.

25 Fit the plain washer and the new

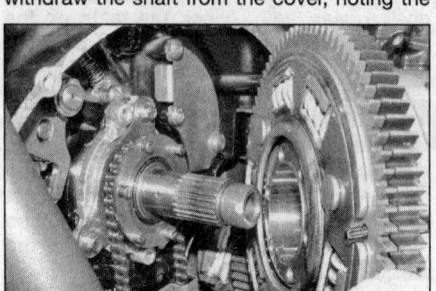

16.23a Align the pegs on the oil pump drive sprocket with the holes in the back of the clutch housing and jiggle the driven sprocket until they are felt to engage

16.23b Slide the bearing into the housing...

16.23c ...then fit the sleeve

16.24a Fit the large thrust washer...

Engine, clutch and transmission 2•33

16.24b ...and slide the clutch centre onto the shaft

16.25a Fit the plain washer and the Belleville washer

16.25b Thread the nut on...

16.25c ...and tighten it to the specified torque

16.25d Stake the rim into the detent

Belleville washer with its OUT marking facing outwards, then thread the clutch nut on **(see illustrations)**. Using the method employed on removal to lock the input shaft, tighten the nut to the torque setting specified at the beginning of the Chapter **(see illustration)**. **Note:** *When the nut has been tightened, check that the clutch centre rotates freely with the transmission in neutral.* Stake the rim of the nut into the detent in the shaft using a small punch **(see illustration)**.

26 The standard clutch pack comprises nine friction plates and eight plain plates. There are three different types of friction plate – the outermost and innermost plates are a different colour (darker) and the innermost has a larger internal diameter. There are two different thicknesses of plain plate (2.0 mm and 1.6 mm), and as standard there are six 2.0 mm plates and two 1.6 mm plates, and the 1.6 mm plates fit outermost.

27 If new clutch plates are being fitted the assembled height of the pack must be measured, and if necessary adjusted, before they are installed. Assemble the pack in the order described in Step 26 and measure its free height using a Vernier caliper **(see illustration)** – if the height is not within the range specified at the beginning of the Chapter, either replace the outermost 2.0 mm plate with a 1.6 mm plate, or replace the innermost 1.6 mm plate with a 2.0 mm plate, as required to bring the height within the specified range. The 1.6 mm plate(s) must always be fitted outermost, and there must be no less than one and no more than three.

28 Fit the anti-judder spring seat into the clutch centre, followed by the anti-judder spring, fitting the spring so that its outer edge is raised off the spring seat **(see illustrations)**.

29 Coat each clutch plate with engine oil prior to installation. Identify the innermost friction

16.27 Measuring the height of the assembled clutch plate pack

16.28a Fit the spring seat and the spring...

16.28b ...making sure they are the correct way round

2•34 Engine, clutch and transmission

16.29a Fit the inner friction plate...

16.29b ...then a plain plate, and so on...

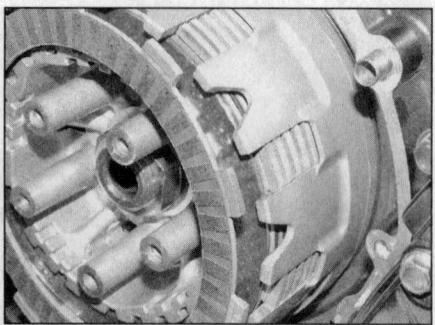

16.29c ...finishing with the outer friction plate

plate – it has a larger internal diameter (i.e. the plate is narrower) and is slightly darker. Build up the clutch plates, starting with the inner friction plate that is narrower, seating it around the anti-judder spring seat and spring **(see illustration)**. Next fit a plain plate, then alternate normal friction and plain plates, making sure the plain plate thicknesses are correctly identified and positioned (see Step 26), until all but the last friction plate are installed **(see illustration)**. Fit the outer friction plate (slightly darker) **(see illustration)**.

30 Insert the pull-rod into the end of the shaft **(see illustration)**. Fit the pressure plate, engaging the notches on its inner rim with the slots in the inside of the clutch centre **(see illustration)**.

31 Fit the springs and bolts and tighten the bolts evenly and a little at a time in a criss-cross sequence to the specified torque setting **(see illustration)**.

32 If the release mechanism shaft has been removed, make sure the spring and washer are on the shaft then grease it and fit it into the cover **(see illustration 16.19a)**. Make sure the spring ends locate correctly **(see illustration 16.19e)**.

33 Apply a dab of sealant to the crankcase joints. Fit the dowels into the crankcase if removed, then fit a new gasket, locating it over the dowels **(see illustration)**. Fit the cover,

16.30a Fit the pull-rod into the shaft...

16.30b ...then fit the pressure plate

16.31 Fit the springs and the bolts then tighten them as described

16.33a Locate a new gasket over the dowels (arrowed)

Engine, clutch and transmission 2•35

16.33b Fit the cover, making sure the shaft and pull-rod engage

16.34 Clutch cover bolt tightening sequence

angling the release shaft arm so it engages with the pull-rod **(see illustration)**.

34 Fit the cover bolts – the longer bolts go into the doweled holes **(see illustration 16.33a)**. Tighten the bolts evenly in the sequence shown to the specified torque setting, then go round the bolts again to the same torque **(see illustration)**. Operate the release lever and make sure it picks up the end of the pull-rod correctly – it should come up solid when it is pointing towards the engine.

35 Attach the clutch cable end to the release lever on the clutch cover, then fit the cable bracket and tighten its bolt **(see illus-**trations 16.2b and a)**. Check and adjust cable freeplay (see Chapter 1).

36 If removed fit the guard onto the cover.

17 Clutch cable

1 Remove the right-hand side panel (see Chapter 7). On XC models remove the left hand guard (see Chapter 7).

2 Pull the rubber boot off the end of the outer cable, then slacken the locknuts securing the cable in the bracket on the clutch cover, and thread the front nut up as far as it will go and thread the rear locknut off **(see illustration)**.

3 Slip the cable end out of the retainer on the release arm, noting how it fits **(see illustration)**. Draw the cable out of the bracket **(see illustration)**.

4 Thread the cable adjuster into the lever bracket on the handlebar **(see illustration)**. Align the slot in the adjuster with the slot in the bracket.

5 Pull the outer cable end from the socket in the adjuster and release the inner cable from the lever **(see illustrations)**. Remove the cable from the machine, noting its routing.

17.2 Slacken the front locknut (A) and thread the rear locknut (B) off the cable

17.3a Detach the cable end...

17.3b ...and draw the cable out of the bracket

17.4 Slacken the lockring (A) and turn the adjuster (B) into the bracket

17.5a Draw the outer cable end from the adjuster and slip the inner cable out via the slots...

17.5b ...then detach the inner cable end from the lever

2•36 Engine, clutch and transmission

HAYNES HiNT *Before removing the cable from the bike, tape the lower end of the new cable to the upper end of the old cable. Slowly pull the lower end of the old cable out, guiding the new cable down into position. Using this method will ensure the cable is routed correctly.*

6 Unless a new cable is being fitted check the cable ends for security of the nipples and any loose strands and fraying. Make sure the inner cable slides smoothly and freely in the outer cable. If required lubricate the cable using a pressure adapter (see Chapter 1).
7 Turn the clutch release mechanism arm to check for smooth operation of the shaft in the cover and any signs of wear or damage. Remove it for inspection if required (see Section 16).

8 Installation is the reverse of removal. Apply grease to the cable ends. Make sure the cable is correctly routed. Make sure the cable lower end is properly located in the retainer on the release mechanism arm.
9 Adjust the clutch lever freeplay (see Chapter 1). Install the side panel, and the hand guard on XC models (see Chapter 7).

18 Sump, oil strainer and pressure relief valve

Removal

1 Remove the sump guard, and its bracket if required (see Chapter 7).
2 Drain the engine oil, and if required remove the oil filter (see Chapter 1).

3 Remove the exhaust system (see Chapter 4).
4 Unscrew the sump bolts, slackening them evenly in a criss-cross sequence to prevent distortion (see illustration). Remove the sump (see illustration). Remove the gasket – a new one must be fitted. Remove the dowels if loose.
5 Remove the drain tube for the water pump – it may have come away with the sump, or otherwise will be in the pump (see illustration). Remove its O-rings (see illustration 18.18) – new ones must be used.
6 Unscrew the oil strainer bolts and remove the strainer (see illustration). Remove the O-ring (see illustration 18.17) – a new one must be used.
7 Unscrew the internal oil pipe bolts and remove the pipe (see illustration). Remove the O-rings (see illustration 18.16) – new ones must be used.
8 Undo the crankcase breather drain tube bolt and remove the tube (see illustration). Remove the O-ring (see illustration 18.15) – a new one must be used.
9 Unscrew the pressure relief valve (see illustration).

Inspection

10 Clean through the water pump drain tube, the internal oil pipe and the breather drain tube with solvent, and blow them through, with compressed air if available.
11 Push the relief valve plunger into the valve body and check that it moves smoothly and freely against the spring pressure (see illustration). If not, remove the circlip, noting

18.4a Unscrew the bolts all round...

18.4b ...and remove the sump

18.5 Remove the drain tube

18.6 Unscrew the bolts (arrowed) and remove the strainer

18.7 Unscrew the bolts (arrowed) and remove the pipe

18.8 Unscrew the bolt (arrowed) and remove the tube

18.9 Pressure relief valve (arrowed)

18.11a Check the plunger moves smoothly and freely

Engine, clutch and transmission 2•37

18.11b Remove the circlip (arrowed) to release the spring and plunger

18.15 Fit the tube using a new O-ring (arrowed)

18.16 Fit new O-rings (arrowed) into the grooves

that it is under spring pressure, and remove the spring seat, spring and plunger **(see illustration)**. Clean all the components in solvent and check them for scoring, wear or damage. If any is found, fit a new relief valve – individual components are not available. Otherwise, coat the inside of the valve body and the plunger with clean engine oil, then insert the plunger, spring and spring seat and secure them with the circlip. Check the action of the valve plunger again – if it is still suspect, replace the valve with a new one.

12 Clean the strainer in solvent and remove any debris caught in the gauze, blowing through it with compressed air if available. The presence of metal caught in the strainer, or in the bottom of the sump, is indicative of engine wear that should be investigated.

Installation

13 Remove all traces of gasket material from the sump and crankcase mating surfaces. Clean the threads of all bolts that had threadlock applied.
14 Apply a drop of non-permanent thread locking compound to the pressure relief valve threads and tighten the valve to the specified torque setting **(see illustration 18.9)**.
15 Fit the crankcase breather drain tube using a new O-ring **(see illustration)**. Apply a drop of non-permanent thread locking compound to the bolt threads and tighten it to the torque setting specified at the beginning of the Chapter **(see illustration 18.8)**.
16 Fit the internal oil pipe using new O-rings **(see illustration)**. Apply a drop of non-permanent thread locking compound to the pipe bolts and tighten them to the specified torque **(see illustration 18.7)**.

17 Fit the strainer using a new O-ring **(see illustration)**. Apply a drop of non-permanent thread locking compound to the bolts and tighten them to the specified torque **(see illustration 18.6)**.
18 Fit new O-rings onto each end of the water pump drain tube and smear them with petroleum jelly (Vaseline) **(see illustration)**. Fit the tube into the sump **(see illustration 18.5)**.
19 Fit the sump dowels if removed **(see illustration)**. Place a new gasket onto the sump if the engine is in the frame, or onto the crankcase if the engine has been removed and is upside down on the bench – use a smear of grease to hold the gasket in place if required. Fit the sump, locating the drain pipe in its hole in the pump **(see illustrations)**. Fit all the bolts finger-tight at first, then tighten them evenly in the sequence shown to the specified torque setting, then go round the bolts again to the same torque **(see illustration)**.
20 Install the exhaust system (see Chapter 4).
21 If removed fit a new oil filter. Fill the engine with the correct type and quantity of oil (see Chapter 1). Start the engine and check that there are no leaks.
22 Install the sump guard (see Chapter 7).

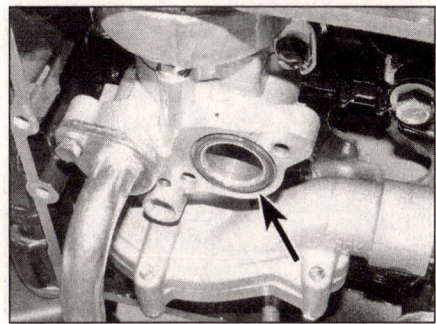

18.17 Fit a new O-ring (arrowed) into the groove

18.18 Fit two new O-rings onto each end of the tube

18.19c Sump bolt tightening sequence

18.19a Make sure the dowels (arrowed) are in place, then fit the gasket

18.19b Make sure the drain tube locates in its hole in the pump (arrowed)

2•38 Engine, clutch and transmission

19.4 Unscrew the bolt (arrowed) and displace or remove the pipe

19.5 Release the clamps (A) and detach the hoses, then unscrew the bolt (B) and withdraw the pipe

19.6 Unscrew the bolts (arrowed) and remove the guide

19 Oil and water pump

Removal

1 Drain the engine oil and coolant (see Chapter 1).
2 Remove the clutch (see Section 16).
3 Remove the sump, then remove the oil strainer and the internal oil pipe (see Section 18).
4 Unscrew the coolant inlet pipe bolt on the left-hand side of the crankcase and displace or remove the pipe – release the clamp and detach the by-pass hose first if you want to remove it **(see illustration)**. Discard the O-ring – a new one must be used.
5 Release the clamps and detach the hoses from the coolant outlet pipe on the front of the crankcase **(see illustration)**. Unscrew the bolt and withdraw the pipe. Discard the O-rings – new ones must be used.
6 Unscrew the pump drive chain guide bolts and remove the guide **(see illustration)**.
7 Slide the drive sprocket and chain off the bearing and sleeve, using a small screwdriver to keep them in place **(see illustration)**.
8 Unscrew the pump mounting bolts and remove the driven sprocket cover **(see illustration)**. Disengage the chain from the driven sprocket and remove the chain and drive sprocket **(see illustration)**. Slide the drive sprocket bearing, sleeve and spacer off the shaft **(see illustrations 19.18b and a)**.
9 Withdraw the roll pin from the front mounting bolt hole to release the pump from the crankcase – to do this locate a hooked tool under the stepped section of the split in the pin and draw it out **(see illustrations)** – also grip the side of the pin with pliers if necessary.

Remove the O-ring from the coolant inlet sleeve to the water pump and discard it – a new one must be used **(see illustration 19.16a)**.

Inspection

Note: *Apart from a rotor set, sprocket and the mounting hardware, individual parts are not available for the combined oil and water pump; if the checks described below indicate that the oil pump rotor tips are worn, you could just fit a new rotor set, but if the outer rotor and pump body are worn as well you will have to fit a new pump. Because the difference in cost between a rotor set and a complete new pump assembly is not that great it is advisable to just fit a complete new pump – if the rotors are worn then other aspects of the pump, such as the bearings and water pump seals are also likely to be worn.*

10 Counter-hold the pump driven sprocket and unscrew the bolt, then remove the sprocket and washer **(see illustration)**.

19.7 Draw the sprocket off the bearing and sleeve to get some slack in the chain

19.8a Unscrew the bolts (arrowed) and remove the cover

19.8b Disengage the chain and remove it along with the drive sprocket

19.9a Hook the roll pin out...

19.9b ...and remove the pump

19.10 Counter-hold the sprocket and unscrew the bolt (arrowed)

Engine, clutch and transmission 2•39

19.11 Unscrew the bolts (arrowed) and remove the body

19.13a Measuring outer rotor-to-body clearance

19.13b Fit the inner rotor...

11 Unscrew the three bolts and remove the oil pump body **(see illustration)**.

12 Remove the inner and outer rotors, noting which way round they fit. Clean them with solvent. Examine them for scoring and wear.

13 Fit the outer rotor into the body and measure the clearance between them **(see illustration)**. Fit the inner rotor over the shaft and locate the cut-outs over the drive pin **(see illustration)**. Fit the outer rotor over the inner rotor, then position them as shown and measure the clearance between the inner rotor tip and the outer rotor tip with a feeler gauge, and record the measurement **(see illustrations)**. Fit both rotors into the body, then lay a straight-edge across the body and measure the rotor end-float (gap between the rotors and straight-edge) with a feeler gauge. If any of the results are outside the limits listed in this Chapter's Specifications, replace the pump with a new one.

19.13c ...and the outer rotor...

19.13d ...and measure rotor tip clearance

14 Before reassembling the pump, make sure that all parts are clean. Lubricate the rotors with new engine oil. Make sure the drive pin is in place **(see illustration)**. Fit the inner and outer rotors **(see illustrations 19.13b and c)**.

Fit the pump body and tighten the bolts to the torque setting specified at the beginning of the Chapter **(see illustration)**. Fit the washer onto the end of the shaft then locate the driven sprocket, OUT mark facing out and aligning the flats **(see illustrations)**. Clean the threads of the bolt and apply a thread locking compound, then counter-hold the sprocket and tighten the bolt to the specified torque **(see illustration 19.10)**.

15 Inspect the oil pump drive and driven sprockets and chain for damage and wear – the sprockets and chain are available separately. Check the needle bearing and sleeve and replace them with new ones if they are worn.

Installation

16 Fit a new O-ring into the coolant inlet sleeve to the water pump **(see illustration)**.

19.14a Set the drive pin (arrowed) centrally

19.14b Fit the body onto the locating pins

19.14c Fit the washer onto the shaft...

19.14d ...then fit the sprocket

19.16a Fit a new O-ring (arrowed) into the groove

2•40 Engine, clutch and transmission

19.16b Prime the pump as described

19.17a Fit the roll pin...

19.17b ...and tap it in

19.18a Slide the spacer on...

19.18b ...then fit the sleeve and bearing

19.20 Fit new O-rings (arrowed) before inserting the pipe

Pour some new engine oil into the pump and turn the sprocket so the rotors are liberally coated **(see illustration)**.

17 Locate the pump on the crankcase **(see illustration 19.9b)**. Insert the roll pin and tap it in until it seats using a punch **(see illustrations)**.

18 Slide the spacer onto the shaft, followed by the sleeve with its collared end innermost, then fit the bearing onto the sleeve **(see illustrations)**. Fit the drive sprocket into the chain and slide the sprocket onto the shaft, but not onto the bearing, then slip the chain around the driven sprocket and slide the drive sprocket onto the bearing **(see illustration 19.8b)**. Check the chain is correctly engaged around each sprocket. Clean the pump mounting bolts and apply some fresh threadlock. Fit the driven sprocket cover then tighten the mounting bolts to the torque setting specified at the beginning of the Chapter **(see illustration 19.8a)**.

19 Clean the pump drive chain guide bolts and apply some fresh threadlock. Fit the guide and tighten the bolts to the specified torque **(see illustration 19.6)**.

20 Clean the coolant outlet pipe bolt and apply some fresh threadlock. Fit new O-rings onto the pipe **(see illustration)**. Insert the pipe, locating it in the pump, and tighten its bolt to the specified torque. Connect the hoses and tighten the clamps **(see illustration 19.5)**.

21 Clean the coolant inlet pipe bolt and apply some fresh threadlock. Fit a new O-ring onto the pipe **(see illustration)**. Fit the pipe and tighten its bolt to the specified torque. If detached connect the hoses and tighten the clamps.

22 Install the oil strainer, the internal oil pipe, and the sump (see Section 18).

23 Install the clutch (see Section 16).

24 Replenish the engine oil and coolant (see Chapter 1).

20 Gearchange mechanism

Removal

1 Make sure the transmission is in neutral.
2 Remove the front sprocket cover (see Chapter 6). Remove the E-clip and washer from the shaft **(see illustration)**. Wrap a single layer of thin insulating tape around the shaft splines to protect the oil seal lips as the shaft is removed.
3 Remove the clutch (see Section 16).
4 Note how the detent arm roller locates in the neutral detent on the selector drum cam, and how the centralising spring ends locate **(see illustration)**. Unhook

19.21 Fit a new O-ring (arrowed) before fitting the pipe

20.2 Remove the E-clip and the washer behind it

20.4a Note how the detent arm roller (A) and the spring ends (B) locate

Engine, clutch and transmission 2•41

20.4b Unhook the spring

20.5 Withdraw the gearchange shaft

20.6 Counter-hold the drum as described and unscrew the bolt (arrowed)

20.7 Check the pawls on the arm and the pins on the plate

20.10a Washer (A), circlip (B), centralising spring (C), washer (D), circlip (E), detent arm (F)

20.10b Circlip (A), washer (B), thrust spring (C), selector arm (D)

and remove the detent arm spring **(see illustration)**.

5 Grasp the shaft/arm assembly and withdraw it from the crankcase, noting the washer **(see illustration)**.

6 If required, undo the camplate bolt, locking the selector drum with a holding tool or using a suitable tool wedged between the plate and the crankcase **(see illustration)**. Remove the plate, using a screwdriver to help ease it off if necessary. Note that there is a locating pin in the end of the selector drum – it should be tight, but take care as it could drop out. Remove it from the drum for safekeeping if it is loose.

Inspection

7 Check the selector arm for cracks, distortion and wear of its pawls, and check for any corresponding wear on the pins on the selector drum camplate **(see illustration)**. Also check the detent arm roller and the detents in the camplate for any wear or damage, and make sure the roller turns freely. Replace any components that are worn or damaged with new ones. If required (and not already done), refer to Step 6 for removal of the camplate, and to Step 13 for installation.

8 Inspect the shaft centralising spring and the detent arm return spring for fatigue, wear or damage. If any is found, they must be replaced with new ones. To replace the shaft spring release the circlip, then slide the spring off the shaft **(see illustration 20.10a)**. Fit the new spring, locating the ends on each side of

the tab, then fit the circlip, using a new one if the old one distorted on removal.

9 Check the gearchange shaft is straight and look for damage to the splines. If the shaft is bent you can attempt to straighten it, but if the splines are damaged the shaft must be replaced with a new one.

10 If you need to disassemble the shaft lay the components out in their correct fitted order and orientation as you remove them: slide the washer off the left-hand end, then release the circlip and slide the centralising spring and washer off the shaft **(see illustration)**. Release the circlip and slide the detent arm off **(see illustration)**. Release the circlip on the right-hand end and remove the washer, thrust spring and selector arm. Reassemble the shaft in reverse order using new components as required – use new circlips if they deformed on removal, and make sure they seat in their grooves.

11 Make sure the centralising spring locating pin in the crankcase is tight **(see illustration)** – if loose, remove it, clean the threads and apply fresh threadlock, then tighten it to the specified torque.

12 Check the condition of the shaft bearings and oil seal in the crankcase **(see illustration 20.11)**. If the seal is damaged or showing signs of leakage or the bearings are worn they must be replaced with new ones. Lever the seal out using a seal hook or screwdriver **(see illustration)**. Draw the bearings out using a puller. Do not reuse the bearings once removed. Press the new bearings into place. Drive the new seal squarely into place with the

20.11 Centralising spring locating pin (A); shaft bearings (B)

20.12a Lever the seal out

2•42 Engine, clutch and transmission

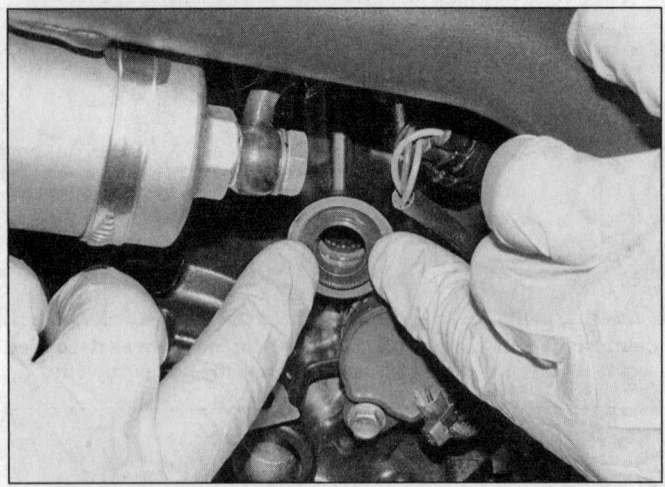

20.12b Press the seal in using your fingers or a socket

20.14 The neutral detent (arrowed) points to the front when the transmission is in neutral

marked side facing out using a suitable socket that bears only on the outer rim, not on the inner lip **(see illustration)**.

Installation

13 If removed, fit the camplate locating pin into the end of the selector drum. Locate the camplate onto the pin, carefully using a drift to tap it into place if necessary. Clean the threads of the bolt, then apply a suitable non-permanent thread locking compound and tighten it to the torque setting specified at the beginning of the Chapter **(see illustration 20.6)** – lock the drum with a holding tool as on removal.
14 Make sure the selector drum is in the neutral position **(see illustration)**.
15 Check that all components are properly positioned on the gearchange shaft **(see illustrations 20.10a and b)**. Apply some oil to the shaft bearings, and some grease to the lips of the oil seal **(see illustration 20.11)**. Slide the shaft into place and push it all the way through until the splined end comes out the other side, and locate the detent arm roller in the neutral detent on the camplate and the selector arm pawls onto the pins on the plate and the centralising spring ends onto each side of the locating pin in the crankcase **(see illustrations 20.5 and 20.4a)**.

Remove the insulating tape from around the gearchange shaft splines. Fit the washer and E-clip onto the left-hand end of the shaft **(see illustrations)**.
16 Fit the detent arm spring **(see illustration 20.4b)**.
17 Check that all components are correctly positioned **(see illustration 20.4a)**.
18 Install the clutch (see Section 16).
19 Fit the front sprocket cover (see Chapter 6).

21 Crankcase separation and reassembly

Separation

1 To access the crankshaft and connecting rods, balancer shaft, transmission shafts, selector drum and forks, and all related bearings, the crankcases must be split.
2 Remove the engine from the frame (see Section 4). Remove the following components, referring to the relevant Sections.
  Camshafts and followers (Section 9)*
  Cam chain, tensioner blade and guide blade (Section 10)*
  Cylinder head (Section 12)*
  Cylinder liners and pistons (Sections 14 and 15)*
  Alternator and starter clutch (see Chapter 8)*
  Clutch (see Section 16)
  Starter motor (Chapter 8)
  Sump, oil strainer, oil pipe and drain tubes (see Section 18)
  Oil/water pump and its drive chain (see Section 19)
  Gearchange mechanism (see Section 20)
**If the crankcase halves are being separated just to examine the crankshaft, balancer shaft or transmission components without removing them, or to just remove the transmission shafts and/or selector drum and forks, then there is no need to remove the camshafts, cam chain, cylinder head, liners and pistons, and alternator, though the right-hand crankcase cover and alternator cover must be removed. The gearchange mechanism need only be removed if the transmission is being removed.*
3 Unscrew the balancer shaft end cover bolts **(see illustration)**. Remove the cover and the gasket – a new gasket must be used.
4 Turn the crankcase upside down, supporting it as required using blocks of wood so it is stable.
5 Slacken and remove all bolts from the lower crankcase half following the numbered

20.15a Fit the washer...

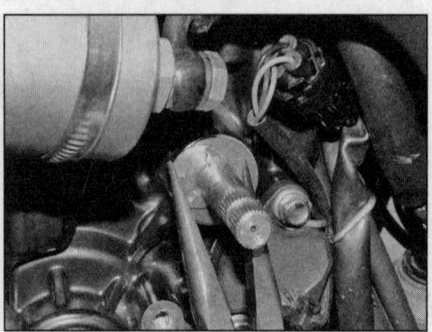

20.15b ...and press the E-clip into the groove

21.3 Unscrew the bolts (arrowed) and remove the cover

Engine, clutch and transmission 2•43

21.5a Crankcase bolt slackening sequence

21.5b Store the bolts in holes punched into a piece of card as shown

sequence **(see illustration)**. *Note: As each bolt is removed, store it in its relative position in a cardboard template of the lower crankcase half* **(see illustration)**. *This will ensure that all bolts are installed in the correct location on reassembly. Also, take note of the washers on the eight crankshaft journal bolts and store them with the bolts to ensure correct reassembly.*

6 Carefully lift the lower crankcase half off the upper half, leaving the crankshaft, balancer shaft and transmission shafts in the upper half of the crankcase **(see illustration)**. As the lower half is lifted away take care not to dislodge or lose any main bearing shells and the three dowels. *Note: If the halves don't separate easily, make sure all fasteners have been removed. Don't lever between the crankcase mating surfaces or they will leak; initial separation can be achieved by tapping gently around the joint with a soft-faced mallet.*

7 Remove the three locating dowels if they are loose – they could be in either crankcase half **(see illustration 21.11)**.

8 Remove all traces of sealant from the crankcase mating surfaces.

Reassembly

9 Ensure that all components are in place in the upper and lower crankcase halves. If the transmission shafts have not been removed, remove the oil seal from the left-hand end of the output shaft and replace it with a new one (see Section 27). Check the position of the selector drum and forks and transmission shafts – make sure they're in the neutral position (i.e. the transmission shafts rotate independently of each other).

10 Lubricate the transmission shaft pinions, selector drum and forks, and crankshaft journals with clean engine oil, then use a rag soaked in high flash-point solvent to wipe over the mating surfaces of both crankcase halves to remove all traces of oil.

11 If removed, fit the three locating dowels into the upper crankcase half **(see illustration)**.

21.6 Lift the lower crankcase half off carefully so as not to dislodge components

21.11 Make sure the dowels (arrowed) are in place

2•44 Engine, clutch and transmission

21.12a Apply sealant...

12 Apply a small amount of suitable silicone sealant (Triumph use ThreeBond 1215) to the indicated areas of the mating surface of the lower crankcase half **(see illustrations)**.
Caution: Take care not to apply an excessive amount of sealant, as it will ooze out when the case halves are assembled and may obstruct oil passages and prevent the bearings from seating.
13 Make sure that the main bearing shells are in position, then carefully fit the lower crankcase half onto the upper half, making sure it locates onto the dowels **(see illustration 21.6)**.
14 Check that the lower crankcase half is correctly seated and that all shafts are free to rotate. *Note: If the cases are not correctly seated, remove the lower crankcase half and investigate the problem. Do not attempt to pull them together using the crankcase bolts as the case will crack and be ruined.*
15 Clean the threads of the lower crankcase bolts and insert them in their original locations, making sure the washers are fitted with the eight crankshaft journal bolts **(see illustration 21.5b)**. Secure all bolts finger-tight at this stage.

21.12b ...to the shaded area as shown

Caution: Note that two sizes of bolt are used, 6 mm and 8 mm. Care must be taken to distinguish between them during the tightening sequence, as the larger 8 mm bolts are set tighter, and if a 6 mm bolt is mistaken for an 8 mm bolt, it may shear or strip threads.
16 Tighten the crankcase bolts as follows: first tighten all crankcase bolts to 12 Nm, tightening them in the correct numbered sequence **(see illustration)**.
17 Now tighten the M8 size crankcase bolts (Nos. 1 to 8, and 14 to 17) to 22 Nm in the correct sequence **(see illustration 21.16)**.
18 With all crankcase fasteners tightened, check that the crankshaft, balancer shaft and transmission shafts rotate smoothly and easily. If there are any signs of undue stiffness or of any other problem, the fault must be rectified before proceeding further.
19 Fit the balancer shaft end cover using a new gasket **(see illustration)**. Tighten the bolts in the sequence shown to the specified torque, then go round the bolts again to the same torque.
20 Install all removed assemblies in the reverse of the sequence in Step 2.

21.16 Crankcase bolt tightening sequence

21.19 Fit the cover using a new gasket

Engine, clutch and transmission 2•45

22 Crankcase inspection

1 After the crankcases have been separated remove the crankshaft and connecting rods, balancer shaft, transmission shafts and oil pipe, selector drum and forks, and all related bearings, referring to the relevant Sections. Remove and the oil pressure switch (see Chapter 8). On models without ABS remove the speed sensor (see Chapter 4). Unscrew the breather chamber cover screws and remove the cover. Discard the gasket – a new one must be used. Remove the oil gallery plugs.
2 Remove all traces of old gasket sealant from the mating surfaces. Minor damage to the surfaces can be cleaned up with a fine sharpening stone or grindstone.
3 Clean the crankcases and oil passages thoroughly with new solvent and dry them with compressed air, blowing through all oil passages and jets.
4 Small cracks or holes in aluminium castings may be repaired with an epoxy resin adhesive as a temporary measure. Permanent repairs can be effected by argon-arc welding, and only a specialist in this process is in a position to advise on the economy or practical aspect of such a repair. Alternatively you could try one of the low temperature aluminium welding kits available. If any damage is found that can't be repaired, renew the crankcase halves as a set.
5 Damaged threads can be economically reclaimed by using a diamond section wire insert, of the Helicoil type, which is easily fitted after drilling and re-tapping the affected thread.
6 Sheared studs or screws can usually be removed with screw extractors, which consist of a tapered, left thread screws of very hard steel. These are inserted into a pre-drilled hole in the stud, and usually succeed in dislodging the most stubborn stud or screw. If a problem arises which seems beyond your scope, it is worth consulting a professional engineering firm before condemning an otherwise sound casing. Many of these firms advertise regularly in the motorcycle press.
7 Fit the breather chamber using a new gasket, and apply some threadlock to the bolts. Apply some thread lock to the oil gallery plugs and tighten them.
8 Install the speed sensor (see Chapter 4) and the oil pressure switch (see Chapter 8).
Caution: Be very careful not to nick or gouge the crankcase mating surfaces or leaks will result. Check both crankcase halves very carefully for cracks and other damage.

 Refer to 'Tools and Workshop Tips' in the Reference section for details of how to install a thread insert and use a screw extractor.

23 Main and connecting rod bearing information

1 Even though main and connecting rod bearings are generally replaced with new ones during the engine overhaul, the old bearings should be retained for close examination as they may reveal valuable information about the condition of the engine.
2 Bearing failure occurs mainly because of lack of lubrication, the presence of dirt or other foreign particles, overloading the engine and/or corrosion. Regardless of the cause of bearing failure, it must be corrected before the engine is reassembled to prevent it from happening again.
3 When examining the bearings, remove the main bearings from the crankcase halves and the rod bearings from the connecting rods and caps and lay them out on a clean surface in the same general position as their location on the crankshaft journals. This will make it possible for you to match any noted bearing problems with the corresponding crankshaft journal.
4 Dirt and other foreign particles get into the engine in a variety of ways. It may be left in the engine during assembly or it may pass through filters or breathers. It may get into the oil and from there into the bearings. Metal chips from machining operations and normal engine wear are often present. Abrasives are sometimes left in engine components after reconditioning operations, especially when parts are not thoroughly cleaned using the proper cleaning methods. Whatever the source, these foreign objects often end up imbedded in the soft bearing material and are easily recognised. Large particles will not imbed in the bearing and will score or gouge the bearing and journal. The best prevention for this cause of bearing failure is to clean all parts thoroughly and keep everything spotlessly clean during engine reassembly. Frequent and regular oil and filter changes are also recommended.
5 Lack of lubrication or lubrication breakdown has a number of interrelated causes. Excessive heat (which thins the oil), overloading (which squeezes the oil from the bearing face) and oil leakage or throw off from excessive bearing clearances, worn oil pump or high engine Streets all contribute to lubrication breakdown. Blocked oil passages will also starve a bearing and destroy it. When lack of lubrication is the cause of bearing failure, the bearing material is wiped or extruded from the steel backing of the bearing. Temperatures may increase to the point where the steel backing and the journal turn blue from overheating.
6 Riding habits can have a definite effect on bearing life. Full throttle low speed operation, or labouring the engine, puts very high loads on bearings, which tend to squeeze out the oil film. These loads cause the bearings to flex, which produces fine cracks in the bearing face (fatigue failure). Eventually the bearing material will loosen in pieces and tear away from the steel backing. Short trip riding leads to corrosion of bearings, as insufficient engine heat is produced to drive off the condensed water and corrosive gases produced. These products collect in the engine oil, forming acid and sludge. As the oil is carried to the engine bearings, the acid attacks and corrodes the bearing material.
7 Incorrect bearing installation during engine assembly will lead to bearing failure as well. Tight fitting bearings which leave insufficient bearing oil clearances result in oil starvation. Dirt or foreign particles trapped behind a bearing insert result in high spots on the bearing which lead to failure.
8 To avoid bearing problems, clean all parts thoroughly before reassembly, double check all bearing clearance measurements and lubricate the new bearings with clean engine oil during installation.

24 Connecting rods and big-end bearings

Note 1: *The connecting rod bolts must be discarded and new ones used on installation – it is best to obtain the new bolts in advance. The old bolts can however be used for the oil clearance check.*
Note 2: *There are a number of different ways in which the connecting rods can be removed, and your best approach will depend on what other work, if any, you are doing on the engine.*
- If the liners have been removed and the pistons have already been separated from the rods, then you can remove the crankshaft with the rods still attached and then separate them afterwards.
- If the pistons have not been separated from the rods, they cannot be removed along with the crankshaft as the pistons will not fit through the crankcase main bearing webs. Remove the rod caps first, then remove the crankshaft, then remove the rod and piston assemblies from the top of the crankcase.

Removal

1 Remove the engine from the frame (see Section 4).
2 Remove the cylinder head (see Section 12).
3 Separate the crankcase halves (see Section 21).
4 Before separating the rods from the crankshaft, measure the side clearance on

each rod with a feeler gauge **(see illustration)**. If the clearance on any rod is greater than the service limit listed in this Chapter's Specifications, replace that rod with a new one.

5 Using paint or a marker pen, mark the relevant cylinder identity across the join between each connecting rod and cap at the front – these ensure that the cap and rod are fitted correctly on reassembly **(see illustration 24.4)**. Cylinders are numbered 1 to 3, from the left to the right-hand side of the engine.

6 Unscrew the connecting rod cap bolts **(see illustration)**.

7 Separate the caps, complete with the lower bearing shells, from the crankpins **(see illustration)**. If a cap appears stuck, tap it lightly on one end with a hammer while pulling it. If necessary thread the bolts part-way back in and tap the heads lightly to dislodge the rod from the cap.

8 Remove the balancer shaft (see Section 26), the crankshaft (Section 25) and the transmission output shaft (Section 27).

9 Position the crankcase on its side or raise and support it at the front. Support the rod to prevent it marking the liner bore or block, push the piston up the bore and remove the rod and piston assembly from the top **(see illustration)**.

HAYNES HiNT *If required, to ease removal of the pistons from the tops of the liners, carefully remove any ridge of carbon built up on the top of each liner bore using a scraper. If there is a pronounced wear ridge, remove it using a ridge reamer.*

Caution: *Do not try to remove the piston/connecting rod from the bottom of the crankcase. The piston will not pass the crankcase main bearing webs.*

10 Fit the relevant bearing shells (if removed), cap, and bolts on each piston/connecting rod assembly so that they are all kept together as a matched set.

11 If required and not already done, separate the pistons from the connecting rods (see Section 15). If the cylinder liners weren't clamped in place after removing the

24.4 Side clearance measuring point (A). Mark the cylinder number on the front of the rod and cap (B)

cylinder head, remove them for resealing (see Section 14).

Inspection

12 Check the connecting rods for cracks and other obvious damage. Refer to Section 15 and check the piston pin and connecting rod small-end bore dimensions for wear. Replace any components that are worn beyond the specified limit with new ones.

13 Refer to Section 23 and examine the connecting rod bearing shells. If they are scored, badly scuffed or appear to have seized, new shells must be installed. Always replace the shells in the connecting rods as a set. If they are badly damaged, check the corresponding crankpin. Evidence of extreme heat, such as discoloration, indicates that lubrication failure has occurred. Be sure to thoroughly check the oil pump and pressure relief valve as well as all oil holes and passages before reassembling the engine.

14 Have the rods checked for twist and bending by a Triumph dealer if you are in doubt about their straightness.

Oil clearance check

15 Whether new bearing shells are being fitted or the original ones are being re-used, the connecting rod bearing oil clearance should be checked prior to reassembly. Work on one rod at a time when checking the clearances.

16 The accuracy of this check is dependant on the rod not turning on the crankpin

24.6 Working on one rod at a time, unscrew the cap bolts...

while it is fitted and tightened – if it does, the Plastigauge will be disturbed and an inaccurate reading will result. To prevent this you ideally need to clamp the crankshaft to the workbench so it cannot move, and after fitting the rod onto its crankpin, but before fitting the cap, also clamp the rod so it can't move.

17 Remove the bearing shells from the rod and cap, keeping them in order **(see illustration 24.18)**. Clean the backs of the shells and the bearing locations in both the connecting rod and cap, and the crankpin journal.

18 Press the bearing shells into their locations, making sure that the tab on each shell engages the notch in the connecting rod/cap **(see illustration)**. Make sure the bearings are fitted in the correct locations and take care not to touch any shell's bearing surface with your fingers. Apply a smear of grease to each crankpin and a smear of silicone release agent to each bearing shell in the rod and cap.

19 Cut a length of the appropriate size Plastigauge (it should be slightly shorter than the width of the crankpin). Place a strand of Plastigauge on the crankpin journal for the rod being checked. Fit the rod onto its crankpin, then fit the cap, making sure it is fitted the correct way around so the previously made markings align. Apply a smear of molybdenum disulphide grease to the bolt threads and to the underside of the heads and tighten them finger-tight.

20 Tighten the bolts in five stages, using a

24.7 ...and remove the connecting rod cap

24.9 Push the rod off the crankpin and withdraw it from the top

24.18 Make sure the tab locates in the notch

Engine, clutch and transmission 2•47

torque wrench and a degree disc, as follows. First tighten them to 22 Nm, then slacken them by 120°. Now tighten them to 10 Nm, then to 14 Nm, and finally tighten them by 120° **(see Haynes Hint)**.

21 Slacken the bolts and remove the connecting rod cap, again taking great care not to rotate the crankshaft.

22 Compare the width of the crushed Plastigauge on the crankpin to the scale printed on the Plastigauge envelope to obtain the connecting rod bearing oil clearance. Be sure to use the appropriate scale as both imperial and metric scales are shown.

23 On completion carefully scrape away all traces of the Plastigauge material from the crankpin and bearing shells using a fingernail or other object which will not score the bearing surfaces.

24 If the clearance is within the range listed in this Chapter's Specifications and the bearing shells are in perfect condition, they can be reused.

25 If the clearance is beyond the specified service limit, first measure the diameter of the crankpin journal with a micrometer and compare the result with the Specifications at the beginning of this Chapter **(see illustration 24.28)**. If the journal diameter is larger than the service limit, new bearing shells can be fitted (see Steps 27 to 29). If the journal diameter is smaller than the service limit, the crankshaft must be replaced with a new one.

26 Repeat the procedure for the remaining connecting rods. If the oil clearance is too great on any one, replace all of the shells (on all three rods) at the same time.

Bearing shell selection

27 The connecting rod big-end bearing oil clearance is controlled in production by selecting one of two grades of bearing shell. The grades are indicated by a colour-coding marked on the edge of each shell. New bearing shells are selected as follows according to the crankpin journal diameter.

28 Measure the crankpin journal diameter using a micrometer and record the result **(see illustration)**.

29 Match the measured journal diameter to the required bearing shells using the following table.

Crankpin journal diameter	Shell colour
32.992 to 33.000 mm	White
32.984 to 32.991 mm	Red

Installation

Note 1: *New connecting rod bolts must be used for final assembly.*

Note 2: *There are a number of different ways in which the connecting rods can be installed, and your best approach will depend on what other work, if any, you are doing on the engine.*

- *If the pistons have not been separated from the rods, install the rod and piston*

24.28 Measure the crankpin width using a micrometer

assemblies from the top of the crankcase then install the crankshaft. You will also have to make a decision regarding installation of the liners, as the rod and piston assemblies can be installed before them, with them or after them – see Section 14 for details.

- *If it makes no difference, we advise fitting the pistons onto the rods first, then fitting the rod and piston assemblies into the liners, then installing the liners. At this point the cylinder head can be installed to avoid the risk of disturbing the liner seals when installing the crankshaft.*

30 Remove the bearing shells from the rods and caps, keeping them in order **(see illustration 24.18)**. Clean the backs of the shells and the bearing locations in both the connecting rod and cap, and the crankpin journal. If new shells are being fitted, ensure that all traces of the protective grease are cleaned off using paraffin (kerosene). Wipe the shells, cap and rod dry with a clean lint free cloth.

31 Press the bearing shells into their locations, ensuring that the tab on each shell engages the notch in the connecting rod/cap **(see illustration 24.18)**. Make sure the bearings are fitted in the correct locations and take care not to touch any shell's bearing surface with your fingers.

32 Decide upon your installation procedure, then assemble the rods, pistons, cylinder liners and crankshaft as required, referring to the relevant Sections. **Note:** *When installing the connecting rods on the crankshaft, refer to the previously made marks to ensure they are fitted in the correct positions (see Step 5).*

33 Lubricate the shells with molybdenum disulphide oil (a 50/50 mixture of molybdenum disulphide grease and engine oil). Fit the rod onto its crankpin, then fit the cap, making sure it is the correct way around so the previously made markings align **(see illustration and 24.7)**. Apply a smear of molybdenum disulphide grease to the bolt threads and to the underside of the heads **(see illustration 24.6)**. Fit the bolts and tighten them finger-tight at this stage. Check to make sure that all components have been returned to their original locations using the marks made on disassembly.

34 Tighten the bolts in five stages, using a

24.33 Pull the rod up onto its crankpin

torque wrench and a degree disc, as follows. First tighten them to 22 Nm, then slacken them by 120°. Now tighten them to 10 Nm, then to 14 Nm, and finally tighten them by 120°.

> **HAYNES HINT** *If a degree disc is not available, the angle can be determined by using the points on the connecting rod bolt. There are six points on the bolt, so the angle between each point is 60°. Select one point as a reference and mark it with paint or a marker. Now select the second point clockwise from it and mark its position on the connecting rod cap. Tighten the nut – when the mark on the first point aligns with the mark made on the connecting rod cap, it will have turned through 120°.*

35 Install the other connecting rods in the same way. Check to make sure that all components have been returned to their original locations using the marks made on disassembly.

36 **Note:** *If the cylinder liners are installed, ensure appropriate measures have been taken to prevent them lifting off their seals (see Section 14)*. Check that the crankshaft rotates freely and that the rods rotate smoothly and freely on the crankpins. If there are any signs of roughness or tightness, remove the rods and re-check the bearing clearance. Sometimes tapping the bottom of the connecting rod cap will relieve tightness, but if in doubt, recheck the clearances.

37 Reassemble the crankcase halves and the rest of the engine according to your removal procedure, referring to the relevant Sections.

25 Crankshaft and main bearings

Removal

1 Remove the engine from the frame (see Section 4) and separate the crankcase halves (see Section 21).

2 Refer to Section 24 and separate the connecting rods from the crankshaft (unless the

25.4 Carefully lift the crankshaft out of the crankcase

25.5 To remove a main bearing shell, push it sideways and lift it out

pistons have been removed, in which case the rods can remain attached for now, and removed later if required). If no work is to be carried out on the piston/connecting rod assemblies there is no need to remove them from the bores (unless the liners have been removed), but clamp the liners in place (see Section 14), then push them up to the top of the bores so that the big-ends are clear of the crankshaft.

3 If required, before removing the crankshaft check the amount of end-float using a dial gauge. If it exceeds the limit specified, the crankshaft and/or the crankcases must be replaced with new ones.

4 Align then remove the balancer shaft (see Section 26). Lift the crankshaft out of the upper crankcase half, taking care not to dislodge the main bearing shells **(see illustration)**.

5 If required, remove the bearing shells from the crankcase halves by pushing their centres to the side, then lifting them out **(see illustration)**. Keep the shells in order.

Inspection

6 Clean the crankshaft with solvent, squirting it through all oil passages. If available, blow it through and dry with compressed air. Check the balancer shaft drive gear teeth and the cam chain drive sprocket teeth for wear and damage, referring to Sections 26 and 10 to also check the driven gear and sprockets and the cam chain.

7 Refer to Section 23 and examine the main bearing shells. If they are scored, badly scuffed or appear to have been seized, new shells must be installed. Always renew the main bearings as a set. If they are badly damaged, check the corresponding crankshaft journals. Evidence of extreme heat, such as discoloration, indicates that lubrication failure has occurred. Be sure to thoroughly check the oil pump and pressure relief valve as well as all oil holes and passages before reassembling the engine.

8 Inspect the crankshaft journals, paying particular attention where damaged bearing shells have been discovered. If the journals are scored or pitted in any way a new crankshaft will be required. Note that oversize shells are not available, precluding the option of re-grinding the crankshaft.

Oil clearance check

9 Whether new bearing shells are being fitted or the original ones are being re-used, the main bearing oil clearance should be checked prior to reassembly.

10 If not already done, remove the bearing shells from the crankcase halves by pushing their centres to the side, then lifting them out **(see illustration 25.5)**. Keep the shells in order. Clean the backs of the shells and their locations in both the crankcase halves.

11 Press the bearing shells back into their locations, making sure that the tab on each shell engages in the notch **(see illustration)**. Make sure the shells are fitted in the correct locations and take care not to touch any shell's bearing surface with your fingers. Apply a smear of grease to each journal and a smear of silicone release agent to each bearing shell.

12 Lay the crankshaft in position in the upper crankcase **(see illustration 25.4)**. Cut several lengths of the appropriate size Plastigauge (they should be slightly shorter than the width of the crankshaft journal). Place a strand of Plastigauge on each crankshaft journal.

13 If removed, fit the three locating dowels into the upper crankcase half **(see illustration 21.11)**. Carefully fit the lower crankcase half onto the upper half, making sure it locates onto the dowels **(see illustration 21.6)**. Check that the lower crankcase half is correctly seated. **Note:** *If the casings are not correctly seated, remove the lower crankcase half and investigate the problem. Do not attempt to pull them together using the crankcase bolts as the casing will crack and be ruined.* Install the eight crankshaft journal bolts with their washers in their original locations and tighten them in the correct numerical sequence (1 to 8) in the two stages and to the torque settings as described in Section 21 **(see illustration 21.16)**. Make sure that the crankshaft is not rotated as the bolts are tightened.

14 Slacken and remove the bolts, working in a criss-cross pattern from the outside in, then carefully lift off the lower crankcase half, making sure the Plastigauge is not disturbed.

15 Compare the width of the crushed Plastigauge on each crankshaft journal to the scale printed on the Plastigauge envelope to obtain the main bearing oil clearance.

16 On completion carefully scrape away all traces of the Plastigauge material from the journals and bearing shells using a fingernail or other object which will not score the bearing surfaces.

17 If the clearance is within the range listed in this Chapter's Specifications and the bearing shells are in perfect condition, they can be reused. If the clearance is beyond the specified service limit, first measure the diameter of the crankshaft journals with a micrometer and compare the results with the Specifications at the beginning of this Chapter **(see illustration)**. If the journal diameters are larger than the service limit, new bearing

25.11 Press each shell into place, locating the tab in the notch (arrowed)

25.17 Measure the crank journal width using a micrometer

shells can be fitted (see Steps 18 and 19). If the journal diameters are smaller than the service limit, the crankshaft must be replaced with a new one.

Bearing shell selection

18 The main bearing oil clearance is controlled in production by selecting one of four grades of bearing shell. The grades are indicated by a colour-coding marked on the edge of each shell. New shells are selected with reference to the following chart, having first measured the crankshaft journal diameter and the crankcase bore diameter.

19 Measure the diameter of each crankshaft journal with a micrometer and record the results (see illustration 25.17). Next, assemble the crankcase halves with the bearing shells and crankshaft removed, and tighten the 8 mm crankshaft journal bolts in the correct numerical sequence in the two stages and to the torque settings as described in Section 21. Measure each crankshaft journal bore diameter using a bore gauge and micrometer and record the results. Refer to *Tools and Workshop Tips* in the Reference Section for details on how to use the measuring equipment.

Crankcase bore diameter	Crankshaft journal diameter	Shell colour
35.973 to 35.982 mm	32.993 to 33.000 mm	White
35.973 to 35.981 mm	32.984 to 32.992 mm	Red
35.981 to 35.989 mm	32.993 to 33.000 mm	Red
35.981 to 35.988 mm	32.984 to 32.992 mm	Blue
35.989 to 35.997 mm	32.993 to 33.000 mm	Blue
35.989 to 35.997 mm	32.984 to 32.992 mm	Green

Installation

20 Clean the backs of the bearing shells and the bearing recesses in both crankcase halves. If new shells are being fitted, make sure that all traces of the protective grease are cleaned off using paraffin (kerosene). Wipe the shells and crankcase halves dry with a lint-free cloth.

26.5a Remove the circlip...

26.2 Balancer shaft driven gear and crankshaft drive gear alignment marks

21 Press the bearing shells into their locations, making sure that the tab on each shell engages in the notch (see illustration 25.11). Make sure the bearings are fitted in the correct locations and take care not to touch any shell's bearing surface with your fingers. Lubricate the shells with molybdenum disulphide oil (a 50/50 mixture of molybdenum disulphide grease and engine oil).

22 Identify the tooth on the balancer drive gear on the crankshaft marked with a dot – this tooth must align with the marked tooth on the balancer shaft driven gear when it is installed (see illustration 26.2). Lower the crankshaft into position in the upper crankcase, with the marked tooth facing forwards (see illustration 25.4). Install the balancer shaft, making sure that it is correctly timed to the crankshaft (see Section 26).

23 If removed, install the connecting rods (see Section 24), then reassemble the crankcase halves and the rest of the engine according to your removal procedure, referring to the relevant Sections.

26 Balancer shaft

Removal

1 Remove the engine from the frame and separate the crankcase halves (see Sections 4 and 21).

2 The balancer shaft is gear driven off the right-hand end of the crankshaft – the

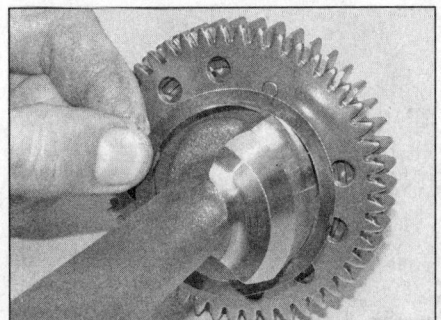

26.5b ...and the wave washer

26.3 Carefully lift the balancer shaft out of the crankcase

crankshaft drive gear and the balancer shaft driven gear are marked so that precise timing of the two shafts can be achieved. Rotate the crankshaft until the teeth marked with dots align (see illustration).

3 Note how the retaining rings on the bearings on each end of the balancer shaft locate in the grooves in the crankcase, and how the bearing locating pins sit in the cut-outs. Carefully lift the balancer shaft out (see illustration). The balancer shaft driven gear incorporates an inner spring-loaded backlash eliminator gear – as the shaft is lifted out, the backlash eliminator gear will spring out of alignment with the main gear.

Inspection, disassembly and reassembly

4 Inspect the teeth of both inner and main driven gears for signs of wear or damage, and check the teeth of the drive gear on the crankshaft. Only the inner backlash eliminator gear is available – if the main outer gear is damaged a complete new shaft must be fitted.

5 The shaft can be disassembled if required – all other components except the main outer gear and the shaft itself are available individually. Slide the needle bearing off the left-hand end of the shaft. Remove the circlip securing the inner gear, then remove the wave washer and the gear, noting how the pin on the inside face locates against one end of the backlash spring (see illustrations). Remove the spring, noting it how it locates against the pin in the main gear (see illustration 26.7a)

26.5c Note how the pin (A) locates against the end of the backlash spring (B)

2•50 Engine, clutch and transmission

26.6 Remove the circlip (arrowed) and the washer behind it

26.7a Fit the spring...

26.7b ...positioning it as shown

– check it for damage and deformation and replace it with a new one if necessary.

6 Check the bearings for wear and damage. If they do not run smoothly and freely, or if there is excessive freeplay between the needle bearing and its sleeve, or between the ball bearing races, replace them with new ones if necessary. To remove the ball bearing remove the circlip and washer, then use a puller to draw the bearing off the shaft or a press to push the shaft out of the bearing **(see illustration)**. Discard the circlip and use a new one. When fitting the new bearing make sure the retaining ring faces the main gear, and either drive it on using a suitable tubular drift that bears only on the inner race, or support the bearing on its inner race and press the shaft into it. In either case make sure the bearing seats against the lip on the shaft. Fit the washer and a new circlip, making sure it locates in the groove.

7 Fit the backlash eliminator gear spring, locating the ends on each side of the pin on the inner face of the main gear **(see illustrations)**. Fit the inner gear, aligning it so its pin is to the left of the main gear pin, and so that both pins are between the spring ends **(see illustration 26.5c)**. Fit the wave washer and the circlip, making sure it locates in the groove **(see illustrations 26.5b and a)**.

8 Lubricate the needle bearing with clean engine oil, then slide it onto the sleeve with its retaining ring to the outside.

Installation

9 Before installing the balancer shaft, ensure the tooth on the drive gear on the crankshaft marked with a dot is facing forwards **(see illustration)**.

10 Now you must align the tooth on the inner face of the main gear marked with a dot with the tooth on the inner gear marked with a line **(see illustration)**. To do this, first mark the top edge of the main gear tooth with paint so that it can be identified when the two gears are aligned **(see illustration)**. Use a holding tool inserted in the holes in the inner gear and a large spanner to draw the gears into position against the tension of the backlash spring **(see illustrations)**. Lock the gears together using a piece of crushed tube or similar between the gear teeth, or make a locking plate out of aluminium as shown **(see illustration)**. Note that the tool must be positioned so that it is not in the way when the balancer shaft is installed in the crankcase **(see illustration 26.11a)**.

26.9 Make sure the dot on the drive gear is correctly positioned

26.10a Inner face of main gear is marked with a dot, inner gear with a line – these must be aligned

26.10b Mark the top of the tooth (arrowed) with paint

26.10c Use the set-up shown...

26.10d ...to align the marked gears as described...

26.10e ...then lock them together

Engine, clutch and transmission 2•51

26.11a Lay the balancer shaft in the crankcase as described

26.11b Make sure the retaining ring and locating pin are correctly seated...

26.11c ...on each end

11 Lay the shaft in the crankcase (see illustration) – make sure that the tooth marked with a dot on the outer face of the main (driven) gear aligns with the tooth marked with a dot on the crankshaft drive gear (see illustration 26.2). Check that the bearing retaining rings locate in their grooves and the locating pins seat in the cut-outs (see illustrations).

12 Remove the locking tool.

⚠ **Warning: If the balancer shaft and crankshaft gears are not correctly aligned, severe engine vibration will occur leading to damage to engine components.**

13 Reassemble the crankcase halves and the rest of the engine according to your removal procedure, referring to the relevant Sections.

27 Transmission shaft removal and installation

Removal

1 Remove the engine from the frame and separate the crankcase halves (see Sections 4 and 21).

2 Lift the output shaft out of the crankcase, noting how the selector forks locate in their pinion grooves, and how the ball bearing retaining ring and locating pin locate in the groove and cut-out respectively, and the needle bearing pin locates in the hole (see illustration). Remove the oil seal from the left-hand end – a new one must be used (see illustration 27.10a).

3 Remove the selector drum and forks (see Section 29).

4 Undo the input shaft ball bearing housing bolts and remove the plate (see illustration). Thread two of the bolts into the threaded holes in the housing and continue to screw them in evenly and a little at a time after they have contacted the crankcase – this will draw the bearing housing and shaft out (see illustrations). Once the housing is free of the crankcase draw the shaft out.

5 If required withdraw the transmission oil pipe, levering it carefully out with a screwdriver (see illustration). New O-rings must be used,

27.2 Lift out the transmission output shaft

27.4a Unscrew the bolts (arrowed) and where fitted remove the plate

27.4b Thread two bolts into the housing as shown...

27.4c ...and use them to draw the housing out

27.5 Remove the oil pipe if required

2•52 Engine, clutch and transmission

27.8a Slide the shaft into the crankcase

27.8b Make sure the tabs do not become disengaged from the slots and out of alignment as shown

27.8c On engines from No. 330119-on fit the plate

27.8d Fit the bolts...

27.8e ...and tighten them as described to draw the housing in

but leave the old ones on for the time being so they can be used as a guide for fitting the new ones – three different sizes are used.

6 If necessary, the transmission shafts can be disassembled and inspected for wear or damage as described in Section 28.

Installation

Note: *Triumph specify to use new bolts for the bearing housing on the input shaft, but to retain the old bolts for use when drawing the housing into the crankcase – once the housing seats remove the old bolts and replace them with the new bolts, tightening them to the specified torque. This is because the new bolts come pre-treated with a thread locking compound. If new bolts are not available you can clean the threads of the old bolts and apply some fresh threadlock to them.*

7 If removed clean the transmission oil pipe with solvent and blow through it, with compressed air if available. Fit the new O-rings onto the pipe in accordance with the layout of the old ones and smear them with oil – the O-ring nearest the flanged (right-hand) end of the pipe is slightly larger (10.1x1.6mm) than the one that sits slightly inwards from it (9.1 x 1.6mm), and the one on the left-hand end is smaller and thicker (5.6 x 2.3mm). Fit the pipe into the crankcase, locating the tab in the cut-out (see illustration 27.5).

8 Slide the input shaft into the crankcase, aligning the ball bearing housing bolt holes with those in the crankcase, locating the inner end in its needle bearing in the crankcase, and pushing the ball bearing housing in as far as it will go by hand (see illustration). Make sure the tabs on the washer behind the 2nd gear pinion remain engaged in the slots in the slotted washer and do not fall out of alignment as shown (see illustration) – if they do the pinions will be pressed tightly together and jam as the bearing housing is pressed in. Clean the threads of the original housing bolts (see **Note** above). If the original bolts are being reused for final assembly apply some fresh threadlock. Fit the plate (see illustration). Fit the bolts and tighten them evenly and a little at a time in a criss-cross pattern to draw the housing squarely in if it wouldn't push in all the way (see illustrations). When the housing seats, if the original bolts are being used for final assembly tighten them to the torque setting specified at the beginning of the Chapter, or if new ones are being used for final assembly remove the original ones, fit the new ones, and tighten them to the specified torque.

9 Install the selector drum and forks (see Section 29).

10 Make sure the bearing retaining ring is in place on the ball bearing on the left-hand end of the output shaft, then fit a new oil seal onto the sleeve (see illustration). Fit the output shaft, making sure the needle bearing pin locates in its hole (see illustration 27.2), the retaining ring and locating pin locate correctly (see illustration), and the selector forks locate in their pinion grooves.

11 Ensure that the gears of both shafts mesh correctly and that they're in the neutral position i.e. the input shaft can be turned whilst the output shaft is held stationary.

12 Reassemble the crankcase halves and the rest of the engine according to your removal procedure, referring to the relevant Sections.

28 Transmission shaft overhaul

1 Remove the shafts from the crankcase as described in Section 27.

27.10a Fit the retaining ring (arrowed) if removed, then fit a new oil seal onto the shaft

27.10b Make sure the ring locates in the groove and the pin in the cut-out

 HAYNES HINT *When disassembling the transmission shafts, place the parts on a long rod or thread a wire through them to keep them in order and facing the proper direction.*

Engine, clutch and transmission 2•53

28.6 1st gear pinion (arrowed)

28.12a Check the bearing on the shaft...

28.12b ...and the bearing (A) in the crankcase. Selector drum bearing (B)

Input shaft disassembly

2 Slide the thrust washer off the left-hand end of the shaft (see illustrations 28.18b). Make a paint mark on the outer face of the 2nd gear pinion then slide it off the shaft (see illustrations 28.18a).

3 Slide the tabbed washer off the shaft, noting how its tabs locate in the slotted washer (see illustrations 28.17c). Turn the slotted washer to align the splines, then slide it off the shaft (see illustrations 28.17b and a).

4 Slide the 6th gear pinion and its splined bush off the shaft, followed by the splined washer (see illustrations 28.16c, b and a).

5 Remove the circlip securing the combined 3rd/4th gear pinion then slide the pinion off the shaft (see illustrations 28.15b and a).

6 Remove the circlip securing the 5th gear pinion, then slide the splined washer, the pinion and its bush off the shaft (see illustrations 28.14d, c, b and a). The 1st gear pinion is integral with the shaft (see illustration).

Input shaft inspection

7 Wash all of the components in clean solvent and dry them off.

8 Check the gear teeth for cracking and other obvious damage. Check the 5th and 6th gear bushes and the surface in the inner diameter of the gears for scoring or heat discolouration. If the gear or bush is damaged, replace it with a new one.

9 Inspect the dogs and the dog holes in related gears for excessive wear. Renew the paired gears as a set if necessary.

10 Measure the selector fork groove width in the 3rd/4th gear pinion as described in Section 29.

11 The shaft is unlikely to sustain damage unless the engine has seized, placing an unusually high loading on the transmission, or the machine has covered a very high mileage. Check the surface of the shaft, especially where a pinion turns on it, and the edges of the splined sections, and replace the shaft with a new one if it has scored or picked up. Damage of any kind can only be cured by renewal.

12 The ball bearing on the left-hand end of the shaft is a press fit on the shaft, and the housing is a press fit on the bearing (see illustration). Press the shaft out of the bearing, then press the bearing out of the housing – note which way round the bearing fits. The bearing cannot be reused. Refer to Tools and Workshop Tips in the Reference Section for more information on bearing checks and removal and installation methods.

When fitting the new bearing press it into the housing until it seats, locating the press only on the outer race. Press the bearing onto the shaft until it seats using a suitable tube that locates only on the inner race. Replace the needle bearing in the crankcase with a new one if it is worn or damaged, or does not run freely (see illustration).

Input shaft reassembly

13 During reassembly, always use new circlips. Lubricate the components with the correct grade of engine oil before assembling them.

14 Slide on the 5th gear pinion bush, then slide the pinion, with its dogs facing away from the integral 1st gear pinion, onto the bush (see illustrations). Slide the splined washer against the pinion (see illustrations). Fit the circlip, making sure it locates in its groove (see illustrations).

28.14a Slide the 5th gear pinion bush on the shaft...

28.14b ...then fit the pinion on the bush

28.14c Slide on the splined washer...

28.14d ...then fit the circlip...

28.14e ...making sure it locates in its groove

2•54 Engine, clutch and transmission

28.15a Slide the 3rd/4th gear pinion onto the shaft, making sure the oil holes (arrowed) do not align...

28.15b ...then fit the circlip...

28.15c ...making sure it locates in its groove

15 Slide the combined 3rd/4th gear pinion with the larger (4th) gear facing the 5th gear pinion, making sure the oil hole does NOT align with the oil hole in the shaft **(see illustration)**. Fit the circlip, making sure it locates in its groove **(see illustrations)**.

16 Slide the splined washer against the circlip, then fit the 6th gear pinion bush making sure the oil hole does NOT align with the oil hole in the shaft **(see illustrations)**. Slide the 6th gear pinion onto the bush with its dogs facing the 3rd gear **(see illustration)**.

17 Slide the slotted washer onto the shaft to its groove then turn it to misalign the splines so the washer is locked **(see illustrations)**. Slide the tabbed washer onto the shaft, locating the tabs into the slots of the slotted washer **(see illustration)**.

18 Fit the 2nd gear pinion with its previously marked side facing away from the 6th gear pinion **(see illustration)**. Slide on the thrust washer **(see illustration)**. The assembled

28.16a Slide the splined washer on...

28.16b ...followed by the bush, making sure the oil holes (arrowed) do not align...

28.16c ...then fit the pinion onto the bush

28.17a Slide the slotted washer into its groove...

28.17b ...then turn it to lock it against the splines...

28.17c ...then slide on the tabbed washer and fit the tabs in the slots

28.18a Slide the 2nd gear pinion onto the shaft...

28.18b ...followed by the thrust washer

28.18c The assembled input shaft

28.31 Check the bearing and replace it with a new one if necessary

input shaft should be as shown (see illustration).

Output shaft disassembly

19 Slide the needle bearing and thrust washer off the right-hand end of the shaft (see illustrations 28.39b and a).
20 Slide the 1st gear pinion off the shaft, followed its bush, the thrust washer and the 5th gear pinion (see illustrations 28.38d, c, b and a).
21 Remove the circlip, then slide off the splined washer, the 4th gear pinion, and its bush (see illustrations 28.37d, c, b and a).
22 Slide the tabbed washer off the shaft, noting how its tabs locate in the slotted washer (see illustrations 28.36c). Turn the slotted washer to align the splines, then slide it off the shaft (see illustrations 28.36b and a).
23 Slide the 3rd gear pinion and its bush off the shaft, and the splined washer (see illustrations 28.35c, b and a).
24 Remove the circlip and slide off the 6th gear pinion (see illustrations 28.34b and a).
25 Remove the circlip, then slide off the splined washer, the 2nd gear pinion and its bush (see illustrations 28.33d, c, b and a).

Output shaft inspection

26 Wash all of the components in clean solvent and dry them off.
27 Check the gear teeth for cracking and other obvious damage. Check the bushes and the surface in the inner diameter of their gears for scoring or heat discoloration. If a gear or bush is damaged, replace them both with new ones.
28 Inspect the dogs and the dog holes in related gears for excessive wear. Renew the paired gears as a set if necessary.
29 Measure the selector fork groove width in the 5th and 6th gear pinions (see Section 29).
30 The shaft is unlikely to sustain damage unless the engine has seized, placing an unusually high loading on the transmission, or the machine has covered a very high mileage. Check the surface of the shaft, especially where a pinion turns on it, and the edges of the splined sections, and replace the shaft with a new one if it has scored or picked up. Damage of any kind can only be cured by renewal.
31 The ball bearing and sleeve on the left-hand end of the shaft are a press fit (see illustration). Support the bearing and press the shaft out of it and the sleeve – note which way round they fit. The bearing cannot be reused. Refer to *Tools and Workshop Tips* in the Reference Section for more information on bearing checks and removal and installation methods. Press the bearing onto the shaft until it seats using a suitable tube that locates only on the inner race. Press the sleeve on, chamfered (narrow) end facing out, until it seats against the bearing. Replace the needle bearing with a new one if it is worn or damaged, or does not run freely.

Output shaft reassembly

32 During reassembly, always use new circlips. Lubricate the components with engine oil before assembling them.
33 Slide the 2nd gear pinion bush onto the shaft, then slide the pinion onto the bush, with its chamfered rim facing away from the ball bearing, followed by the splined washer (see illustrations). Fit the circlip,

28.33a Slide the 2nd gear pinion bush onto the shaft...

28.33b ...then fit the pinion onto the bush

28.33c Slide on the splined washer...

28.33d ...then fit the circlip...

28.33e ...making sure it locates in its groove

28.34a Slide the 6th gear pinion onto the shaft, making sure the oil holes (arrowed) do not align...

making sure it locates in its groove **(see illustration)**.

34 Slide 6th gear pinion onto the shaft with its selector fork groove facing away from the 2nd gear pinion, making sure the oil holes in the gear do NOT align with the oil hole in the shaft **(see illustration)**. Secure the gear with the circlip, making sure it locates in the shaft groove **(see illustrations)**.

35 Slide the splined washer onto the shaft, followed by the 3rd gear pinion bush, making sure the oil hole in the bush does NOT align with the hole in the shaft **(see illustrations)**. Slide the 3rd gear pinion onto the bush with its recessed side facing the 6th gear pinion **(see illustration)**.

36 Slide the slotted washer onto the shaft to its groove then turn it to misalign the splines so the washer is locked **(see illustrations)**. Slide the tabbed washer onto the shaft, locating the tabs into the slots of the slotted washer **(see illustration)**.

37 Slide on the 4th gear pinion splined bush, making sure the oil holes do NOT align, then

28.34b ...then fit the circlip...

28.34c ...making sure it locates in its groove

28.35a Slide the splined washer on...

28.35b ...followed by the bush, making sure the oil holes (arrowed) do not align...

28.35c ...then fit the pinion onto the bush

28.36a Slide the slotted washer to its groove...

28.36b ...then turn it to lock it against the splines...

28.36c ...then slide on the tabbed washer and fit the tabs in the slots

Engine, clutch and transmission 2•57

28.37a Slide the 4th gear pinion bush onto the shaft, making sure the oil holes (arrowed) do not align...

28.37b ...then fit the pinion onto the bush

28.37c Slide on the splined washer...

28.37d ...then fit the circlip...

28.37e ...making sure it locates in its groove

28.38a Slide the 5th gear pinion onto the shaft, making sure the oil holes (arrowed) do not align,...

slide the pinion onto the bush, with its recessed side facing away from the 3rd gear, followed by the splined washer (see illustrations). Fit the circlip, making sure it locates in its groove (see illustrations).

38 Slide the 5th gear pinion onto the shaft with its selector fork groove facing the 4th gear pinion, making sure the oil holes in the gear do NOT align with the hole in the shaft (see illustration). Fit the thrust washer (see illustration). Slide the 1st gear pinion bush onto the shaft, again making sure the oil holes do NOT align, then fit the 1st gear pinion onto the bush, with the deeper recessed side facing the 5th gear pinion (see illustrations).

39 Fit the thrust washer and needle bearing (see illustrations).

28.38b ...followed by the thrust washer...

28.38c ...the bush...

28.38d ...then fit the 1st gear pinion onto the bush

28.39a Fit the thrust washer...

28.39b ...and the needle bearing

2•58 Engine, clutch and transmission

28.40 The assembled output shaft

29.5 Unscrew the bolts (arrowed) and remove the retainers

40 The assembled output shaft should be as shown (see illustration).

29 Selector drum and forks

Removal

1 Remove the engine from the frame and separate the crankcase halves (see Sections 4 and 21).

2 Remove the gear position sensor (see Chapter 4).
3 Remove the transmission output shaft (see Section 27).
4 Mark each selector fork for identification using paint or a felt pen, i.e. 1 to 3 from left to right, with the marks facing the left-hand side of the engine, as an aid to installation. Note how the guide pin on each fork locates in the groove in the selector drum.
5 Unscrew the bolts securing the selector fork shaft/selector drum bearing retainers and remove them, noting how they fit (see illustration).

6 Support the output shaft selector forks and withdraw their shaft from the right-hand side of the crankcase, then remove the forks (see illustration). Slide the forks back on the shaft in their correct order and way round.
7 Withdraw the input shaft selector fork shaft, then move the fork guide pin out of its track in the selector drum (see illustration). Withdraw the selector drum (see illustration). Remove the input shaft selector fork (see illustration). Slide the fork the correct way round back on the shaft.

Inspection

8 Check the selector forks and shaft for wear and damage.
9 Locate each selector fork in its corresponding gear pinion groove and measure the fork-to-groove clearance using a feeler gauge (see illustration). If the clearance is outside the service limit, measure the selector fork end widths and the groove in the gear using a Vernier caliper. Replace any component that is worn beyond the service limit with a new one (see Specifications).
10 Check the fit of each fork on the shaft – they should slide freely but with no freeplay

29.6 Withdraw the shaft and remove the forks

29.7a Withdraw the shaft and displace the fork...

29.7b ...then withdraw the drum...

29.7c ...and remove the fork

29.9 Measure the fork-to-groove clearance using a feeler gauge

Engine, clutch and transmission 2•59

29.10 Check the fit of each fork on the shaft

29.11 Check the fork guide pins and the grooves they run in

29.12 Use a rod through the drum to hold it while unscrewing the camplate bolt

29.15 Align the hole (arrowed) as shown

between them (see illustration). Check the selector fork shaft for bend by rolling it along a flat surface. A bent shaft will cause difficulty in selecting gears and make the gearchange action heavy. Replace the shaft with a new one if necessary.

11 Inspect the selector drum grooves and selector fork guide pins for wear and damage (see illustration). If they show signs of wear or damage the selector fork(s) and drum must be replaced with new ones.

12 Check that the selector drum ball bearing rotates freely and has no sign of freeplay between its inner and outer race. Fit a new bearing if necessary – refer to Section 20, Step 6 to remove the camplate, holding the drum as shown (see illustration). Also check the needle bearing in the crankcase.

Installation

13 Clean the fork shaft/selector drum bearing retainer plate screw threads to remove all old threadlock. Apply molybdenum disulphide oil (a 50/50 mixture of molybdenum disulphide grease and engine oil) to the selector fork ends, guide pins and shafts and to the tracks in the selector drum before installing them. Lubricate the drum bearings with oil.

14 Fit the input shaft selector fork into its pinion groove, making sure it is the correct way round – see Step 7 (see illustration 29.7c).

15 Slide the selector drum into the crankcase (see illustration 29.7b). Rotate the drum so the hole for the gear position sensor pin is aligned as shown (see illustration).

16 Pivot the input shaft selector fork to locate its guide pin the in its track in the selector drum then insert the fork shaft (see illustration 29.7a).

17 Slide the output shaft selector fork shaft into its bore in the crankcase and through each fork in turn, making sure they are correctly fitted (see Step 6), locating each fork guide pin in its track in the selector drum (see illustration 29.6).

18 Fit the selector fork shaft/selector drum bearing retainers and bolts, applying a suitable non-permanent thread locking compound to the threads and tightening them to the torque setting specified at the beginning of the Chapter (see illustration 29.5).

19 Install the transmission output shaft (see Section 27).

20 Install the gear position sensor (see Chapter 4).

30 Running-in procedure

1 Make sure the engine oil and coolant levels are correct (see Pre-ride checks).

2 Make sure there is fuel in the tank.

3 Start the engine and let it run until it reaches normal operating temperature.

Warning: If the oil pressure warning light doesn't go off, or it comes on while the engine is running, stop the engine immediately.

4 Check carefully that there are no oil or coolant leaks, and make sure the transmission and controls, especially the brakes, function properly before road testing the machine.

5 Treat the machine gently for the first few miles to make sure oil has circulated throughout the engine and any new parts installed have started to seat.

6 Upon completion of the road test, and after the engine has cooled down completely, recheck the valve clearances and check the engine oil and coolant levels (see *Pre-ride checks*).

 If a lubrication failure is suspected, stop the engine immediately and try to find the cause. If an engine is run without oil, even for a short period of time, severe damage will occur.

7 If new pistons and liners or new main and/or big-end bearings have been installed, the bike will have to be run in as if when new. This means greater use of the transmission and a restraining hand on the throttle. There's no point in keeping to any set road speed limit – it's the engine revs and load that are important. For the first 500 miles (800 km) the main idea is to keep from labouring the engine and to gradually increase performance, but do not exceed 3/4 of maximum engine speed – and allow the engine to warm up gently. It is best to vary engine and road speed as much as possible, so use the gearbox. Between 500 and 1000 miles (800 and 1600 km) gradually work engine speed up to the maximum, again avoiding labouring or straining the engine, or being in the wrong gear. Experience is the best guide, since it's easy to tell when an engine is running freely.

Chapter 3
Cooling system

Contents

	Section number		Section number
Coolant change	see Chapter 1	Cooling system checks	see Chapter 1
Coolant hoses, pipes and unions	8	General information	1
Coolant level check	see *Pre-ride checks*	Oil cooler	see Chapter 2
Coolant reservoir	3	Radiator	6
Coolant temperature gauge	see Chapter 8	Radiator pressure cap	2
Coolant temperature sensor	see Chapter 4	Thermostat	5
Cooling fan and relay	4	Water pump	7

Degrees of difficulty

Easy, suitable for novice with little experience	Fairly easy, suitable for beginner with some experience	Fairly difficult, suitable for competent DIY mechanic	Difficult, suitable for experienced DIY mechanic	Very difficult, suitable for expert DIY or professional

Specifications

Coolant
Coolant type.. Triumph HD4X Hybrid OAT pre-mixed coolant
Coolant capacity... 2.4 litres

Radiator
Cap valve opening pressure.................................. 16 psi (1.1 Bar)

Cooling fan
Cooling fan cut-in temperature.............................. 103°C

Thermostat
Opening temperature.. 66 to 76°C

Torque wrench settings
Coolant inlet union bolts
    Left-hand bolt (M6 x 25 mm)............................ 9 Nm
    Right-hand and upper bolts (M6 x 20 mm)................ 8 Nm
Radiator bolts.. 6 Nm
Thermostat housing bolts.................................... 9 Nm

3•2 Cooling system

1 General information

The cooling system uses a water/antifreeze coolant to carry away excess energy in the form of heat. The cylinders are surrounded by a water jacket from which the heated coolant is circulated by thermo-syphonic action in conjunction with a water pump. The water pump is an integral unit with the oil pump and is driven by a chain running off the back of the clutch. The hot coolant passes upwards to the thermostat and through to the radiator. The coolant then flows across the radiator core, where it is cooled by the passing air, to the water pump and back to the engine, where the cycle is repeated.

A thermostat is fitted in the system to prevent the coolant flowing through the radiator when the engine is cold, therefore accelerating the speed at which the engine reaches normal operating temperature. A coolant temperature sensor transmits information to the engine management system. This information is used to help optimise the fuelling of the engine at all temperatures. The engine management system also controls the temperature gauge and the cooling fan, via a relay. Because the control side of these cooling system functions is integral with the engine management system, it is dealt with in Chapter 4. The function side of the cooling fan and relay are in this Chapter, while the function of the temperature gauge is in Chapter 8.

The complete cooling system is partially sealed and pressurised, the pressure being controlled by a valve contained in the spring-loaded radiator cap. By pressurising the coolant the boiling point is raised, preventing premature boiling in adverse conditions. The overflow pipe from the system is connected to a reservoir into which excess coolant is expelled under pressure. The discharged coolant automatically returns to the radiator when the engine cools.

⚠️ **Warning: Do not remove the pressure cap from the radiator when the engine is hot. Scalding hot coolant and steam may be blown out under pressure, which could cause serious injury. When the engine has cooled, place a thick rag, like a towel over the pressure cap; slowly rotate the cap anti-clockwise to the first stop. This procedure allows any residual pressure to escape. When the steam has stopped escaping, press down on the cap while turning it anti-clockwise and remove it. Do not allow antifreeze to come into contact with your skin or painted surfaces of the motorcycle. Rinse off any spills immediately with plenty of water. Antifreeze is highly toxic if ingested. Never leave antifreeze lying around in an open container or in puddles on the floor; children and pets are attracted by its sweet smell and may drink it. Check with the local authorities about disposing of used antifreeze. Many communities will have collection centres which will see that antifreeze is disposed of safely.**

Caution: At all times use the specified type of antifreeze, and always mix it with distilled water in the correct proportion. The antifreeze contains corrosion inhibitors which are essential to avoid damage to the cooling system. A lack of these inhibitors could lead to a build-up of corrosion which would block the coolant passages, resulting in overheating and severe engine damage. Distilled water must be used as opposed to tap water to avoid a build-up of scale which would also block the passages.

2 Radiator pressure cap

1 If problems such as overheating and/or loss of coolant occur, check the entire system as described in Chapter 1.
2 Remove the fairing left-hand side panel (see Chapter 7).
3 Clamp the hose from the reservoir close to its union on the radiator filler neck **(see illustration)** – this is because the coolant reservoir is mounted higher than the radiator, so it will start to empty itself via the hose into the filler neck, which will then overflow (assuming the radiator is full) as soon as you remove the pressure cap.
4 Remove the pressure cap from the filler neck in the radiator as follows: turn the cap anti-clockwise until it reaches a stop – if you hear a hissing sound (indicating there is still pressure in the system), wait until it stops; now press down on the cap and continue turning it until it can be removed **(see illustration)**. Check the cap seals – if you are in any doubt as to their effectiveness replace the cap with a new one – maintaining a good seal to retain the pressure in the cooling system is essential to the efficient function of the system.
5 If no obvious problems can be found have the radiator cap opening pressure checked by a Triumph dealer equipped with the special tester required for the job. If the cap is defective, replace it with a new one.

3 Coolant reservoir

Removal

1 Remove the fuel tank (see Chapter 4). Remove the reservoir cover if required, noting how the clutch cable fits into the front of it **(see illustration)**.
2 Detach the overflow hose from the top of

2.3 Clamp the hose (arrowed)...

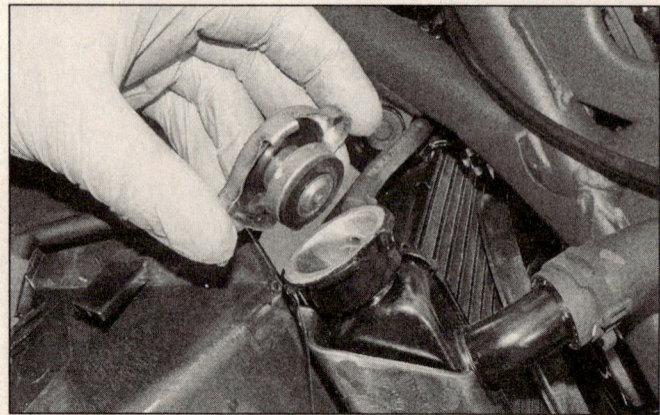

2.4 ...or the reservoir will drain itself when you remove the cap

3.1 Reservoir cover screw (A) – note the routing of the clutch cable (B)

Cooling system 3•3

3.2a Reservoir overflow hose (A) and mounting bolts (B)

3.2b Release the clamp (arrowed), detach the hose...

3.2c ...and drain the reservoir

3.4 Add coolant via the filler cap (A) to the UPPER level line (B)

the reservoir **(see illustration)**. Hold a suitable container to collect the coolant under the reservoir, then release the clamp and detach the hose from the bottom and allow the coolant to drain **(see illustrations)**.

3 Unscrew the bolts and remove the reservoir, releasing the clutch cable from the cover if you didn't remove it **(see illustrations 3.2a and 3.1)**.

Installation

4 Installation is the reverse of removal. Make sure the hoses are fully pushed onto their unions and the bottom hose is secured with the clamp. Fill the reservoir to the UPPER level line with the specified coolant **(see illustration)**.

4 Cooling fan and relay

Cooling fan
Check

1 If the engine is overheating and the cooling fan isn't coming on, first check the fan fuse (see Chapter 8). Next check the fan relay as described in Steps 7 to 9.

2 If the fuse and relay are good and the fan still

does not come on, the fault could be in either the cooling fan motor itself, or the relevant wiring and connectors. Check all the wiring and connections, referring to *Electrical system fault finding* at the beginning of Chapter 8 and to the Wiring Diagram for your model at the end of it.

3 For best access to the cooling fan wiring connector remove the radiator's left-hand outer cover, and if required the side panel (see Chapter 7). Trace the wiring from the fan and disconnect it at the connector **(see illustration)**.

4 Using a 12 volt battery and two jumper wires, connect the positive (+) battery lead to the black/blue wire terminal on the fan side of

4.3 Cooling fan wiring connector (arrowed)

the wiring connector and the negative (-) lead to the black wire terminal. Once connected the fan should operate. If it does not, and the wiring is all good, then the fan motor is faulty. Replace the fan assembly with a new one (Step 5) – individual components are not available. If all tests so far have shown no problems, test the ECT (Engine Coolant Temperature) sensor (see Chapter 4, Section 14).

Renewal

5 Remove the radiator (see Section 6). Undo the screws and remove the fan **(see illustration)**.
6 Installation is the reverse of removal.

4.5 Fan motor screws (arrowed)

3•4 Cooling system

4.8 Cooling fan relay (arrowed)

5.4a Unscrew the bolts (arrowed), detach the cover...

5.4b ...and withdraw the thermostat

Cooling fan relay

Note: *Refer to the Wiring Diagrams at the end of Chapter 8 for relay terminal identification.*

7 If the engine is overheating and the cooling fan isn't coming on, first check the fan fuse (see Chapter 8). If the fuse is blown, check the fan circuit for a short to earth (see the wiring diagrams at the end of this book).

8 If the fuse is good, remove the rider's seat (see Chapter 7). Disconnect the relay from its connector block **(see illustration)**. Check the terminals and sockets for damage and corrosion.

9 Referring to the Wiring Diagrams at the end of Chapter 8 for terminal identification, connect a continuity tester or a multimeter set to the ohms x 1 scale between the No. 3 and No. 5 wire terminals on the relay – there should be no continuity or infinite resistance. If there is continuity or zero resistance replace the relay with a new one.

10 Leaving the tester in place, use two insulated jumper wires to connect a fully-charged 12 volt battery – positive (+) terminal of the battery to the No. 1 wire terminal on the relay, and negative (–) terminal to the No. 2 wire terminal on the relay. At this point the relay should be heard to click and there should be continuity or zero resistance. If this is the case the relay is proved good. If the relay does not click when battery voltage is applied and the tester or meter indicates no continuity (infinite resistance), the relay is faulty and must be replaced with a new one. If the relay is good, test the fan motor (see Step 4).

5.6 Thermostat testing set-up

5 Thermostat

1 The thermostat is automatic in operation and shouldn't ever require attention. In the event of a failure, the valve will probably jam open, in which case the engine will take much longer than normal to warm up. Conversely, if the valve jams shut, the coolant will be unable to circulate and the engine will overheat. Neither condition is acceptable, and the fault must be investigated promptly.

Removal

2 Drain the cooling system (see Chapter 1).
3 Remove the throttle bodies (see Chapter 4).
4 Unscrew the thermostat housing bolts, then detach the housing from the cylinder head and remove the thermostat, noting how it fits **(see illustrations)**. Remove the seal – a new one must be used **(see illustration 5.7)**.

Check

5 Examine the thermostat visually before carrying out the test. If it remains in the open position at room temperature, it should be replaced with a new one.
6 Suspend the thermostat by a piece of wire in a container of cold water. Place a thermometer in the water so that the bulb is close to the thermostat, and not in contact with the container **(see illustration)**. Heat the water, noting the temperature when the thermostat opens, and compare the result with the specified

5.7 Fit a new seal over the rim of the thermostat

opening temperature given at the beginning of the Chapter. If the thermostat opens at a different temperature, does not open at all, or is permanently open, it is faulty and must be replaced with a new one. **Note:** *In the event of thermostat failure, as an emergency measure only, it can be removed and the machine used without it. Take care when starting the engine from cold as it will take much longer than usual to warm up. Ensure that a new unit is installed as soon as possible.*

Installation

7 Fit a new seal onto the thermostat **(see illustration)**.
8 Fit the thermostat into the cylinder head with the toggle pin at the top, then fit the housing and tighten the bolts to the torque setting specified at the beginning of the Chapter **(see illustrations 5.4b and a)**.
9 Install the throttle bodies (see Chapter 4).
10 Refill the cooling system (see Chapter 1 and *Pre-ride checks*).

6 Radiator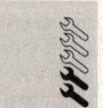

Removal

> ⚠ **Warning:** *The engine must be completely cool before carrying out this procedure.*

Note: *Car type hose clamps are used on the large bore coolant hoses. To release the clamps squeeze the ends together using large pliers, or use a dedicated automotive clamp tool (see Chapter 1, Section 5) – they are available from good tool suppliers.*

1 Remove the side panels, and if required the radiator inner panels and guard (where fitted) (see Chapter 7).
2 Drain the cooling system (see Chapter 1). Leave the reservoir hose disconnected and remove it along with the radiator, noting its routing – this saves having to remove the single-use clamp from the filler neck and having to fit a new one. If you need to detach it from the radiator refer to Section 8, Step 2.
3 If you haven't removed the radiator inner panels release the clutch cable guide from the right-hand side **(see illustration)**.

Cooling system 3•5

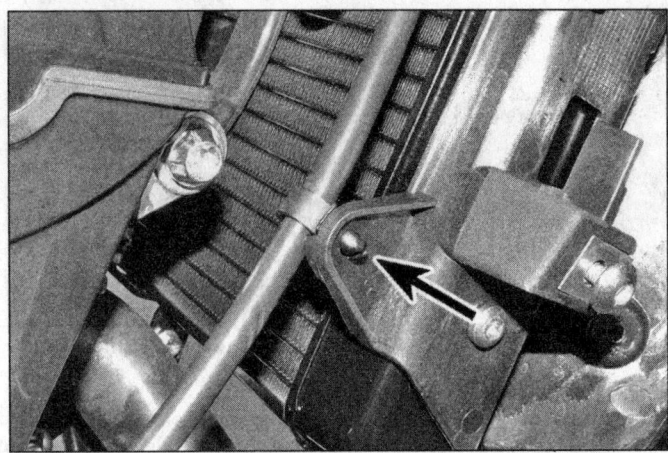

6.3 Squeeze the protruding ends (arrowed) together and draw the guide out of the panel

6.4 Release the clamps (arrowed) and detach the hoses

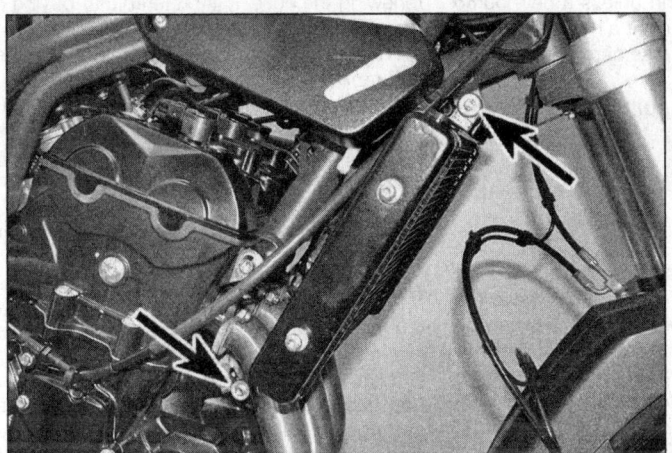

6.6a Unscrew the bolts (arrowed)...

6.6b ...then displace the radiator from the lug (arrowed)

4 Release the radiator hose clamps and slide them along the hoses, then detach the hoses **(see illustration)**.

5 Disconnect the cooling fan wiring connector **(see illustration 4.3)**.

6 Unscrew the radiator bolts **(see illustration)**. Move the radiator to the left until it clears the mounting lug and remove it **(see illustration)**. Note the collars with the bolts **(see illustration 6.9)**.

7 If necessary, remove the cooling fan (see Section 4).

8 Check the radiator for signs of damage and clear any dirt or debris that might obstruct airflow and inhibit cooling. If the radiator fins are badly damaged or broken the radiator must be replaced with a new one. Also check the rubber mounting grommets, and replace them with new ones if necessary **(see illustration)**.

Installation

9 Installation is the reverse of removal, noting the following.
● *Make sure the collars are fitted with the bolts – the longer bolt is for the bottom mount, and its collar has a rounded inner end **(see illustration 6.9)**. Tighten the bolts to the torque setting specified at the beginning of the Chapter.*
● *Make sure that the wiring connector is securely connected **(see illustration 4.3)**.*
● *Check the coolant hoses are in good condition (see Chapter 1), and are retained by their clamps, using new ones if necessary. Make sure there is 3 to 7 mm of hose exposed between the clamp and the end of the hose.*

6.8 Make sure the grommets (arrowed) are in good condition

● On completion refill the cooling system as described in Chapter 1.

7 Water pump

Check

1 The water pump is located on the left-hand side of the engine.

6.9 Upper bolt and collar (A), lower bolt and collar (B)

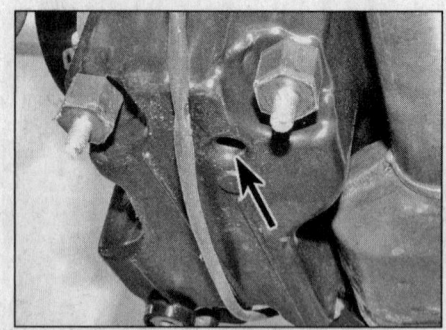

7.2 Water pump drain tube (arrowed) – shown with sump guard removed

7.6 Water pump cover bolts (arrowed)

8.4 Coolant inlet union bolts (arrowed)

2 To prevent leakage of water from the cooling system to the lubrication system and vice versa, two seals are fitted on the water pump shaft. There is a drain hole between the seals in the seal housing section of the pump. If either seal fails, the drain allows the coolant or oil to escape via a tube through a hole in the bottom of the sump and prevents them mixing (see illustration). The seal on the water pump side is of the mechanical type and bears on the rear face of the impeller. The second seal, which is mounted behind the mechanical seal is of the normal feathered lip type. If on inspection the drain hole shows signs of coolant and/or oil leakage, remove the pump assembly and replace it with a new one (see Chapter 2) – the seals are not available separately.

3 With the pump removed, remove the cover and wiggle the water pump impeller back-and-forth and in-and-out, and turn it by hand. If there is excessive movement, or the pump is noisy or rough when turned, or if any damage is found, replace the pump assembly with a new one – individual components are not available.

4 Check the pump housing and cover, and the impeller and shaft for cracks, deformation and any other damage. Check that the shaft is straight – if it is bent, replace the pump assembly with a new one. Also check for corrosion or a build-up of scale in the pump body and clean or renew the pump as necessary.

Removal and installation

5 The water pump is an integral assembly with the oil pump, and no individual components are available. Refer to Chapter 2, Section 19 for removal and installation of the pump assembly.

6 If you just want to remove the cover to inspect the pump, unscrew the bolts, then hold the housing and detach the cover (see illustration). Note that the cover seal is available separately, and unless a new pump is being fitted you should fit a new one.

7 Installation is the reverse of removal.

8 Coolant hoses, pipes and unions

Removal

Note: *Car type hose clamps are used on the large bore coolant hoses. To release the clamps squeeze the ends together using large pliers, or use a dedicated automotive clamp tool (see Chapter 1, Section 5) – they are available from good tool suppliers.*

1 Before removing a hose, pipe or union, drain the coolant (see Chapter 1).

2 Release the hose clamps, then slide them back along the hose. The small-bore hose on the reservoir is secured by a spring clamp, which can be expanded by squeezing its ears together with pliers (see illustration 3.2b). Where the reservoir hose connects to the radiator filler neck a single-use crimp-type clamp is fitted, which you can release using pliers, but take care not to bend the union on the filler neck as it could snap off (see illustration 2.3). It is best to secure the hose with a screw-type clamp on installation – they are available in a number of sizes from automotive factors.

Caution: The radiator unions are fragile. Do not use excessive force when attempting to remove the hoses.

3 If a hose proves stubborn, release it by rotating it on its union before working it off. If all else fails, cut the hose with a sharp knife then slit it at each union so that it can be peeled off in two pieces. Whilst this means renewing the hose, it is preferable to buying a new radiator.

4 Remove the coolant inlet union on the engine by detaching the hose (see above), then unscrewing the bolts (see illustration) – note how the radiator bracket mount is secured. Remove the gasket – a new one must be used. See Section 5 for removal of the thermostat housing.

5 For removal of the water pump pipes refer to Section 19 in Chapter 2.

Installation

6 For installation of the water pump pipes refer to Section 19 in Chapter 2.

7 If the inlet union has been removed, fit a new gasket and tighten the bolts to the torque settings specified at the beginning of the Chapter, not forgetting the radiator bracket mount (see illustration 8.4). See Section 5 for installation of the thermostat housing.

8 Slide the clamps onto the hose and then work the hose onto its unions, making sure it is correctly orientated so the hose aligns correctly at each end.

> **HAYNES HiNT**: *If the hose is difficult to push on its union, it can be softened by soaking it in very hot water, or alternatively a little soapy water can be used as a lubricant.*

9 Slide the clamps into place. Make sure there is 3 to 7 mm of hose exposed between the clamp and the end of the hose.

Chapter 4
Engine management system (fuel and ignition)

Contents

	Section number		Section number
Air filter	see Chapter 1	Fuel tank	2
Airbox	3	General information and precautions	1
Catalytic converter	17	Idle air control unit	15
Clutch switch	see Chapter 8	Idle speed adjustment	see Chapter 1
EMS relay	13	Ignition coils	11
Engine management system and ECM	12	Ignition switch	see Chapter 8
EVAP system – California models	16	Immobiliser	18
Exhaust system	10	Sensors	14
Fuel hoses	see Chapter 1	Sidestand switch	see Chapter 8
Fuel level sensor	6	Spark plugs	see Chapter 1
Fuel pressure check	5	Throttle bodies	7
Fuel pump and relay	4	Throttle body synchronisation	see Chapter 1
Fuel rail and injectors	8	Throttle cable check and adjustment	see Chapter 1
Fuel system check	see Chapter 1	Throttle cable removal and installation	9

Degrees of difficulty

| Easy, suitable for novice with little experience | Fairly easy, suitable for beginner with some experience | Fairly difficult, suitable for competent DIY mechanic | Difficult, suitable for experienced DIY mechanic | Very difficult, suitable for expert DIY or professional |

Specifications

Fuel
Grade.. Unleaded, minimum 91 RON (Europe Research Octane Number), or minimum 87 (R+M)/2 (US CLC or AKI Octane rating)
Fuel tank capacity..................................... 19 litres
Fuel quantity remaining when low level warning light comes on...... 4.0 litres
Fuel level sensor resistance
  Full tank.. 8 to 10 ohms
  Empty tank.. 120 to 125 ohms

Fuel injection system
Operating pressure (nominal).......................... 43.5 psi (3.0 Bar) @ 1200 rpm
Idle air control unit stepper motor resistance........... 4 to 12 ohms
Fuel injector resistance................................ 11 to 12.5 ohms
EVAP system purge valve resistance (California models)... 24 to 28 ohms

Engine management system
Type... Electronic
Control sensors...................................... atmospheric pressure, engine coolant temperature, crankshaft position, gear position, manifold absolute pressure, intake air temperature, throttle position, oxygen content (lambda), speed (road), tip-over

ECT (Engine Coolant Temperature) sensor resistance
  Warm engine.. 200 to 400 ohms
  Cold engine
    20°C ambient..................................... 2.35 to 2.65 K-ohms
    -10°C ambient.................................... 8.5 to 10.25 K-ohms
IAT (Intake Air Temperature) sensor resistance
  80°C ambient....................................... 200 to 400 ohms
  20°C ambient....................................... 2.35 to 2.65 K-ohms
  -10°C ambient...................................... 8.5 to 10.25 K-ohms

4•2 Engine management system (fuel and ignition)

Ignition system

Type	Digital inductive
Firing order	1–2–3
Cylinder identification	1–2–3, from left to right
Spark plugs	see Chapter 1
Ignition coil resistance	
Primary	0.8 to 1.2 ohms
Secondary	11.5 to 12.0 K-ohms (see Section 11)
Crankshaft position (CKP) sensor resistance	240 ohms ± 10% @ 20°C
Rev limiter cut-in	10,000 rpm

Torque settings

Air intake duct bolts in airbox	6 Nm
Crankshaft position (CKP) sensor bolts	4 Nm
Engine coolant temperature (ECT) sensor	18 Nm
Exhaust system	
Silencer mounting bolt	15 Nm
Silencer-to-downpipe clamp bolt	10 Nm
Downpipe assembly nuts (see Text)	
Initial setting	2 Nm
Final setting	19 Nm
Downpipe assembly mounting bolt	19 Nm
Fuel pump mounting plate bolts	9 Nm
Fuel rail screws	3.5 Nm
Fuel tank bolts	12 Nm
Gear position sensor bolts	5 Nm
Idle air control unit mounting screws	3.5 Nm
Immobiliser control unit bolts	9 Nm
Intake stub screws	
Up to engine No. 617516	12 Nm
From engine No. 617517	8 Nm
Oxygen sensor	25 Nm
Speed sensor bolt	
Up to VIN 574315	9 Nm
From VIN 574316, and if retro-fitted to earlier VINs	4 Nm
Throttle position sensor screws	2 Nm
Tip-over sensor screws	3 Nm

1 General information and precautions

General information

The Tiger 800 has an electronic engine management system that controls both the fuel and ignition system functions. The system is controlled by an electronic control module, or ECM. The ECM receives information from various sensors around the motorcycle, which it uses to determine the optimum fuel requirements for the fuel injection system and the optimum timing for the ignition system for all engine speeds and loads.

The sensors used are for atmospheric pressure, crankshaft position, engine coolant temperature, manifold absolute pressure, intake air temperature, oxygen (lambda), road speed, throttle position, gear position, and tip-over. Information on the function of these sensors is in Section 14.

The fuel system consists of the fuel tank, the fuel pump with integral filter, pressure regulator and level sensor, the fuel hose, fuel rail and injectors, the throttle bodies and throttle control cables, and the air intake system. The fuel pump is housed inside the tank. There is an injector for each cylinder, housed in the throttle body. Cold starting and idle speed is controlled by the ECM which reacts to the information sent by the intake air temperature sensor and the coolant temperature sensor, and adjusts the fuel requirements accordingly via a throttle stepper motor on the right-hand end of the throttle bodies – there is no manual method (i.e. a choke) for assisting cold starting, or for adjusting engine idle speed. The low fuel warning circuit is operated by a level sensor that is an integral part of the fuel pump.

The exhaust system is a three-into-one.

The ignition system type is digital inductive, which due to its lack of mechanical parts is totally maintenance free. The coil for each spark plug is incorporated in the spark plug cap. The system incorporates an electronic advance system controlled by the ECM, which reacts to the information sent to it from the various sensors to provide the spark at the optimum time. A rev limiter prevents the engine exceeding its maximum rpm. The system incorporates a starter safety circuit that will cut the ignition if the sidestand is put down whilst the engine is running and in gear, or if a gear is selected whilst the engine is running and the sidestand is down. The tip-over sensor will cut the ignition if it detects that the machine has fallen over.

The engine management system has an in-built two-stage diagnostic function. The initial stage is fault detection, whereupon the system notes the fault and counts the occurrences, looking for repetition. If the fault was a temporary glitch that does not reoccur, no DTC (diagnostic trouble code, or fault code) is registered. If the fault continues a DTC is registered, and the ECM records and stores all engine and system data at that moment, and the malfunction indicator lamp (MIL) in the instrument cluster illuminates. Recorded faults can then be checked using Triumph's diagnostic tool, which reads the data and lists a code to indicate the exact fault. If this happens, the management system in most cases switches itself into 'limp home' mode, so that in theory you should not be left stranded, or in some cases switches itself off, in which case you will be left stranded, depending on the severity of the fault – with minor faults it is possible that you will notice no difference in the running of the motorcycle. If after the DTC has been logged and the MIL comes on the fault clears itself, the MIL will remain on until the engine has been through three engine warm-up and system power-down cycles

Engine management system (fuel and ignition) 4•3

without the fault recurring, and the DTC will self-erase after forty such cycles. If the fault does not clear itself but is repaired the DTC can be erased using Triumph's tool and the MIL will turn itself off.

All models are fitted with an immobiliser that will only allow the engine to be started if the signal sent from a transponder in the ignition key is recognised by the ECM. The signal from the transponder is picked up and transmitted by a receiver fitted around the top of the ignition switch to the immobiliser control unit, which in turn corresponds with the ECM. The system has its own self-diagnostic function. The immobiliser system components must be paired with the ECM and this can only be done using the Triumph diagnostic tool. The tool is also required for fault code retrieval.

Because of their nature, the individual system components can be checked but not repaired. If system troubles occur, and the faulty component can be isolated, the only cure for the problem is to replace the part with a new one. Keep in mind that most electrical parts, once purchased, cannot be returned. To avoid unnecessary expense, make very sure the faulty component has been positively identified before buying a new part.

A number of the bolts used are of the Torx type. Unless you are already equipped with a good range of Torx bits, you are advised to obtain a set. Make sure you get bits that can be used in conjunction with a socket set so that a torque wrench can be applied – a Torx key set will not be adequate on its own, though will be useful in addition to the bits.

Precautions

> **Warning: Petrol (gasoline) is extremely flammable, so take extra precautions when you work on any part of the fuel system. Don't smoke or allow open flames or bare light bulbs near the work area, and don't work in a garage where a natural gas-type appliance is present. If you spill any fuel on your skin, rinse it off immediately with soap and water. When you perform any kind of work on the fuel system, wear safety glasses and have a fire extinguisher suitable for a class B type fire (flammable liquids) on hand.**

Always perform fuel-related procedures in a well-ventilated area to prevent a build-up of fumes.

Never work in a building containing a gas appliance with a pilot light, or any other form of naked flame. Ensure that there are no naked light bulbs or any sources of flame or sparks nearby.

Do not smoke (or allow anyone else to smoke) while in the vicinity of petrol (gasoline) or of components containing it. Remember the possible presence of vapour from these sources and move well clear before smoking.

Check all electrical equipment belonging to the house, garage or workshop where work is being undertaken (see the Safety first! section of this manual). Remember that certain electrical appliances such as drills, cutters etc. create sparks in the normal course of operation and must not be used near petrol (gasoline) or any component containing it. Again, remember the possible presence of fumes before using electrical equipment.

Always mop up any spilt fuel and safely dispose of the rag used.

Any stored fuel that is drained off during servicing work must be kept in sealed containers that are suitable for holding petrol (gasoline), and clearly marked as such; the containers themselves should be kept in a safe place. Note that this last point applies equally to the fuel tank if it is removed from the machine; also remember to keep its filler cap closed at all times.

Read the Safety first! section of this manual carefully before starting work.

Owners of machines used in the US, particularly California, should note that their machines must comply at all times with Federal or State legislation governing the permissible levels of noise and of pollutants such as unburnt hydrocarbons, carbon monoxide etc. that can be emitted by those machines. All vehicles offered for sale must comply with legislation in force at the date of manufacture and must not subsequently be altered in any way which will affect their emission of noise or of pollutants.

In practice, this means that adjustments may not be made to any part of the fuel, ignition or exhaust systems by anyone who is not authorised or mechanically qualified to do so, or who does not have the tools, equipment and data necessary to properly carry out the task. Also if any part of these systems is to be replaced it must be replaced with only genuine Triumph components or by components which are approved under the relevant legislation. The machine must never be used with any part of these systems removed, modified or damaged.

2 Fuel tank

> **Warning: Refer to the precautions given in Section 1 before starting work.**

Raise

1 Remove the rider's seat, the radiator outer covers, the side panels, the cockpit trim panel and the fuel tank trim panels (see Chapter 7).
2 Disconnect the battery (see Chapter 8). Make sure the fuel cap is secure.
3 Get a suitable prop such as a piece of 4 x 2 wood 8 to 10 inches long to place between the tank and the airbox.
4 Unscrew the bolts securing the tank **(see illustration)**. Lift the back of the tank and disconnect the breather and overflow hoses – they are different sizes so there is no need to note which goes where **(see illustration)**.
5 Draw the tank back a little until the front support brackets are clear of the supporting rubbers, then lift the front and seat the support brackets on the top of the rubbers, and fit the piece of wood under the back of the tank, as shown **(see illustrations)**.

2.4a Unscrew the bolt (arrowed) on each side

2.4b Raise the tank and disconnect the hoses (arrowed)

2.5a Seat the support brackets on top of the front supporting rubbers...

2.5b ...then support the rear of the tank

4•4 Engine management system (fuel and ignition)

2.8 Fuel pump wiring connector (A – brown), fuel level sensor connector (B – black)

2.9a Slide the orange cover down...

2.9b ...press the clips in...

2.9c ...and pull the hose connector off

2.11 Check the front support rubber (A) and mounting bolt collar and rubber (B) on each side

Removal

Note: *If the tank is full of fuel it will be quite heavy – either make sure the tank is nearly empty, or siphon any excess fuel out and into a suitable container before removal (siphons are cheaply available from a good automotive store), or have an assistant to help.*

6 Make sure the fuel cap is secure. Have some rag to hand to catch any residual fuel in the connector and its union as the fuel hose is disconnected – the tank and hose are both self-sealing so there won't be much.

7 Lift and support the tank as described above to access the hoses and connectors on the underside.

8 Disconnect the wiring connectors – the brown one is for the fuel pump and the black one is for the fuel level sensor **(see illustration)**. Pull the clutch lever in and turn the engine over on the starter for a few seconds – this reduces any pressure in the fuel rail.

9 Slide the orange fuel hose connector cover down to reveal the clips, then press the clips in and pull the hose off its union **(see illustrations)**.

10 Carefully lift the tank off the bike and remove it.

11 Inspect the tank support rubbers and the mounting bolt rubbers for signs of damage or deterioration and replace them with new ones if necessary – note the collars fitted in the mounting bolt rubbers **(see illustration)**.

Installation – all models

12 Installation is the reverse of removal, noting the following:

- Check the condition of the rubber grommets and supports and replace them with new ones if they are damaged, deformed or deteriorated **(see illustration 2.11)**. Fit the collars into the mounting bolt grommets. Make sure all components are correctly located before fitting the tank and stay located while fitting it.
- Initially position the tank in the raised position, with the front support brackets on the top of each rubber **(see illustration 2.5a)**.
- Each end of the fuel hose is colour-coded – the orange end connects to the fuel pump, the grey end to the fuel rail. Make sure the connector is fully pushed onto the union until the clips locate, then push the connector cover up to cover the clips **(see illustration 2.12a)** – if the cover won't push up the connector is not properly located.
- Make sure the electrical connectors are secure – the brown one goes into the right hand socket on the pump, the black into the left **(see illustration 2.8)**.
- Reposition the tank so the front support brackets seat around the rubbers **(see illustration 2.12b)**. Keep the rear raised and connect the drain and breather hoses to the correct unions **(see illustration 2.4b)**.
- Tighten the bolts to the torque setting specified at the beginning of the Chapter.
- Before fitting the body panels, switch the ignition ON and check that there are no leaks around the hose unions as the pump pressurises the system.

Cleaning and repair

13 All repairs to the fuel tank should be carried out by a professional who has experience in this critical and potentially dangerous work. Even after cleaning and flushing, explosive fumes can remain and ignite during repair of the tank.

14 If the fuel tank is removed from the bike, it should not be placed in an area where sparks or open flames could ignite the fumes coming out of the tank. Be especially careful inside garages where a natural gas-type appliance is located, because the pilot light could cause an explosion.

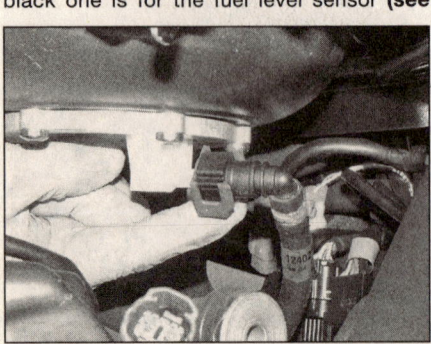

2.12a Push the cover up over the clips

2.12b Seat the support brackets in their correct positions around the rubbers

Engine management system (fuel and ignition) 4•5

3.2a IAT sensor wiring connector (arrowed)

3.2b MAP sensor wiring connector (A) and hose (B)

3.3 Airbox cover screws (arrowed)

3.4a Undo the screws (arrowed)...

3 Airbox

Removal

1 Remove the fuel tank (see Section 2).

2 Disconnect the intake air temperature (IAT) sensor wiring connector **(see illustration)**. Disconnect the manifold absolute pressure (MAP) sensor wiring connector and hose **(see illustration)**.

3 Undo the airbox cover screws and remove the cover **(see illustration)**.

4 Undo the filter element screws then lift the filter out **(see illustrations)**.

5 Unscrew the air intake trumpet bolts and remove the trumpets **(see illustration)**.

6 Unscrew the bolt securing the rear of the airbox **(see illustration)**.

7 Lift the airbox, then disconnect the

3.4b ...and lift the filter out

3.5 Unscrew the bolts (arrowed) and remove the trumpets

3.6 Unscrew the bolt (arrowed)

4•6 Engine management system (fuel and ignition)

3.7a Disconnect the crankcase breather hose...

3.7b ...and release the intake duct

3.8 Check the O-rings (arrowed)

3.9 Check the seal (arrowed) in the rim

Fuel pump

Check

1 The fuel pump is located inside the fuel tank.

2 The fuel pump runs for a few seconds when the ignition is switched ON, then cuts out when the system is up to operating pressure, and cuts in again when the engine is started. If you can't hear anything, first check the No. 3 fuse in the rear fusebox (see Chapter 8). Next check the wiring and wiring connectors in the fuel pump and relay circuit, referring to Section 2 for access to the pump wiring connector, and to *Electrical system fault finding* at the beginning of Chapter 8 and to the Wiring Diagram for your model at the end of it. Next, check the relay (see below). If they are all good, remove the pump (see below) and check the internal connections **(see illustration)**.

3 If the pump still does not work, using a fully charged 12 volt battery and two insulated jumper wires, connect the negative (-) lead to the black wire terminal, then briefly touch the positive (+) lead to the purple/white wire terminal – the pump should operate. If the pump does not operate, replace it with a new one. The pump relay is controlled by the ECM. Refer to Section 12 for further information on the ECM.

4 If the pump operates but is thought to be delivering an insufficient amount of fuel, first check that the fuel tank breather hose is unobstructed, and that the fuel hose is in good condition and not pinched or trapped. If all is good, check the fuel pressure (see Section 5).

Removal

5 Make sure the ignition is switched OFF. Using a siphon pump, drain the fuel from the tank into a suitable container. Remove the fuel tank (see Section 2). Turn the tank upside down and rest it on some rag.

6 Note the orientation of the fuel pump and its mounting plate. Unscrew the bolts, then remove the plate and withdraw the pump assembly, then unhook and disconnect the fuel level sensor wiring **(see illustrations)**. Remove the pump seal, noting which way round it fits – a new one must be used **(see illustration 4.8a)**.

crankcase breather hose from the underside and feed the intake duct rim out of the back of the airbox, noting how it locates **(see illustrations)**. Block the throttle bodies with a clean rag to prevent anything falling in.

8 If required remove the IAT sensor and MAP sensor (see Section 14). Check the O-rings on the underside of the airbox and replace them with new ones if required **(see illustration)**.

Installation

9 Installation is the reverse of removal, noting the following:
- Do not forget to remove the rag from the throttle bodies.
- Make sure the O-rings are seated in their grooves on the underside of the airbox **(see illustration 3.8)**.
- Do not forget to connect the crankcase breather hose, and make sure the intake duct rim is correctly seated in the back of the airbox **(see illustrations 3.7a and b)**.
- Tighten the air intake duct bolts before the rear mounting bolt, and tighten them to the torque setting specified at the beginning of the Chapter.
- Make sure the cover sealing ring is in good condition and correctly seated in its groove **(see illustration 3.9)**.
- Make sure all hoses and wiring connectors are correctly and securely attached.

4 Fuel pump and relay

Warning: *Refer to the precautions given in Section 1 before starting work.*

4.2 Make sure the wiring connectors are secure

4.6a Unscrew the bolts (arrowed) and remove the plate

4.6b Lift the pump and release the wire from the hook (A) and disconnect the connector (B)

Engine management system (fuel and ignition) 4•7

4.8a Fit a new seal and make sure it is the correct way up

4.8b Locate the tab on the pump in the cut-out (arrowed) in the plate

4.8c Tighten the bolts evenly and a little at a time in this sequence to the specified torque

7 The pump assembly comes as a sealed unit for which no individual parts are available. If the pump or one of its components fails the complete unit must be replaced with a new one.

Installation

8 Installation is the reverse of removal, noting the following:
- Make sure the fuel tank and pump mounting plate mating surfaces are clean.
- Check that the fuel level sensor wiring is not looped over the sensor arm, which will restrict its movement (see illustration 6.6).
- Fit a new seal onto the pump with the raised lip facing up (see illustration 4.8a).
- The pump and its mounting plate can only fit one way – the pump has a tab that locates in a cut-out in the plate, and the plate has an offset mounting bolt hole (see illustration 4.8b). Manoeuvre the pump into the tank, making sure it is correctly orientated and the seal remains in place, and connect the level sensor wiring and hook it into its guide (see illustration 4.6b).
- Fit the mounting plate, locating the cut-out over the tab and aligning the bolt holes (see illustration 4.8b). Make sure everything is correctly aligned and seated, then tighten the mounting plate bolts evenly and a little at a time in the sequence shown to the torque setting specified at the beginning of the Chapter (see illustration 4.8c).
- On completion, start the engine and check carefully that there is no leakage from around the pump mounting plate and from the hose connection.

Fuel pump relay

Note: *Refer to the Wiring Diagrams at the end of Chapter 8 for relay terminal identification.*

9 Remove the rider's seat (see Chapter 7). Disconnect the relay from its connector block (see illustration). Check the terminals and sockets for damage and corrosion.
10 Connect a continuity tester or a multimeter set to the ohms x 1 scale between the No. 3 and No. 5 wire terminals on the relay – there should be no continuity or infinite resistance. If there is continuity or zero resistance replace the relay with a new one. Using a fully-charged 12 volt battery and two insulated jumper wires, connect the positive (+) terminal of the battery to the No. 1 wire terminal on the relay, and the negative (–) terminal to the No. 2 wire terminal on the relay. At this point the relay should be heard to click and there should be continuity or zero resistance. If this is the case the relay is proved good. If the relay does not click when battery voltage is applied and the tester or meter indicates no continuity or infinite resistance, the relay is faulty and must be replaced with a new one. If the relay is good, test the pump (see above).

5 Fuel pressure check

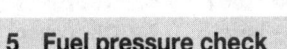
Warning: *Refer to the precautions given in Section 1 before starting work.*

1 To check the fuel pressure, the Triumph tool (Pt. No. T3880001) is needed. The tool comprises a gauge and two adapter hoses, marked A and B – use adapter hose B. A commercial pressure gauge will not be of any use. If required you can also use the wiring harness adapter (Pt. No. 3880123) that allows the fuel pump to be connected to the wiring loom with the fuel tank removed and supported next to the bike – this allows easier connection and use of the gauge and hose adapter, but is not essential.
2 Make sure the ignition switch is in the OFF position. If the wiring harness adapter is not being used, refer to Section 2, raise the tank and detach the fuel hose from the fuel pump mounting plate. If the wiring harness adapter is being used, refer to Section 2 and remove the tank and place it on a suitable support next to the bike.
3 Connect the adapter hose between the bike's fuel hose and the fuel pump union on the underside of the tank. Press each connector onto its union until it is felt and heard to click

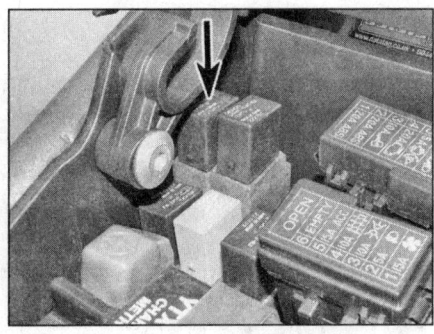
4.9 Fuel pump relay (arrowed)

into place. Fit the pressure gauge into its union, again until it is felt to click into place.
4 If the tank has been removed connect the pump using the wiring harness adapter.
5 Turn the ignition switch ON and check the pressure reading on the gauge. Start the engine and allow it to idle. The operating pressure should be as specified at the beginning of the Chapter.
6 Turn the ignition OFF. Have some rag ready to catch residual fuel in the adapter hose. Release the pressure gauge by sliding its outer ferrule down – the gauge will spring out of the union. Release the adapter hose by pressing the clips on the connectors in. Install the fuel tank (see Section 2).
7 If the pressure is too low, either the pressure regulator is stuck open, the fuel pump is faulty, the strainer or filter is blocked, or there is a leak in the system, probably from a hose joint. Firstly check the system for leaks. If none are found, fit a new fuel pump – all other possible causes are due to components within the pump assembly, which is a sealed unit.
8 If the pressure is too high, there could be a blockage somewhere in the system, and/or the pressure regulator could be stuck closed, or the fuel pump check valve could be faulty. First check the fuel rail and injectors for a blockage (see Section 8). Next fit a new fuel hose. If the pressure is still too high fit a new fuel pump – all other possible causes are due to components within the pump assembly, which is a sealed unit.

4•8 Engine management system (fuel and ignition)

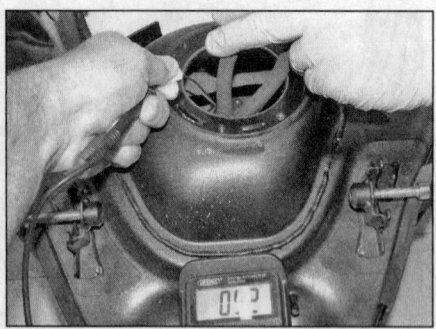

6.2a Connect the meter and use pliers to move the arm from the full position...

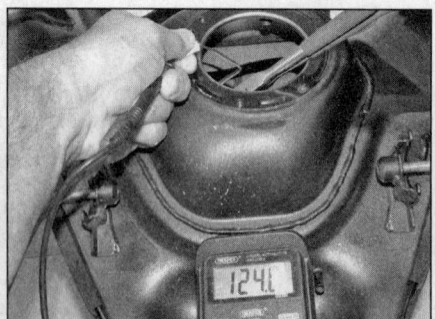

6.2b ...to the empty position

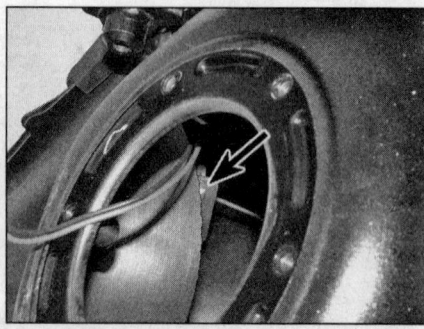

6.5 The three clips (one of which arrowed) that secure the sensor are not easy to see, and must be released by feel

6.6 Make sure the wiring is under, not over, the float arm – here the tank is upside down, so the wiring is effectively under the arm

7.2 Disconnect the injector wiring connectors (A), the idle unit wiring connector (B) and the throttle sensor wiring connector (C)

6 Fuel level sensor

Warning: Refer to the precautions given in Section 1 before starting work.

Check

1 If the low fuel level warning light fails to come on either when the ignition is first turned on or if the fuel level is low, first check the level sensor and instrument cluster wiring connectors (see Section 2 and Chapter 8 respectively), then check the wiring between the connectors for continuity, referring to the *Electrical system fault finding* at the beginning of Chapter 8 and to the wiring diagrams at the end of it.

2 If the wiring is good, remove the pump from the tank (Section 4), then connect a multimeter set to read resistance (ohms) to the sensor wiring connector. Reach inside the tank with a pair of long nose pliers and manually move the float arm up and down between the full and empty positions **(see illustrations)** – as the float moves the resistance will change, and the readings we measured are given in the Specifications at the beginning of the Chapter.

3 If the sensor does not behave as described fit a new one. If everything appears to be working correctly it is possible the fault lies in the instrument cluster – refer to Chapter 8.

Removal and installation

4 Refer to Section 4 and remove the fuel pump.

5 Reach inside the tank and release the three clips securing the sensor to its bracket, then manoeuvre the sensor out, taking care not to snag the float arm **(see illustration)**.

6 Fit the new sensor onto the bracket, making sure all three clips click into place. Make sure the wiring is not looped over the float arm **(see illustration)**.

7 Refer to Section 4 and install the fuel pump.

7 Throttle bodies

Warning: Refer to the precautions given in Section 1 before starting work.

Removal

1 Remove the fuel tank and the airbox (see Sections 2 and 3).

2 Disconnect the fuel injector wiring connectors **(see illustration)**.

3 Disconnect the idle air control unit wiring connector **(see illustration 7.2)**.

4 Disconnect the throttle position sensor wiring connector **(see illustration 7.2)**.

5 Release the throttle body clamps, then ease the assembly out of the intake stubs **(see illustrations)**.

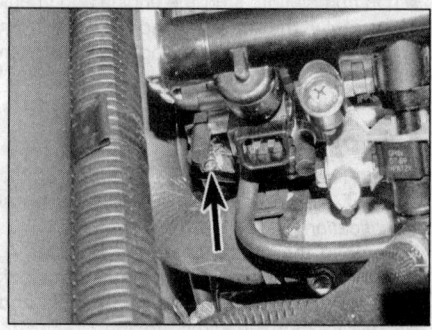

7.5a Slacken the left-hand clamp (arrowed)...

Engine management system (fuel and ignition) 4•9

7.5b ...and the middle and right-hand clamps (arrowed)...

7.5c ...and displace the throttle body

6 Disconnect the throttle cables from the throttle bodies (see Section 9, Step 2) – they can remain connected at the handlebar end.

7 Unless you are removing the intake stubs (Step 11) plug them with clean rags to prevent anything dropping inside. Note the location of the clamps on the stubs to aid reassembly.

8 If required, remove the fuel rail and injectors (see Section 8), but read the **Note** under the removal heading first.

9 If required, detach and remove the MAP sensor hoses, noting which fits where **(see illustration)**.

10 Do not remove the throttle position sensor or idle air control unit from the throttle bodies unless you know there is a fault and are fitting a new one, or unless you are replacing the throttle bodies with new ones. If you do need to remove them, note that correct set-up is essential and can only be done using the Triumph diagnostic tool. There is no alternative, unless you want to run the risk of having the bike running incorrectly. Refer to Section 12 for further information on the engine management section, and to Section 14 for the throttle position sensor and Section 15 for the idle air control valve.

11 If required undo the screws securing each intake stub to the cylinder head and remove them **(see illustration)**. On models with engine No. up to 617516 remove the O-rings – new ones must be used. On models with engine No. from 617517-on check the condition of the sealing bead on each stub and if it is damaged replace the stub with a new one. Plug the intakes in the cylinder head with clean rag.

Cleaning

Caution: Use only a dedicated spray cleaner (such as a carburettor and injector cleaner) for throttle body cleaning.

12 Spray the cleaner over the throttle bodies to remove any dirt and grime, paying particular attention to the throttle cam assembly and spring. Use a nylon brush if required, but be careful not to embed dirt particles into the cam assembly as this could cause the throttles to stick. Ensure no dirt is lodged in the bores for the throttle body synchronising screws. Take great care not to disturb any screw settings.

> **HAYNES HiNT** *If the motorcycle is constantly used in wet, dirty or dusty conditions, or the idle speed becomes erratic, clean the throttle linkage and the idle air control valve linkage regularly, and lubricate them with a light spray lubricant.*

13 If you have removed the intake stubs clean them and their mating surfaces on the cylinder head.

Inspection

14 Check the throttle bodies for cracks or any other damage that may result in air getting in.

15 Check that the throttle butterflies move smoothly and freely in the bodies, and make

7.9 Remove the MAP sensor hose assembly (arrowed) if required

7.11 Intake stub screws (arrowed)

sure that the inside of each body is completely clean.

16 Check that the throttle cable cam moves smoothly and freely, taking into account spring pressure. Clean any grit and dirt from around the cam. Check the spring for signs of damage and distortion.

17 If a body or the butterfly linkage assembly is damaged, the whole assembly must be replaced with a new one – individual components are not available.

Installation

18 Installation is the reverse of removal, noting the following:
- Do not forget to remove the rag from the intakes.
- On models with engine No. up to 617516, if removed, fit the intake stubs using new O-rings and tighten the screws to the torque setting specified at the beginning of the Chapter for your engine number **(see illustration 7.11)**.
- On models with engine No. from 617517-on, if removed, clean the threads of the intake stub screws and apply some fresh threadlock. Fit the intake stubs and tighten the screws to the torque setting specified at the beginning of the Chapter for your engine number **(see illustration 7.11)**.

8.2 Measure the resistance between the terminals

- If removed fit the fuel injectors and fuel rail onto the throttle bodies as described in Section 8 before installing the throttle bodies.
- Connect the throttle cables before installing the throttle bodies.
- If removed connect each MAP sensor hose to its union as noted on removal **(see illustration 7.9)**.
- Make sure the throttle body clamps are correctly positioned on the intake stubs **(see illustration 7.11)**, and that the throttle bodies are fully engaged with the intake stubs before tightening the clamps.
- Make sure all wiring connectors are reconnected **(see illustration 7.2)**.
- Check the operation of the throttle cables and adjust as necessary (see Chapter 1).

8 Fuel rail and injectors

⚠ **Warning: Refer to the precautions given in Section 1 before proceeding.**

Check

1 If the MIL light has come on, and you suspect an injector to be faulty, you can either have a Triumph dealer confirm this using the diagnostic tool, or, if the engine runs, start it and allow it to idle, then check the operation of each injector in the throttle bodies using a sounding rod; an injector will emit a 'clicking' noise when functioning. If any injector is silent, either the injector or its wiring harness is faulty.

2 If the engine does not run, remove the fuel tank (Section 2). Disconnect the wiring connector from each injector in turn **(see illustration 7.2)**. Connect an ohmmeter between the terminals of the injector and measure the resistance **(see illustration)**. Compare each reading to that given in the Specifications. If the resistance of any injector differs greatly from that specified replace it with a new one.

3 If the injectors are good check for continuity in the wiring from each injector to the ECM and the EMS (engine management system) relay (see Section 13 for location), referring to electrical system fault finding at the beginning of Chapter 8 and to the wiring diagram for your model at the end of it. If all is good, check the EMS fuse (the No. 4 fuse in the rear fusebox – see Chapter 8), the EMS relay (Section 13), then the ECM (Section 12).

Removal

Note: *The fuel injectors have an O-ring on each end to seal them in the fuel rail and throttle bodies, and prevent fuel leakage under pressure. Removal of the injectors could cause the seals to lose their effectiveness, and Triumph do not list them as being available separately from the injectors themselves, which are expensive. It is therefore best not to remove the fuel rail and injectors from the throttle bodies unless you have to fit a new injector.*

4 Remove the throttle body assembly (see Section 7). Slide the grey fuel hose connector cover down to reveal the clips, then press the clips in and pull the hose off its union **(see illustration)**.

5 Undo the fuel rail screws, then ease the fuel rail and injectors off the throttle bodies **(see illustration)**.

6 If required carefully pull the injector(s) out of the fuel rail.

7 Check the condition of the injector O-rings – if they are damaged or deformed they must be replaced with new ones, but note that they are not listed as being available separately from the injectors themselves. It is best to consult a Triumph dealer, who may be able to supply them separately, or alternatively take the old O-rings to a good aftermarket O-ring supplier who may be able to match the exact size, although check that they suit the purpose.

8.4 Disconnect the fuel hose (arrowed) as described

8.5 Undo the screws (arrowed) and carefully remove the fuel rail with the injectors attached

Engine management system (fuel and ignition) 4•11

8 Modern fuels contain detergents that should keep the rail and injectors clean and free of gum or varnish from residue fuel. Clean the rail in a dedicated cleaner and blow it through with compressed air. If an injector is suspected of being blocked, flush it out with injector cleaner, and if necessary have it ultrasonically cleaned by a specialist.

Installation

9 Fit new O-rings onto each injector. Push each injector into its socket in the fuel rail, aligning the tab on the injector with the slot in the socket, and making sure you do not turn it whilst doing so, and that it is properly seated.
10 Fit the fuel rail and injector assembly onto the throttle bodies, making sure each injector seats correctly. Fit the fuel rail screws and tighten them to the torque setting specified at the beginning of the Chapter **(see illustration 8.5)**.
11 Connect the fuel hose: each end of the hose is colour-coded – the orange end connects to the fuel pump, the grey end to the fuel rail. Make sure the connector is fully pushed onto the union until the clips locate, then push the connector cover up to cover the clips **(see illustration 8.4)** – if the cover won't push up the connector is not properly located.
12 Install the throttle bodies (see Section 7).

9 Throttle cable removal and installation

Warning: Refer to the precautions given in Section 1 before proceeding.

Removal

1 Remove the fuel tank and the airbox (see Sections 2 and 3). On XC models remove the right handguard (see Chapter 7). Note the routing of the cables and mark them according to their location at each end. Displace the throttle bodies (see Section 7, Steps 2 to 5).

9.2a Fully slacken the locknuts (arrowed)…

9.2b …and free the cables from the bracket

9.2c Detach the closing cable end…

9.2d …and the opening cable end

2 Slacken the locknuts securing the opening and closing cables in the bracket and thread them up **(see illustration)**. Slip the outer cables out of the bracket and detach the inner cable ends from the throttle cam **(see illustrations)**.
3 Pull the rubber boot off the throttle pulley housing on the handlebars, then undo the housing screws **(see illustration)**. Separate the halves, then detach the inner cable ends from the pulley and free the cable elbows, noting how it all fits **(see illustrations)**.
4 Remove the cables from the machine noting their correct routing. Inspect the area around the cable sockets in the twistgrip for cracks – some have been known to break when the there has been too little or no cable freeplay.

Installation

5 Installation is the reverse of removal. If necessary, lubricate the cables (see Chapter 1). Make sure the cables are correctly routed – they must not interfere with any other component and should not be kinked or bent sharply. At the throttle body end the opening cable elbow has silver coloured nuts and the closing cable has black nuts. Lubricate the end of each inner cable with multi-purpose grease.
6 Adjust the cables as described in Chapter 1. Turn the handlebars back and forth to make sure the cables don't cause the steering to bind.
7 Start the engine and check that the engine speed does not rise as the handlebars are turned. If it does, correct the problem before riding the motorcycle.

9.3a Pull back the rubber boot (A) then undo the screws (B)…

9.3b …separate the housing halves…

9.3c …and free the cable ends from the throttle pulley and the elbows from the housings

4•12 Engine management system (fuel and ignition)

10.1 Slacken the clamp bolt (arrowed)

10.2a Unscrew the nut...

10.2b ...withdraw the bolt...

10 Exhaust system

Warning: *If the engine has been running the exhaust system will be very hot. Allow the system to cool before carrying out any work.*
Caution: *The exhaust downpipe assembly incorporates a catalytic converter and oxygen sensor. Take care when handling it, and do not strike or drop it because the delicate catalytic converter element could be damaged.*

10.2c ...and remove the silencer

10.2d Remove the collars and rubber bushes

Silencer

Removal

1 Note the orientation of the clamp securing the silencer to the intermediate pipe, then slacken the bolt **(see illustration)**.
2 Unscrew the nut on the silencer mounting bolt, noting the washer **(see illustration)**. Support the silencer, then withdraw the bolt and draw the silencer out of the intermediate pipe **(see illustrations)**. Remove the collars and rubber bushes for safekeeping if required **(see illustration)**.
3 Check the condition of the sealing ring between the silencer and intermediate pipe and replace it with a new one if necessary **(see illustration)** – unless it is obviously in need of renewal it is best to leave it in place as it will be ruined when you dig it out, and bear in mind it is easy to damage a new one when fitting it.

Installation

4 Installation is the reverse of removal. Fit a new sealing ring into the intermediate pipe if necessary **(see illustration 10.3)**. When inserting the silencer make sure it does not catch on the rim of the sealing ring as it is easily damaged. Make sure the clamp is correctly orientated and located **(see illustration 10.1)**. Tighten the silencer mounting bolt to the torque setting specified at the beginning of the Chapter, then tighten the clamp bolt to the specified torque. Run the engine and check that there are no leaks from the exhaust system.

Downpipe assembly

Removal

5 Remove the silencer.
6 Remove the sump guard, and where fitted the engine protection bars (see Chapter 7). Remove the radiator (see Chapter 3).
7 Trace the wiring from the oxygen sensor and disconnect it at the connector **(see illustration)**.
8 Unscrew the six downpipe assembly nuts from the cylinder head **(see illustration)**. Triumph specifies to use new nuts on installation.
9 Unscrew the bolt securing the rear of the downpipe assembly, noting the arrangement

10.3 Check the sealing ring (arrowed)

10.7 Oxygen sensor wiring connector is between the engine and the shock absorber

10.8 Unscrew the nuts (arrowed)...

Engine management system (fuel and ignition) 4•13

10.9a ...then unscrew the bolt...

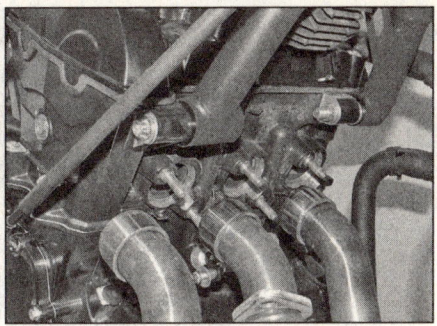

10.9b ...and remove the downpipe assembly

10.10a Remove the old gaskets

of the collars and rubber bushes **(see illustration)**. Draw the downpipes off the cylinder head **(see illustration)**.

10 Remove the gasket from each port in the cylinder head **(see illustration)** – new ones must be fitted. Remove the collars and bushes from the rear mounting. Check the condition of the rubber bushes and replace them with new ones if hardened or cracked **(see illustration)**. If required remove the sensor (see Section 14).

Installation

11 Installation is the reverse of removal. Install the oxygen sensor if removed (Section 14). Fit a new gasket into each of the cylinder head ports **(see illustration)** – they should have small tabs on them to keep them in place, but if required apply a smear of grease to assist. Fit a bush and collar into the inner end of the rear mounting **(see illustration 10.12a)**. Fit the other bush and collar onto the bolt **(see illustration 10.10b)**.

12 Manoeuvre the assembly into position so that the head of each downpipe is located in its port in the cylinder head **(see illustration 10.9b)**. Fit the rear mounting bolt, but do not yet tighten it **(see illustration)**. Fit the flanges onto the studs, then fit the new downpipe nuts and tighten them in the sequence shown (1 to 6), first to the initial torque setting specified at the beginning of the Chapter, then in the same sequence to the final setting **(see illustrations)**.

10.10b Check the bushes for the rear mount

13 Reconnect the sensor wiring connector **(see illustration 10.7)** – make sure the wiring is correctly routed and secured.
14 Install the radiator (see Chapter 3).
15 Install the silencer.
16 Run the engine and check that there are no leaks from the exhaust system. Install the sump guard and any other components removed (see Chapter 7).

11 Ignition coils

Warning: The energy levels in electronic systems can be very high. On no account should the

10.11 Fit the new gaskets with the tabs innermost

ignition be switched on whilst the coils are connected and being held. Shocks from the HT circuit can be most unpleasant. Secondly, it is vital that the plugs are soundly earthed (grounded) when the system is checked for sparking. The ignition system components can be seriously damaged if the HT circuit becomes isolated.

Removal

1 Remove the fuel tank (see Section 2).
2 The ignition coils, one for each cylinder, are integral with the spark plug caps. Clean the area around each coil to prevent any dirt falling into the spark plug channels.
3 Disconnect the ignition coil wiring

10.12a Fit the rear mounting bolt, taking care not to dislodge the inner bush

10.12b Fit the flanges and the nuts...

10.12c ...and tighten them as described in the sequence shown

4•14 Engine management system (fuel and ignition)

11.3a Disconnect the wiring connector...

11.3b ...and pull the coil off the spark plug

11.7 A typical ignition spark testing tool

connectors (see illustration). Pull the coils off the spark plugs (see illustration).

4 Fit the coils onto the spark plugs (see illustration 11.3b). Connect the coil wiring connectors, making sure each goes to its correct cylinder (see illustration 11.3a). Install the fuel tank (see Section 2).

Ignition system check

5 Remove the coil (Steps 1 to 3), then reconnect the wiring connector. Fit a new spark plug into the cap and hold the coil so the plug threads rest against a valve cover bolt head. Do not hold the plug against the valve cover.

⚠ **Warning:** *Do not remove any of the spark plugs from the engine to perform this check – atomised fuel being pumped out of the open spark plug hole could ignite, causing severe injury!*

6 Check that the kill switch is in the RUN position and the transmission is in neutral, then turn the ignition switch ON, pull the clutch lever in and turn the engine over on the starter motor. If the system is in good condition a regular, fat blue spark should be evident at the plug electrodes. If the spark appears thin or yellowish, or is non-existent, further investigation will be necessary. Turn the ignition OFF. Repeat the check for the other coils.

7 The ignition system must be able to produce a spark that is capable of jumping a particular size gap. Triumph provide no specification, but a healthy system should produce a spark capable of jumping at least 6 mm. Ignition spark gap testing tools are available from good suppliers (see illustration) – follow the manufacturer's instructions.

8 If the system is in good condition a regular, fat blue spark should be seen to jump the gap on the tool. If the test results are good the entire ignition system can be considered good. If the spark appears thin or yellowish, or is non-existent, further investigation is necessary.

9 Using an ohmmeter or multimeter set to the ohms x 1 scale, measure the primary circuit resistance between the terminals on the coil (see illustration). The resistance should be as specified at the beginning of the Chapter. If not, the coil is faulty and must be replaced with a new one. Remove the rubber end piece from the bottom of the coil. Set the ohmmeter or multimeter to the K-ohms scale and measure the secondary circuit resistance between one of the terminals on the coil and the plug contact in the base (see illustration). Triumph does not specify a resistance but the coil we tested showed just over 11 K-ohms. If the value deviates from this figure by +/- 10%, the coil is faulty and must be replaced with a new one. The coil is a sealed unit and cannot therefore be repaired.

10 If the coils and spark plugs are good, then there is a fault elsewhere in the system. The likely faults are listed below, starting with the most probable source of failure. Work through the list systematically, referring to the subsequent sections for full details of the necessary checks and tests. **Note:** *Before checking the following items ensure that the battery is fully charged and that all fuses are in good condition.*

- Loose, corroded or damaged wiring connections, broken or shorted wiring between any of the component parts of the ignition system – refer to 'Electrical system fault finding' at the beginning of Chapter 8 and to the wiring diagram for your model at the end of it.
- Faulty spark plug, dirty, worn or corroded plug electrodes, or incorrect gap between electrodes (see Chapter 1).
- Blown EMS relay fuse (see Chapter 8) or faulty EMS relay (see Section 13).
- Faulty ignition switch or engine kill switch (see Chapter 8).
- Faulty clutch, neutral or sidestand switch (see Chapter 8).
- Faulty crankshaft position sensor (see Section 14).
- Faulty ECM.

11.9a To test the coil primary resistance, connect the meter as shown

11.9b To test the coil secondary resistance, remove the rubber end piece and connect the meter as shown

Engine management system (fuel and ignition) 4•15

11 If the above checks don't reveal the cause of the problem, have the engine management system tested by a Triumph dealer. Triumph produces a diagnostic tool that can perform a complete analysis of the engine management system. Refer to Sections 1 and 12 for more information.

12 Engine management system and ECM

Warning: *Refer to the precautions given in Section 1 before starting work.*

1 For a general description of the system, see Section 1.

Diagnostic tool and fault codes

2 To diagnose the exact cause of a failure in the system, either the Triumph diagnostic tool or an EOBD (OBD2) fault code reader is essential – both of these plug into the socket under the passenger seat **(see illustration 12.4)**.

3 The ECM has in-built diagnostic functions which record and store all data should a permanent fault occur. Diagnostic trouble codes (DTCs) can then be read using the diagnostic tool, which lists a P-code to indicate the exact fault. Should a fault occur, the malfunction indicator light or symbol (MIL) in the instrument cluster illuminates. If this happens, the management system switches itself into 'limp home' mode, so that in theory you should not be left stranded. Depending on the problem, it is possible that you will notice no difference in the running of the motorcycle.

4 The socket for the diagnostic tool is located under the seat **(see illustration)**. With the ignition off, plug the code reader into the socket. Turn the ignition on and allow the code reader to process any stored fault codes – these will be displayed as a four digit number prefixed by the letter P. Turn off the ignition and disconnect the code reader once the P-code has been noted. Refer to the accompanying table to link the code with the faulty circuit. Once the fault has been rectified the code reader can be used to delete the stored code from the ECM's memory.

12.4 After-market EOBD (OBD2) fault code reader plugged into the socket (arrowed)

5 If you don't have access to a code reader it is possible to perform certain tests and checks to identify a particular fault, but the difficulty is knowing in which part of the system the fault has occurred, and therefore where to start checking. Further details on the functions of and checks that can be made to the individual sensors and components and the wiring between them are detailed below and in other Sections of this Chapter.

P-code	Circuit affected
P0030	Oxygen sensor heater – circuit fault
P0031	Oxygen sensor heater – open circuit to battery/short to earth
P0032	Oxygen sensor heater – short circuit to battery
P0107	MAP sensor low voltage
P0108	MAP sensor high voltage
P0112	Intake air temperature too high
P0113	Intake air temperature too low
P0117	Engine coolant temperature too high – sensor short circuit to earth
P0118	Engine coolant temperature too low – sensor open circuit or short circuit to battery+
P0122	Throttle position sensor low input – short to earth or open circuit
P0123	Throttle position sensor high input – short circuit to sensor supply
P0136	Oxygen sensor circuit fault
P0201/P1201	Injector cyl 1 circuit fault – misfire = open circuit, flooding = short circuit
P0202/P1202	Injector cyl 2 circuit fault – misfire = open circuit, flooding = short circuit
P0203/P1203	Injector cyl 3 circuit fault – misfire = open circuit, flooding = short circuit
P0335	Crankshaft position sensor circuit fault
P0351	Ignition coil circuit fault cyl 1
P0352	Ignition coil circuit fault cyl 2
P0353	Ignition coil circuit fault cyl 3
P0444	EVAP purge control valve short circuit to earth or open circuit
P0445	EVAP purge control valve short circuit to battery
P0460	Fuel level sensor circuit fault
P0500	Speed (speedometer) sensor fault or ABS sensor fault
P0505	Idle speed control system fault
P0560	System voltage problem – battery circuit malfunction
P0616	Starter relay coil short circuit to earth or open circuit
P0617	Starter relay short circuit to battery+
P0630	EEPROM fault
P0654	Tachometer circuit fault
P0705	Gear position sensor fault
P1105	MAP sensor vacuum hose fault
P1107	Ambient air pressure sensor circuit low voltage
P1108	Ambient air pressure sensor circuit high voltage
P1115	Temperature gauge circuit fault
P1231	Fuel pump relay short circuit to earth or open circuit
P1232	Fuel pump relay short circuit to battery+
P1500	Speedometer circuit fault
P1508	Immobiliser (or tyre pressure sensor system) and ECM unmatched
P1520	ABS modulator ID incompatible
P1521	No signal to ABS modulator
P1552	Cooling fan – short or open circuit
P1553	Cooling fan – short to battery voltage/over temperature
P1602	Tunelock
P1614	ECM and instruments incorrect matched
P1628	Fuel pump short circuit to earth or open circuit
P1629	Fuel pump short circuit to battery
P1631	Tip-over sensor circuit low voltage
P1632	Tip-over sensor circuit high voltage
P1659	Ignition voltage input circuit fault
P1685	EMS relay fault
P1690	CAN-bus network communication fault between ECM and instruments
P1698	5 volt sensor supply circuit fault

4•16 Engine management system (fuel and ignition)

12.7 ECM wiring connector pin identification

Fault tracing

Note: *Refer to 'Electrical system fault finding' at the beginning of Chapter 8 and to the wiring diagram for your model at the end of it.*

6 If a fault is indicated, check the wiring and connectors to and from the ECM (electronic control module) and the various sensors and all their related components – see Steps 9 to 11 for access to the ECM and its connectors. It may be that a connector is dirty or corroded or has come loose – a dirty or corroded terminal or connector will affect the resistance in that circuit, which will upset the information going to the ECM, and therefore affect the decisions it makes in controlling the system. Electrical contact cleaners are available in aerosol cans from good suppliers.

7 A wire could be pinched and is shorting out – a continuity test of all wires from connector to connector will locate this. Albeit a fiddly and laborious task, the only way to determine any wiring faults is to systematically work through the Wiring Diagrams at the end of Chapter 8 and test each individual wire and connector for continuity – all wires are colour-coded. When making continuity checks, isolate the wire being tested by disconnecting the wiring connectors at each end. The Wiring Diagrams show the terminal identification for each wire on the ECM with the letter given on the wiring diagram indicating the relevant ECM connector, and the number referring to the terminal within that connector, as shown **(see illustration)** – match these to the terminals on the ECM connector(s) when making the tests.

8 If all the wiring and connectors appear good, remove the relevant sensor and make sure its sensing tip or head is clean and undamaged, as this can often be the cause of inaccurate signals being sent to the ECM.

ECM removal and installation

Note: *Before removing the ECM, make sure the ignition has been switched OFF for at least one minute to allow the system to power down, then disconnect the battery (see Chapter 8).*

9 Remove the rider's seat (see Chapter 7).
10 Remove the battery (see Chapter 8).
11 Remove the ECM cover, then disconnect the wiring **(see illustrations)**.
12 Release the retaining clip and lift the ECM out **(see illustrations)**.
13 Installation is the reverse of removal. Check the terminal pins and connectors for damage and corrosion. The connectors are colour-coded and shaped so they cannot be re-connected the wrong way round.

13 EMS relay

Note: *Before disconnecting the relay, make sure the ignition has been switched OFF for at least one minute to allow the system to power down, then disconnect the battery (see Chapter 8). Refer to the Wiring Diagrams at the end of Chapter 8 for relay terminal identification.*

1 The engine management system (EMS) has its own power relay which is designed to provide a steady voltage supply to the ECM. The ECM holds the relay open after the ignition is switched off to enable it perform various power-down functions, such as writing data to the memory, referencing the position of the idle air control valve, and if necessary, running the cooling fan.

2 Remove the rider's seat (see Chapter 7). Disconnect the relay from its connector block **(see illustration)**. Check the terminals and sockets for damage and corrosion.

3 Connect a continuity tester or a multimeter set to the ohms x 1 scale between the No. 3 and No. 5 wire terminals on the relay – there should be no continuity or infinite resistance. If there is continuity or zero resistance replace the relay with a new one. Using a fully-charged 12 volt battery and two insulated jumper wires, connect the positive (+) terminal of the battery to the No. 1 wire terminal on the relay, and the negative (–) terminal to the No. 2 wire terminal on the relay. At this point the relay should be heard to click and there should be

12.11a Lift the cover off...

12.11b ...and disconnect the connectors (arrowed)

12.12a Release the clip...

12.12b ...and remove the ECM

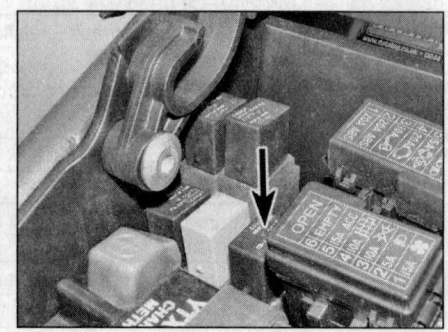

13.2 EMS relay (arrowed)

Engine management system (fuel and ignition) 4•17

continuity or zero resistance. If this is the case the relay is proved good. If the relay does not click when battery voltage is applied and the tester or meter indicates no continuity (infinite resistance), the relay is faulty and must be replaced with a new one.

14 Sensors

Note: *Before disconnecting the wiring connector from any sensor, make sure the ignition is switched OFF, and disconnect the battery (see Chapter 8).*

Atmospheric pressure (AP) sensor

1 The sensor reads the atmospheric (barometric) pressure (i.e. air density). The ECM combines this with other information to determine fuelling requirements.
2 Remove the battery (see Chapter 8).
3 Disconnect the wiring connector from the sensor, then unscrew the bolt securing it **(see illustration)**. Installation is the reverse of removal.

Crankshaft position (CKP) sensor

Function

4 The sensor reads the position of the crankshaft and how fast it is turning; this information is used by the ECM to determine which cylinder is on its ignition stroke and when it should fire. The ECM combines engine speed with information from other sensors to determine fuelling and ignition requirements.

Test

5 On models with engine numbers up to 612713 and from 613308 to 613370 the crankshaft position sensor is mounted on the crankcase next to the alternator rotor and has its own wiring sub-loom. On all other engines the sensor is mounted in the alternator cover and is wired into the stator sub-loom, and is not available separately from it **(see illustration 14.7)**.
6 To check the sensor, first make sure the ignition is switched OFF, then remove throttle bodies (see Section 7). Release the sensor wiring connector from its bracket on the starter motor and disconnect it **(see illustrations)**. Using an ohmmeter or multimeter set to the K-ohms scale, measure the resistance between the terminals on the sensor side of the connector **(see illustration)**. If the result is as specified, check that there is no continuity between each terminal and earth (ground).
7 Remove the alternator cover (see Chapter 8). Inspect the sensor and the sensor triggers on the alternator rotor for damage. Make sure the sensor head is clean, and the bolts are tight **(see illustration)**.

Removal

8 Remove the throttle bodies (see Section 7). Release the sensor wiring connector from its

14.3 Atmospheric pressure sensor (arrowed)

14.6b ...then disconnect it...

bracket on the starter motor and disconnect it **(see illustrations 14.6a and b)**. Feed it down to the sensor, releasing it from any ties or guides and noting its routing.
9 On models with engine numbers up to 612713 and from 613308 to 613370 remove the alternator cover (see Chapter 8). Unscrew the upper wiring guide bolt and free the wiring. Unscrew the sensor bolts and remove it along with the lower wiring guide.
10 On all other engines (from 612714-on but excluding 613308 to 613370) refer to Chapter 8, remove the alternator stator and replace it with a new one – the CKP sensor is integral with it.

Installation

11 On models with engine numbers up to 612713 and from 613308 to 613370, installation is the reverse of removal. Clean the threads of the sensor and guide bolts

14.7 Crankshaft position sensor (arrowed) – engines from 612714-on but excluding 613308 to 613370

14.6a Release the wiring connector from the bracket using a small screwdriver...

14.6c ...and measure the resistance of the sensor

and apply some fresh threadlock. Tighten the sensor bolts to the torque setting specified at the beginning of the Chapter. Make sure the wiring is correctly routed and secured.
12 On all other engines (from 612714-on but excluding 613308 to 613370) refer to Chapter 8 and install the alternator stator.

Engine coolant temperature (ECT) sensor

Function

13 The sensor reads the temperature of the engine coolant, and the ECM uses the information to determine fuelling requirements, particularly for hot and cold starting.

Test

14 The sensor is located in the back of the cylinder head **(see illustration)**.

14.14 ECT sensor (arrowed)

4•18 Engine management system (fuel and ignition)

14.16a Push the clip in to release the wiring connector

14.16b Measure the resistance across the terminals (arrowed)

15 Make sure the ignition is switched OFF. Remove the throttle bodies (see Section 7).
16 To test the sensor resistance, disconnect the wiring connector **(see illustration)**. Measure the resistance between the sensor terminals **(see illustration)** using an ohmmeter or multimeter set to the relevant scale for the temperature of the engine if warm, or the air if the engine is cold – see Specifications. If the result is not as specified, the sensor is faulty.

Removal and installation

17 The sensor is located in the back of the cylinder head **(see illustration 14.14)**. Remove the throttle bodies (see Section 7). Drain the cooling system (see Chapter 1). Disconnect the wiring connector **(see illustration 14.16a)**.
18 Unscrew the sensor from the cylinder head. Remove the sealing washer – a new one must be used.
19 Fit a new sealing washer onto the sensor, then thread it into the head and tighten it to the torque setting specified at the beginning of the Chapter. Reconnect the wiring connector.
20 Fill the cooling system (see Chapter 1).
21 Install the throttle bodies (see Section 7).

Gear position (GP) sensor

22 The sensor tells the ECM which gear the engine is in, and the ECM then operates the neutral light and gear position indicator in the instrument cluster.
23 Remove the sensor (see below), and check that the contact pin is not damaged, and that the switch plate turns freely in the body **(see illustration 14.26)**.

Removal and installation

Note: *The sensor fitted to models from engine No. 598650 is different from earlier models and can be retro-fitted to earlier models, but a wiring adapter is needed and is supplied with the sensor as a kit. If you are fitting a new sensor check your engine number and tell the supplier when ordering the new part.*

24 The sensor is on the left-hand side of the engine. Remove the front sprocket cover (see Chapter 6). On models with engine numbers up to 598649, remove the fuel tank and the airbox (see Sections 2 and 3).
25 Trace the wiring from the sensor and disconnect it at the wiring connector **(see illustration)**.
26 Unscrew the bolts, noting the wiring/hose guide, and remove the sensor. Remove the O-rings – new ones should be used **(see illustration)**.
27 Fit the sensor using new O-rings smeared with petroleum jelly (Vaseline) or grease. Clean the threads of the bolts and apply some fresh threadlock. Tighten the bolts to the torque setting specified at the beginning of the Chapter.
28 Connect the wiring connector, using the adapter lead where necessary (see **Note**) – if you are fitting the new sensor to an engine with number up to 598649, connect the four-pin connector of the adapter lead to the sensor connector, then connect the other connector (at the same end of the lead) to the connector that the old sensor connected to. Now route the adapter lead along the back of the engine breather chamber cover, behind the hose, and towards the throttle position sensor (TPS) on the right-hand end of the throttle body. Disconnect the TPS wiring connector, connect the female connector on the adapter lead to the sensor side of the connector and the male connector on the lead to the loom side of the connector. Check the operation of the neutral light and gear position readout. Install the airbox and fuel tank (see Sections 3 and 2) where necessary, and the sprocket cover (see Chapter 6).

Intake air temperature (IAT) sensor

Function

29 The sensor reads the temperature of the air in the airbox. As changes in temperature affect air density, the ECM uses the information to determine fuelling requirements.

Test, removal and installation

30 The sensor is threaded into the airbox cover. Make sure the ignition is switched OFF. Remove the fuel tank (see Section 2).
31 To test the sensor resistance, disconnect the wiring connector **(see illustration 3.2a)**. Measure the resistance between the sensor terminals using an ohmmeter or multimeter set to the K-ohms scale. If the result is not as specified for the relevant temperature, the sensor is faulty.
32 To remove the sensor, undo the screw. Installation is the reverse of removal.

Manifold absolute pressure (MAP) sensor

Function

33 The sensor reads the pressure of the air in the throttle bodies. The ECM combines this with other information to determine engine load and adjusts fuelling requirements accordingly.

Removal and installation

34 The sensor is mounted on the front of the airbox **(see illustration 3.2b)**. Make sure the ignition is switched OFF. Remove the fuel tank (see Section 2). Disconnect the wiring connector and the vacuum hose, then unscrew the bolt securing the sensor – if you can't access the bolt, remove the airbox (see Section 3) **(see illustration)**.
35 Installation is the reverse of removal. Make

14.25 Gear position sensor (A) and its connector (B – late model shown)

14.26 The sensor has two O-rings (arrowed)

14.34 MAP sensor bolt (arrowed)

Engine management system (fuel and ignition) 4•19

sure the vacuum hoses are in good condition and securely fitted at each end.

Oxygen (lambda) sensor

Function

36 The sensor measures oxygen left in the un-burnt exhaust gases and generates a signal voltage that is fed back to the ECM. In this way the ECM can correct the mixture supplied to the engine to ensure that the oxygen content of the exhaust gases remains within a narrow range and suitable for the operation of the catalytic converter. This type of system is called closed-loop control.

Removal and installation

37 The sensor is in the exhaust downpipe assembly. Remove the sump guard and its bracket (see Chapter 7).
38 Trace the wiring from the sensor and disconnect it at the connector **(see illustration 10.7)**.
39 Unscrew and remove the sensor **(see illustration)** – the sensor is fragile so care must be taken not to apply undue force. If the sensor is difficult to unscrew or the area around it is badly corroded, apply a penetrating fluid.
40 When installing the sensor, apply copper grease to the sensor threads and tighten it to the torque setting specified at the beginning of the Chapter – a special tool is required for this because of the wiring. Reconnect the sensor wiring connector – make sure the wiring is correctly routed and secured.

Speed sensor

Note: *The sensor is fitted to models without ABS. On models with ABS a blanking plug is fitted in place of the sensor and the ABS wheel speed sensors provide the information to the ECM – see Chapter 6. The bolt that secures the sensor or blanking plug was changed from VIN 574316 and requires a different torque to the bolt fitted to earlier models. The new bolt can be fitted to the early models, so if you buy a new bolt you must check which one is being supplied and tighten to the appropriate torque.*

Function

41 The sensor reads the road speed of the bike by counting the rate at which the transmission output shaft is turning. This information is used by the ECM in conjunction

14.39 Oxygen sensor (arrowed)

with engine speed information to determine which gear the bike is in, and controls fuelling and ignition accordingly, and also to provide road speed display at the instruments. The information also helps to determine the idle air control valve setting.

Removal and installation

42 The speed sensor is located in the top of the crankcase. Make sure the ignition is switched OFF. Remove the throttle bodies (see Section 7). Trace the wiring from the sensor and disconnect the connector. Unscrew the bolt and remove the sensor **(see illustration)**.
43 Installation is the reverse of removal – check the condition of the O-ring and replace it with a new one if it is deformed or has deteriorated, or there is evidence of oil leakage from it **(see illustration)**. Clean the threads of the bolt and apply some fresh threadlock. Tighten the bolt to the torque setting specified at the beginning of the Chapter for your VIN, noting that if you are fitting the new type bolt to an early engine (see **Note**) it must be tightened to the torque for the later VINs.

Throttle position (TP) sensor

Function

44 The sensor reads the amount of throttle being used, and the ECM uses this in conjunction with the information from other sensors to determine fuelling and ignition requirements.

Removal and installation

45 The sensor is located on the left-hand end of the throttle body. Do not remove the throttle position sensor unless you know it is faulty

14.42 Speed sensor location (arrowed) – model with blanking plug shown

and are replacing it with a new one, or unless you are replacing the throttle body with a new one. If you do remove it, it has to be set up using the Triumph diagnostic tool. There is no alternative, unless you want to run the risk of having the bike running incorrectly.
46 Remove the throttle body (see Section 7). Undo the screws, then rotate the sensor 45° clockwise and draw it off the end of the throttle shaft, noting the position of the O-ring **(see illustration)**.
47 Fit the O-ring onto the sensor, using a new one if necessary. Locate the sensor onto the end of the throttle shaft, making sure the O-ring seats correctly, then turn it anti-clockwise 45° to align the screw holes; secure the screws just finger-tight.
48 Install the throttle body (see Section 7). The sensor must now be set up correctly using the Triumph diagnostic tool. On completion tighten the screws to the torque setting specified at the beginning of the Chapter.

Tip-over (TO) sensor

Function

49 The sensor is basically a safety switch that tells the ECM if the bike has fallen over, in which case the ECM will shut down the fuel pump and stop the engine. The switch can be reset by picking the bike up and turning the ignition off, then on again.

Removal and installation

50 The sensor is mounted in front of the tail light **(see illustration)** – remove the luggage rack for access (see Chapter 7).

14.43 Fit a new O-ring if necessary

14.46 Throttle position sensor screws (arrowed)

14.50 Tip-over sensor (arrowed)

4•20 Engine management system (fuel and ignition)

15.4 Idle air control unit wiring connector (arrowed)

15.7 Unscrew the nut (arrowed) and remove the washers

15.8 Undo the screws (arrowed) and remove the unit

51 Disconnect the wiring connector. Unscrew the bolts and remove the sensor.
52 Clean the threads of the bolts and apply some fresh threadlock. Fit the sensor with the UP mark at the top and tighten the bolts to the torque setting specified at the beginning of the Chapter.

15 Idle air control unit

Check

1 The idle air control unit, located on the throttle body, is actuated by the ECM and set according to information received by the ECM from the various sensors. The unit is used to control the engine idle speed, to adjust the air supply on engine overrun, to correct for altitude, and for cold starting. The idle speed cannot be adjusted manually.
2 The ECM actuates a stepper motor which moves an arm connected to a lever that contacts the throttle cam and varies the closed throttle position setting. If a fault in the valve is suspected check the wiring connector for loose, corroded or damaged terminals, and the wiring between the valve and the ECM for continuity, referring to *Electrical system fault finding* at the beginning of Chapter 8 and the *Wiring Diagrams* at the end of it.
3 Remove the fuel tank and the airbox (see Sections 2 and 3).
4 To test the stepper motor resistance, first make sure the ignition is switched OFF. Disconnect the wiring connector **(see illustration)**. First measure the resistance between the orange/brown and orange/white wire terminals in the sensor side of the connector using an ohmmeter or multimeter set to the ohms x 10 scale. Next, measure the resistance between the orange/blue and orange/pink wire terminals in the sensor side of the connector. If either of the results is not as specified at the beginning of this Chapter, the stepper motor is faulty.

Removal

5 The idle air control unit is located on the throttle body. Do not remove it unless you know it is faulty and are replacing it with a new one, or unless you are replacing the throttle body assembly with a new one. If you do remove it, it has to be set up using the Triumph diagnostic tool. There is no alternative, unless you want to run the risk of having the bike running incorrectly.
6 Remove the throttle body (see Section 7). Make a careful note of the how the actuating lever locates in relation to the throttle cam **(see illustration 15.9a)**.
7 Unscrew the nut securing the arm in the lever and remove the metal and plastic washers **(see illustration)**.
8 Undo the screws securing the unit to its bracket, then draw the sensor down to free the arm from the lever **(see illustration)**. Note the plastic collar and spring on the arm, and leave them there.

Installation

9 Make sure the actuating lever is correctly engaged with the throttle cam **(see illustration)**. Make sure the spring and plastic collar are in place on the arm, then fit the unit, locating the arm in the lever, and tighten the screws to the torque setting specified at the beginning of the Chapter **(see illustration)**. Fit the plastic and metal washers and the nut to secure the arm in the lever **(see illustration 15.7)**. Make sure everything is correctly positioned.
10 Install the throttle body (see Section 7). The sensor must now be set up correctly using the Triumph diagnostic tool.

15.9a Correct fitting of actuating lever against throttle cam (arrowed)

15.9b Correct fitting of spring and collar against the lever (arrowed)

Engine management system (fuel and ignition) 4•21

16 EVAP system (California models)

1 This system prevents the escape of fuel vapour into the atmosphere by storing it in a charcoal-filled canister located under the front of the swingarm.

2 When the engine is stopped, fuel vapour from the tank is directed into the canister where it is absorbed and stored whilst the motorcycle is standing. When the engine is started, the purge control valve next to the canister opens, thus drawing vapours which are stored in the canister into the throttle bodies to be burned during the normal combustion process.

3 The tank vent pipe also incorporates a roll-over valve which closes and prevents any fuel from escaping through it in the event of the bike falling over. The tank filler cap has a one-way valve that allows air into the tank as the volume of fuel decreases, but prevents any fuel vapour from escaping.

4 The system is not adjustable and can be properly tested only by a Triumph dealer, as the diagnostic tool is required. However the owner can check that all the hoses are in good condition and are securely connected at each end. Replace any hoses that are cracked, split or generally deteriorated with new ones.

5 You can also check the purge valve by disconnecting the wiring connector and measuring the resistance of the valve using an ohmmeter. If the result is not as specified at the beginning of the Chapter, in particular if there is infinite or no resistance, replace the valve with a new one.

17 Catalytic converter

General information

1 The catalytic converter minimises the level of exhaust pollutants released into the atmosphere. It consists of a canister containing a fine mesh impregnated with a catalyst material, over which the hot exhaust gases pass. The catalyst speeds up the oxidation of harmful carbon monoxide, unburned hydrocarbons and soot, effectively reducing the quantity of harmful products released into the atmosphere via the exhaust gases.

2 The catalytic converter is housed in the exhaust downpipe assembly.

3 It operates under closed-loop control with an oxygen (Lambda) sensor feeding back gas oxygen content information to the ECM; information on the sensor can be found in Section 14.

Precautions

4 The catalytic converter is a reliable and simple device which needs no maintenance in itself, but there are some precautions the owner should note if the converter is to function properly for its full service life.
- DO NOT use leaded or lead replacement petrol (gasoline) – the additives will coat the precious metals, reducing their converting efficiency and will eventually destroy the catalytic converter.
- Always keep the ignition and fuel systems well-maintained in accordance with the manufacturer's schedule – if the fuel/air mixture is suspected of being incorrect have it checked on an exhaust gas analyser.
- If the engine develops a misfire, do not ride the bike at all (or at least as little as possible) until the fault is cured.
- DO NOT use fuel or engine oil additives – these may contain substances harmful to the catalytic converter.
- DO NOT continue to use the bike if the engine burns oil to the extent of leaving a visible trail of blue smoke.
- Remember that the catalytic converter is FRAGILE – do not strike it with tools during servicing work.

18 Immobiliser

General information

Note: *The immobiliser control unit also controls the tyre pressure monitoring system (TPMS), if fitted. Refer to Chapter 6 for details on the TPMS.*

1 The immobiliser system will only allow the engine to be started if the signal sent from a transponder in the ignition key is recognised by the ECM. The signal from the transponder is picked up and transmitted by a receiver fitted around the top of the ignition switch to the immobiliser control unit, which in turn corresponds with the ECM. The system has its own self-diagnostic function. The immobiliser

18.6a Unscrew the bolts (arrowed)...

18.5 Handlebar switch connectors (A), control unit connector (B)

system components must be paired with the ECM and this can only be done using the Triumph diagnostic tool. The bike comes from the factory with two paired keys. A further two keys can be paired with the system.

2 An immobiliser light in the instrument cluster flashes for twenty-four hours when the immobiliser is active. When the ignition is turned on, and the key transponder is recognised by the ECM, the light goes out.

3 If the light comes on and stays on when the ignition is turned on there is a fault in the system. The Triumph diagnostic tool is required for fault code retrieval.

Immobiliser control unit

4 The immobiliser control unit is mounted behind the steering head. Remove the fuel tank for access (see Section 2).

5 Disconnect the handlebar switch and control unit wiring connectors and free them from the bracket **(see illustration)**. Disconnect the control unit wiring connector.

6 Unscrew the two bolts and displace the control unit, then draw the wiring out, noting its routing **(see illustrations)**.

7 Installation is the reverse of removal. Tighten the bolts to the torque setting specified at the beginning of the Chapter.

Immobiliser receiver

8 The receiver is an integral part of the ignition switch and is not available separately. Refer to Chapter 8 for removal and installation of the switch.

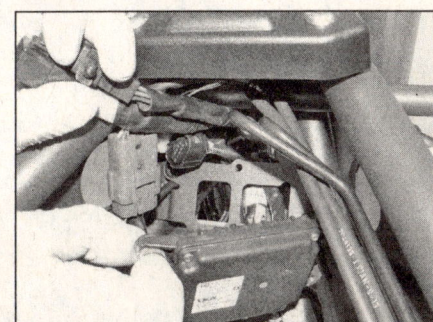

18.6b ...and remove the control unit

Chapter 5
Frame and suspension

Contents

	Section number		Section number
Footrests, brake pedal and gearchange lever	3	Rear suspension linkage	12
Fork oil change	7	Sidestand	4
Fork overhaul	8	Sidestand and starter safety circuit check	see Chapter 1
Fork removal and installation	6	Sidestand switch	see Chapter 8
Frame	2	Steering head bearing check and adjustment	see Chapter 1
General information	1	Steering head bearing overhaul	10
Handlebar switches	see Chapter 8	Steering stem	9
Handlebars and levers	5	Suspension check	see Chapter 1
Rear shock absorber	11	Swingarm	13
Rear shock absorber adjustment	14		

Degrees of difficulty

Easy, suitable for novice with little experience	**Fairly easy,** suitable for beginner with some experience	**Fairly difficult,** suitable for competent DIY mechanic	**Difficult,** suitable for experienced DIY mechanic	**Very difficult,** suitable for expert DIY or professional

Specifications

Front forks
Fork oil type	Showa SS-8 or equivalent
Fork oil capacity	
Tiger 800	553 cc
Tiger 800XC	619 cc
Fork oil level*	
Tiger 800	103 mm
Tiger 800XC	107 mm

*Oil level is measured from the top of the tube with the fork spring removed and the leg fully compressed.

Torque wrench settings
Clutch lever pivot bolt locknut	3.5 Nm
Clutch lever bracket clamp bolts	12 Nm
Fork clamp bolts – top and bottom yokes	20 Nm
Fork damper cartridge bolt	20 Nm
Fork top bolt	35 Nm
Front brake lever pivot bolt	1 Nm
Front brake lever pivot bolt locknut	6 Nm
Front brake master cylinder bracket clamp bolts	12 Nm
Gearchange lever pivot bolt	22 Nm
Handlebar clamp bolts	
Front (M10) bolts	35 Nm
Rear (M8) bolts	26 Nm
Handlebar end-weight screws	5 Nm
Rear brake pedal pivot bolt	22 Nm
Rear shock absorber	
Upper mounting bolt nut	48 Nm
Lower mounting bolt nut	80 Nm
Rear suspension linkage bolts/nuts	80 Nm
Sidestand bracket bolts	45 Nm
Sidestand pivot bolt	20 Nm
Sidestand pivot bolt nut	20 Nm
Steering head bearing adjuster nut	
Initial (pre-load) setting	40 Nm
Final setting	10 Nm
Steering head bearing adjuster locknut	40 Nm
Steering stem nut	90 Nm
Swingarm pivot bolt nut	110 Nm

5•2 Frame and suspension

3.2a Remove the E-clip (arrowed) and withdraw the pivot pin...

3.2b ...note how the return spring ends (arrowed) locate

3.3 The front rubbers are a push-fit into the holes, and are easily removed for off-road use if required

1 General information

All models have a steel trellis frame that uses the engine as a stressed member.

Front suspension is by a pair of upside-down oil-damped telescopic forks with a cartridge-type damper. The forks are not adjustable.

At the rear, an aluminium alloy twin-sided swingarm acts on a single shock absorber via a three-way linkage. The shock absorber has adjustable spring pre-load on standard models, and adjustable spring pre-load and rebound damping on XC models.

2 Frame

1 The frame should not require attention unless accident damage has occurred. In most cases, fitment of a new frame is the only satisfactory remedy for such damage. A few frame specialists have the jigs and other equipment necessary for straightening the frame to the required standard of accuracy, but even then there is no simple way of assessing to what extent the frame may have been over stressed.
2 After the machine has accumulated a lot of miles, the frame should be examined closely for signs of cracking or splitting at the welded joints. Loose engine mounting bolts can cause ovaling or fracturing of the mounts themselves. Minor damage can often be repaired by welding, depending on the extent and nature of the damage, but this is a task for an expert.
3 Remember that a frame that is out of alignment will cause handling problems. If misalignment is suspected as the result of an accident, it will be necessary to strip the machine completely so the frame can be thoroughly checked.

3 Footrests, brake pedal and gearchange lever

Footrests

1 If you are removing the rider's right-hand footrest, remove the master cylinder pushrod clevis pin retaining clip, then withdraw the pin and separate the pedal from the pushrod (see illustration 3.6) – this allows the pedal to be raised so the footrest pivot pin can be withdrawn.
2 Remove the E-clip from the bottom of the footrest pivot pin, then withdraw the pivot pin and remove the footrest (see illustration). On the rider's footrests, note the fitting of the return spring (see illustration). On the passenger footrests, note the fitting of the detent plate.
3 The footrest rubbers, and the lean angle pegs on the front footrests, can be replaced with new ones (see illustration).
4 Installation is the reverse of removal.

Brake pedal

Removal

5 Unscrew the heel guard bolts and remove the guard (see illustration).
6 Remove the master cylinder pushrod clevis pin retaining clip, then withdraw the pin and separate the pedal from the pushrod (see illustration).
7 Unscrew the pedal pivot bolt and remove the pedal and the return spring, noting how its ends locate (see illustration).

Installation

8 Installation is the reverse of removal, noting the following:
- Clean and grease the brake pedal pivot and the bush in the pedal (see illustration). If the bush is worn it can be replaced with a new one.
- Make sure the return spring ends locate correctly (see illustration 3.7).
- Tighten the pedal pivot bolt to the torque setting specified at the beginning of the Chapter.
- If necessary use a new retaining clip on the clevis pin securing the brake pedal to the master cylinder pushrod (see illustration 3.6).

3.5 Heel guard bolts (arrowed)

3.6 Remove the clip and withdraw the pin (arrowed)

3.7 Brake pedal pivot bolt (A) – note how the spring ends (B) locate

Frame and suspension 5•3

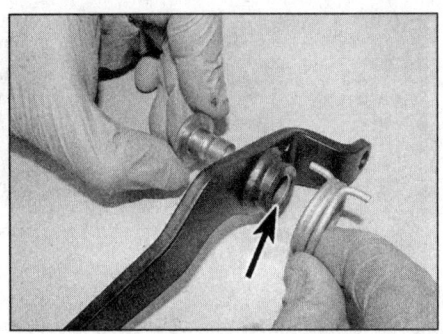

3.8 Clean and grease the pivot bolt and bush (arrowed), and assemble the bolt and spring before fitting the pedal

3.9 Slacken the linkage rod locknuts (arrowed), then unscrew the rod

3.10 Heel guard bolts (arrowed)

3.11 Gearchange lever pivot bolt (arrowed)

3.12a Note the alignment of the punch mark (arrowed)...

3.12b ...then unscrew the bolt and slide the arm off

Gearchange lever and linkage

Removal

9 Note how far the linkage rod is threaded into the gearchange lever and linkage arm by counting or measuring the exposed threads – this determines the height of the lever relative to the footrest. Slacken the locknuts on the rod **(see illustration)**. Unscrew the rod and separate it from the lever and the arm – the rod is reverse-threaded on one end and so will simultaneously unscrew from both lever and arm when turned in the one direction.

10 Unscrew the heel guard bolts and remove the guard **(see illustration)**.

11 Unscrew the gearchange lever pivot bolt and remove the lever **(see illustration)**.

12 Note the alignment of the punch mark on the gearchange shaft end with the slit in the linkage arm clamp **(see illustration)**. Unscrew the pinch bolt and slide the arm off the shaft **(see illustration)**.

Installation

13 Installation is the reverse of removal, noting the following:
- Align the slit in the linkage arm clamp with the mark on the shaft **(see illustration 3.12a)**.
- Clean and grease the brake pedal pivot and the bush in the pedal. If the bush is worn replace the pedal with a new one.
- Tighten the lever pivot bolt to the torque setting specified at the beginning of the Chapter.
- Adjust the gear lever height as required by screwing the linkage rod in or out of the lever and arm. Tighten the locknuts securely **(see illustration 3.9)**.

4 Sidestand

1 Support the motorcycle on its centrestand if fitted, or securely in an upright position using an auxiliary stand.

2 Unhook the stand springs **(see illustration)**.

3 Unscrew the pivot bolt nut **(see illustration)**. Unscrew the pivot bolt and remove the stand, noting how it locates against the switch plunger.

4 If required unscrew the sidestand bracket nuts, withdraw the bolts and remove the bracket **(see illustration)**.

5 On installation apply grease to the pivot section of the bolt and to the contact surfaces

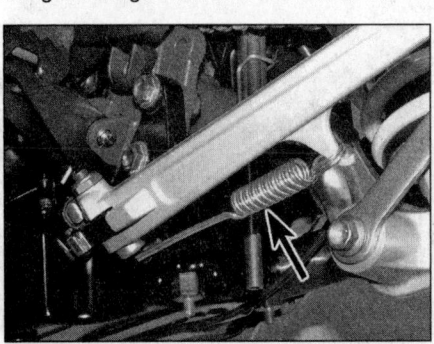

4.2 Unhook the springs (arrowed)

4.3 Unscrew the nut (A), then unscrew the bolt (B) and remove the stand

4.4 Sidestand bracket bolt nuts (arrowed)

5•4 Frame and suspension

5.4a Disconnect the wiring (arrowed)...

5.4b ...then unscrew the two bolts and displace the master cylinder

5.4c Undo the screws (arrowed) and displace the right switch housing

5.5a Undo the screws (arrowed) and displace the left switch housing

5.5b Unscrew the two bolts and displace the clutch lever bracket

7 Slide the throttle twistgrip off the right-hand bar. Remove the grip from the left-hand bar – it may be necessary to slit it open using a sharp blade as it may have been glued in place, though a suitable tool inserted between the grip and the handlebar and some aerosol lubricant directed into the grip will usually work – whatever you do take care not to scratch the handlebar. Depending on your removal method and its success, a new grip may be required on assembly.

8 Note the setting of the handlebars in the holders, and the positions of the holders on the top yoke – the positions can be adjusted to suit the rider if required.

9 Unscrew the handlebar holder clamp bolts, then remove the clamps and either remove the handlebars, or displace them and lay them on the towel (see illustration). If required remove the holders, but they are fairly tight on their dowels and so can be left in place without fear of them falling off.

Installation

10 Installation is the reverse of removal, noting the following.

- If removed, fit the holders onto the top yoke. To change their position once installed just turn each one round 180° – they pivot on the locating dowel (see illustration 5.10a).
- Make sure the handlebars are central in the holders, and align the central etched lines on the front of the handlebar with the mating surfaces of the holder, or you can rotate the bars so the ends sit slightly lower or higher as required to suit (see

of the stand and bracket. If removed tighten the bracket nuts/bolts to the torque setting specified at the beginning of the Chapter. Tighten the pivot bolt to the specified torque, then hold it and tighten the nut to the specified torque. Reconnect the sidestand springs and check the stand is held securely up when not in use – an accident is almost certain to occur if the stand extends while the machine is in motion.

6 Check the operation of the sidestand switch (see Chapter 1).

5 Handlebars and levers

Handlebars

Removal

Note: *The handlebars can be displaced from the top yoke without having to remove the lever or switch assemblies.*

1 Cover the fuel tank and surrounding trim panels with an old towel to prevent accidental damage.

2 Remove the mirrors (see Chapter 7).

3 On XC models remove the handguards (see Chapter 7).

4 On the right-hand side, disconnect the brake light switch wiring connectors and displace the front brake master cylinder (see illustrations) – there is no need to disconnect

the hydraulic hose, but keep the reservoir upright to prevent possible fluid leakage, and make sure no strain is placed on the hose. Displace the handlebar switch housing (see illustration) – there is no need to disconnect the loom wiring connector. Detach the throttle cables from the twistgrip (see Chapter 4) – there is no need to detach them from the throttle bodies.

5 On the left-hand side, displace the handlebar switch housing (see illustration) – there is no need to disconnect the loom wiring connector. Unscrew the clutch lever bracket bolts and displace it (see illustration) – there is no need to detach the clutch cable.

6 On standard models undo the handlebar end-weight screws and remove the weights from the ends of the handlebars, noting how they fit.

5.9 Handlebar holder clamp bolts (arrowed)

5.10a Position the holders as required

Frame and suspension

5.10b Align the handlebars as described

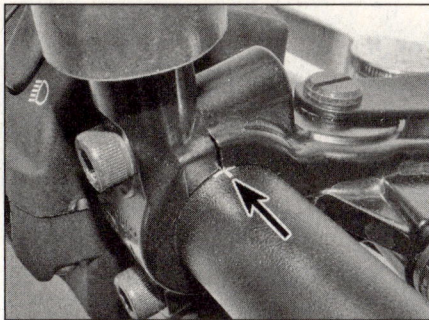

5.10c Align the clamp mating surfaces with the + mark (arrowed)

5.12a Slacken the lockring (A) and turn the adjuster (B) fully in

illustration 5.10b). Tighten the (M10) clamp bolts first, then the (M8) bolts, to the torque settings specified at the beginning of the Chapter.
- Apply some rubber adhesive to the left-hand bar before fitting the grip. Apply some grease to the right-hand bar before sliding on the throttle twistgrip. On standard models fit the end-weights.
- Fit the clutch lever bracket and front brake master cylinder clamps with the UP mark facing up (see illustrations 5.4b and 5.5b), and align the clamp/bracket mating surfaces with the + marks on the handlebar (see illustration 5.10c). Tighten the upper clamp bolt first, then the lower bolt, to the specified torque setting.
- When fitting each switch housing locate its pin in the hole in the handlebar.
- Refer to Chapter 4 for installation of the throttle cables.
- Adjust throttle and clutch cable freeplay (see Chapter 1).
- Check the operation of the switches, the throttle, the front brake and the clutch before taking the machine on the road.

Clutch lever

11 On XC models remove the handguard (see Chapter 7).
12 Slacken the clutch cable adjuster lockring and thread the adjuster fully into the bracket to provide maximum freeplay in the cable (see illustration). Unscrew the lever pivot bolt locknut (see illustration). Remove the pivot bolt, on XC models remove the handguard

6.2 Unscrew the brake hose holder bolt (arrowed)

5.12b Clutch lever pivot bolt locknut (arrowed)

bracket, then remove the lever, detaching the cable end as you do so.
13 Installation is the reverse of removal. Clean and grease the pivot bolt shaft, the bush in the lever and the contact areas between the lever and its bracket, and the clutch cable end. Check the bush for wear and replace it with a new one if necessary. Fit the pivot bolt, then fit the locknut and tighten it to the torque setting specified at the beginning of the Chapter. Adjust the clutch cable freeplay (see Chapter 1).

Front brake lever

14 On XC models remove the handguard (see Chapter 7).
15 Unscrew the lever pivot bolt locknut, then unscrew the pivot bolt, on XC models remove the handguard bracket, and remove the lever (see illustration).

6.6 Slacken the clamp bolts (arrowed) in the top yoke

5.15 Brake lever pivot bolt locknut (A), pivot bolt (B)

16 Installation is the reverse of removal. Clean and grease the pivot bolt shaft and the contact areas between the lever and its bracket. Tighten the pivot bolt to the torque setting specified at the beginning of the Chapter, then fit the locknut, hold the pivot bolt, and tighten the nut to the specified torque.

6 Fork removal and installation

Removal

Caution: Although not strictly necessary, and where applicable, before removing the forks it is recommended that the fairing side panels and/or fairing are removed (see Chapter 7). This will prevent accidental damage to the paintwork should a tool slip.

1 Remove the side panels and the cockpit trim panel (see Chapter 7).
2 Displace the front brake calipers (see Chapter 6) – there is no need to disconnect the hydraulic hoses from the calipers, but on XC models release the hose from the left-hand fork (see illustration).
3 Remove the front wheel (see Chapter 6).
4 Remove the front mudguard (see Chapter 7).
5 Work on each fork individually. Mark each fork according to which side it fits. Note the routing of the cables, wiring and hoses around the forks.

5•6 Frame and suspension

6.7 Slacken the fork top bolt if required

6.8a Note the setting of the forks in the top yoke

6.8b Slacken the clamp bolts (arrowed) in the bottom yoke...

6.8c ...then draw the fork down and out of the yokes

6 Slacken the fork clamp bolts in the top yoke **(see illustration)**.
7 If the fork oil is being changed or the forks are being overhauled, wrap some masking tape around the fork top bolt to protect the finish, then slacken the bolt now whilst it is still clamped in the bottom yoke **(see illustration)**.
8 Measure the protrusion of the tops of the fork tubes from the top yoke **(see illustration)**. Slacken the fork clamp bolts in the bottom yoke **(see illustrations)**. Remove the fork by twisting it and pulling it downwards **(see illustration)**.

 If the fork legs are seized in the yokes, spray the area with penetrating oil and allow time for it to soak in before trying again.

Installation

9 Remove all traces of corrosion from the fork tubes and the yokes. Make sure you fit the fork to its correct side as noted on removal.
10 Slide the fork up through the bottom yoke and up into the top yoke, making sure the wiring, cables and hoses are the correct side of the fork as noted on removal **(see illustration 6.8c)**. Set the fork in the top yoke so the joint between the fork top bolt and the top of the fork tube is 4 mm above the top surface of the top yoke **(see illustration 6.8a)**. Note that this is the standard setting specified by Triumph – if the setting you measured on removal is different because you have knowingly altered it, and you are aware of the implications this has on the geometry and handling of the bike, then set the forks as you prefer. With the fork positioned as required tighten the fork clamp bolts in the bottom yoke to the torque setting specified at the beginning of the Chapter **(see illustration 6.8b)**.
11 If the fork leg has been dismantled or if the fork oil has been changed, tighten the fork top bolt to the specified torque setting **(see illustration 6.7)**.
12 Tighten the fork clamp bolts in the top yoke to the specified torque setting **(see illustrations 6.6)**.
13 Install the front mudguard (see Chapter 7), front wheel and brake calipers (see Chapter 6). On XC models secure the brake hose to the left-hand fork **(see illustration 6.2)**.
14 Install the body panels (see Chapter 7).
15 Check the operation of the front forks and brakes before taking the machine out on the road.

7 Fork oil change

1 Over time the fork oil will deteriorate and its damping and lubrication qualities will be impaired. Triumph recommends changing the fork oil every four years or every 24,000 miles (40,000 km). Always change the oil in both forks, but work on one fork at a time.
2 Remove the fork – make sure the top bolt is loosened while the leg is still clamped in the bottom yoke (see Section 6).
3 Support the fork upright and unscrew the top bolt from the top of the outer tube **(see illustration)**. Slide the outer tube down over the inner tube.
4 Counter-hold the locknut and loosen the top bolt, then thread the top bolt assembly off the damper rod **(see illustration)**. Thread the locknut up to the top of the damping rod, but not off it – this makes compressing the spring easier.
5 Push down on the spacer to compress the spring and remove the slotted washer from under the locknut **(see illustration)**. Slowly release the pressure on the spacer and allow the spring to relax.
6 Remove the spacer **(see illustration 7.13b)** – note the collar on the bottom of the spacer, where fitted **(see illustration 7.13a)**. Withdraw the spring from the tube **(see illustration 7.12)**.

7.3 Unscrew the top bolt

7.4 Hold the locknut and thread the top bolt off

7.5 Push the spacer down and remove the washer from under the locknut

Frame and suspension 5•7

7.7 Drain and pump the oil from the fork

7.9 Pour in the correct type and quantity of oil and pump the damper rod to circulate it

7.10 Measure the oil level and adjust if necessary

7.12 Fit the spring, on XC models with the tapered end at the top

7.13a Fit the collar if removed...

7.13b ...then fit the spacer

7 Invert the fork leg over a suitable container and pump the fork and damper rod to expel as much oil as possible **(see illustration)**.

8 Support the leg and allow it to drain for several minutes, pumping it again. Wipe any excess oil off the spring and spacer. If the fork oil contains metal particles inspect the fork components for signs of wear (see Section 8).

9 Slowly pour in the correct quantity and type of fork oil as specified at the beginning of this Chapter **(see illustration)**. Draw the damper rod out of the fork using long-nosed pliers and pump the rod several times to circulate the oil and expel air from the damper cartridge. Secure the fork leg upright and allow it to stand for several minutes to allow all the air to escape. Now pump the rod several times again – once all the air is expelled you should feel stiff resistance when pumping the rod. Take great care to ensure that all air is expelled from the damper cartridge at this stage.

10 Fully compress the fork and damper rod and measure the oil level from the top of the tube **(see illustration)**. Add or subtract oil until it is at the level specified at the beginning of this Chapter for your model.

11 Draw the damper rod out.

12 Fit the spring into the fork – on standard models the spring is uniformly shaped and can fit either way up, on XC models fit the spring with the tapered end at the top **(see illustration)**.

13 Where fitted make sure the collar is on the bottom end of the spacer **(see illustration)**. Fit the spacer into the fork **(see illustration)**.

14 Keeping the damper rod fully extended, press down on the spacer to compress the spring, then insert the slotted washer under the locknut **(see illustration 7.5)**. Now thread the locknut back down so there is 10.5 mm of exposed thread above it on standard models and 12 mm of thread on XC models **(see illustration)**.

15 Make sure the top bolt O-ring is in good condition then smear some fork oil onto it. Fit the top bolt and thread it all the way down to the locknut **(see illustration)** – do not thread the locknut up to the top bolt. Counter-hold the locknut and tighten the top bolt against it **(see illustration 7.4)**.

17 Pull the outer tube all the way out of the inner tube and carefully screw the top bolt into the tube making sure it is not cross-threaded **(see illustration 7.3)**. Tighten the top bolt to the specified torque when the fork leg has been installed and is securely clamped in the bottom yoke.

18 Install the fork (see Section 6).

| 8 | Fork overhaul | |

Disassembly

1 Remove the fork – make sure that the top bolt is loosened while the leg is still clamped in the bottom yoke (see Section 6). Always dismantle the fork legs separately to avoid interchanging parts. Store all components in

7.14 Thread the locknut down and set it to the correct position

7.15 Check and lubricate the O-ring (arrowed), then thread the top bolt onto the rod

5•8 Frame and suspension

8.2 Slacken the damper rod bolt

8.4 Prise out the dust seal using a flat-bladed screwdriver...

8.5 ...then remove the retaining clip

8.6a Repeatedly draw the tubes apart...

8.6b ...until the bush and seal are displaced

separate, clearly marked containers. When working on the right-hand fork first remove the axle clamp bolts.

2 If you want to remove the damper cartridge from the fork (this is not necessary if for example you are just fitting new seals) lay the fork flat on the bench with the caliper mounting lugs to the left, slacken the damper cartridge bolt in the bottom of the fork, then lightly re-tighten it to prevent oil coming out **(see illustration)**. If the bolt does not loosen, turn the leg upside down and compress the fork so that the spring exerts maximum pressure on the damper cartridge assembly to prevent it turning, then try to loosen the bolt. If you still have no luck, use an air wrench.

3 Refer to Section 7, Steps 3 to 8, and drain the fork oil.

4 Carefully prise out the dust seal from the bottom of the outer tube **(see illustration)**.

5 Carefully prise out the oil seal retaining ring, taking care not to scratch the surface of the inner tube **(see illustration)**. Triumph specifies to use a new retaining ring on reassembly – they are not expensive.

6 To separate the inner and outer tubes it is necessary to displace the bottom bush and oil seal from the bottom of the outer tube. The top bush on the inner tube will not pass through the bottom bush, and this can be used to good effect. Grasp the inner tube in one hand and the outer tube in the other and compress them slightly, then pull them apart so that the top bush strikes the bottom bush **(see illustration)**. Repeat this operation until the bottom bush and seal are tapped out **(see illustration)**.

7 To remove the top bush carefully lever its ends apart using a screwdriver and slide it off the tube **(see illustration)**. Slide the bottom bush, the oil seal washer, the oil seal, the retaining ring and the dust seal off the inner tube, noting which way up they fit **(see illustration 8.16b)**. A new oil seal and dust seal must be fitted. New bushes should also be fitted as they are not expensive, but they can be reused if there are no signs of wear – see Step 11.

8 If required remove the previously loosened damper cartridge bolt and its sealing washer from the bottom of the inner tube **(see illustration 8.2)**. A new sealing washer must be fitted on reassembly. Withdraw the damper cartridge from the tube **(see illustration 8.15b)**. Remove the damper cartridge seat from the bottom of the cartridge, or if not there tip it out of the tube **(see illustration 8.15a)**.

Inspection

9 Clean all parts in a suitable solvent and blow them dry with compressed air, if available.

10 Check the outer surface of the fork inner tube for score marks, scratches, pitting and flaking of the finish, and excessive or abnormal wear. Look for creases and dents. Check the tube for runout using V-blocks and a dial gauge. If the condition of either inner tube is suspect have it checked by a Triumph dealer or suspension specialist. Triumph provides no specifications for runout.

11 Inspect the inside surface of the outer tube and the working surface of each bush for score marks, scratches and signs of excessive wear (in which case the grey Teflon outer surface will have worn away to reveal the copper inner surface) **(see illustration)**. Replace the bushes with new ones if worn, though as they are not expensive it is worth fitting new ones anyway as part of the overhaul.

12 Check the fork oil seal seat for nicks, gouges and scratches. If damage is evident, leaks will occur. Also check the oil seal washer for damage or distortion and replace it with a new one if necessary.

13 Check the spring for cracks and other damage. If the spring is defective or has sagged, fit new springs in both forks. Never fit only one new spring.

14 Check the damper cartridge for damage and wear. Hold the cartridge and gently pump the rod in and out. If the rod does not move smoothly the damper must be replaced with a new one.

8.7 Remove the top bush, then slide all other components off

8.11 Check the working surface (arrowed) of each bush

Frame and suspension 5•9

8.15a Fit the seat onto the bottom of the cartridge

8.15b Insert the cartridge...

8.15c ...then use a small screwdriver to centre it...

8.15d ...into its recess

8.15e Use a new sealing washer and threadlock on the bolt

8.16a Wrap some tape over the bottom edge of the recess

Reassembly

15 If removed fit the damper cartridge seat onto the bottom of the cartridge **(see illustration)**. Lay the inner tube flat on the bench with the caliper mounting lugs to the right. Insert the damper cartridge into the inner tube until it contacts the bottom, then use a screwdriver inserted in the bolt hole to centre it and simultaneously push down on the top so the seat drops into its recess **(see illustrations)**. Clean the threads of the damper cartridge bolt. Fit a new sealing washer onto the bolt and apply a few drops of a suitable non-permanent thread locking compound to the threads, then fit the bolt into the bottom of the inner tube, thread it into the bottom of the damper cartridge and tighten it to the torque setting specified at the beginning of the Chapter **(see illustration)**. If the damper cartridge rotates inside the tube, fit the slotted washer under the damper rod locknut and use it to pull up on the rod which should help the bolt to tighten, or wait until the fork is fully reassembled and tighten it then (the pressure of the spring on the cartridge should prevent it from turning, especially if you compress the fork).

16 Wrap a layer of insulating tape over the bottom edge of the recess for the top bush in the inner tube to protect the seal lips **(see illustration)**. Smear some oil over the tape, and also over the oil seal lips. Slide the new dust seal, retaining ring, new oil seal (with its marked side facing the retaining ring and dust seal), and oil seal washer onto the inner tube, making sure they are the correct way round **(see illustration)**. Remove the tape. Lubricate the inner surface of the bottom bush and slide it on. Fit the top bush into its recess **(see illustration)**. Apply a smear of the specified clean fork oil to the bushes.

17 Slide the inner tube fully into the outer tube **(see illustration)**. Support the fork upside down, and have an assistant hold the inner tube and the components on it up. Slide the bottom bush into the bottom of the outer tube, then squeeze the ends together using two suitable plastic or wooden tools to close the gap to allow the bush the drop in (if you are lucky), or at least to start to go in.

18 To get the bush fully in slide the oil seal washer onto it. Using the narrow end of the special service tool (part No. T3880003 for standard models and T3880157 for XC models), or a suitable drift, carefully drive the bottom bush fully into its recess until the bush and washer seat – the washer prevents damaging the edges of the bush **(see illustration 8.20b)**. If using a drift, wrap tape around it to prevent scratching the inner tube. Make sure the bush enters the recess squarely. It is best to make sure that the inner tube is

8.16b Fit all components as shown...

8.16c ...then fit the top bush

8.17 Slide the inner tube into the outer tube

5•10 Frame and suspension

8.20a Use a section of the old seal as an interface…

8.20b …to prevent damage to the new seal when driving it in

8.20c Remove the piece of old seal

8.21 Fit the retaining ring

8.22 You can slide the inner tube down and use the bottom section to press the dust seal in

9.1 Unscrew the bolt

withdrawn as much as possible from the outer tube so that any accidental scratching is confined to the area that does not affect the oil seal. Lift the washer to check the bush is seated fully and squarely in its recess in the outer tube, then wipe the recess clean.

19 Slide the oil seal washer back onto its seat.
20 Slide the oil seal down and into the outer tube. Push the seal into place, driving it in as in Step 18 if you have the tool, until the retaining clip groove is visible. If you don't have the tool cut the old seal in half and use it as an interface between the drift and the new seal, and then drive the seal in **(see illustrations)**. When the old seal is about flush with the rim of the fork tube the new seal is seated – remove the piece of old seal and check the retaining clip groove is visible **(see illustration)**.
21 Fit the retaining ring, making sure it is correctly located in its groove **(see illustration)**.

22 Press the dust seal into the top of the outer tube **(see illustration)**.
23 Pour in the correct quantity and type of fork oil, and finish assembling the fork (see Section 7, Steps 9 to 17).
24 Install the fork (see Section 6).

9 Steering stem

Removal

1 Remove the side panels and the cockpit trim panel (see Chapter 7). It is advisable to also remove the fuel tank to avoid the possibility of damage should a tool slip (see Chapter 4). Unscrew the brake hose guide bolt **(see illustration)**.
2 Displace the handlebars from the top yoke

and rest them behind the ignition switch on some rag (see Section 5).
3 Remove the front forks (see Section 6).
4 Wrap some masking tap around the steering stem nut to protect its finish. Unscrew the nut, and where fitted remove the washer **(see illustration)**. **Note:** *The washer is fitted on models from VIN 515213-on, and Triumph specifies that a new washer should be used each time it is removed. On models up to VIN 515212 Triumph specify to use a new nut each time it is removed, but will supply you with the new nut/washer arrangement, so that in the future you only have to replace the washer, which is much cheaper.*
5 Ease the top yoke up off the forks **(see illustration)**.
6 Using either the Triumph service tool (Part No. T3880023) or a C-spanner, unscrew the locknut, then lift off the tabbed washer **(see illustration)**.

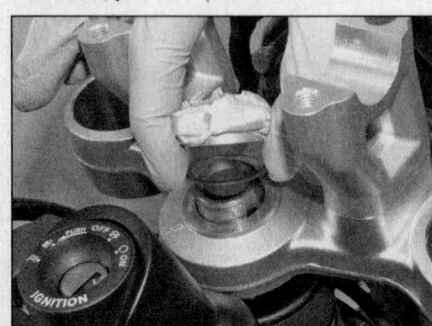

9.4 Unscrew the steering stem nut and remove the washer, where fitted

9.5 Remove the top yoke

9.6 Unscrew the locknut and remove the washer, noting how it locates

Frame and suspension 5•11

9.7a Unscrew the adjuster nut...

9.7b ...then lower the bottom yoke and draw the stem out of the head

7 Support the bottom yoke, then unscrew the bearing adjuster nut and gently lower the bottom yoke and steering stem out of the frame **(see illustrations)**. The bearing cover should come away with the nut, but if not remove it from the top of the steering head.

8 Remove the dust seal, the inner race and upper bearing from the top of the steering head **(see illustration)**. Remove the lower bearing from the bottom of the steering stem **(see illustration)**.

9 Remove all traces of old grease from the bearings and races and check them for wear or damage as described in Section 10. **Note:** *Do not attempt to remove the outer races from the steering head or the lower bearing inner race from the steering stem unless they are to be replaced with new ones.*

Installation

10 Smear a liberal quantity of lithium-based grease (see Chapter 1 Specifications) onto the bearing outer races in the steering head. Work grease well into the upper and lower bearings.

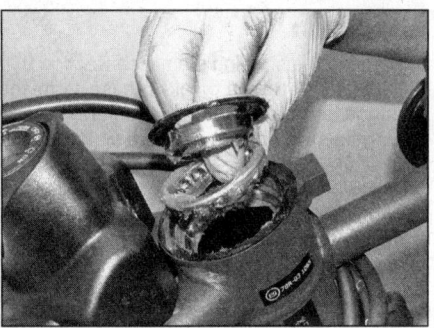

9.8a Remove the seal, inner race and bearing from the top of the head...

Fit the lower bearing onto the steering stem **(see illustration 9.8b)**. Fit the upper bearing and its inner race and the dust seal into the top of the steering head **(see illustration 9.8a)**.

11 If separated fit the bearing cover onto the bottom of the adjuster nut. Carefully lift the steering stem/bottom yoke up through the steering head, holding the upper bearing

9.8b ...and the lower bearing from the base of the stem

assembly so you don't accidentally knock it out, and support it **(see illustration)**. Thread the nut onto the steering stem and tighten it finger-tight **(see illustration)**.

12 Triumph specify a torque setting for the adjuster nut, which can only be applied using their service tool (Part No. T3880023), or a suitable peg spanner, either bought

9.11a Slide the stem up into the head and through the upper bearing assembly

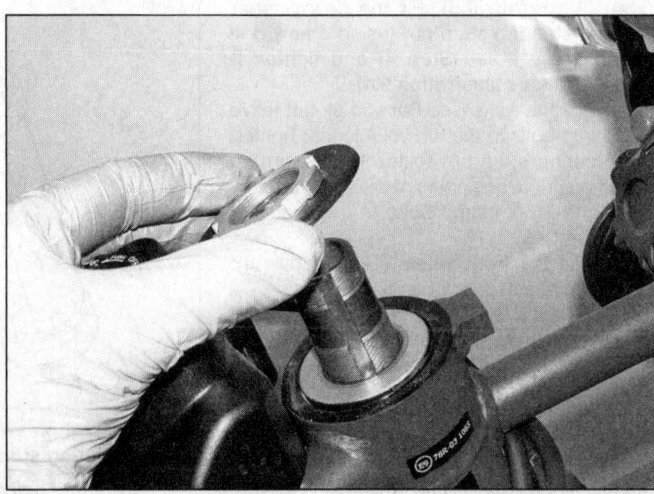

9.11b ...and thread the adjuster nut onto the stem

5•12 Frame and suspension

10.3 Check the inner and outer races for wear and damage

10.5a Drive the outer races from the steering head using a drift...

10.5b ...located in the cut-outs provided (arrow – there are two, opposite each other)

commercially or fabricated by cutting castellations into an old 36 mm socket to fit the adjuster nut slots – note that two castellations opposite each other should be sufficient. With the tool fitted to a torque wrench, apply a torque of 40 Nm to the adjuster nut – this will preload the bearings. Now slacken the nut and tighten it to the final torque setting of 10 Nm.

13 If a tool isn't available tighten the adjuster nut using a C-spanner until all freeplay is removed, then tighten it a little more **(see illustration 9.7a)**. This pre-loads the bearings. Now slacken the nut, then tighten it again, setting it so that all freeplay is just removed yet the steering is able to move smoothly (though it may feel a bit tight, but this is normal as the weight of the forks and wheel is not influencing the feel) from lock-to-lock. To do this, tighten the nut only a little at a time, and after each tightening repeat the checks for freeplay and freedom of movement until the bearings are correctly set. The object is to set the adjuster nut so that the bearings are under a very light loading, just enough to remove any freeplay.

14 Fit the tabbed washer, locating the tab in the slot **(see illustration 9.6)**. Fit the locknut and tighten it to 40 Nm if the tool is available, or using a C-spanner if not.

15 Fit the top yoke onto the steering stem **(see illustration 9.5)**. Fit the new washer and the steering stem nut (using a new one if necessary – see Step 4) and tighten it finger-tight **(see illustration 9.4)**.

16 Install the forks (see Section 6), but leave the clamp bolts in the top yoke loose. Tighten the steering stem nut to the torque setting specified at the beginning of the Chapter. Now tighten the fork clamp bolts to the specified torque setting.

17 Install the front wheel (see Chapter 6). Install the handlebars (see Section 5).

18 Carry out a final check of the steering head bearing freeplay as described in Chapter 1, and if necessary re-adjust – this is especially important if the correct torque settings were not applied to the adjuster nut and locknut as the extra weight and inertia of the forks, front wheel and handlebars will make a difference to the feel of the freeplay and movement checks.

19 Install the fuel tank and body panels as required.

10 Steering head bearing overhaul

Inspection

1 Remove the steering stem (see Section 9).
2 Remove all traces of old grease from the bearings and races and check them for wear or damage, referring to *Tools and Workshop Tips* in the Reference Section for information on bearing checks.
3 The bearing races should be polished and free from indentations **(see illustration)**. Inspect the bearing rollers for signs of wear, damage or discoloration, and examine their cage for signs of cracks or splits. Spin the bearings by hand. They should spin freely and smoothly. If there are any signs of wear on any of the above components both upper and lower bearing assemblies should be replaced with a new set, complete with new outer races. Only remove the outer races in the steering head and the lower bearing inner race from the steering stem if new ones are being fitted – do not re-use them once they have been removed.

Renewal

4 Remove the steering stem (see Section 9).
5 The bearing outer races are an interference fit in the steering head and can be tapped from position with a suitable drift located in the two cut-outs in the race seat **(see illustrations)**. Move the drift from one cut-out to the other so that the race is driven out squarely.
6 Alternatively, the races can be removed using a slide-hammer type bearing extractor – these can often be hired from tool shops.
7 Draw the new outer races into the steering head using a drawbolt arrangement **(see illustration)**, or by using a large diameter tubular drift. Ensure that the drawbolt washer or drift (as applicable) bears only on the outer edge of the race and does not contact the working surface.

> **HAYNES HINT** *Installation of new bearing outer races is made much easier if they are left overnight in the freezer. This causes them to contract slightly making them a looser fit. Alternatively, use a freeze spray.*

8 Only remove the lower bearing inner race from the steering stem if a new one is being fitted **(see illustration)**. To remove the race,

10.7 Drawbolt arrangement for fitting steering stem bearing races

1 Long bolt or threaded bar
2 Thick washer
3 Guide for lower race

10.8a Lower bearing inner race (A) and seal (B)

Frame and suspension 5•13

10.8b If necessary remove the inner race using a puller

10.9 Drive the new bearing on using a suitable driver or a length of pipe

11.1a Sidestand switch wiring connector (arrowed)

thread a suitable nut onto the top of the stem to protect the threads, then place the stem on its side and tap under the race using a cold chisel to dislodge it, then use two screwdrivers placed on opposite sides of the race to work it fully free, using blocks of wood to improve leverage and protect the yoke. If the race is firmly in place it will be necessary to use a puller **(see illustration)**, or a press, or to carefully cut it off. Take the steering stem to a Triumph dealer if required. Remove the dust seal.

9 Fit a new dust seal onto the steering stem **(see illustration 10.8a)**. Fit the new race onto the stem and drive it into place using a length of tubing with an internal diameter slightly larger than the steering stem but not so large it contacts the bearing surface **(see illustration)**.

10 Install the steering stem (see Section 9).

11 Rear shock absorber

Note: *Locknuts are used on all shock absorber and suspension linkage bolts. Triumph specifies that the nuts should only be used once, so new ones are needed for installation. If new nuts are not available apply some threadlock to the threads of the old nuts.*

Removal

1 Support the motorcycle on level ground, on its centrestand if fitted, or securely in an upright position using an auxiliary stand or stands under the frame, passenger footrest brackets or engine (do not use a rear paddock stand), so the rear wheel is off the ground – the accompanying photograph shows axle stands positioned under the frame, but to do this you need to disconnect the sidestand switch wiring connector **(see illustration)**, then remove the complete sidestand and switch assembly, secured by two bolts **(see illustration 4.4)**, so the stands are equally set **(see illustration)**. If you place a support under the engine it needs to be as far back as possible so the centre of gravity is ahead of it, and you should tie the front end down. Place a support (such as a block of wood) under the rear wheel so that it does not drop when the shock absorber upper bolt is removed, but also making sure that the weight of the machine is off the rear suspension so that the shock is not compressed. Note from which side the bolts are fitted before removing them.

2 On XC models remove the fuel tank trim panels (see Chapter 7). Remove the front sprocket cover (see Chapter 6). Release the clamps holding the remote reservoir **(see illustrations)** – if you find that the clamp screws are pointing up and difficult to release, reposition them on installation. When the reservoir is free remove the clamps from it.

11.1b Bike supported under the frame using axle stands

11.2a Slacken the clamp screws...

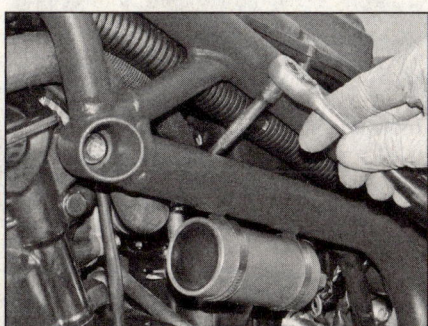

11.2b ...accessing them as shown from the top using a universal drive bit

5•14 Frame and suspension

11.3 Detach the drop links from the swingarm and pivot them down

11.4 Detach the drag link from the shock absorber and pivot it down

11.5a Unscrew the bolt (arrowed)...

11.5b ...then lift and support the rear wheel

11.6a Unscrew the nut (arrowed), withdraw the bolt...

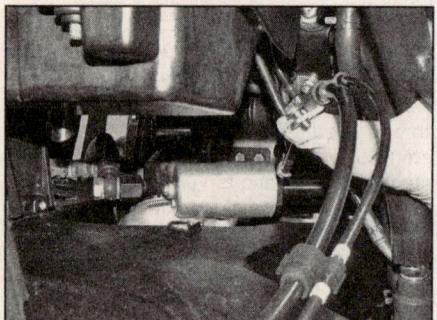

11.6b ...manoeuvre the shock absorber under the brake hose...

3 Unscrew the nut and withdraw the bolt securing the drop links to the swingarm, then pivot the links down (see illustration).

4 Unscrew the nut and withdraw the bolt securing the bottom of the shock absorber to the drag link (see illustration). Pivot the drag link down.

5 Release the brake hose from the front of the swingarm (see illustration). Lift the rear wheel about six inches and support it with a block of wood.

6 Unscrew the nut on the shock absorber upper mounting bolt, then withdraw the bolt, rotate the shock absorber so the adjuster mechanism is at the front and under the brake hose, and manoeuvre the shock down and out, on XC models bringing the reservoir with it and noting its routing (see illustrations).

7 Discard the nuts – new ones should be used.

Inspection

8 Inspect the shock absorber for obvious physical damage and the coil spring for looseness, cracks or signs of fatigue. Inspect the damper rod for signs of bending, pitting and oil leakage.

9 Check the bush in the upper mounting, and check the mountings themselves for cracks (see illustration). Refer to Section 12 and check the bearings and seals in the drag link and swingarm.

10 Replacement parts for the shock absorber itself are not available from Triumph. If the shock is damaged or leaking, consider having it rebuilt by a suspension specialist before buying a new shock.

Installation

11 Installation is the reverse of removal, noting the following:
- Apply lithium-based grease to NLGI 2 specification to the linkage bearings, sleeves and seals.
- Insert all bolts from the left-hand side. Use

11.6c ...and lower it out

11.9 Upper mounting bush (arrowed)

Frame and suspension 5•15

12.2 Detach the drop link plates from the drag link

12.3a Detach the drag link from the shock absorber...

12.3b ...and the frame

new nuts, and tighten them all finger-tight only at first (see **Note**).
- Tighten the nuts on the drop and drag link bolts to the torque setting specified at the beginning of the chapter. Take the bike off the stand(s) so the weight is through the suspension, then tighten the upper mounting bolt nut to the specified torque setting.
- Check the operation of the rear suspension and adjust the shock absorber settings as required before taking the machine on the road.

12 Rear suspension linkage

Note: *Locknuts are used on all shock absorber and suspension linkage bolts. Triumph specifies that the nuts should only be used once, so new ones are needed for installation. If new nuts are not available apply some threadlock to the threads of the old nuts.*

Removal

1 Support the motorcycle as described in Section 11, Step 1.
2 Unscrew the nut and withdraw the bolt securing the drop links to the swingarm **(see illustration 11.3)**. Unscrew the nut and withdraw the bolt securing the drop links to the drag link and remove the drop links **(see illustration)**.
3 Unscrew the nuts and withdraw the bolts securing the drag link to the shock absorber and frame and remove the link, noting which way round it fits **(see illustrations)**.

Inspection

4 Withdraw the bearing sleeves from the drag link and the drop link mount on the swingarm **(see illustrations)**. Thoroughly clean all components, removing all traces of dirt, corrosion and grease. If the bearings are dirty or rusty, indicating the seals have failed, lever the seals out, and after checking and if necessary fitting new bearings (see Steps 6 and 7), replace them with new ones **(see illustration)**.
5 Inspect all components closely, looking for obvious signs of wear such as heavy scoring, or for damage such as cracks or distortion **(see illustration)**. Slip each sleeve back into its bearing and check that there is not an excessive amount of freeplay between the two components. Replace any components as required with new ones.

12.4a Withdraw the sleeves from the bearings in the drag link...

6 To check the needle bearings, and for details of removal and installation methods, refer to 'Tools and workshop tips' (Section 5) in the Reference section. The needle bearings can be drawn or driven out of their bores – note that once a needle bearing has been removed it cannot be re-used. New bearings should be obtained before work commences.
7 Fit the new bearings with the marked side facing out. The bearings must be pressed or drawn into their bores and not driven into position, as doing so will ruin the cage. In the absence of a press, a suitable drawbolt tool can be made up as described in the Reference section. The bearings must sit centrally in the bores.
8 Lubricate the bearings with the recommended grease (see Chapter 1 Specifications). Press the new seals in using your fingers, or tap them in using a suitable socket **(see illustration)**. Grease the seal

12.4b ...and the swingarm

12.4c If required lever the seals out

12.5 Check all bearings and components as described

12.8 Press the new seals in using your fingers

5•16 Frame and suspension

13.5a Main chainguard screws (arrowed)

13.5b Lower chainguard screws (arrowed)

lips and the sleeves, then fit the sleeves **(see illustrations 12.4a and b)**.

Installation

9 Installation is the reverse of removal, noting the following:
- If not already done clean off old grease and apply new grease to all sleeves, bearings and seals, as described above. Make sure the sleeves are correctly fitted.
- Insert all bolts from the left-hand side. Use new nuts (see **Note**).

13.6 Unscrew the bolts (arrowed) to free the hose

- Install the bolts and new nuts finger-tight only until all components are in position, then tighten the nuts to the torque setting specified at the beginning of the Chapter.
- Check the operation of the rear suspension before taking the machine on the road.

13 Swingarm

Removal

Note: *A locknut is used on the suspension drop link bolt and the swingarm pivot bolt. Triumph specifies that the nuts should only be used once, so new ones are needed for installation. If new nuts are not available apply some threadlock to the threads of the old nuts.*

1 Support the motorcycle as described in Section 11, Step 1.
2 Remove the exhaust silencer (see Chapter 4).
3 Remove the rear wheel (see Chapter 6). Place a support under the rear of the swingarm.

4 Unscrew the nut and withdraw the bolt securing the drop links to the swingarm, then pivot the links down **(see illustration 11.3)**.
5 Remove the front sprocket cover (see Chapter 6). Remove the main chainguard, and if required the lower chainguard **(see illustrations)**.
6 Release the brake hose guides from the swingarm **(see illustration)**. Support or tie the brake caliper clear, making sure no strain is placed on the hose.
7 Before removing the swingarm it is advisable to re-check for play in the bearings (see Chapter 1). Any problems that may have been overlooked with the other suspension components attached to the frame are highlighted with them loose.
8 Unscrew the nut on the left-hand end of the swingarm pivot bolt and remove the washer – counter-hold the bolt head if required **(see illustration)**. Push the end of the pivot bolt in.
9 Support the swingarm, then withdraw the pivot from the right-hand side, using a drift to knock it through if required, and remove the swingarm **(see illustration)**. Make sure the drive chain does not drag on the floor.
10 Refer to Section 1 in Chapter 1 and

13.8 Unscrew the nut and remove the washer

13.9 Withdraw the bolt and remove the swingarm

Frame and suspension 5•17

13.12a Withdraw the sleeves...

13.12b ...and lever out the covers

remove the chain slider from the swingarm if necessary, noting how it fits. If the chain slider is badly worn or damaged, replace it with a new one.

11 Inspect all components for wear or damage as described below.

Inspection

12 Withdraw the sleeve from each bearing and remove the bearing cover from each side **(see illustrations)**. Thoroughly clean the swingarm, removing all traces of dirt, corrosion and grease.

13 Inspect all components closely, looking for obvious signs of wear such as heavy scoring, and cracks or distortion due to accident damage. Check the condition of the grease seals, and check the bearings for roughness, looseness and any other damage, referring to *Tools and Workshop Tips* (Section 5) in the Reference section. Slip each sleeve back into its bearing and check that there is not an excessive amount of freeplay between the two components. Any damaged or worn component must be replaced with a new one.

14 Check the swingarm pivot bolt is straight by rolling it on a flat surface such as a piece of plate glass (first wipe off all old grease and remove any corrosion using wire wool). If the equipment is available, place the pivot in V-blocks and measure the runout using a dial gauge. If the pivot is bent, replace it with a new one.

Seal and bearing renewal

15 Lever out the grease seal from each side **(see illustration)**. New seals must be used.

16 To check the needle bearings, and for details of removal and installation methods, refer to *'Tools and workshop tips' (Section 5)* in the Reference section at the end of the book. The needle bearings can be drawn or driven out of their bores – note that once a needle bearing has been removed it cannot be re-used. New bearings should be obtained before work commences.

17 Fit the new bearings with the marked side facing out. The bearings must be pressed or drawn into their bores and not driven into position, as doing so will ruin the cage. In the absence of a press, a suitable drawbolt tool can be made up as described in the Reference section. The bearings must sit centrally in the bores.

18 Lubricate the bearings with lithium-based multi-purpose grease to NLGI 2. Press the new seals in using your fingers, or tap them in using a suitable socket **(see illustration)**. Grease the seal lips and the sleeves, then fit the sleeves.

Installation

19 If not already done, remove the sleeve from each bearing and remove the bearing cover from each side, and lubricate the bearings, sleeves and seal lips with grease **(see illustrations 13.12a and b)**. Refit the covers and sleeves.

20 If removed, refer to Section 1 in Chapter 1 and fit the chain slider.

21 Offer up the swingarm and have an assistant hold it in place, making sure drive chain is looped over the chain slider at the front. Grease the pivot bolt and insert it from the right-hand side **(see illustration 13.9)**.

22 Fit the washer and a new nut onto the left-hand end of the pivot bolt **(see illustration 13.8)**. Counter-hold the bolt on the right-hand end and tighten the nut to the torque setting specified at the beginning of the Chapter.

23 Install all remaining components and assemblies in a reverse of the removal procedure, referring to the relevant Sections and Chapters where necessary. Fit the drop links using a new nut and tighten it to the specified torque **(see illustration 11.3)**. Make sure the front mount on the main chainguard locates correctly between the chain slider and the lug **(see illustration)**.

24 Check and adjust the drive chain slack (see Chapter 1). Check the operation of the rear suspension and brake before taking the machine on the road.

13.15 If required lever the seals out

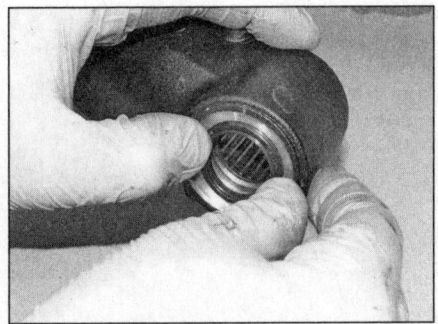

13.18 Press the new seals in using your fingers

13.23 Seat the front mount between the slider and the lug

5•18 Frame and suspension

14.3 Spring pre-load adjuster (arrowed)

14.5 Rebound damping adjuster (arrowed)

14 Rear shock absorber adjustment

Note: *Refer to the owners handbook supplied with the machine for recommended front and rear suspension settings to suit loading.*

Standard models

1 Spring pre-load is adjusted using a screwdriver in the slot in the adjuster on the back of the shock absorber on the right-hand side **(see illustration 14.3)**. The amount of pre-load is indicated by the number of clicks out from the fully screwed-in position. The standard position for solo riding is 30 clicks turns out. For all other loads Triumph specifies the standard setting is zero clicks out (i.e. fully screwed in), but you may wish to compromise between the two settings according to the load being carried.

2 Turn the adjuster clockwise to increase pre-load and anti-clockwise to decrease it. To establish the current setting, turn the adjuster in (clockwise) until it seats (do not force it tight), counting the number of clicks, then reset it as required by turning it out.

XC models

Spring pre-load

3 Pre-load is adjusted using a screwdriver in the slot in the adjuster on the back of the shock absorber on the right-hand side **(see illustration)**. The amount of pre-load is indicated by the number of clicks out from the fully screwed-in position. The standard position for solo riding is 24 clicks out. For all other loads Triumph specify the standard setting is zero clicks out (i.e. fully screwed in), but you may wish to compromise between the two settings according to the load being carried.

4 Turn the adjuster clockwise to increase pre-load and anti-clockwise to decrease it. To establish the current setting, turn the adjuster in (clockwise) until it seats (do not force it tight), counting the number of clicks, then reset it as required by turning it out.

Rebound damping

5 Damping is adjusted using a screwdriver in adjuster screw slot in the bottom of the shock **(see illustration)**. The amount of damping is indicated by the number of turns out from the fully screwed-in position. The standard position for solo riding is 1.5 turns out, for solo plus luggage 1 turn out, for two-up with or without luggage and for off-road riding 0.5 turn out.

6 Turn the adjuster clockwise to increase damping and anti-clockwise to decrease it. To establish the current setting, turn the adjuster in (clockwise) until it seats (do not force it tight), counting the number of turns, then reset it as required by turning it out.

Chapter 6
Brakes, wheels and final drive

Contents

	Section number		Section number
Anti-lock brake system – ABS	11	Rear brake caliper	6
Brake bleeding and fluid change	10	Rear brake disc	7
Brake fluid level check	see *Pre-ride checks*	Rear brake master cylinder	8
Brake hoses and fittings	9	Rear sprocket coupling/rubber dampers	21
Brake light switches	see Chapter 8	Rear wheel	15
Brake pads	2	Sprockets	20
Brake pad wear check	see Chapter 1	Tyre information and fitting	17
Brake system check	see Chapter 1	Tyre pressure monitoring system (TPMS)	18
Drive chain and sprockets check	see Chapter 1	Tyre pressures, tread depth and condition	see *Pre-ride checks*
Drive chain removal, cleaning and installation	19	Wheel alignment check	13
Front brake calipers	3	Wheel bearing check	see Chapter 1
Front brake discs	4	Wheel checks	see Chapter 1
Front brake master cylinder	5	Wheel inspection and repair	12
Front wheel	14	Wheel and sprocket coupling bearings	16
General information	1		

Degrees of difficulty

Easy, suitable for novice with little experience	**Fairly easy**, suitable for beginner with some experience	**Fairly difficult**, suitable for competent DIY mechanic	**Difficult**, suitable for experienced DIY mechanic	**Very difficult**, suitable for expert DIY or professional

Specifications

Brakes
Brake fluid type	DOT 4
Brake pad minimum thickness	1.5 mm
Front caliper piston OD	27.00 mm
Front disc diameter	305 mm
Front disc thickness	
Standard	4.5 mm
Service limit	4.0 mm
Front disc maximum runout	0.15 mm
Front master cylinder bore ID	14.00 mm
Rear caliper piston OD	38.18 mm
Rear disc diameter	255 mm
Rear disc thickness	
Standard	6.0 mm
Service limit	5.5 mm
Rear disc maximum runout	0.5 mm
Rear master cylinder bore ID	12.7 mm

ABS components
Wheel speed sensor air gap	0.1 to 1.5 mm

Wheels

Runout – axial (side-to-side) and radial (out-of round)
    Standard models .... 0.5 mm max
    XC models .... 1.0 mm max

Tyres

Tyre pressures .... see *Pre-ride checks*
Tyre sizes*
    Standard models
        Front 100/90-19
        Rear 150/70-17
    XC models
        Front 90/90-21
        Rear 150/70-17

*Refer to the owner's handbook, the tyre information label on the swingarm, or your Triumph dealer or a tyre specialist for approved tyre brands and ratings.

Final drive

Chain size 525
No. of links
    Standard models 122
    XC models 124
Drive chain slack and stretch limit .... see Chapter 1
Sprocket size .... 16T front, 50T rear

Torque wrench settings

ABS components
    Brake pipe nuts on modulator (models) .... 15 Nm
    Front wheel pulse ring/brake disc bolts .... 22 Nm
    Rear wheel pulse ring bolts .... 5 Nm
    Wheel speed sensor bolt .... 9 Nm
Brake caliper bleed valves .... 6 Nm
Brake hose banjo bolts .... 25 Nm
Front brake caliper mounting bolts .... 28 Nm
Front brake disc bolts .... 22 Nm
Front brake master cylinder clamp bolts .... 12 Nm
Front brake pad retaining pin .... 18 Nm
Front sprocket nut .... 85 Nm
Front wheel axle .... 65 Nm
Front wheel axle clamp bolts .... 22 Nm
Rear brake caliper mounting bolts
    Front .... 27 Nm
    Rear .... 22 Nm
Rear brake disc bolts .... 22 Nm
Rear brake light switch .... 15 Nm
Rear brake master cylinder bolts .... 16 Nm
Rear brake pad retaining pin .... 18 Nm
Rear sprocket nuts .... 55 Nm
Rear wheel axle nut .... 110 Nm

1 General information

Standard models are fitted with cast alloy wheels designed for tubeless tyres only. XC models have steel rimmed spoke wheels and tubed tyres.

Both front and rear brakes are hydraulically operated disc brakes. The front brake has two twin piston sliding calipers. The rear brake has a single piston sliding caliper. Some models are fitted with an ABS system.

The drive to the rear wheel is by chain and sprockets.

Caution: Disc brake components rarely require disassembly. Do not disassemble components unless absolutely necessary. If an hydraulic brake line is loosened, the system must be thoroughly bled. Do not use solvents on internal brake components. Solvents will cause the seals to swell and distort. Use only clean brake fluid or denatured alcohol for cleaning. Use care when working with brake fluid as it can injure your eyes and it will damage painted surfaces and plastic parts.
Note: *Before draining or changing the brake fluid on ABS models, bear in mind that the system must be bled on completion of work, and although this is done initially in the same way as models without ABS, to complete the procedure effectively the Triumph Diagnostic tool must be used to open and close the solenoids within the ABS modulator, and this can only be carried out by a dealer. The tool should not be needed in the case of a caliper overhaul as the hose need only be disconnected at the caliper, and any air that gets into the end of the hose or caliper will not reach the ABS modulator and so can be bled out in the conventional way.*

Some of the bolts used on Triumph motorcycles are of the Torx type. Unless you are already equipped with a good range of Torx bits, you are advised to obtain a set. Make sure you get bits that can be used in

Brakes, wheels and final drive 6•3

conjunction with a socket set so that a torque wrench can be applied – a Torx key set will not be adequate on its own, though will be useful in addition to the bits.

2 Brake pads

⚠️ **Warning:** *The dust created by the brake system may contain asbestos, which is harmful to your health. Never blow it out with compressed air and don't inhale any of it. An approved filtering mask should be worn when working on the brakes.*

Front

1 Release the brake hose(s) from the mudguard and from the clip holding the ABS sensor wire where fitted, to give more freedom of movement.
2 Unscrew the pad retaining pin plug and slacken the pin **(see illustration)**.
3 Unscrew the caliper mounting bolts and slide the caliper off the disc **(see illustration)**.
4 Unscrew the pad retaining pin and remove the pads **(see illustrations)**.
5 Inspect the surface of each pad for contamination and check that the friction material has not worn beyond its service limit (see Chapter 1). If either pad is worn down to or beyond the service limit wear indicator or the minimum thickness specified, is fouled with oil or grease, or is heavily scored or damaged by dirt and debris, both pads in each caliper must be replaced with new ones. Note that it is not possible to fully degrease the friction material; if the pads are contaminated in any way new ones must be fitted. Check that the wear on each pad is even – uneven wear is a sign of a sticking or seized piston or pistons (see Steps 10 and 11).

2.2 Remove the plug then slacken the pad pin (arrowed)

2.3 Caliper mounting bolts (arrowed)

2.4a Unscrew the pin...

2.4b ...and remove the pads

6 If the pads are in good condition and not worn to the limit clean them carefully, using a fine wire brush that is completely free of oil and grease, to remove all traces of road dirt and corrosion. Using a pointed instrument, clean out the grooves in the friction material and dig out any embedded particles of foreign matter. Spray with a dedicated brake cleaner to remove any dust.
7 Check the condition of the brake disc (see Section 4).
8 Remove all traces of corrosion from the pad pin. Check for signs of damage and wear.
9 Separate the bracket from the caliper by sliding them apart **(see illustration)**. Clean off all traces of corrosion and hardened grease from the slider pins and rubber boots. Check the rubber boots. If they are damaged, deformed or deteriorated, they should be replaced with new ones (but check with a Triumph dealer as they do not list them as being available separately). Note how the pad spring is fitted and remove it for cleaning if required **(see illustration)**.

2.9a Slide the caliper off the bracket and clean and check the boots (A) and pins (B)

2.9b Check and clean the spring (arrowed)...

2.9c ...and the guide (arrowed) if required

2.10a You should be able to push the pistons in using finger pressure

2.10b This shows a purpose-made tool in use

Also clean the pad guide on the bracket **(see illustration)**.

10 Clean around the exposed section of each piston to remove any dirt or debris that could cause the seals to be damaged. If new pads are being fitted, now push the pistons all the way back into the caliper to create room for them; if the old pads are still serviceable push the pistons in a little way. To push the pistons back use finger pressure or a piece of wood as leverage, or place the old pads back in the caliper and use a metal bar or a screwdriver inserted between them, or use grips and a piece of wood, with rag or card to protect the caliper body **(see illustration)**. Alternatively obtain a proper piston-pushing tool from a good tool supplier **(see illustration)**. If there is too much brake fluid in the reservoir it may be necessary to remove the cover and diaphragm and siphon some out (see *Pre-ride checks*). If a piston is difficult to push back, remove the bleed valve cap, then attach a length of clear hose to the bleed valve and place the open end in a suitable container, then open the valve and try again (see Section 10). Take great care not to draw any air into the system. If in doubt, bleed the brake afterwards.

11 If a piston appears seized, apply the brake lever and check whether the piston in question moves at all – first block or hold the other piston using wood or cable-ties. If it moves out but can't be pushed back in the chances are there is some hidden corrosion stopping it. If it doesn't move at all, or to fully clean and inspect the pistons, disassemble the caliper and overhaul it (see Section 3).

12 If removed, fit the pad spring into the caliper, making sure it is clean and correctly located **(see illustration 2.9b)**. Make sure the guide is clean and correctly fitted on the bracket **(see illustration 2.9c)**. Apply a smear of silicone based grease to the slider pins and inside the boots **(see illustration 2.9a)**. Slide the caliper onto the bracket. Check that the caliper is able to slide freely.

13 Make sure the shims are correctly fitted to the back of each pad. Lightly smear the pad retaining pin with copper grease. Fit the pads into the caliper **(see illustration 2.4b)** – make sure their ends locate against the guide on the bracket **(see illustration)**. Press the pads against the spring and slide the pad pin through **(see illustration 2.4a)**. Make sure the pin passes through the hole in each pad. Tighten the pin finger-tight.

14 Slide the caliper onto the disc, making sure the pads sit squarely on each side **(see illustration)**. Fit the caliper mounting bolts and tighten them to the torque setting specified at the beginning of the Chapter. Now tighten the retaining pin to the specified torque. Smear the pad pin plug threads with copper grease and fit the plug **(see illustration 2.2)**. Secure the brake hose(s).

15 Operate the brake lever until the pads contact the disc. Check the fluid level in the reservoir (see *Pre-ride checks*).

16 Check the operation of the brake before riding the motorcycle.

Rear

17 On models with ABS release the clip holding the ABS sensor wire from the brake hose, to give more freedom of movement **(see illustration)**.

18 Unscrew the pad retaining pin plug and slacken the pin **(see illustration)**.

19 Unscrew the caliper mounting bolts and slide the caliper off the disc **(see illustration)**.

2.13 Make sure the pad ends locate correctly against the guide (arrowed)

2.14 Make sure there is sufficient gap between the pads so the disc slides easily between them

2.17 Release the clip (arrowed)

2.18 Remove the plug then slacken the pad pin (arrowed)

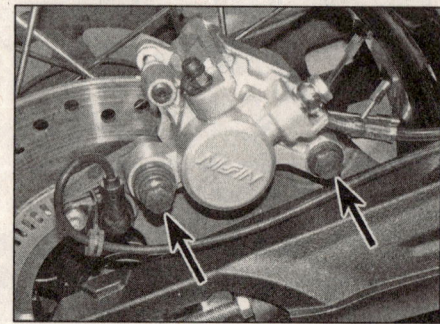

2.19 Caliper mounting bolts (arrowed)

Brakes, wheels and final drive 6•5

2.20a Unscrew the pin...

2.20b ...and remove the pads

2.22a Rubber boot (A) and spring (B) in the caliper

2.22b Rubber boot (A) and guide (B) in the bracket

2.27a Make sure the pads seat against the guide (arrowed)...

2.27b ...then fit the bolts

20 Unscrew and remove the pad pin, then remove the pads, noting how they fit (see illustrations).
21 Refer to Steps 5, 6, 7 and 8 above and inspect the pads and caliper components.
22 Clean off all traces of corrosion and hardened grease from the bolts and boots, and from the sleeve in the caliper boot (see illustrations). Check the rubber boots. If they are damaged, deformed or deteriorated, they should be replaced with new ones – they come as a set along with the sleeve and mounting bolts. Note how the pad spring is fitted and remove it for cleaning if required. Also do the pad guide on the bracket.
23 Clean around the exposed section of the piston to remove any dirt or debris that could cause the seals to be damaged. If new pads are being fitted, push the piston all the way back into the caliper to create room for them; if the old pads are still serviceable push the piston in a little way. To push the piston back use finger pressure or a piece of wood as leverage, or two pieces of wood and a metal bar or a screwdriver inserted between them, or use grips and a piece of wood, with rag or card to protect the caliper body (see illustration 2.10a). Alternatively obtain a proper piston-pushing tool from a good tool supplier (see illustration 2.10b). If there is too much brake fluid in the reservoir it may be necessary to remove the cap, plate and diaphragm and siphon some out (see Pre-ride checks). If the piston is difficult to push back, remove the bleed valve cap, then attach a length of clear hose to the bleed valve and place the open end in a suitable container, then open the valve and try again (see Section 10). Take great care not to draw any air into the system. If in doubt, bleed the brake afterwards.
24 If the piston appears seized, apply the brake pedal and check whether the piston moves at all. If it moves out but can't be pushed back in the chances are there is some hidden corrosion stopping it. If it doesn't move at all, or to fully clean and inspect the piston, disassemble and overhaul the caliper (see Section 6).
25 If removed, fit the pad spring into the caliper, making sure it is clean and correctly located (see illustration 2.22a). Make sure the guide is clean and correctly fitted on the bracket (see illustration 2.22b). Lightly smear the pad retaining pin with copper grease. Apply a smear of silicone based grease to the caliper bolts and inside the boots and sleeve.
26 Fit the pads into the caliper and slide the pad pin through (see illustrations 2.20b and a). Tighten the pin finger-tight.
27 Slide the caliper onto the disc, making sure the pads sit squarely on each side and locate correctly in the bracket and against the guide (see illustration). Fit the bolts and tighten them to the torque settings specified at the beginning of the Chapter (see illustration). Now tighten the pad pin to the specified torque. Smear the pad pin plug threads with copper grease and fit the plug (see illustration 2.18). Secure the brake hose (see illustration 2.17).
28 Operate the brake pedal until the pads contact the disc. Check the fluid level in the reservoir (see Pre-ride checks).
29 Check the operation of the brake before riding the motorcycle.

3 Front brake calipers

Warning: Overhaul must be done in a spotlessly clean work area to avoid contamination and possible failure of the brake hydraulic system components. Do not, under any circumstances, use petroleum-based solvents to clean brake parts. Use clean DOT 4 brake fluid, dedicated brake cleaner or denatured alcohol only, as described. To prevent damage from spilled brake fluid, always cover paintwork when working on the braking system, and have plenty of absorbent rag to hand to catch and wipe off any spilled fluid..
Note: *If the caliper is being overhauled (usually due to sticking pistons or fluid leaks) read through the entire procedure first and make sure that you have obtained all the new parts required, including some new DOT 4 brake fluid.*

Removal

1 On models with ABS, either displace the wheel speed sensor from the fork (see Section 11), or release the sensor wire from the clips joining it to the brake hose, as

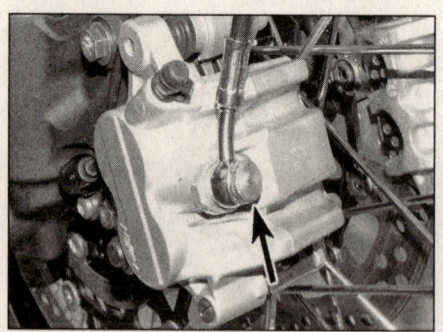

3.3a Brake hose banjo bolt (arrowed)

3.3b Seal the banjo using a nut and bolt and the sealing washers

3.8a Position the wood as shown then apply compressed air...

3.8b ...until both pistons are displaced...

3.8c ...then remove the wood and withdraw the pistons

6 Mark the inside of each piston with its location in the caliper (upper and lower) using a felt marker to ensure that the pistons can be matched to their original bores on reassembly.

7 To remove the pistons you need either a supply of compressed air, or a piston removal tool, or if neither are available a good pair of external circlip removal pliers.

8 If you are using compressed air make sure the bleed valve is tight. Place a piece of wood or a wad of rag between the pistons and the caliper, then apply compressed air gradually and progressively, starting with a fairly low pressure, to the fluid inlet in the caliper and allow the pistons to ease out of the bores **(see illustrations)**. If one piston is being pushed out before the others, block that one so more pressure is applied to the sticking one(s), but do not use your fingers.

9 If you are using a dedicated tool or the circlip pliers, grip the inner wall of the piston then twist and pull the piston out, keeping it square to the bore wall until it is free **(see illustration 6.8)**. Do not try to remove a piston by levering it out or by using pliers or other grips that may scratch the outer wall.

10 If a piston is stuck in its bore due to corrosion replace the caliper with a new one.

11 Remove the dust seals and fluid seals from the bores, preferably using a soft wooden or plastic tool to avoid scratching the bores **(see illustration)**. New seals must be fitted on reassembly.

12 Clean the pistons and bores with DOT 4 brake fluid. If compressed air is available, blow it through the fluid passages in the caliper to ensure they are clear.

Caution: Do not, under any circumstances, use a petroleum-based solvent to clean brake parts.

13 Inspect the caliper bores and pistons for signs of corrosion, nicks and burrs and loss of plating **(see illustration)**. If surface defects are present, the pistons and/or caliper must be replaced with a new one. If the caliper is in poor condition, the other front caliper and the master cylinder should also be checked.

14 Lubricate the new fluid seals with clean

required. Free the brake hose(s) from the mudguard, and from the fork on the left-hand side if required.

2 If the calipers are just being displaced, unscrew the caliper mounting bolts and slide the caliper off the disc **(see illustration 2.3)**. Secure the caliper to the bike with a cable-tie. **Note:** *Do not operate the brake lever while either caliper is off the disc.*

3 If the caliper is being completely removed or overhauled, place some rag around the brake hose banjo bolt, then unscrew the bolt and detach the banjo union(s), noting the alignment with the caliper, and catching any residual fluid with the rag **(see illustration)**. When working on the right-hand caliper, note the double hose arrangement. Seal the banjo union and secure the hose upright to minimise fluid loss and prevent air getting in **(see illustration)**. New sealing washers must be fitted on reassembly. Remove the brake pads (see Section 2) – this involves detaching the caliper.

Overhaul

4 Separate the bracket from the caliper by sliding them apart **(see illustration 2.9a)**. Remove the pad spring from the caliper, noting how it fits **(see illustration or 2.9b)**.

5 Clean all dirt and dust off the caliper with denatured alcohol or brake system cleaner. Have some clean rag ready to catch any spilled brake fluid.

3.11 Remove the seals and discard them

3.13 Check the surfaces of the pistons and bores – the plating on this piston is lifting off

Brakes, wheels and final drive 6•7

3.14a Lubricate the new piston seals with brake fluid...

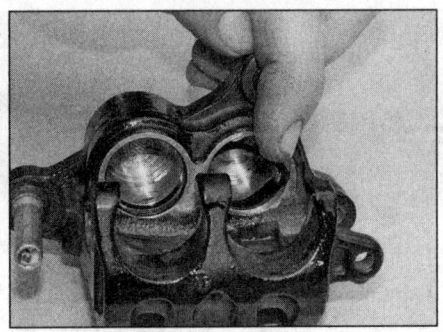
3.14b ...then fit them into their grooves...

3.15 ...followed by the new dust seals

3.16a Fit the pistons...

3.16b ...and push them all the way in

brake fluid and fit them into the inner grooves in the bores **(see illustrations)**.

15 Lubricate the new dust seals with clean brake fluid and fit them into the outer grooves in the bores **(see illustration)**.

16 Lubricate the outside of the pistons with clean brake fluid and push them, closed-end first, squarely all the way into the caliper bores, taking care not to displace the seals **(see illustrations)**.

17 Clean off all traces of corrosion and hardened grease from the slider pins and rubber boots **(see illustration 2.9a)**. Check the rubber boots - If they are damaged, deformed or deteriorated, they should be replaced with new ones (but check with a Triumph dealer as they do not list them as being available separately). Fit the pad spring into the caliper, making sure it is correctly located **(see illustration 2.9b)**. Apply a smear of silicone based grease to the slider pins and inside the boots. Slide the caliper onto the bracket. Check that the caliper is able to slide freely.

Installation

18 If the caliper has been overhauled, check and install the brake pads (see Section 2) – this procedure involves installing the caliper.
19 If the calipers have just being displaced slide them onto the discs, making sure the pads fit on each side **(see illustration 2.14)**. Fit the caliper mounting bolts and tighten them to the torque setting specified at the beginning of the Chapter.
20 If detached, connect the brake hose(s) to the caliper, using new sealing washers on each side of each banjo fitting **(see illustration**

6.20). Align the fitting as noted on removal **(see illustration 3.3a)**. Tighten the banjo bolt to the specified torque setting.
21 Secure the brake hose(s), and where fitted the ABS wheel speed sensor wire, or fit the sensor if displaced (Section 11).
22 Top up the hydraulic reservoir with DOT 4 brake fluid (see *Pre-ride checks*) and bleed the system as described in Section 10. Check that there are no fluid leaks and test the operation of the brake before riding the motorcycle.

4 Front brake discs

Inspection

1 Inspect the surface of each disc for score marks and other damage. Light scratches are normal after use and won't affect brake operation, but deep grooves and heavy score marks will reduce braking efficiency and accelerate pad wear. If a disc is badly grooved replace both discs with new ones – never fit only one new disc.
2 The discs must not be allowed to wear down to a thickness less than the service limit as listed in this Chapter's Specifications. The minimum thickness is also stamped on the disc. Check the thickness of each disc in the middle of the pad contact area using a micrometer, and replace both discs with new ones if worn **(see illustration)**.
3 To check if a disc is warped, position the bike on an auxiliary stand with the front wheel raised off the ground. Mount a dial gauge to the fork leg, with the gauge plunger touching the surface of the disc about 10 mm from the outer edge **(see illustration)**. Rotate the wheel and watch the gauge needle, comparing the reading with the limit listed in the Specifications at the beginning of this Chapter. If the runout is greater than the service limit, check the wheel bearings for play (see Chapter 1). If the bearings are worn, fit new ones (see Section 16) and repeat this check. If the disc runout is still excessive, a new pair of discs must be fitted.

4.2 Using a micrometer to measure disc thickness

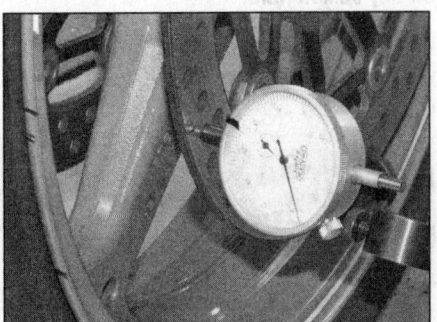
4.3 Set up a dial gauge with the probe contacting the brake disc, then rotate the wheel to check for runout

6•8 Brakes, wheels and final drive

4.5 Unscrew the bolts (arrowed) and remove the disc

5.3 Brake light switch wiring connectors (A) and screw (B)

Removal

4 Remove the wheel (see Section 14).

Caution: *Do not lay the wheel down and allow it to rest on the disc – the disc could become warped. Set the wheel on wood blocks so the disc doesn't support the weight of the wheel.*

5 If you are not replacing the discs with new ones, mark their alignment with the wheel, so they can be installed in the same position and on the same side as originally fitted. Unscrew the disc bolts, loosening them evenly and a little at a time in a criss-cross pattern to avoid distorting the disc, then remove the disc **(see illustration)** – note that on models with ABS the left-hand disc bolts also secure the wheel sensor pulse ring (see Section 11) **(see illustration 11.18)**. Triumph specify that new bolts should be used as they are pre-treated with a threadlock, but if necessary clean the threads of the old bolts and apply some fresh threadlock to them on installation.

Installation

6 Before fitting the discs, make sure there is no dirt or corrosion where they seat on the hub, particularly right in the angle of the seat, as this will not allow them to sit flat when bolted down, and they will appear to be warped when checked or when using the front brake.

7 Fit the disc on the wheel with its marked side facing out, aligning the previously applied matchmarks (if you're reinstalling the original disc). On models with ABS fit the pulse ring onto the left-hand disc **(see illustration 11.18)**.

8 Either fit the new bolts, or clean the threads of the original bolts and apply fresh thread locking compound, and tighten them evenly and a little at a time in a criss-cross pattern to the torque setting specified at the beginning of this Chapter. Clean the disc using acetone or brake system cleaner. If a new disc has been installed, remove any protective coating from its working surfaces and fit new brake pads.

9 Install the wheel (see Section 14). If new discs have been fitted, you will have to push the caliper pistons in a little (see Section 2 for details on ways of doing this) before fitting the calipers.

10 Operate the brake lever several times to bring the pads into contact with the disc. Check the fluid level in the reservoir (see *Pre-ride checks*). Check the operation of the brake carefully before riding the bike.

5 Front brake master cylinder

Warning: *Overhaul must be done in a spotlessly clean work area to avoid contamination and possible failure of the brake hydraulic system components. Do not, under any circumstances, use petroleum-based solvents to clean brake parts. Use clean DOT 4 brake fluid, dedicated brake cleaner or denatured alcohol only, as described. To prevent damage from spilled brake fluid, always cover paintwork when working on the braking system, and have plenty of absorbent rag to hand to catch and wipe off any spilled fluid.*

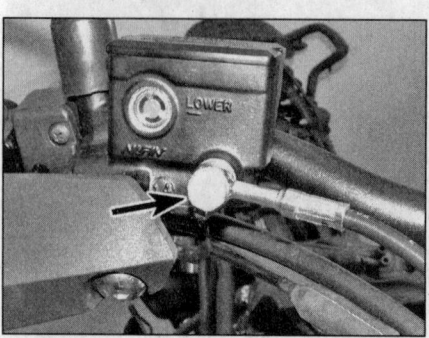

5.4 Brake hose banjo bolt (arrowed)

Note: *If the master cylinder is being overhauled (usually due to sticking or poor action, or fluid leaks) read through the entire procedure first and make sure that you have obtained all the new parts required, including some new DOT 4 brake fluid.*

Removal

1 Remove the mirror (see Chapter 7).

2 Remove the brake lever (see Chapter 5).

3 Disconnect the brake light switch wiring connectors, and if required remove the switch **(see illustration)**.

4 Have some rag to catch the brake fluid, then unscrew the brake hose banjo bolt and detach the hose, noting its alignment with the master cylinder **(see illustration)**. Seal the banjo union and secure the hose upright to minimise fluid loss and prevent air getting in **(see illustration 3.3b)**. Note that new sealing washers will be required later.

5 Unscrew the two clamp bolts and remove the master cylinder **(see illustration)**. Drain and fluid any in the master cylinder into a suitable container.

6 Remove the reservoir cover and diaphragm, and drain the fluid in the reservoir into the container.

5.5 Master cylinder clamp bolts

Brakes, wheels and final drive 6•9

5.7 Remove the boot from the end of the master cylinder piston...

5.8a ...then depress the piston, remove the circlip...

5.8b ...and draw out the piston...

Overhaul

7 Remove the rubber boot from the master cylinder **(see illustration)**.

8 Push the piston in and use circlip pliers to remove the circlip, then slide out the piston assembly and spring **(see illustrations)**. Lay the parts out in the proper order to prevent confusion during reassembly.

9 Clean the inside of the master cylinder and reservoir with clean brake fluid. If compressed air is available, blow it through the fluid galleries to ensure they are clear.

Caution: Do not, under any circumstances, use a petroleum-based solvent to clean brake parts.

10 Check the master cylinder bore for corrosion, scratches, nicks and score marks. If damage or wear is evident, the master cylinder must be replaced with a new one. If the master cylinder is in poor condition, then the caliper should be checked as well.

11 The dust boot, circlip, piston, cup, seal, and spring are all included in a master cylinder rebuild kit. Use all of the new parts, regardless of the apparent condition of the old ones. Lubricate the master cylinder bore with new brake fluid.

12 Fit the cup onto the narrow end of the spring, locating the peg in the hole **(see illustration)**. Lubricate the spring and cup with clean brake fluid and fit the wide end of the spring into the bore, then push the cup in, making sure it does not turn inside out **(see illustration)**.

13 Smear the seal with new brake fluid and if not already in place fit it into its groove in the piston so the wider end will fit into the master cylinder first **(see illustration)**. Slide the piston in, making sure the seal does not turn inside out **(see illustration)**. Push the piston in to compress the spring and fit the new circlip, making sure it locates in the groove **(see illustration)**.

14 Smear the outer end of the piston and the inside of the boot with silicone grease. Carefully push the wide rim of the boot onto its seat in the master cylinder and locate the

5.8c ...and spring

5.12a Fit the cup onto the end of the spring

5.12b Fit the spring into the master cylinder

5.13a Make sure the seal is correctly installed on the piston

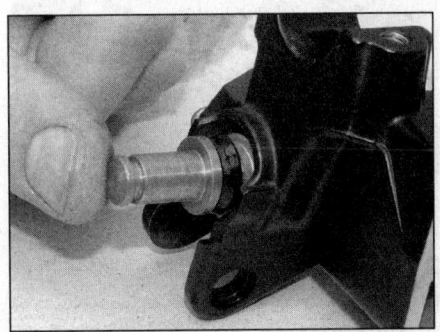

5.13b Push the piston into the bore...

5.13c ...then fit the circlip

6•10 Brakes, wheels and final drive

5.14a Fit the boot onto the pushrod...

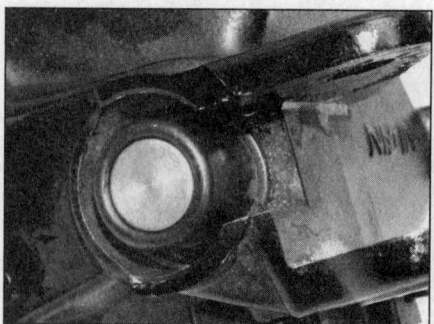

5.14b ...and locate its rim in the groove

5.15 Align the mating surfaces of the clamp with the + mark (arrowed) on the handlebar

narrow end lips in the groove in the piston **(see illustrations)**.

Installation

15 Fit the master cylinder onto the handlebar, aligning the clamp joint with the + mark on the top of the handlebar, then fit the back of the clamp with its UP mark facing up **(see illustration)**. Tighten the upper bolt to the torque setting specified at the beginning of this Chapter, followed by the lower bolt.
16 Connect the brake hose to the master cylinder, using new sealing washers on each side of the banjo fitting. Align the hose as shown and tighten the banjo bolt to the specified torque **(see illustration 5.4)**.
17 Fit the brake light switch if removed, and connect the wiring connectors **(see illustration 5.3)**.
18 Install the brake lever (see Chapter 5). Install the mirror (see Chapter 7).
19 Refer to Section 10 to fill and bleed the system.
20 Check that there are no fluid leaks and test the brake before riding the motorcycle.

6 Rear brake caliper

 Warning: *Overhaul of the brake caliper must be done in a spotlessly clean work area to avoid contamination and possible failure of the brake hydraulic system components. Do not, under any circumstances, use petroleum-based solvents to clean brake parts. Use clean DOT 4 brake fluid, dedicated brake cleaner or denatured alcohol only, as described. To prevent damage from spilled brake fluid, always cover paintwork when working on the braking system, and have plenty of absorbent rag to hand to catch and wipe off any spilled fluid.*
Note: *If the caliper is being overhauled (usually due to a sticking piston or fluid leak) read through the entire procedure first and make sure that you have obtained all the new parts required, including some new DOT 4 brake fluid.*

Removal

1 On models with ABS, either displace the wheel speed sensor from the caliper bracket (see Section 11), or release the sensor wire from the clips joining it to the brake hose, as required. Unscrew the brake hose guide bolts **(see illustration)**.
2 If the caliper is just being displaced, unscrew the caliper bolts and slide the caliper off the disc **(see illustration 2.19)**. Tie or support it clear, making sure no strain is placed on the hose. **Note:** *Do not operate the brake pedal while the caliper is off the disc.*
3 If the caliper is being completely removed or overhauled, place some rag around the brake hose banjo bolt, then unscrew the bolt and detach the banjo union, noting its alignment with the caliper, and catching any residual fluid with the rag **(see illustration)**. Seal the banjo union and secure the hose upright to minimise fluid loss and prevent air getting in **(see illustration 3.3b)**. New sealing washers must be fitted on reassembly. Remove the brake pads (see Section 2) – this involves detaching the caliper.

Overhaul

4 Remove the pad spring from the caliper, noting how it fits **(see illustration 2.22a)**.
5 Clean all dirt and dust off the caliper with denatured alcohol or brake system cleaner. Have some clean rag ready to catch any spilled brake fluid.
6 To remove the piston you need either a supply of compressed air, or a piston removal tool, or if neither are available a good pair of external circlip removal pliers. Note that a new piston is supplied with the seal kit.
7 If you are using compressed air make sure the bleed valve is tight. Place a piece of wood or a wad of rag between the piston and the caliper, then apply compressed air gradually and progressively, starting with a fairly low pressure, to the fluid inlet in the caliper and allow the piston to ease out of the bore **(see illustration)**.
8 If you are using a dedicated tool or the

6.1 Brake hose guide bolts (arrowed)

6.3 Brake hose banjo bolt (arrowed)

6.7 Fit the wood, then apply the compressed air as described until the piston is displaced

Brakes, wheels and final drive 6•11

circlip pliers, grip the inner wall of the piston then twist and pull the piston out, keeping it square to the bore wall until it is free **(see illustration)**.

9 If the piston is stuck in its bore due to corrosion replace the caliper with a new one.

10 Remove the dust seal and fluid seal from the bore, preferably using a soft wooden or plastic tool to avoid scratching the bore **(see illustration)**. New seals must be fitted on reassembly, and come in a kit along with a new piston.

11 Clean the bore with DOT 4 brake fluid. If compressed air is available, blow it through the fluid passage in the caliper to ensure it is clear.

Caution: Do not, under any circumstances, use a petroleum-based solvent to clean brake parts.

12 Inspect the caliper bore for signs of corrosion, nicks and burrs. If surface defects are present and cannot be cleaned up, the caliper must be replaced with a new one. If the caliper is in poor condition, the master cylinder should also be checked.

13 Lubricate the new fluid seal with clean brake fluid and fit it into the inner groove in the bore **(see illustration)**.

14 Lubricate the new dust seal with clean brake fluid and fit it into the outer groove in the bore **(see illustration)**.

15 Lubricate the outside of the piston with clean brake fluid and push it, closed-end first, into the caliper bore, taking care not to displace the seals **(see illustration)**. Push the piston all the way in, making sure it enters the bore squarely **(see illustration)**.

16 Fit the pad spring into the caliper, making sure it is correctly located **(see illustration 2.22a)**.

17 Clean off all traces of corrosion and hardened grease from the bolts and from the boots in the caliper and bracket **(see illustrations 2.22a and b)** – remove the sleeve from the boot in the caliper. Replace the rubber boots with new ones if they are damaged, deformed or deteriorated – they come as a set along with the sleeve and mounting bolts. Apply a smear of silicone-based grease to the boots and sleeve, and fit them if removed.

Installation

18 If the caliper has been overhauled, check and install the brake pads (see Section 2) – this procedure involves installing the caliper.

19 If the caliper has just being displaced slide it onto the brake disc, making sure the pads fit on each side **(see illustration 2.27a)**. Fit the bolts and tighten them to the torque settings specified at the beginning of the Chapter **(see illustration 2.27b)**.

20 If detached, connect the brake hose to the caliper, using new sealing washers on each side of the banjo fitting **(see illustration)**. Align the fitting as noted on removal **(see illustration 6.3)**. Tighten the banjo bolt to the specified torque setting.

21 Secure the brake hose, and where fitted the ABS wheel speed sensor wire, or fit the sensor if displaced (Section 11) **(see illustration 6.1)**.

22 Top up the hydraulic reservoir with DOT 4 brake fluid (see *Pre-ride checks*) and bleed the system as described in Section 10. Check that there are no fluid leaks and test the operation of the brake before riding the motorcycle.

7 Rear brake disc

Inspection

1 Refer to Section 4 of this Chapter, noting that the dial gauge should be attached to the swingarm.

Removal

2 Remove the wheel (see Section 15).

Caution: Do not lay the wheel down and allow it to rest on the disc – the disc could become warped. Set the wheel on wood

6.8 Using circlip pliers to extract a piston

6.10 Remove the seals and discard them

6.13 Fit the new piston seal into its groove...

6.14 ...followed by the new dust seal

6.15a Fit the piston...

6.15b ...and push it all the way in

6.20 Use new sealing washers (arrowed)

6•12 Brakes, wheels and final drive

7.4 Rear brake disc bolts (arrowed)

8.1a Heel guard bolts (arrowed)

8.1b Reservoir mounting bolt (arrowed)

blocks so the disc doesn't support the weight of the wheel.

3 On models with ABS remove the pulse ring from the wheel (see Section 11).

4 If you are not replacing the disc with a new one, mark its alignment with the wheel, so it can be installed in the same position. Unscrew the disc bolts, loosening them evenly and a little at a time in a criss-cross pattern to avoid distorting the disc, then remove the disc **(see illustration)**. Triumph specify that new bolts should be used as they are pre-treated with a threadlock, but if necessary clean the threads of the old bolts and apply some fresh threadlock to them on installation.

Installation

5 Before fitting the disc, make sure there is no dirt or corrosion where it seats on the hub, particularly right in the angle of the seat, as this will not allow it to sit flat when bolted down, and it will appear to be warped when checked or when using the front brake.

6 Fit the disc on the wheel with its marked side facing out, aligning the previously applied alignment marks (if you're reinstalling the original disc).

7 Either fit the new bolts, or clean the threads of the original bolts and apply fresh thread locking compound, and tighten them evenly and a little at a time in a criss-cross pattern to the torque setting specified at the beginning of this Chapter. Clean the disc using acetone or brake system cleaner. If a new disc has been installed, remove any protective coating from its working surfaces and fit new brake pads.

8 On models with ABS fit the pulse ring onto the wheel (see Section 11).

9 Install the wheel (see Section 15). If a new disc has been fitted, you will have to push the caliper piston in a little (see Section 2 for details on ways of doing this) before fitting the caliper.

10 Operate the brake pedal several times to bring the pads into contact with the disc. Check the fluid level in the reservoir (see *Pre-ride checks*). Check the operation of the brake carefully before riding the bike.

8 Rear brake master cylinder

⚠️ *Warning: Overhaul must be done in a spotlessly clean work area to avoid contamination and possible failure of the brake hydraulic system components. Do not, under any circumstances, use petroleum-based solvents to clean brake parts. Use clean DOT 4 brake fluid, dedicated brake cleaner or denatured alcohol only, as described. To prevent damage from spilled brake fluid, always cover paintwork when working on the braking system, and have plenty of absorbent rag to hand to catch and wipe off any spilled fluid.*

Note: If the master cylinder is being overhauled (usually due to sticking or poor action, or fluid leaks) read through the entire procedure first and make sure that you have obtained all the new parts required, including some new DOT 4 brake fluid.

Removal

1 Remove the heel guard **(see illustration)**. Unscrew the bolt securing the reservoir to the frame **(see illustration)**.

2 Remove the retaining clip from the clevis pin securing the master cylinder pushrod to the brake pedal **(see illustration)**. Withdraw the clevis pin and separate the pushrod from the pedal.

3 Remove the brake light switch from the top of the master cylinder (see Chapter 8).

4 Unscrew the bolts securing the master cylinder and remove it along with the reservoir **(see illustration)**. Drain any fluid in the master cylinder into a suitable container.

5 Remove the reservoir cap, diaphragm plate and diaphragm, and drain the fluid in the reservoir cylinder into the container. If required release the clamp securing the reservoir hose to the union on the master cylinder and detach the hose.

Overhaul

6 Dislodge the rubber dust boot from the base of the master cylinder to reveal the pushrod retaining circlip **(see illustration)**. If a new rubber boot is needed you have to get a complete pushrod assembly.

8.2 Remove the retaining clip and withdraw the clevis pin (arrowed)

8.4 Master cylinder bolts (arrowed)

8.6 Pull the boot out...

Brakes, wheels and final drive 6•13

8.7a ...then release the circlip...

8.7b ...and remove the pushrod assembly...

8.7c ...the piston...

8.7d ...and the spring

8.10 Remove the circlip (arrowed) to release the union

8.11 Make sure the seal is correctly fitted on the piston

7 Depress the pushrod and, using circlip pliers, remove the circlip (see illustration). Remove the pushrod, then slide out the piston assembly and spring (see illustrations). Lay the parts out in the proper order to prevent confusion during reassembly.

8 Clean the inside of the master cylinder with clean brake fluid. If compressed air is available, blow it through the fluid galleries to ensure they are clear.

Caution: Do not, under any circumstances, use a petroleum-based solvent to clean brake parts. If compressed air is available, use it to dry the parts thoroughly.

9 Check the master cylinder bore for corrosion, scratches, nicks and score marks. If damage is evident, the master cylinder must be replaced with a new one. If the master cylinder is in poor condition, then the caliper should be checked as well.

10 Inspect the reservoir hose for cracks or splits and replace it with a new one if necessary (see illustration 8.15). If required, remove the hose union from the master cylinder (see illustration). Discard the O-ring as a new one must be used.

11 The piston, cup, seal and spring are included in the rebuild kit. Use all of the new parts, regardless of the apparent condition of the old ones. Fit them according to the layout of the old piston assembly. If the seal is not already fitted onto the piston, lubricate it with new brake fluid before fitting it, and make sure the wider end will fit into the master cylinder first (see illustration).

12 Fit the cup onto the narrow end of the spring (see illustration). Fit the spring, wide-end first, into the master cylinder, and push the cup in, making sure the lip does not turn inside out (see illustrations).

13 Lubricate the piston with clean brake fluid and push it into the master cylinder up against the spring, making sure the lip on the seal does not turn inside out (see illustration).

8.12a Fit the cup onto the spring...

8.12b ...then fit the spring into the cylinder...

8.12c ...and push the cup in

8.13 Fit the piston into the cylinder

6•14 Brakes, wheels and final drive

8.14a Locate the pushrod and push it in...

8.14b ...then fit the circlip...

8.14c ...and push it into its groove

8.14d Make sure the boot lips locate correctly

8.15 Fit the reservoir hose and its clamp

8.16 Distance x should measure 75.5mm in the base position

14 Fit the circlip, using a new one if necessary, on the rod if removed and make sure the lower rim of the boot is in its groove. Locate the pushrod against the piston and push it in, then fit the circlip, making sure it is properly seated in the groove **(see illustrations)**. Fit the upper rim of the boot into the groove in the master cylinder **(see illustrations)**.
15 If removed, fit a new reservoir hose union O-ring, then push the union into the master cylinder and secure it with the circlip **(see illustration 8.10)**. Connect the reservoir hose to the union and secure it with the clamp **(see illustration)**.
16 If the position of the clevis on the end of the pushrod has been disturbed it can be reset to base setting by slackening the locknut and rotating the clevis on the threaded pushrod end so that the distance from the clevis eye to the centre of the lower mounting bolt hole is 75.5 mm **(see illustration)**. Changing this setting affects brake pedal height relative to the footrest.

Installation

17 Fit the master cylinder and tighten the bolts to the torque setting specified at the beginning of the Chapter **(see illustration 8.4)**.
18 Fit the reservoir, making sure the hose is correctly routed, and secure it with the bolt **(see illustration 8.1b)**.
19 Install the brake light switch (see Chapter 8).
20 Align the brake pedal with the master cylinder pushrod clevis, then slide in the clevis pin, and secure it with the retaining clip **(see illustration 8.2)**. Fit the heel guard **(see illustration 8.1a)**.

21 Refer to Section 10 to fill and bleed the system.
22 Check that there are no fluid leaks and test the brake before riding the motorcycle.

9 Brake hoses and fittings

Inspection

1 Check brake hose condition regularly (see Chapter 1). Twist and flex the hoses, looking for cracks and seeping fluid. Check extra carefully around the areas where the hoses connect with the banjo fittings, as these are common areas for hose failure.
2 On models with ABS remove the fuel tank (see Chapter 4) and check the brake pipes, the pipe/hose joints and the ABS modulator for signs of fluid leakage and for any dents or cracks in the pipes **(see illustration 11.30)**.
3 Inspect the banjo fittings connected to the brake hoses and the pipe joints on ABS models. If the fittings are rusted, scratched or cracked, fit new ones.

Removal and installation

Note: *On ABS models, before draining the brake fluid from the system, changing the fluid, or disconnecting any brake hoses or pipes from the master cylinders and ABS modulator or between them, bear in mind that the system must be bled on completion of work, and although this is done initially in the same way as models without ABS, to complete the procedure effectively the Triumph Diagnostic tool must be used to open and close the solenoids within the ABS modulator, and this can only be carried out by a dealer with the diagnostic tool. The bike should be transported, not ridden, to the dealer. It is OK to disconnect the hoses from the calipers, provided they are supported upright to minimise fluid loss and air ingress, as they come after the modulator in the system and so any air that gets into the end of the hose or caliper does not have to bleed through the modulator.*

4 Drain all old brake fluid from the system (see Section 10).
5 The brake hoses have banjo fittings on each end. Cover the surrounding area with plenty of rags. When working on the rear master cylinder lift the rubber boot off the top and disconnect the rear brake light switch wiring connector **(see illustration)**. Unscrew the banjo bolt, or in the case of the rear master cylinder fitting

9.5 Disconnect the wiring connector (arrowed)

Brakes, wheels and final drive 6•15

the rear brake light switch, at each end of the hose, noting the alignment of the fitting with the master cylinder or brake caliper **(see illustration 3.3a, 5.4, and 6.3)**. Free the hose from any clips or guides and remove it, noting its routing. Discard the sealing washers. **Note:** *Do not operate the brake lever or pedal while a brake hose is disconnected.*

6 Position the new hose, making sure it isn't twisted or otherwise strained, and ensure that it is correctly routed through any clips or guides and is clear of all moving components.

7 Check that the fittings align correctly, then fit the banjo bolts or brake light switch, using new sealing washers on both sides of the fittings **(see illustration 6.20)**. Tighten the banjo bolts or brake light switch to the torque setting specified at the beginning of this Chapter.

8 On models with ABS the hoses join to pipes that connect the system components to the ABS modulator. The pipes are secured to the modulator by nuts **(see illustration 11.30)**. There are no sealing washers. Unscrew the nuts to detach the pipes from the modulator. When refitting them tighten the nuts to the specified torque setting if the correct tools are available.

9 Refill the system with new DOT 4 brake fluid (see *Pre-ride checks*) and bleed the air from it (see Section 10).

10 Check the operation of the brakes before riding the motorcycle.

10 Brake bleeding and fluid change

Note: *On ABS models, before draining the brake fluid from the system, changing the fluid, or disconnecting any brake hoses or pipes from the master cylinders and ABS modulator or between them, bear in mind that the system must be bled on completion of work, and although this is done initially in the same way as models without ABS, to complete the procedure effectively the Triumph Diagnostic tool must be used to open and close the solenoids within the ABS modulator, and this can only be carried out by a dealer with the diagnostic tool. The bike should be transported, not ridden, to the dealer. It is OK to disconnect the hoses from the calipers, provided they are supported upright to minimise fluid loss and air ingress, as they come after the modulator in the system and so any air that gets into the end of the hose or caliper does not have to bleed through the modulator.*

Bleeding principles

1 Bleeding a brake is the process of removing aerated brake fluid from the master cylinder, the hose and the caliper. Bleeding is necessary whenever a brake system hydraulic connection is loosened, after a component

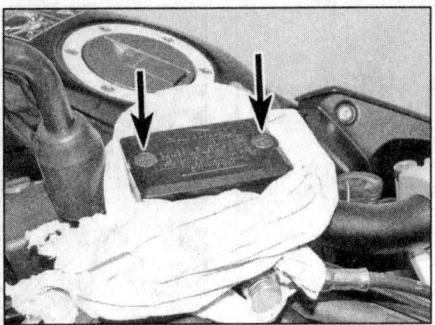

10.5a Undo the screws (arrowed)...

10.5b ...and remove the cover and diaphragm

or hose is replaced with a new one, when a master cylinder or a caliper is overhauled, or when there is a spongy feel to the lever or pedal and it travels all the way to its stop, and where braking force is less than it should be, and it is not due to any mechanical fault in the system (i.e. a sticking piston in the caliper, or a pad that is not moving as it should due to corrosion, for example on the pad pin). Leaks in the system may also allow air to enter, but leaking brake fluid will reveal their presence and warn you of the need for repair.

2 Brake bleeding is considered by some to be a bit of a black art – seasoned professionals sometimes have trouble getting a good firm feel in the brake lever, while a first timer may have no trouble at all. One of the problems, particularly with the front brake system, is that you are working against natural principles – science dictates that air bubbles in a liquid will rise to the top, but the process entails pumping the brake fluid and any air bubbles it contains down, from the master cylinder at the top to the bleed valve in the caliper at the bottom, so while the fluid is moving down the air bubbles will try to rise. Air bubbles can also get trapped, particularly where there are high points in its path, as with the front caliper hose(s).

3 To bleed the brakes using the conventional method, you will need some new DOT 4 brake fluid, a length of clear flexible hose, a small container partially filled with clean brake fluid, some rags, and a spanner to fit the brake

caliper bleed valve. Bleeding kits that include the hose, a one-way valve and a container are available relatively cheaply from a good auto store, and simplify the task.

4 Cover painted components to prevent damage in the event that brake fluid is spilled. *Caution: Brake fluid attacks painted finishes and some plastics – to prevent damage from spilled fluid, always cover paintwork when working on the braking system, and clean up any spills immediately using brake cleaner.*

Bleeding the front brake system

5 Turn the handlebars so the brake fluid reservoir is level. Note the current setting on the brake lever span adjuster, then set it to the No. 1 position – this gives maximum fluid displacement on each stroke. Remove the reservoir cover and diaphragm **(see illustrations)**. Slowly pump the brake lever a few times to dislodge any air bubbles from the holes in the bottom of the reservoir.

6 Pull the dust cap off the bleed valve on the right-hand caliper **(see illustration)**. If using a ring spanner (which is preferable to an open-ended one) fit it onto the valve **(see illustration)**. Attach one end of the bleed hose to the bleed valve and, if not using a kit, submerge the other end in the clean brake fluid in the container. . Support the container or kit at a suitable height according to the length of hose.

7 Check the fluid level in the reservoir – keep

10.6a Pull the cap off the bleed valve

10.6b Fit the ring spanner over the valve then connect the hose

6•16 Brakes, wheels and final drive

10.7 Keep the reservoir topped up

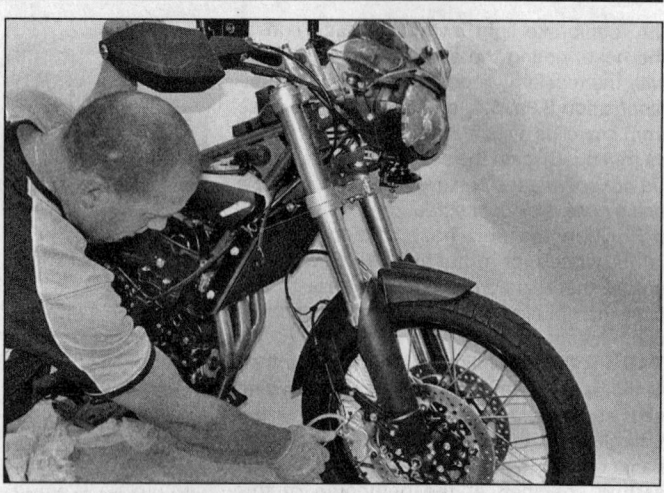

10.8 Bleeding the front brake

it topped up and do not allow the level to drop below the bottom of the window during the procedure **(see illustration)**.

8 Slowly pump the brake lever three or four times, then hold it in and open the bleed valve a quarter turn **(see illustration)**. When the valve is opened, brake fluid will flow out into the clear tubing, and the lever will move toward the handlebar. Tighten the bleed valve, then release the brake lever gradually.

9 If there is air in the system there will be air bubbles visible in the brake fluid, but not necessarily on the first pump. Repeat the process until no air bubbles have been seen for a few pumps, and the lever is firm when applied, topping the reservoir up when necessary. On completion remove the equipment and make sure the bleed valve is tight (but do not overtighten it as the threads in the caliper are easily stripped), then fit the dust cap. Transfer the equipment to the left-hand caliper and repeat the process.

10 When the system has been successfully bled there should be a good and progressively firm feel as the lever is applied, and the lever should not be able to travel all the way back to the handlebar.

11 On completion remove the equipment and make sure the bleed valve is tight (but do not overtighten it as the threads in the caliper are easily stripped), then fit the dust cap. Top-up the reservoir, then fit the diaphragm and cover **(see illustration 10.5b)**. Check for spilled brake fluid and clean up as required. Check that there are no fluid leaks from the system. On models with ABS refer to the **Note** above and if necessary take the bike to a Triumph dealer to complete the bleeding of the modulator. Check the operation of the brake before riding the motorcycle.

Bleeding the rear brake system

12 Unscrew the reservoir cap and remove the diaphragm plate and diaphragm **(see illustrations)**. Slowly pump the brake pedal a few times to dislodge any air bubbles from the holes in the bottom of the reservoir.

13 Pull the dust cap off the bleed valve on the caliper **(see illustration)**. If using a ring spanner (which is preferable to an open-ended one) fit it onto the valve **(see illustration)**.

10.12a Unscrew the cap...

10.12b ...and remove the diaphragm plate and diaphragm

10.13a Pull the cap (arrowed) off the bleed valve

10.13b Fit the ring spanner over the valve then connect the hose

Brakes, wheels and final drive 6•17

10.13c Bleeding kit set up for use, container supported on wood blocks

10.14 Keep the reservoir topped up

Attach one end of the bleed hose to the bleed valve and, if not using a kit, submerge the other end in the clean brake fluid in the container. Support the container or kit at a suitable height according to the length of hose **(see illustration)**.

14 Check the fluid level in the reservoir – keep it topped up and do not allow the level to drop below the lower level line during the procedure **(see illustration)**.

15 Slowly pump the brake pedal three or four times, then hold it down and open the bleed valve a quarter turn **(see illustration)**. When the valve is opened, brake fluid will flow out into the clear tubing, and the pedal will move down. Tighten the bleed valve, then release the brake pedal gradually.

16 If there is air in the system there will be air bubbles visible in the brake fluid, but not necessarily on the first pump. Repeat the process until no air bubbles have been seen for a few pumps, and the pedal is firm when applied, topping the reservoir up when necessary.

17 When the system has been successfully bled there should be a good and progressively firm feel as the pedal is applied.

18 On completion remove the equipment used and make sure the bleed valve is tight (but do not overtighten it as the threads in the caliper are easily stripped), then fit the dust cap. Top-up the reservoir, then fit the diaphragm, diaphragm plate and cap **(see illustration 10.12b)**. Check for spilled brake fluid and clean up as required. Check that there are no fluid leaks from the system. On models with ABS refer to the **Note** above and if necessary take the bike to a Triumph dealer to complete the bleeding of the modulator. Check the operation of the brake before riding the motorcycle.

Bleeding problems

19 If it is not possible to produce a firm feel to the lever or pedal look for any high point in the system in which a pocket of air may become trapped. Displace and move the hose so the bubble can be dislodged – tapping it may help. If necessary displace the master cylinder and/or the caliper, and free the brake hose from its guides and move the parts around to dislodge the air and encourage it towards the bleed valve – refer to the relevant Sections as required to displace components.

20 If you are still having trouble the fluid may be full of many tiny air bubbles rather than a few big ones. To remedy this apply some pressure to the system, for the front brake by tying the front brake lever lightly back to the handlebar, and for the rear by tying a weight to the brake pedal – do not apply too much pressure or the cup and seals in the master cylinder and caliper may fail. Let the fluid stabilise for a few hours, after which the tiny bubbles should either have risen to the top in the reservoir, or have formed into one or more big bubbles that can be more easily bled out by repeating the bleeding procedure.

21 If bleeding the system using the conventional tools and methods stated does not give satisfactory results, you can use a vacuum-type brake bleeding tool, such as the Mity-vac shown, following the manufacturer's instructions **(see illustration)**. This type of tool literally sucks the fluid out by creating a vacuum at the bleed valve. You may find that air is sucked past the bleed valve threads (air provides less resistance to the vacuum than the brake fluid) where it mixes with the fluid being drawn out. If this is the case the vacuum applied may be too great, or the bleed valve

10.15 Bleeding the rear brake

10.21 Vacuum-type brake bleeding tool

6•18 Brakes, wheels and final drive

may have been loosened too much. One way to get round this is to remove the bleed valve and thread some PTFE tape around its threads, but note that doing so will be a bit messy, so have some rag to hand. Also make sure the hose from the brake bleeding tool forms an air-tight fit over the bleed valve head, otherwise air will be drawn in from around the valve head.

Fluid change

22 Changing the brake fluid is a similar process to bleeding the brake and requires the same materials plus a suitable tool (such as a syringe, or alternatively lots of absorbent rag or paper) for siphoning the fluid out of the reservoir.
23 Remove the reservoir cover or cap, diaphragm plate (rear reservoir) and diaphragm and siphon the old fluid out **(see illustrations 10.5a and b (front) or 10.12a and b (rear))**. Wipe the reservoir clean. Fill the reservoir with new brake fluid **(see illustration 10.7 (front) or 10.14 (rear))**.
24 Connect the brake bleeding hose to the bleed valve (see Step 6 (front) and Step 13 (rear)). Slowly pump the brake lever or pedal three or four times then hold it in and open the bleed valve. When the valve is opened, brake fluid will flow out of the valve into the clear tubing, and the lever will move toward the handlebar, or the pedal will move down.
25 Tighten the bleed valve, then release the brake lever or pedal gradually. Keep the reservoir topped-up with new fluid at all times or air may enter the system and greatly increase the length of the task. Repeat the process until new fluid can be seen emerging from the caliper bleed valve.

 Old brake fluid is invariably much darker in colour than new fluid, making it easy to see when all old fluid has been expelled from the system.

26 On models with ABS refer to the **Note** above and take the bike to a Triumph dealer to complete the bleeding of the modulator. Check the operation of the brakes before riding the motorcycle. If the lever or pedal action is spongy, carry out the bleeding operation as described above.

Draining the system for overhaul

27 Draining the brake fluid is again a similar process to bleeding the brakes. The quickest and easiest way is to use a vacuum-type brake bleeding tool (see Step 21). Otherwise follow the procedure described above for changing the fluid, but quite simply do not put any new fluid into the reservoir – the system fills itself with air instead.
28 When it comes to refilling the system start by adding new fluid from a sealed container to the reservoir, then perform the bleeding procedure as described above until the fluid comes out of the bleed valve, and keep at it until you are certain there is no more air left in the system. On models with ABS refer to the **Note** above and take the bike to a Triumph dealer to complete the bleeding of the modulator. Check the operation of the brakes before riding the motorcycle. If the lever or pedal action is spongy, carry out the bleeding operation as described above.

11 Anti-lock brake system – ABS

General information

⚠ **Warning: The ABS system works by comparing the relative speed of the wheels, and is programmed using the wheel and tyre sizes specified and fitted as standard. If non-specified wheels or tyres are fitted the control unit may become confused and the system will not function correctly.**

1 The anti-lock braking system (ABS) prevents the wheels from locking up under hard braking or on uneven road surfaces. A sensor on each wheel picks up information about the speed of wheel rotation from a pulse ring mounted on the wheel and transmits to an electronic control unit in the modulator, and if it senses that a wheel is about to lock, it activates the solenoids in the modulator which releases brake pressure momentarily to that wheel, preventing a skid. When the system is active a pulsing can be felt through the lever or pedal as the fluid pressure is released and reapplied as required. The front and rear systems are entirely independent of each other, even though they function through the same control module and modulator.
2 The ABS system is self-checking, and is automatically switched on with the ignition. ABS will not function at speeds of less than 6 mph (10 km/h), with the ignition off, if a fault is indicated (ABS warning light remains on after start-up or comes on during use), or if the battery is flat.
3 When the ignition switch is turned on, the ABS indicator light on the instrument panel flashes, then goes off when a speed of 6 mph (10 km/h) is reached. If the indicator light stays on, or comes on while riding, then there is probably a fault in the system, in which case it will record a fault code. Stop the motorcycle and switch the ignition switch off. Switch it on again, start the engine and ride the bike - if the light goes off then the system is OK and will work, but the fault code is till stored. Depending on the severity or continuity of a fault the system may or may not switch itself off, but if it doesn't, if the fault still exists when the bike is next ridden, it will not switch itself on. If the light remains on or comes on again, take the machine to a Triumph dealer for testing – fault codes can only be read and diagnosed by the Triumph special tool, and every main dealer has one.
4 Note that under certain conditions, the indicator light could come on and a fault code could be registered, even though there is no actual problem with the system. This is when the effects of the conditions themselves simulate an actual fault. This can occur if the machine is ridden continuously on very bumpy roads, or if the rider does a wheelie, or if the air pressure on one tyre is extremely low, or if the machine is placed on the centrestand or an auxiliary stand with the engine running and the rear wheel is turning when the front is not. If this happens stop the bike and turn the engine off, then restart and ride the bike – the light may not come on again when the system realises everything is OK, but if it does the fault code must be retrieved and then erased before the indicator light will go out.
5 The only actions the owner can take in the case of a fault, and the only maintenance that can be applied, is firstly to make sure there is no dirt or debris on each wheel speed sensor tip or between the poles on the sensor rotor **(see illustration)**. Secondly check the air gap between the sensor tip and one of the poles on the rotor, though once set, this is unlikely to change. Check the gap by inserting a feeler gauge between the sensor and the tip of one of the poles **(see illustrations)**. Check the gap in different places by rotating the wheel. If the gap is not within the range specified at the beginning of the Chapter, remove the sensor (see below) and adjust the air gap by inserting

11.5a Check the sensor tip (A) and pulse ring poles (B) are clean

11.5b Checking the air gap on the front sensor

Brakes, wheels and final drive 6•19

11.5c Checking the air gap on the rear sensor

11.5d A shim can be fitted, changed or removed to restore the correct air gap

11.9 Front wheel speed sensor (arrowed)

11.10a Displace the ignition switch connector (arrowed)...

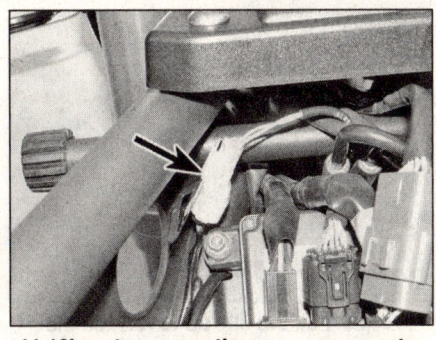

11.10b ...to access the sensor connector (arrowed)

11.11 Removing the front wheel speed sensor

a shim of the required thickness to bring the gap within specifications **(see illustration)**. Shims are available in sizes of 0.8 and 1.6 mm. On completion tighten the bolt to the specified torque setting.

6 Also make a check of all the system wiring and connectors, looking for chafed wires or broken connector pins, damp or corroded terminals, and if required refer to electrical system fault finding at the beginning of Chapter 8 and to the wiring diagrams at the end of it and check all wiring for continuity. Make sure the ignition is OFF before disconnecting any wiring connectors or making any tests.

7 If the indicator light does not come on when the ignition is switched on, check the ABS fuses (see Chapter 8) and the instrument panel and the control module wiring connectors. If all is good, take the machine to a Triumph dealer for testing.

8 Fault diagnosis and any other work on the system, including the final stage of bleeding it and changing the brake fluid, must be undertaken by a Triumph dealer.

Component removal and installation

Front wheel sensor

9 The sensor is mounted in the bottom of the left-hand fork **(see illustration)**.
10 Remove the fuel tank (see Chapter 4). Displaced the ignition switch wiring connector from its bracket **(see illustration)**. Displace and disconnect the sensor wiring connector **(see illustration)**. Free the wiring from any ties and the clips and feed it down to the sensor, noting its routing.
11 Unscrew the bolt securing the sensor and withdraw it from the fork, collecting any shim fitted behind the sensor plate **(see illustration)**.
12 Installation is the reverse of removal. Make sure the sensor tip is clean and undamaged, and that the mounting plate is not distorted. Make sure any shim previously fitted is positioned between the mounting plate and the fork. Tighten the bolt to the torque setting specified at the beginning of the Chapter. Check the air gap (see Step 5).

Rear wheel sensor

13 The sensor is mounted in the rear brake caliper bracket **(see illustration)**.
14 Remove the battery (see Chapter 8). Disconnect the sensor wiring connector **(see illustration)**. Free the wiring from any ties and the clips and feed it down to the sensor, noting its routing.
15 Unscrew the bolt securing the sensor and withdraw it from the bracket, collecting any shim fitted behind the sensor plate **(see illustration 11.5d)**.
16 Installation is the reverse of removal. Make sure the sensor tip is clean and undamaged, and that the mounting plate is not distorted. Make sure any shim previously fitted is positioned between the mounting plate and the caliper bracket. Tighten the bolt to the torque setting specified at the beginning of the Chapter. Check the air gap (see Step 5).

Front wheel pulse ring

17 Remove the wheel (see Section 14). Support the wheel using wooden blocks so no weight is on the disc.

11.13 Rear wheel speed sensor (arrowed)

11.14 Rear wheel sensor connector (arrowed)

6•20 Brakes, wheels and final drive

11.18 Front wheel pulse ring bolts (arrowed)

11.21 Rear wheel pulse ring bolts (arrowed)

11.24a Undo the bolts (arrowed), release the battery strap and remove the bracket

11.24b Unscrew the bolt (arrowed) and remove the duct

11.25 Pull the clip up to release the connector

11.26 Release the guides (arrowed) and clips

18 Unscrew the bolts securing the pulse ring and lift it off **(see illustration)** – note that the bolts also secure the brake disc.

19 Before installing the ring, make sure there is no dirt or corrosion between the mating surfaces as this will not allow the ring to sit flat when bolted down and it will be warped and could cause the ABS system to indicate a fault. Tighten the bolts evenly in a criss-cross pattern to the torque setting specified at the beginning of the Chapter.

Rear wheel pulse ring

20 Remove the wheel (see Section 15).
21 Unscrew the bolts securing the pulse ring and lift it off, along with the spacer ring **(see illustration)**.
22 Before installing the ring, make sure there is no dirt or corrosion between the mating surfaces as this will not allow the ring to sit flat when bolted down and it will be warped and could cause the ABS system to indicate a fault. Tighten the bolts evenly in a criss-cross pattern to the torque setting specified at the beginning of the Chapter.

Modulator

Note: *Before removing the modulator, bear in mind that the system must be bled on completion of work, and although this is done initially in the same way as models without ABS, to complete the procedure the Triumph Diagnostic tool must be used to open and close the solenoids within the modulator, and this can only be carried out by a dealer. The bike should be transported, not ridden, to the dealer.*

23 Have some clean rag to hand to catch any spilled brake fluid and some clingfilm to wrap around the end of each pipe as it is disconnected. Drain the brake fluid from the system (see Section 10).

24 Remove the seat (see Chapter 7). Disconnect the battery (Chapter 8). Remove the airbox (see Chapter 4). Remove the seat bracket and the air intake duct **(see illustrations)**.
25 Release the security clip and disconnect the wiring connector from the control module **(see illustration)**.
26 Release the rear brake hose guides from the swingarm and modulator bracket **(see illustration)**. Release the rear wheel speed sensor wire clips from the hose.
27 Unscrew the engine earth lead bolt **(see illustration)**.
28 Remove the rear brake light switch (see Chapter 8).
29 Release the brake pipe clips from the inside of the frame **(see illustration)**.
30 Loosen the pipe nuts, being prepared with some rag to catch any residual fluid **(see illustration)**.

11.27 Unscrew the bolt (arrowed)

11.29 Release the clips (arrowed)

11.30 Slacken the nuts (arrowed)

Brakes, wheels and final drive 6•21

31 Unscrew the two remaining modulator bracket mounting bolts (one has already been removed with the seat bracket) **(see illustrations)**. Carefully lift the modulator, bringing the brake pipes and the engine earth lead (which routes between the modulator and its bracket) with it, taking great care not to bend the pipes, until you can access the underside.
32 Unscrew the pipe nuts, then release the pipes from the clips on the underside of the modulator, being prepared with some rag to catch any residual fluid, and taking care not to bend the pipes. Wrap the end of each pipe in clingfilm to prevent fluid loss and dirt getting in. Remove the modulator.
33 If required remove the modulator bracket, noting the routing of the earth lead. Make sure the grommets in the bracket are in good condition.
34 Installation is the reverse of removal. Make sure the collars are fitted in the mounting bracket grommets. Initially tighten the brake pipe nuts finger-tight only for correct alignment until the modulator is mounted, then fully tighten them. If the correct tools are available tighten the nuts to the torque setting specified at the beginning of the Chapter.
35 Bleed the hydraulic system following the procedure in Section 10, then transport the bike to a Triumph dealer for bleeding of the modulator. Check the operation of both front and rear brakes carefully before riding the motorcycle.

12 Wheel inspection and repair

1 In order to carry out a proper inspection of the wheels, it is necessary to support the bike upright so that the wheel being inspected is raised off the ground. Position the motorcycle on an auxiliary stand. Clean the wheels thoroughly

11.31a Unscrew the bolt (arrowed)...

11.31b ...and the bolt (arrowed)

to remove mud and dirt that may interfere with the inspection procedure or mask defects. Make a general check of the wheels (see Chapter 1) and tyres (see *Pre-ride checks*).
2 Attach a dial gauge to the fork or the swingarm and position its tip against the side of the wheel rim. Spin the wheel slowly and check the axial (side-to-side) runout of the rim **(see illustration)**.
3 In order to accurately check radial (out of round) runout with the dial gauge, remove the wheel from the machine, and the tyre from the wheel. With the axle clamped in a vice and the dial gauge positioned on the top of the rim, the wheel can be rotated to check the runout **(see illustration 12.2)**.
4 An easier, though slightly less accurate, method is to attach a stiff wire pointer to the fork or the swingarm and position the end a fraction of an inch from the wheel rim where the wheel and tyre join. If the wheel is true, the distance from the pointer to the rim will be constant as the wheel is rotated. **Note:** *If wheel runout is excessive, check the wheel bearings very carefully before renewing the wheel.*
5 If wheel runout is excessive, first check the wheel bearings. If they are good, on XC models it should be possible to realign the wheel by adjusting the spokes, but to do this accurately takes some knowledge and skill, and should be left to an experienced wheel builder. On standard models you will have to replace the wheel with a new one.
6 The wheels should also be inspected for cracks, flat spots on the rim and other damage. Look very closely for dents in the area where the tyre bead contacts the rim. On standard models (with tubeless tyres) dents in this area may prevent complete sealing of the tyre against the rim, which leads to deflation

of the tyre over a period of time. If damage is evident, the wheel will have to be replaced with a new one. Never attempt to repair a damaged cast alloy wheel.

13 Wheel alignment check

1 Misalignment of the wheels, which may be due to a cocked rear wheel or a bent frame or fork yokes, can cause strange and possibly serious handling problems. If the frame or yokes are at fault, repair by a frame specialist or replacement with new parts are the only alternatives.
2 To check the alignment you will need an assistant, a length of string or a perfectly straight piece of wood or metal bar and a ruler. A plumb bob or other suitable weight will also be required.
3 In order to make a proper check of the wheels it is necessary to support the bike in an upright position, using an auxiliary stand (or on its centrestand if fitted). First ensure that the chain adjuster markings coincide on each side of the swingarm (see Chapter 1, Section 1). Measure the width of both tyres at their widest points. Subtract the smaller measurement from the larger measurement, then divide the difference by two. The result is the amount of offset that should exist between the front and rear tyres on both sides.
4 If a string is used, have your assistant hold one end of it about halfway between the floor and the rear axle, touching the rear sidewall of the tyre.
5 Run the other end of the string forward and pull it tight so that it is roughly parallel to the floor **(see illustration)**. Slowly bring the string

12.2 Check the wheel for radial (out-of-round) runout (A) and axial (side-to-side) runout (B)

13.5 Wheel alignment check using string

6•22 Brakes, wheels and final drive

13.7 Wheel alignment check using a straight-edge

into contact with the front sidewall of the rear tyre, then turn the front wheel until it is parallel with the string. Measure the distance from the front tyre sidewall to the string.

6 Repeat the procedure on the other side of the motorcycle. The distance from the front tyre sidewall to the string should be equal on both sides.

7 As previously mentioned, a perfectly straight length of wood or metal bar may be substituted for the string (see illustration). The procedure is the same.

8 If the distance between the string and tyre is greater on one side, or if the rear wheel appears to be out of alignment, have your machine checked by a Triumph dealer or frame specialist.

9 If the front-to-back alignment is correct, the wheels still may be out of alignment vertically.

10 Using a plumb bob, or other suitable weight, and a length of string, check the rear wheel to make sure it is vertical. To do this, hold the string against the tyre upper sidewall and allow the weight to settle just off the floor. When the string touches both the upper and lower tyre sidewalls and is perfectly straight, the wheel is vertical. If it is not, place thin spacers under one leg of the stand until it is.

11 Once the rear wheel is vertical, check the front wheel in the same manner. If both wheels are not perfectly vertical, the frame and/or major suspension components are bent.

14 Front wheel

Removal

1 Support the motorcycle securely on level ground using the centrestand if fitted, and/or an auxiliary stand or stands, so the front wheel is off the ground.

2 Unbolt the front brake calipers (see illustration 2.3). Support them with a piece of wire, string, a cable-tie or a bungee cord so that no strain is placed on the hoses. There is no need to disconnect the hoses. Note: *Do not operate the front brake lever with the calipers displaced.*

3 Slacken the axle clamp bolts on the bottom of the right-hand fork (see illustration). Unscrew the axle – you need a dedicated motorcycle axle bit, readily available from good suppliers, or a large hex bit or car sump key.

4 Support the wheel, then withdraw the axle and lower the wheel to the ground (see illustration). Use a drift to drive the axle out if required. Roll the wheel out from between the forks.

5 Remove the spacer from each side of the wheel for safekeeping if required (see illustration).

Caution: *Don't lay the wheel down and allow it to rest on a disc – the disc could become warped. Set the wheel on wood blocks so the disc doesn't support the weight of the wheel, or keep it upright.*

6 Clean off all old grease from the axle and spacers and remove any corrosion using a scouring pad or wire wool. Check the axle is straight by rolling it on a flat surface. If the equipment is available, place the axle in V-blocks and check for runout using a dial gauge. If the axle is bent, replace it with a new one.

7 Check the condition of the wheel bearings (see Section 16).

Installation

8 Apply lithium-based grease to the lips of the bearing seals, to the axle and to the spacers. Fit a spacer into each side of the wheel – they are the same (see illustration 14.5).

9 Manoeuvre the wheel into position, making sure the directional arrow on the tyre points in the direction of forward rotation. Lift the wheel into place between the forks, making sure the spacers remain in position, and slide the axle in from the right-hand side (see illustration 14.4).

10 Tighten the axle to the torque setting specified at the beginning of the Chapter. Tighten the axle clamp bolts on the bottom of the right-hand fork to the specified torque setting (see illustration 14.3). Wipe any excess grease off the spacers and forks. Make sure the wheel spins freely.

11 Install the brake calipers (see Section 2). Apply the front brake a few times to bring the pads back into contact with the discs.

12 Check the operation of the front brake before riding the bike.

14.3 Slacken the clamp bolts (A) then unscrew the axle (B) using a large hex bit

14.4 Withdraw the axle and remove the wheel

14.5 Remove the spacer from each side

Brakes, wheels and final drive 6•23

15 Rear wheel

Removal

1 Support the motorcycle securely on level ground using the centrestand if fitted, or an auxiliary stand (a paddock stand is ideal), so the rear wheel is off the ground.
2 Refer to Chapter 1 and slacken the drive chain.
3 Unbolt the rear brake caliper (see illustration 2.19). Support it with a piece of wire, string, a cable-tie or a bungee cord so that no strain is placed on the hose. There is no need to disconnect the hose from the caliper. **Note:** *Do not operate the brake pedal with the caliper removed.*
4 Unscrew the nut from the left-hand end of the axle and remove the washer and the adjustment position marker (see illustrations). Note that Triumph specifies to use a new nut.
5 Disengage the chain from the sprocket (see illustration). Support the wheel then withdraw the axle along with the right-hand adjustment position marker and lower the wheel to the ground (see illustration). Remove the wheel from between the swingarm ends.
6 Remove the caliper bracket, noting how it locates on the swingarm (see illustration). Remove the plain spacer from the left-hand side of the wheel and the shouldered spacer from the right-hand side for safekeeping if required (see illustrations).

15.4a Unscrew the axle nut and remove the washer...

15.4b ...adjustment position marker

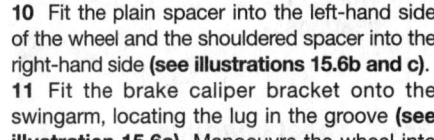 *Tie the chain to the rear sub-frame, or lay some paper or rag on the ground for the chain to rest on, to prevent any dust and grit sticking to it.*

7 Clean off all old grease from the axle and spacers and remove any corrosion using a scouring pad or wire wool. Check the axle is straight by rolling it on a flat surface. If the equipment is available, place the axle in V-blocks and check for runout using a dial gauge. If the axle is bent, replace it with a new one.
8 Check the wheel bearings and sprocket coupling bearings (see Section 16).

Installation

9 Apply a thin coat of lithium-based grease to the lips of each grease seal, and also to the spacers and the axle.

10 Fit the plain spacer into the left-hand side of the wheel and the shouldered spacer into the right-hand side (see illustrations 15.6b and c).
11 Fit the brake caliper bracket onto the swingarm, locating the lug in the groove (see illustration 15.6a). Manoeuvre the wheel into place between the ends of the swingarm.
12 Slide the right-hand adjustment position marker (the one with the raised sections, which must face out) onto the axle. Lift the wheel into position, making sure the caliper bracket and the spacers remain in place, and slide the axle through from the right-hand side (see illustration 15.5b). Make sure it passes through the caliper bracket. Make sure the adjustment marker is correctly positioned with the raised sections horizontal and fit the flats on the axle head between them (see illustration). Fit the drive chain around the sprocket (see illustration 15.5a).

15.5a Slip the chain off the sprocket...

15.5b ...then withdraw the axle and lower the wheel

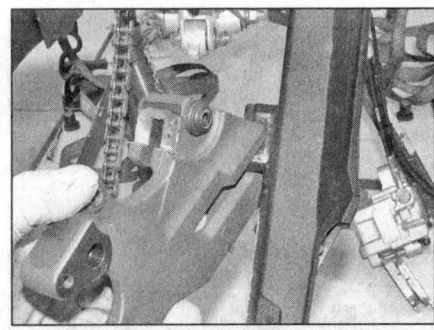

15.6a Remove the caliper bracket

15.6b Remove the plain spacer...

15.6c ...and the shouldered spacer

15.12 Make sure the axle head and adjustment marker locate correctly

6•24 Brakes, wheels and final drive

13 Check that everything is correctly aligned, then fit the left-hand adjustment position marker (see illustration 15.4b). Fit the washer and the axle nut (see illustration 15.4a). Adjust the chain slack as described in Chapter 1. Tighten the axle nut to the torque setting specified at the beginning of the Chapter, making sure the adjustment markers are butted against the adjuster bolt heads.
14 Install the brake caliper (see Section 2). Apply the brake pedal several times to bring the pads into contact with the disc.
15 Check the operation of the rear brake before riding the bike.

16 Wheel and sprocket coupling bearings

Front wheel bearings

Note: *Always renew the wheel bearings in pairs, never individually. Avoid using a high pressure cleaner on the wheel bearing area.*
1 Remove the wheel (see Section 14). Lay the wheel on wood blocks. A caged ball bearing is fitted in each side of the wheel, with a circlip retaining the left-hand bearing.
2 Inspect the seals and bearings – check that each bearing inner race turns smoothly and that the outer race is a tight fit in the hub (see *Tools and Workshop Tips* (Section 5) in the Reference Section). **Note:** *Do not remove the bearings unless they are going to be replaced with new ones.*
3 If new components are needed lever out the bearing seal from each side of the hub, using a flat-bladed screwdriver or a seal hook (see illustration). Take care not to damage the hub. New seals must be fitted on reassembly.

> **HAYNES HiNT** *Position a piece of wood against the wheel to prevent the screwdriver shaft damaging it when levering the seal out.*

4 Remove the circlip from the left-hand side of the wheel (see illustration) - Triumph specifies to use a new one.
5 Move the bearing spacer aside to expose the inner race on the lower bearing (see illustration 16.16a). Using a metal rod (preferably a brass punch) inserted through the centre of the upper bearing drive the lower bearing from the hub, moving the spacer around and relocating the drift so it's driven out squarely (see illustration 16.16b). The bearing spacer will also come out. Turn the wheel over so that the remaining bearing faces down. Drive the bearing out of the wheel using a socket on the inner race and an extension bar. If you can't move the spacer, or if you can't get sufficient purchase with the drift, remove the bearings using an internal expanding puller with slide-hammer attachment, which can be obtained commercially - select the correct attachment and locate it between the inner race of the upper bearing and the spacer, then tighten the inner bolt to expand and lock the puller (see illustration). Attach the slide-hammer, hold the wheel firmly down and jar the bearing out (see illustration).
6 Thoroughly clean the hub area of the wheel and inspect the bearing housings for damage. If a housing is damaged, consult a Triumph dealer or wheel specialist before reassembling the wheel.
7 Fit the new bearings with the marked side facing out. Drive the first bearing in using a bearing driver or suitable socket that bears only on the outer race, and make sure the bearing fits squarely and all the way onto its seat (see illustration). Alternatively draw it in using a drawbolt arrangement (see *Tools and Workshop Tips*).
8 Turn the wheel over then fit the bearing spacer and the other new bearing.
9 Fit a new circlip into its groove outside the left-hand bearing (see illustration 16.4).
10 Fit the new seals into the hub using finger pressure or a suitable driver that bears on the outer rim, setting them flush with the hub (see illustration). Smear the seal lips with grease.
11 Clean the brake discs using acetone or brake system cleaner, then install the wheel (see Section 14).

Rear wheel bearings

12 Remove the wheel (see Section 15). Set the wheel on wood blocks. Lift the sprocket coupling out of the wheel, noting how it fits, and remove the spacer inside it (see illustrations 16.24a and b). A caged ball bearing is fitted in each side of the wheel, with a circlip retaining the right-hand bearing.
13 Inspect the seal and bearings – check that each bearing inner race turns smoothly and that the outer race is a tight fit in the hub (see *Tools and Workshop Tips* (Section 5) in the Reference Section). **Note:** *Do not remove the bearings unless they are going to be replaced with new ones.*

16.3 Lever out the grease seals

16.4 Remove the circlip

16.5a Locate the knife edge of the puller in the gap between the bearing and the spacer, then expand it...

16.5b ...and use the slide-hammer to dislodge the bearing

16.7 A socket can be used to drive in the bearing

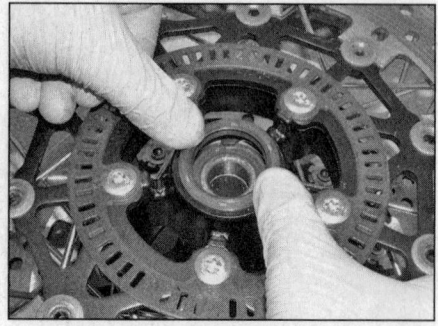

16.10 Fit the grease seal and press or tap it into place

Brakes, wheels and final drive 6•25

16.14 Lever out the grease seal

16.15 Remove the circlip

16.16a Move the spacer to the side to expose the inner race...

14 If new components are needed lever out the bearing seal from the right-side of the hub, using a flat-bladed screwdriver or a seal hook (see illustration). Take care not to damage the hub. A new seal must be fitted on reassembly.

 Haynes Hint: *Position a piece of wood against the wheel to prevent the screwdriver shaft damaging it when levering the seal out.*

15 Remove the circlip from the right-hand side of the wheel (see illustration) - Triumph specify to use a new one.
16 Move the bearing spacer aside to expose the inner race on the lower bearing (see illustration). Using a metal rod (preferably a brass punch) inserted through the centre of the upper bearing drive the lower bearing from the hub, moving the spacer around and relocating the drift so it's driven out squarely (see illustration). The bearing spacer will also come out. Turn the wheel over so that the remaining bearing faces down. Drive the bearing out of the wheel using a socket on the inner race and an extension bar. If you can't move the spacer, or if you can't get sufficient purchase with the drift, remove the bearings using an internal expanding puller with slide-hammer attachment, which can be obtained commercially - select the correct attachment and locate it between the inner race of the upper bearing and the spacer, then tighten the inner bolt to expand and lock the puller (see illustration 16.5a). Attach the slide-hammer, hold the wheel firmly down and jar the bearing out (see illustration 16.5b).
17 Thoroughly clean the hub area of the

16.16b ...then locate the drift on it and drive the bearing out

wheel and inspect the bearing housings for damage. If a housing is damaged, consult a Triumph dealer or wheel specialist before reassembling the wheel.
18 Fit the new bearings with the marked side facing out. Drive the first bearing in using a bearing driver or suitable socket that bears only on the outer race, and make sure the bearing fits squarely and all the way onto its seat (see illustration 16.7). Alternatively draw it in using a drawbolt arrangement (see *Tools and Workshop Tips*).
19 Turn the wheel over then fit the bearing spacer and the other new bearing.
20 Fit a new circlip into its groove outside the right-hand bearing (see illustration 16.15).
21 Fit the new seal into the right-hand side of the hub using finger pressure or a suitable driver that bears on the outer rim, setting it flush with the hub (see illustration). Smear the seal lips with grease.

16.21 Fit the grease seal and press or tap it into place

22 Make sure the spacer is in place, then fit the sprocket coupling into the wheel (see illustrations 16.24b and a).
23 Clean the brake disc using acetone or brake system cleaner, then install the wheel (see Section 15).

Sprocket coupling bearing

24 Remove the rear wheel (see Section 15). Lift the sprocket coupling out of the wheel, noting how it fits, and remove the spacer inside it (see illustrations).
25 Inspect the seal and bearing – check that the bearing inner races turn smoothly and that the outer race is a tight fit in the coupling (see *Tools and Workshop Tips (Section 5)* in the Reference Section). **Note:** *Do not remove the bearing unless it is being replaced with a new one.*
26 If new components are needed lever out the bearing seal using a flat-bladed screwdriver or a seal hook (see illustration). Take care not

16.24a Lift the sprocket coupling out of the wheel...

16.24b ...and remove the spacer from inside it

16.26 Lever out the grease seal

6•26 Brakes, wheels and final drive

16.27 Remove the circlip (arrowed)

16.28 Drive the bearing out from the inside

16.30 A socket can be used to drive in the bearing

16.31 Press or drive the seal into the coupling

to damage the rim of the coupling. Discard the seal – a new one must be fitted.

27 If the bearing is worn, remove the circlip **(see illustration)** – Triumph specifies to use a new one.

28 Support the coupling on blocks of wood, sprocket side down, and drive the bearing out from the inside using a bearing driver or socket **(see illustration)**.

29 Thoroughly clean the sprocket coupling and inspect the bearing housing for damage. If the housing is damaged, consult a Triumph dealer or wheel specialist before reassembling the wheel.

30 Fit the new bearing with the marked side facing out. Drive the bearing in using a bearing driver or suitable socket that bears only on the outer race, and make sure the bearing fits squarely and all the way onto its seat **(see illustration)**. Fit a new circlip into its groove.

31 Fit the new seal into the coupling using finger pressure or a suitable driver that bears on the outer rim, setting it flush with the hub **(see illustration)**. Smear the seal lips with grease.

32 Check the sprocket coupling/rubber dampers (see Section 21).

33 Fit the spacer, then fit the sprocket coupling into the wheel **(see illustrations 16.24b and a)**. Clean the brake disc using acetone or brake system cleaner then install the wheel (see Section 15).

17 Tyre information and fitting

General information

1 The wheels on standard models are designed to take tubeless tyres. The wheels on XC models are designed to take tubed tyres. Tyre sizes are given in the Specifications at the beginning of this chapter.

2 Refer to the *Pre-ride checks* listed at the beginning of this manual for tyre maintenance.

Fitting notes

Note: *On standard models fitted with the TPMS refer to Step 5 in Section 18.*

3 When selecting new tyres, refer to the tyre information in the Owner's Handbook. Ensure that front and rear tyre types are compatible, the correct size and correct speed rating; if necessary seek advice from a Triumph dealer or tyre fitting specialist **(see illustration)**.

4 Have the tyres fitted by a motorcycle tyre specialist rather than attempting to do it yourself. This is particularly relevant in the case of tubeless tyres because the force required

17.3 Common tyre sidewall markings

to break the seal between the wheel rim and tyre bead is substantial, and is usually beyond the capabilities of an individual working with normal tyre levers. Additionally, the specialist will be able to balance the wheels after tyre fitting.

5 Note that punctured tubeless tyres can in some cases be repaired. External repairs made using a repair kit should only ever be considered as a temporary measure to get you to a dealer for a new tyre, and riding at speed or with any extra load should be avoided. Internal repairs carried out by a motorcycle tyre fitting specialist are better. Make sure a wheel with a repaired tyre is balanced before it is fitted back on the bike. A repaired tyre should not be used at speeds above 50 mph (80 kmh) for the first 24 hours, and not above 80 mph (130 kmh) thereafter, and carrying heavy loads should be avoided.

6 A punctured tubed tyre can be repaired by fitting a new inner tube having removed the cause of the puncture from the tyre itself. Don't resort to patching the inner tube.

18 Tyre pressure monitoring system (TPMS)

General information

1 A tyre pressure monitoring system (TPMS) may be fitted as an optional extra on standard models only with tubeless tyres – the system cannot be fitted to XC models with tubed tyres. A sensor inside each wheel measures the pressure of air in the tyre and transmits to a read-out on the instrument panel via the immobiliser/TPMS control unit (covered in Section 18, Chapter 4). The system will only transmit a read-out when the bike reaches a speed of 12 mph (20 km/h) – until then the read-out will only show two dashes. Each sensor is powered by its own internal battery, but as the sensors are sealed units new sensors must be fitted when the batteries run out.

2 The system monitors real-time pressures, so as the tyre warms up with use the pressure displayed will increase. Tyre pressures should always be checked and set when the tyres are cold, so do not re-adjust the pressure when the tyre is warm because the read-out says it is higher than it should be. The cold pressures specified by Triumph take into account the fact that pressures will increase as the tyres warm.

3 Triumph state that cold tyre pressures should only be set using an accurate tyre gauge, and not using the TPMS read-out. Refer to the *Pre-ride checks* listed at the beginning of this manual for tyre pressure check details and tyre maintenance.

4 The system performs its own self-diagnosis, and in the event of a fault the read warning light will come on and the tyre symbol will flash. The Triumph diagnostic tool is required for fault code retrieval.

5 It is advisable to inform whoever may be fitting new tyres of the presence of a sensor in each wheel, as they are easily damaged – an adhesive label on each wheel rim identifies the position of the sensor, but the label may well have come off, or been taken off. Note

6•28 Brakes, wheels and final drive

that the use of 'get-you-home' puncture repair sealants injected via the valve may well damage the sensor beyond use.

19 Drive chain removal, cleaning and installation

Note: *The drive chain has a riveted-type soft (joining) link so it can be split using one of several commercially-available chain cutting/staking tools (but the cheap ones are best avoided - Triumph can supply one, part No. T3880027). The soft joining link can be recognised by the sideplate's different colour, as well as by the riveted ends of the link's two pins which look as if they have been deeply centre-punched, instead of peened over as with all the other pins.*

Removal

1 Remove the front sprocket cover (see Section 20).
2 Identify the soft link and move it to a suitable position to work on by rotating the back wheel **(see illustration)**.
3 Slacken the drive chain as described in Chapter 1.
4 Split the chain at the soft link using a chain breaker tool - refer to Section 8 'Chains' of *Tools and Workshop Tips* in the Reference section at the end of this manual for details of how to use the tool, or follow the tool manufacturer's instructions. Remove the chain

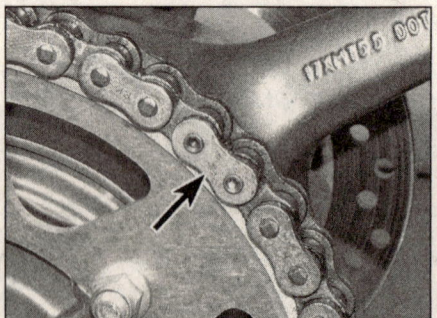

19.2 The soft link (arrowed) is visibly different from the others

from the bike, noting its routing around the swingarm and through the chainguard. Note that it is essential to use a new soft link when re-joining the chain.

Installation

⚠ **Warning:** *NEVER fit a drive chain that uses a clip-type master (split) link. Use ONLY the correct service tools to secure the staked-type master link – if you do not have access to such tools, have the chain replaced by a Triumph dealer.*

5 Route the drive chain around the sprockets and through the chainguard, leaving the two ends mid-way between the sprockets along the bottom run.
6 Referring to Section 8 in *Tools and Workshop Tips* in the Reference Section, fit the new joining link from the inside using

new O-rings. Fit the new sideplate using new O-rings and with its identification marks facing out. Using the chain tool to press the sideplate into position. Stake the new link using the chain tool, following carefully the instructions of both the chain manufacturer and the tool manufacturer. DO NOT re-use old joining link components.
7 After riveting, check the soft link and pin ends for any signs of cracking. If there is any evidence of cracking, the soft link, O-rings, and sideplate must be replaced with new ones. Measure the diameter of the riveted pin ends in two directions and check that each pin has been evenly riveted.
8 Install the sprocket cover.
9 On completion, adjust and lubricate the chain following the procedures described in Chapter 1.

Caution: *Don't use gasoline (petrol), solvent or other cleaning fluids which might damage the chain's internal sealing properties. Don't use high-pressure water. Remove the chain, wipe it off, then blow dry it with compressed air immediately. The entire process shouldn't take longer than ten minutes – if it does, the sealing rings in the chain rollers could be damaged.*

20 Sprockets

Front sprocket cover

1 Note the alignment of the punch mark on the gearchange shaft end with the slit in the linkage arm clamp **(see illustration)**. Unscrew the pinch bolt and slide the arm off the shaft **(see illustration)**.
2 Unscrew the sprocket cover bolts and remove the cover **(see illustration)**.
3 Installation is the reverse of removal. Clean all old chain lube off the sprocket cover and crankcase. Make sure the coolant by-pass hose seats in its cut-out **(see illustration)**. Align the slit in the linkage arm with the mark on the shaft **(see illustration 20.1a)**.

Sprocket check

4 Remove the front sprocket cover (Steps 1 and 2).
5 Check the wear pattern on both sprockets (see Chapter 1, Section 1). If the sprocket teeth are worn excessively, replace the chain and both sprockets as a set. Whenever the sprockets are inspected, the drive chain should be inspected also (see Chapter 1). Always replace the chain and sprockets as a set – worn sprockets can ruin a new drive chain and vice versa.
6 Adjust and lubricate the chain following the procedures described in Chapter 1.

Front sprocket

Note: *Slacken the front sprocket nut before disengaging the chain from the rear sprocket*

20.1a Note the alignment of the punch mark (arrowed)…

20.1b …then unscrew the bolt and slide the arm off

20.2 Unscrew the bolts (arrowed) and remove the cover – note the routing of the by-pass hose

20.3 Fit the hose in the front of the cover

20.8 Bend back the lockwasher tab(s) then unscrew the nut and remove the washer

20.9 Slide the sprocket off the shaft and remove it

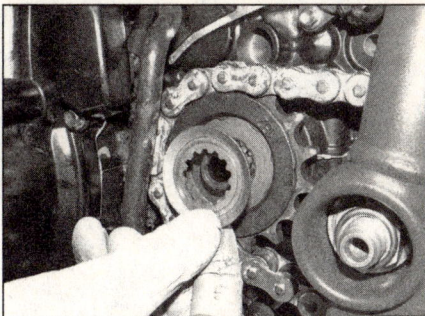

20.11a Fit the new lockwasher...

20.11b ...and the nut, and tighten it to the specified torque

20.11c Bend the tabs up against the nut

20.14 Rear sprocket nuts (arrowed)

so the rear brake can be used to prevent the front sprocket turning.

7 Remove the front sprocket cover (Steps 1 and 2).

8 Bend down the raised tab(s) on the sprocket nut lockwasher **(see illustration)**. Have an assistant apply the rear brake hard, then unscrew the nut and remove the washer **(see illustrations 20.11b and a)**. Discard the washer - a new one should be used. Refer to Chapter 1 and adjust the chain so that it is fully slack.

9 Slide the sprocket and chain off the shaft and slip the sprocket out of the chain **(see illustration)**. If there is not enough slack in the chain to remove the sprocket, disengage the chain from the rear wheel.

10 Engage the sprocket with the chain, making sure the marked side is facing out, and slide it on the shaft **(see illustration 20.9)**. Take up the slack in the chain (see Chapter 1).

11 Slide on the new lockwasher, locating it on the splines **(see illustration)**. Fit the nut with its shouldered side facing in and tighten it to the torque setting specified at the beginning of the Chapter, applying the rear brake to prevent the sprocket from turning **(see illustration)**. Bend one side of the lockwasher against a flat on the nut **(see illustration)**.

12 Install the front sprocket cover and gearchange linkage.

Rear sprocket

13 Remove the rear wheel (see Section 15).

14 Unscrew the nuts securing the sprocket to the coupling **(see illustration)**. Remove the sprocket, noting which way round it fits.

15 Fit the sprocket onto the coupling with the stamped mark facing out, then fit the nuts. Tighten the nuts evenly and in a criss-cross sequence to the torque setting specified at the beginning of the Chapter.

16 Install the rear wheel (see Section 15).

21 Rear sprocket coupling/ rubber dampers

1 Remove the rear wheel (see Section 15). Lift the sprocket coupling out of the wheel, noting how it fits, and remove the spacer inside it **(see illustrations 16.24a and b)**.

2 Check the coupling for cracks or any obvious signs of damage.

3 Lift the rubber damper piece from the wheel hub, noting how it fits. Check it for cracks, hardening and general deterioration **(see illustration)**. Replace the damper piece with a new one if necessary.

4 Checking and replacement procedures for the sprocket coupling bearing are described in Section 16.

5 Installation is the reverse of removal. Make sure the damper assembly is correctly fitted.

21.3 Lift the damper piece out and check the segments

Chapter 7
Bodywork

Contents

	Section number		Section number
Body panels	3	Hand guards (XC models)	6
Engine protection bars	7	Mirrors	4
Front mudguard	5	Seats	2
General information	1		

Degrees of difficulty

Easy, suitable for novice with little experience	Fairly easy, suitable for beginner with some experience	Fairly difficult, suitable for competent DIY mechanic	Difficult, suitable for experienced DIY mechanic	Very difficult, suitable for expert DIY or professional

1 General information

This Chapter covers the procedures necessary to remove and install the body parts. Since many service and repair operations on these motorcycles require their removal, the procedures are grouped here and referred to from other Chapters.

In the case of damage to the body parts, it is usually necessary to remove the broken component and replace it with a new (or used) one. The material that the body panels are composed of doesn't lend itself to conventional repair techniques. There are however some shops that specialise in 'plastic welding', so it may be worthwhile seeking the advice of one of these specialists before scrapping an expensive component. There are also DIY kits available for making small repairs.

When attempting to remove any body panel, first study it closely, noting any fasteners and associated fittings, to be sure of returning everything to its correct place on installation. In some cases the aid of an assistant will be required when removing panels, to help avoid the risk of damage to paintwork. Once the evident fasteners have been removed, try to withdraw the panel as described but DO NOT FORCE IT – if it will not release, check that all fasteners have been removed and try again. Where a panel engages another by means of tabs, be careful not to break the tab or its mating slot or to damage the paintwork. Remember that a few moments of patience at this stage will save you a lot of money in replacing broken fairing panels! To undo quick-release fasteners, turn them 90° anti-clockwise.

When installing a body panel, first study it closely, noting any fasteners and associated fittings removed with it, to be sure of returning everything to its correct place. Check that all fasteners and damping/rubber mounts are in good condition; any of these must be replaced with new ones if faulty before the panel is reassembled. Check also that all mounting brackets are straight and repair or renew them if necessary before attempting to install the panel. Where assistance was required to remove a panel, make sure your assistant is on hand to install it. To install quick-release fasteners, turn them 90° clockwise.

Tighten the fasteners securely, but be careful not to overtighten any of them or the panel may break (not always immediately) due to the uneven stress.

7•2 Bodywork

2.1 Turn the key, then lift the rear of the seat and remove it

2.2 Locate the prongs in the hooks

Rider's seat

3 Remove the passenger seat (Step 1).
4 Lift the back of the seat and draw it back and up, noting how the bars locate in the supports **(see illustration)**.
5 Installation is the reverse of removal – make sure the seat height is adjusted as required by positioning the support bars in the required slots **(see illustration)**. Fit the seat, locating the bars in the supports.

2 Seats

3 Body panels

Passenger seat

1 Insert the ignition key into the seat lock located below the tail light, and turn it anti-clockwise **(see illustration)**. Lift up the rear of the seat and draw it backwards, noting how the prongs at the front locate.
2 Installation is the reverse of removal – slide the prongs at the front under the hooks, then push down on the back of the seat to engage the latch **(see illustration)**.

Radiator covers

Outer covers

1 Undo the three screws **(see illustrations)**.
2 Release the top of the outer cover from the tab on the inner cover, then draw the outer

2.4 The adjustable bars locate in the supports

2.5 Position the support bars (arrowed) as required

3.1a Undo the screw (arrowed)...

3.1b ...and the screws (arrowed)

cover back to release it from the side panel **(see illustrations)**.

3 Installation is the reverse of removal.

Inner covers and radiator guard

4 Remove the outer covers (Steps 1 and 2).
5 Remove the side panels (Steps 13 and 14).
6 On the right-hand side release the clutch cable guide **(see illustration)**.
7 If heated grips and/or spotlights are fitted, release the wiring ties and the relay(s) as required.
8 Undo the two screws securing the first cover being removed, then on XC models release the radiator guard clips and remove the cover **(see illustration)**.
9 On XC models release the radiator guard clips from the other panel and remove the guard.
10 Remove the second cover by undoing the screws.
11 Installation is the reverse of removal.

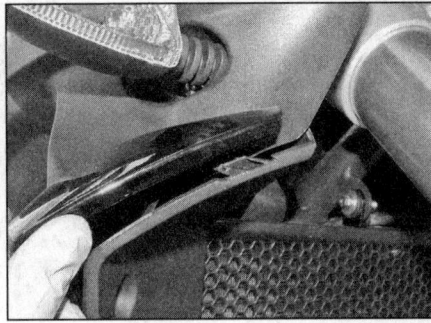

3.2a Release the top from the inner cover tab…

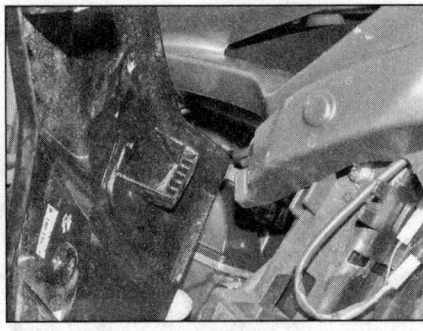

3.2b …and the side panel

Side panels

12 Remove the radiator outer cover (Steps 1 and 2).

13 Undo the two screws **(see illustrations)**.
14 Lift the panel to release the pegs from the grommets in the fuel tank, then slide it back to

3.6 Press the clip ends (arrowed) together and draw the clip out

3.8 Inner cover screws (A), radiator guard clips (B)

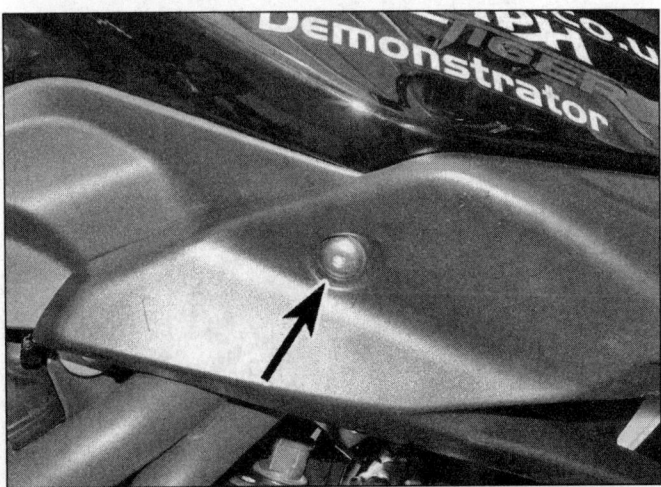

3.13a Undo the screw (arrowed)…

3.13b …and the screw (arrowed)

7•4 Bodywork

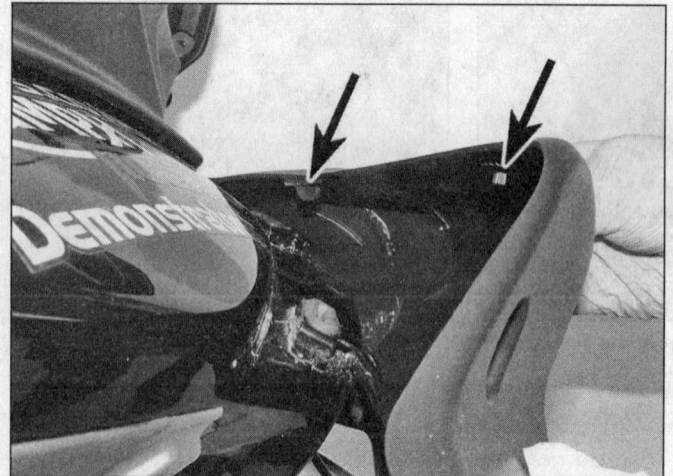

3.14a Release the pegs (arrowed)…

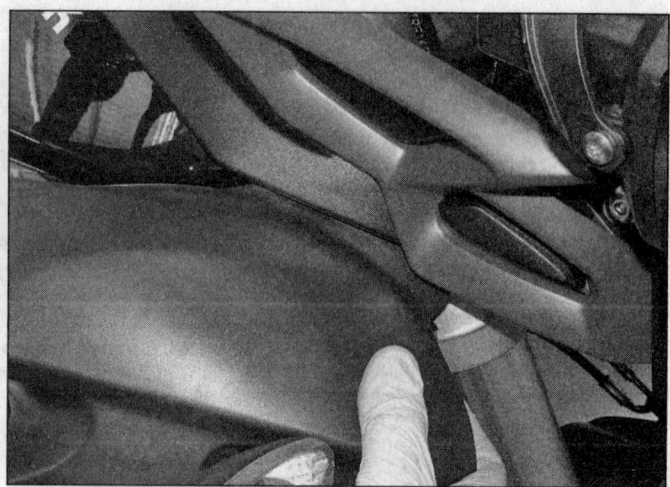

3.14b …and the front edge…

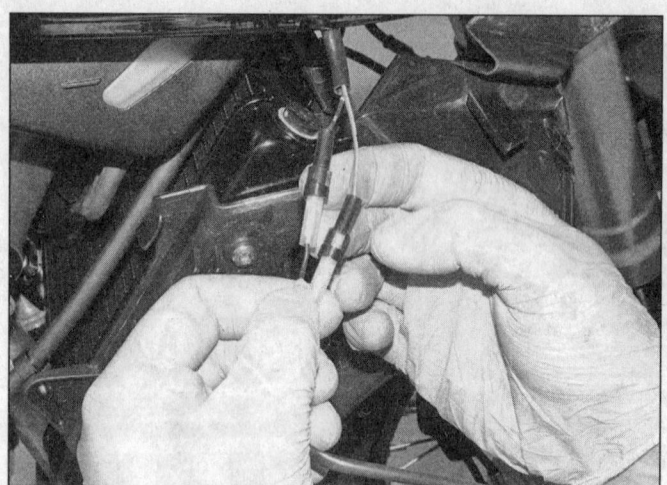

3.15 …then disconnect the wiring

3.18 Undo the screws on the top (arrowed)

3.19 Undo the screws underneath (arrowed)

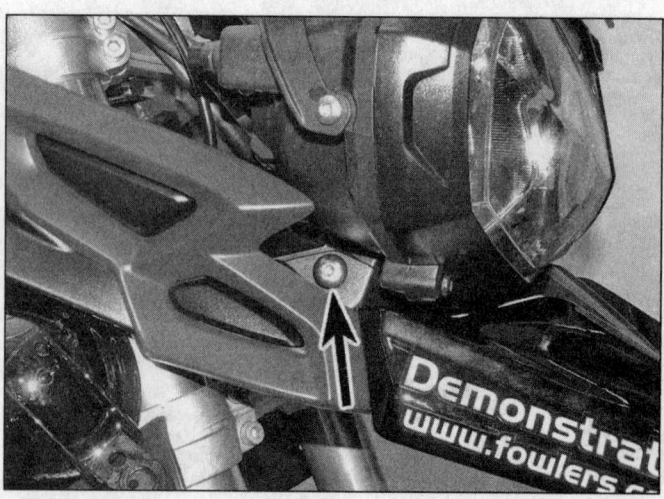

3.20 Undo the screw (arrowed) on each side

Bodywork 7•5

3.21 Lift the sides and remove the panel to the front

3.22 Separate the panel into its component parts by undoing the various screws

release the front edge from behind the cockpit panel **(see illustrations)**.

15 Disconnect the turn signal wiring connector and remove the panel **(see illustration)**.

16 If required remove the turn signal from the cowl (see Chapter 8).

17 Installation is the reverse of removal.

Cockpit panel

18 Undo the two screws on the top **(see illustration)**.

19 On XC models undo the two screws on the underside **(see illustration)**.

20 Undo the nut and remove the screw on each side **(see illustration)**.

21 Lift the rear sides off the fuel tank and draw the panel forwards and off the bike **(see illustration)**.

22 If required separate the panel sections **(see illustration)**.

23 Installation is the reverse of removal.

Fuel tank trim panels

24 Remove the seats (see Section 2).

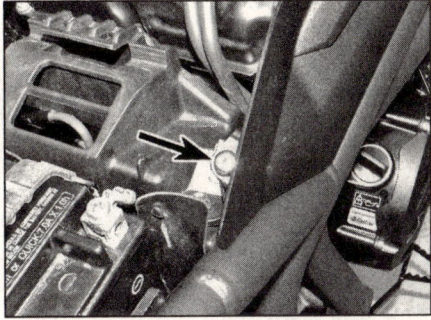

3.25 Undo the screw (arrowed)

25 Undo the screw **(see illustration)**.

26 Lift the rear of the panel to release the rear tab from the grommet, then slide it back to release the front from the rubber covered bracket **(see illustration)**.

27 Installation is the reverse of removal.

3.26 Release the tab from the grommet (A) then draw the panel off the rubber (B)

Sump guard and bracket

28 To remove the guard unscrew the two bolts and the four nuts **(see illustration)**.

29 To remove the bracket unscrew the three bolts **(see illustration)**.

3.28 Sump guard bolts (A) and nuts (B)

3.29 Sump guard bracket bolts (arrowed)

7•6 Bodywork

3.31 Luggage rack bolts (arrowed)

3.32 Grab-rail bolts (arrowed)

3.34 Windshield is secured by four screws with nuts (arrowed)

4.1 Lift the cover to access the base hex (A) for removal and the conical nut (B) for adjustment

5.3 Front mudguard screws (arrowed) – XC models

6.1a Undo the screws (arrowed)...

Bodywork 7•7

6.1b ...and remove the guard and the end-weight

7.1 Engine protection bar joining screws (A) and mounting bolts (B)

30 Installation is the reverse of removal. Tighten the nuts to 10 Nm and the bolts to 6 Nm.

Luggage rack and grab-rails

31 To remove the rack first remove the passenger seat (see Section 2). Unscrew the four bolts **(see illustration)**.
32 To remove the grab rails first remove the luggage rack. Unscrew the two bolts securing each rail **(see illustration)**.
33 Installation is the reverse of removal – tighten the grab handle bolts/nut to 20 Nm. Tighten the luggage rack bolts to 3 Nm.

Windshield

34 Undo the nuts on the four screws, remove the screws and lift the windshield off **(see illustration)**.
35 Installation is the reverse of removal. Check the rubber grommets are all in good condition and the collars are fitted in them. Do not overtighten the screws.

4 Mirrors
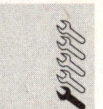

1 Lift the rubber cover off the base of the mirror, then unscrew it from its mount using the bottom hex **(see illustration)**.
2 Installation is the reverse of removal. To adjust the position of the mirror, counter-hold the base hex, then slacken the conical nut above it, reposition the mirror as required, then tighten the nut **(see illustration 4.1)**.

5 Front mudguard

1 Release the brake hoses and ABS sensor wiring (where fitted) from the clips or guides on the mudguard as required according to model.
2 On standard models undo the two screws on each side and remove the fork protectors. Draw the mudguard forwards from between the forks.

3 On XC models undo the three screws on each side and draw the mudguard forwards from between the forks **(see illustration)**.
4 Installation is the reverse of removal.

6 Hand guards

1 Undo the two screws and remove the guard, collecting the end-weight from the handlebar **(see illustrations)**.
2 Remove the brake or clutch lever to release the guard bracket (see Chapter 5).
3 Installation is the reverse of removal.

7 Engine protection bars

1 Undo one of the screws joining the bars together at the front **(see illustration)**.
2 Unscrew the three bolts and remove the protection bar **(see illustration 7.1)**.
3 Installation is the reverse of removal.

Notes

Chapter 8
Electrical system

Contents

	Section number		Section number
Alternator	27	Horn	22
Battery charging	4	Ignition switch	17
Battery removal and installation	3	Ignition system components	see Chapter 4
Brake light switches	14	Instrument cluster	15
Brake and tail light LEDs	10	Lighting system check	6
Charging system testing	26	Gear position sensor (neutral switch)	see Chapter 4
Clutch switch	20	Oil pressure switch	21
Electrical system fault finding	2	Regulator/rectifier	28
Fuel pump and relay	see Chapter 4	Sidestand switch	19
Fuses	5	Speed sensor	see Chapter 4
General information	1	Starter motor overhaul	25
Handlebar switches	18	Starter motor removal and installation	24
Headlight aim	9	Starter relay	23
Headlight and sidelight bulbs	7	Tail light unit	11
Headlight relay and starter circuit relay	16	Turn signal bulbs and assemblies	13
Headlight unit	8	Turn signal circuit check and relay	12

Degrees of difficulty

| Easy, suitable for novice with little experience | Fairly easy, suitable for beginner with some experience | Fairly difficult, suitable for competent DIY mechanic | Difficult, suitable for experienced DIY mechanic | Very difficult, suitable for expert DIY or professional |

Specifications

Battery
Type	Yuasa YTX-16BS
Capacity	12V, 14Ah
Current leakage	1 mA (max)
Charging rate	1.4 A (max)
Charging time (flat battery)	see Section 4

Alternator
Nominal output	41.5A @ 4000 rpm
Regulated output	13.5 to 15 volts DC
Stator coil resistance	0.14 to 0.18 ohms

8•2 Electrical system

Fuses
Fuse identity is marked on the fusebox lids

Main fuse (in starter relay)	30A
Front fusebox	
Fuse 1	15A (cooling fan)
Fuse 2	15A (accessory lights)
Fuse 3	10A (side light, turn signals, tail lights, horn)
Fuse 4	10A (heated grips, where fitted)
Fuse 5	15A (accessory sockets)
Fuse 6	not used
Rear fusebox	
Fuse 1	20A (ABS)
Fuse 2	20A (ABS)
Fuse 3	10A (fuel pump relay, immobiliser, instruments, kill switch)
Fuse 4	20A (ECM relay – engine management)
Fuse 5	5A (alarm, diagnostic connector, instruments)
Fuse 6	Headlights, starter relay
Standard model	15A up to VIN 560913, 20A from VIN 560914
Standard model with ABS	15A up to VIN 558558, 20A from VIN 558559
XC model	15A up to VIN 558558, 20A from VIN 558559

Bulbs
Headlight	12V 60/55W H4 x 2
Sidelight	5W
Brake/tail light	LED
Turn signal light	12V 10W (amber)
Instrument lights	LED

Torque wrench settings
Alternator cover bolts	12 Nm
Alternator rotor bolt	120 Nm
Alternator stator bolts	12 Nm
Alternator stator/CKP sensor wiring guide bolt(s)	6 Nm
CKP sensor bolts	6 Nm
Oil pressure switch	13 Nm
Rear brake light switch	15 Nm
Starter motor mounting bolts	10 Nm

1 General information

All models have a 12 volt electrical system charged by a three-phase alternator, with the rotor mounted on the left-hand end of the crankshaft and the stator located in the alternator cover.

The system incorporates a combined regulator/rectifier, mounted above the radiator. The regulator maintains the charging system output within the specified range to prevent overcharging, and the rectifier converts the ac (alternating current) output of the alternator to dc (direct current) to power the lights and other components and to charge the battery.

The starter motor is mounted on the top of the crankcase, and the starter clutch is mounted on the back of the alternator rotor. The starting system includes the motor, the battery, the relay and the various wires and switches.

Note: *Keep in mind that electrical parts, once purchased, cannot be returned. To avoid unnecessary expense, make very sure the faulty component has been positively identified before buying a replacement part.*

2 Electrical system fault finding

1 A typical electrical circuit consists of an electrical component, the switches, relays, etc, related to that component and the wiring and connectors that link the component to the battery and the frame.

2 Before tackling any troublesome electrical circuit, first study the wiring diagram thoroughly to get a complete picture of what makes up that individual circuit. Trouble spots can often be located by noting if other components related to that circuit are operating properly or not. If several components or circuits fail at one time, chances are the fault lies either in the fuse or in a common earth (ground) connection, as several circuits are often routed through the same fuse and earth (ground) connections **(see illustration)**.

3 Electrical problems often stem from simple causes, such as loose or corroded connections or a blown fuse. Prior to any electrical fault finding, always visually check the condition of the fuse, wires and connections in the problem circuit. Intermittent failures can be especially frustrating, since you can't always duplicate the failure when it's convenient to test. In such situations, a good practice is to clean all connections in the affected circuit, whether or not they appear to be good – where possible use a dedicated electrical cleaning spray along with sandpaper, wire wool or other abrasive material to remove corrosion, and a dedicated electrical protection spray to prevent further problems. All of the connections and wires should also be wiggled to check for looseness that can cause intermittent failure.

4 If you don't have a multimeter it is highly advisable to obtain one – they are not

2.2 Common earth point (arrowed) – remove the airbox to check it

Electrical system

2.4a A digital multimeter can be used for all electrical tests

2.4b A battery-powered continuity tester

2.4c A simple test light is useful for voltage tests

expensive and will enable a full range of electrical tests to be made **(see illustration)**. Go for a modern digital one with an LCD display, as they are easier to use. A continuity tester and/or test light are useful for certain electrical checks as an alternative, though are limited in their usefulness compared to a multimeter **(see illustrations)**.

Continuity checks

5 The term continuity describes the uninterrupted flow of electricity through an electrical circuit. Continuity can be checked with a multimeter set either to its continuity function (a beep is emitted when continuity is found), or to the resistance (ohms / Ω) function, or with a dedicated continuity tester. Both instruments are powered by an internal battery; therefore the checks are made with the ignition OFF. As a safety precaution, always disconnect the battery negative (-) lead before making continuity checks, particularly if ignition switch checks are being made.

6 If using a multimeter, select the continuity function if it has one, or the resistance (ohms) function. Touch the meter probes together and check that a beep is emitted or the meter reads zero, which indicates continuity. If there is no continuity there will be no beep or the meter will show infinite resistance. After using the meter, always switch it OFF to conserve its battery.

7 A continuity tester can be used in the same way – its light should come on or it should beep to indicate continuity in the switch ON position, but should be off or silent in the OFF position.

8 Note that the polarity of the test probes doesn't matter for continuity checks, although care should be taken to follow specific test procedures if a diode or solid-state component is being checked.

Switch continuity checks

9 If a switch is at fault, trace its wiring to the wiring connectors. Separate the connectors and inspect them for security and condition. A build-up of dirt or corrosion here will most likely be the cause of the problem – clean up and apply a water dispersant such as WD40, or alternatively use a dedicated contact cleaner and protection spray.

10 If using a multimeter, select the continuity function if it has one, or the resistance (ohms) function, and connect its probes to the terminals in the connector **(see illustration)**. Simple ON/OFF type switches, such as brake light switches, only have two wires whereas combination switches, like the handlebar switches, have many wires. Study the wiring diagram to ensure that you are connecting to the correct pair of wires. Continuity should be indicated with the switch ON and no continuity with it OFF.

Wiring continuity checks

11 Many electrical faults are caused by damaged wiring, often due to incorrect routing or chaffing on frame components. Loose, wet or corroded wire connectors can also be the cause of electrical problems.

12 A continuity check can be made on a single length of wire by disconnecting it at each end and connecting the meter or continuity tester probes to each end of the wire **(see illustration)**. Continuity (low or no resistance – 0 ohms) should be indicated if the wire is good. If no continuity (high resistance) is shown, suspect a broken wire.

13 To check for continuity to earth in any earth wire connect one probe of your meter or tester to the earth wire terminal in the connector and the other to the frame, engine, or battery earth (-) terminal. Continuity (low or no resistance – 0 ohms) should be indicated if the wire is good. If no continuity (high resistance) is shown, suspect a broken wire or corroded or loose earth point (see below).

Voltage checks

14 A voltage check can determine whether power is reaching a component. Use a multimeter set to the dc voltage scale, or a test light. The test light is the cheaper component, but the meter has the advantage of being able to give a voltage reading.

15 Connect the meter or test light in parallel, i.e. across the load **(see illustration)**.

16 First identify the relevant wiring circuit by referring to the wiring diagram at the end of this manual. If other electrical components share the same power supply (i.e. are fed from the same fuse), take note whether they are working correctly – this is useful information in deciding where to start checking the circuit.

17 If using a meter, check first that the meter

2.10 Continuity should be indicated across switch terminals when lever is operated

2.12 Wiring continuity check. Connect the meter probes across each end of the same wire

2.15 Voltage check. Connect the meter positive probe to the component and the negative probe to earth

8•4 Electrical system

2.23 A selection of insulated jumper wires

3.2 Disconnect the negative terminal first, then the positive terminal (arrowed)

leads are plugged into the correct terminals on the meter (red to positive (+), black to negative (-). Set the meter to the dc volts function, where necessary at a range suitable for the battery voltage – 0 to 20 vdc. Connect the meter red probe (+) to the power supply wire and the black probe to a good metal earth (ground) on the bike's frame or directly to the battery negative terminal. Battery voltage should be shown on the meter with the ignition switch, and if necessary any other relevant switch, ON.

18 If using a test light, connect its positive (+) probe to the power supply terminal and its negative (-) probe to a good earth (ground) on the bike's frame. With the switch, and if necessary any other relevant switch, ON, the test light should illuminate.

19 If no voltage is indicated, work back towards the fuse continuing to check for voltage. When you reach a point where there is voltage, you know the problem lies between that point and your last check point.

Earth (ground) checks

20 Earth connections are made either directly to the engine or frame via the mounting of the component, or by a separate wire into the earth circuit of the wiring harness. Alternatively a short earth wire is sometimes run from the component directly to the bike's frame.

21 Corrosion is a common cause of a poor earth connection, as is a loose earth terminal fastener.

22 If total or multiple component failure is experienced, check the security of the main earth lead from the negative (-) terminal of the battery, the earth lead bolted to the engine, and the main earth point on the frame (see illustrations 2.2). If corroded, dismantle the connection and clean all surfaces back to bare metal. Remake the connection and prevent further corrosion from forming by smearing battery terminal grease over the connection.

23 To check the earth of a component, use an insulated jumper wire to temporarily bypass its earth connection (see illustration) – connect one end of the jumper wire to the earth terminal or metal body of the component and the other end to the bike's frame. If the circuit works with the jumper wire installed, the earth circuit is faulty.

24 To check an earth wire first check for corroded or loose connections, then check the wiring for continuity (Step 13) between each connector in the circuit in turn, and then to its earth point, to locate the break.

3 Battery removal and installation

Caution: Be extremely careful when handling or working around the battery. The electrolyte is very caustic and an explosive gas (hydrogen) is given off when the battery is charging.

Removal and installation

1 Remove the rider's seat (see Chapter 7).
2 Unscrew the negative (–) terminal bolt first and disconnect the lead from the battery (see illustration). Lift up the insulating cover to access the positive (+) terminal, then unscrew the bolt and disconnect the lead.
3 Release the battery strap (see illustration).
4 Carefully lift the battery from the bike (see illustration).
5 On installation, clean the battery terminals and lead ends with a wire brush, fine sandpaper or steel wool. Reconnect the leads, connecting the positive (+) terminal first.

> **HAYNES HiNT** Battery corrosion can be kept to a minimum by applying a layer of petroleum jelly (Vaseline) or dielectric grease (available as a spray) to the terminals after the cables have been connected. DO NOT use mineral based grease.

Inspection and maintenance

6 The battery is of the maintenance free (sealed) type, therefore requiring no regular maintenance. However, the following checks should still be performed.
7 Check the state of charge by measuring the voltage at the battery terminals (see illustration). Connect the voltmeter positive (+) probe to the battery positive (+) terminal, and the negative (–) probe to the battery negative (–) terminal. When fully charged there should be 12.8 to 13.0 volts present. If the voltage falls below 12.5 volts remove the battery (see above), and recharge it as described below in Section 4.
8 Check the battery terminals and leads are tight and free of corrosion. If corrosion is evident, clean the terminals as described in Step 5, then protect them from further corrosion (see **Haynes Hint**).
9 Keep the battery case clean to prevent current leakage, which can discharge the battery over a period of time (especially when it sits unused). Wash the outside of the case with a solution of baking soda and water. Rinse the battery thoroughly, then dry it.
10 Look for cracks in the case and replace the battery with a new one if any are found. If acid has been spilled on the frame or battery

3.3 Unhook the strap (arrowed)

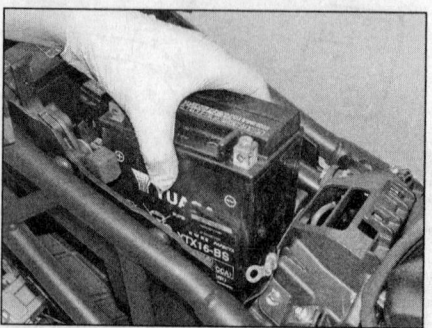

3.4 Carefully lift the battery out – it is quite heavy

3.7 Checking battery voltage – connect the meter as shown

Electrical system 8•5

box, neutralise it with a baking soda and water solution, then dry it thoroughly.
11 If the motorcycle sits unused for long periods of time, disconnect the leads from the battery terminals, negative (–) terminal first. Refer to Section 4 and charge the battery once every month to six weeks.

4 Battery charging

Caution: Be extremely careful when handling or working around the battery. The electrolyte is very caustic and an explosive gas (hydrogen) is given off when the battery is charging.

1 Remove the battery (see Section 3).
2 Connect the charger to the battery, making sure that the positive (+) lead on the charger is connected to the positive (+) terminal on the battery, and the negative (–) lead is connected to the negative (–) terminal **(see illustration)**.
3 The battery should be charged at the specified rate for up to 12 hours if it is completely flat, or until the voltage across the terminals reaches 12.8V – disconnect the charger and allow the battery to stabilise for 30 minutes after charging before taking a voltage reading. The actual time required depends on the initial voltage present (Section 3, Step 7). Exceeding this can cause the battery to overheat, buckling the plates and rendering it useless. It is best to use a dedicated motorcycle battery charger, preferably one of the 'intelligent' ones that constantly monitors the state of charge and controls its output accordingly. If a normal car type charger is used check that after a probable initial peak, the charge rate falls to a safe level consistent with the charge rate specified for your model at the beginning of the Chapter. If the battery becomes hot during charging **stop**. Further charging will cause damage. There are many bike-specific chargers available from good suppliers that are designed for the maintenance and recovery of motorcycle batteries, in particular catering for the requirements of heavily discharged MF batteries. They are not too expensive, and are a worthwhile investment, especially if the bike is not used over winter. Follow the manufacturer's instructions.
4 If the recharged battery discharges rapidly when left disconnected it is likely that an internal short caused by physical damage or sulphation has occurred. A new battery will be required. A sound battery will tend to lose its charge at about 1% per day.
5 Install the battery (see Section 3).
6 If the motorcycle sits unused for long periods of time, charge the battery once every month to six weeks and leave it disconnected.

5 Fuses

1 The electrical system as a whole is protected by the main fuse, and individual circuits are protected by other fuses of different ratings (see Specifications). The main fuse is housed in the starter relay, which is under the battery. All other fuses are housed in two fuseboxes, which are under the rider's seat.
2 To access the main fuse, remove the battery (see Section 3), and the ECM (see Chapter 4). Disconnect the AP sensor wiring connector, then displace the starter relay, turn it upside down and disconnect the wiring connector **(see illustrations)**. Remove the plastic cover – the fuse is between the wiring socket and the leads **(see illustration)**. A spare main fuse is housed in the relay sleeve **(see illustration)**.
3 To access the fusebox fuses, remove the rider's seat (see Chapter 7). The identity, location and rating of each fuse is marked on the top of each fusebox lid – unclip the relevant lid **(see illustrations)**. A spare fuse of each rating is housed in the fusebox.

4.2 Battery connected to a charger

5.2a Disconnect the wiring connector (A), then displace the relay (B)…

5.2b …and disconnect the connector, using a screwdriver to release the tab

5.2c Remove the terminal cover to access the fuse (arrowed)

5.2d Spare main fuse (arrowed)

5.3a Fuseboxes (arrowed) – the identity, location and rating of each fuse is marked on the lid

5.3b Unclip the lid to access the fuses

8•6 Electrical system

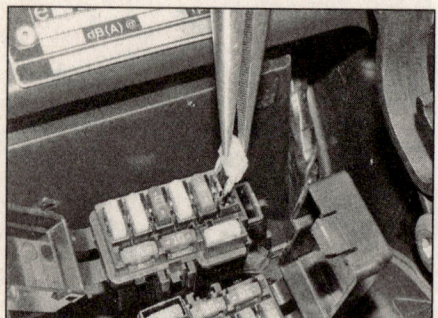

5.4a Use suitable pliers to remove a fuse

5.4b A blown fuse can be identified by a break in its element

4 The fuses can be removed and checked visually. If you can't pull the fuse out with your fingertips, use a suitable pair of pliers **(see illustration)**. A blown fuse is easily identified by a break in the element **(see illustration)**, or can be tested for continuity using an ohmmeter or continuity tester – if there is no continuity, it has blown. Each fuse is clearly marked with its rating and must only be replaced by a fuse of the same rating. If a spare fuse is used, always replace it with a new one so that a spare of each rating is carried on the bike at all times.

 Warning: *Never put in a fuse of a higher rating or bridge the terminals with any other substitute, however temporary it may be. Serious damage may be done to the circuit, or a fire may start.*

5 If the new fuse blows, you need to check the relevant circuit and its components for evidence of a short-circuit. Look for bare wires and chafed, melted or burned insulation.

6 Sometimes fuses blow for no specific reason, in which case replacing it with a new one is the only action required. Also corrosion of the fuse ends and fusebox terminals may occur and cause poor fuse contact. If this happens, remove the corrosion with a wire brush or emery paper, then spray the fuse end and terminals with electrical contact cleaner.

6 Lighting system check

Note: *Refer to Electrical system fault finding (Section 2) and to the Wiring Diagrams at the end of the Chapter when making electrical tests on any part of the system.*

1 If a light fails first check the bulb (see relevant Section), the bulb terminals in the holder, and the wiring connector. Bulbs are used for the headlight, sidelight and turn signal lights. When checking for a blown filament in a bulb, it is advisable to back up a visual check with a continuity test of the filament as it is not always apparent that a bulb has blown. When testing for continuity, remember that on single terminal bulbs it is the metal body of the bulb that is the earth (ground). LED (Light Emitting Diodes) are used for the brake/tail light and instrument lights; an LED is unlikely to fail.

2 Next check the fuse (Section 5). If none of the lights work, check battery voltage – low voltage indicates either a faulty battery or a defective charging system. Refer to Section 3 for battery checks and Section 26 for charging system tests. If there is a problem with more than one circuit at the same time, or with all circuits, it is likely to be a fault relating to a multi-function component, such as the fuse or the ignition switch.

Headlight

2 Two twin filament bulbs, one filament in each bulb for high beam and one for low beam.

3 If a single beam or a single bulb fails first check the relevant bulb and the bulb terminals, and wiring connector (see Section 7). If both bulbs do not work first check the fuse (see Section 5). If they are all good, check for battery voltage at the blue/white (high beam) or blue/red (low beam) supply wire terminal in the headlight wiring connector, with the ignition switch ON, and the dip beam/main beam switch set appropriately. If voltage is present, check for continuity between the black (earth or ground) wire terminal and the battery negative (-) terminal. If there is no continuity, check the earth (ground) circuit for an open or poor connection.

4 If no voltage is indicated, check the wiring and connectors between the headlight, switch, headlight relay, starter circuit relay, fusebox, and the ignition switch, and check the dimmer switch and ignition switch (see Sections 18 and 17).

5 If no problem can be found refer to Section 16 and check the headlight relay, and if that is good check the starter circuit relay. Make sure each relay is secure in its connector and that the terminals are corrosion free and not bent or broken. Then check the function of the relay itself as described.

Tail light

Note: *The tail and brake lights consist of a number of LEDs. If an individual LED fails it cannot be replaced with a new one (the only solution is to fit a complete new tail light unit), but the rest should continue to function. If none of them work, it is more likely to be a circuit problem – follow Steps 6 and 7.*

6 If the tail light fails to work, check the wiring connector first (see Section 10), then the circuit fuse (see Section 5). If they are all good, check for battery voltage at the yellow wire terminal in the loom side of the tail light wiring connector, with the ignition switch ON. If voltage is present, check for continuity between the black (earth or ground) wire terminal and the battery negative (-) terminal. If there is no continuity, check the earth (ground) circuit for an open or poor connection.

7 If no voltage is indicated, check the wiring and connectors in the tail light circuit.

Sidelight

8 If the sidelight fails to work, check the bulb and the bulb terminals and wiring connector first (see Section 7), then the circuit fuse. If they are all good, check for battery voltage at the yellow wire terminal in the socket, with the ignition switch ON. If voltage is present, check for continuity between the black (earth or ground) wire terminal and the battery negative (-) terminal. If there is no continuity, check the earth (ground) circuit for an open or poor connection.

9 If no voltage is indicated, check the wiring and connectors in the sidelight circuit.

Brake light

Note: *The tail and brake lights consist of a number of LEDs. If an individual LED fails it cannot be replaced with a new one (the only solution is to fit a complete new tail light unit), but the rest should continue to function. If none of them work, it is more likely to be a circuit or switch problem – follow Steps 10 and 11.*

10 If the brake light fails to work, check the wiring connector first (see Section 10), then the circuit fuse (see Section 5). If they are all good, check for battery voltage at the green/violet wire terminal in the loom side of the tail light wiring connector, with the ignition switch ON, and the brake lever or pedal applied. If voltage is present, check for continuity between the black (earth or ground) wire terminal and the battery negative (-) terminal. If there is no continuity, check the earth (ground) circuit for an open or poor connection.

11 If no voltage is indicated, check the brake light switches (see Section 14), then the wiring and connectors between the tail light and the switches.

Turn signal lights

12 If one light fails to work, check the bulb and the bulb terminals first, then the wiring connectors (see Section 13). If none of the turn signals work, first check the signal circuit fuse (see Section 5).

13 If the fuse is good, see Section 12 for the turn signal circuit check.

7.1 Remove the cover...

7.2 ...and disconnect the wiring connector

7.3a Release the clips...

7.3b ... and remove the bulb

7.6 Undo the screws (arrowed) and remove the trim

7.7 Pull the bulbholder out of the headlight...

7 Headlight and sidelight bulbs

Note: *The headlight bulbs are the quartz-halogen type. Do not touch the bulb glass as skin acids will shorten the bulb's life. If the bulb is accidentally touched, it should be wiped carefully when cold with a rag soaked in methylated spirit and dried before fitting.*

Headlight

1 Remove the cover by turning it anti-clockwise (see illustration).
2 Disconnect the wiring connector from the bulb (see illustration).
3 Release the bulb retaining clips, then remove the bulb (see illustrations).
4 Fit the new bulb in reverse order, bearing in mind the information in the **Note** above.
5 Make sure the cover sealing ring is correctly seated, then align the tabs and turn the cover clockwise to lock it. Check the operation of the headlight.

Sidelight

6 Remove the headlight trim (see illustration).
7 Carefully pull the bulbholder out – do not pull it out by the wires (see illustration).
8 Carefully pull the bulb out of the holder (see illustration).
9 Fit the new bulb in reverse order.
10 Check the operation of the sidelight.

8 Headlight unit

1 Remove the cockpit panel (see Chapter 7).
2 Undo the two windshield bracket screws on each side, then unscrew the two headlight mounting bolts on each side, displace the headlight forwards and disconnect the wiring connector (see illustrations).
3 If required, remove the headlight and sidelight bulbs (see Section 7).
4 Installation is the reverse of removal. Check the operation of the headlights and sidelight. Check the headlight aim (see Section 9).

7.8 ...then pull the bulb out of the holder

8.2a Windshield bracket screws (A), headlight mounting bolts (B) – right-hand side

8.2b Displace the headlight and disconnect the wiring

9.2 Vertical adjustment lever (A) and screw (B), horizontal adjustment screw (C)

11.2 Tail light wiring connector (arrowed)

9 Headlight aim

Note: *An improperly adjusted headlight may cause problems for oncoming traffic or provide poor, unsafe illumination of the road ahead. Before adjusting the headlight aim, be sure to consult with local traffic laws and regulations – for UK models refer to MOT Test Checks in the Reference section.*

1 The headlight beams can be adjusted both horizontally and vertically. Before making any adjustment, check that the tyre pressures are correct and the suspension is adjusted as required. Make any adjustments to the headlight aim with machine on level ground, with the fuel tank half full, with an assistant sitting on the seat, and with the headlight on and shining against a dark vertical surface such as a garage wall, and set to dipped beam. If the bike is usually ridden with a passenger on the back, have a second assistant do this – note that there is a two-position lever on the vertical adjuster that moves the vertical height of the beams between two pre-set conditions, one for solo riding (lever horizontal) and the other for two-up and/or loaded riding (lever downwards) **(see illustration 9.2)**. Make sure this lever is set in the horizontal position before making any adjustment.

2 To raise the beam turn the vertical adjustment screw clockwise, and to lower it turn it anti-clockwise **(see illustration)**.

3 To move the beam to the right turn the horizontal adjustment screw clockwise, and to move it to the left turn it anti-clockwise **(see illustration 9.2)**.

10 Brake/tail LEDs

1 The brake and tail lights consist of a number of LEDs. If an individual LED fails it cannot be replaced with a new one (the only solution is to fit a complete new tail light unit), but the rest should continue to function. If none of them work, it is more likely to be a circuit problem (see Section 6).

11 Tail light unit

1 Remove the luggage rack (see Chapter 7). Displace the turn signal relay **(see illustration 12.3)**.

2 Release and disconnect the wiring connector **(see illustration)**.

3 Undo the tail light screws and draw the light out **(see illustrations)** – a ball-ended hex key is best to get on the bottom screw, or alternatively use a short hex bit and a spanner.

4 Installation is the reverse of removal. Check the operation of the tail and brake lights.

12 Turn signal circuit check and relay

1 Most turn signal problems are the result of a burned out bulb or corroded socket. This is especially true when the turn signals function properly in one direction, but fail to flash in the other direction. Check the bulbs, sockets and wiring connectors (see Section 13). Also, check the turn signal circuit fuse (see Section 5) and the switch (see Section 18).

2 If the bulbs, sockets, connectors, fuse, switch and battery are good, check the turn signal relay – to access it remove the luggage rack (see Chapter 7).

3 Displace the relay and disconnect the wiring connector **(see illustration)**. Short between the terminals in the loom side of the connector

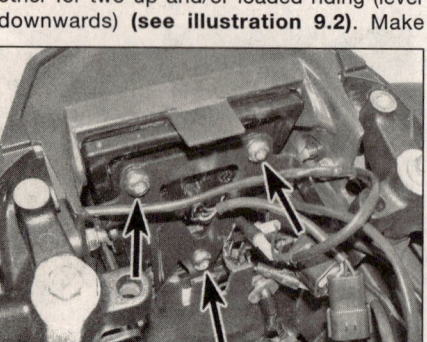

11.3a Undo the screws (arrowed)...

11.3b ...then draw out the light with the wiring

12.3 Turn signal relay

Electrical system 8•9

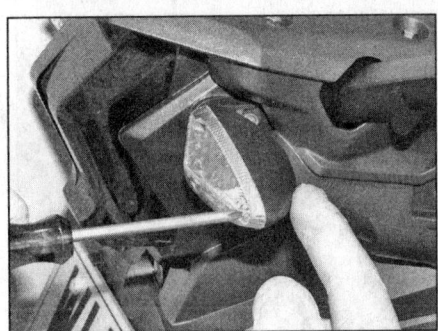
13.1 Lens is secured by a single screw

13.2 Release and remove the bulb

13.3 Make sure the tab (arrowed) locates correctly when fitting the lens

using the ends of a paper clip or a jumper wire. Turn the ignition ON and operate the turn signal switch, first in one direction then the other. If the lights come on (they won't flash), the relay is faulty and must be replaced with a new one.

4 If the lights do not come on check for voltage at the orange/green wire in the relay wiring connector with the ignition ON. Turn the ignition OFF when the check is complete. If no voltage is present, using the appropriate wiring diagram at the end of this Chapter check the wiring between the relay and the fusebox. If voltage was present, check for continuity in the other wire from the relay to the turn signal switch and turn signal lights for continuity.

13 Turn signal bulbs and assemblies

Turn signal bulbs

1 Undo the turn signal lens screw and remove the lens, noting how it fits (see illustration).
2 Push the bulb in and twist it anti-clockwise to remove it (see illustration). Check the socket terminals for corrosion and clean them if necessary. Line up the pins of the new bulb with the slots in the socket, then push the bulb in and turn it clockwise until it locks into place. Note that the pins on amber bulbs are not set 180° apart – take care to line them up with the slots in the bulbholder.
3 Fit the lens, making sure the tab locates correctly (see illustration). Do not overtighten the screw as the lens or threads could be damaged.

Front turn signals

4 Remove the side panel (see Chapter 7).
5 Unscrew the nut, withdraw the bolt and remove the turn signal, taking care not to snag the wiring (see illustration).
6 Installation is the reverse of removal. Check the operation of the turn signals.

Rear turn signals

7 Remove the luggage rack (see Chapter 7).
8 Disconnect the turn signal wiring connectors (see illustration).
9 Unscrew the nut, withdraw the bolt and

13.5 Front turn signal nut/bolt (arrowed)

remove the turn signal, taking care not to snag the wiring (see illustration 13.8).
10 Installation is the reverse of removal. Check the operation of the turn signals.

14 Brake light switches

Circuit check

1 Before checking the switches, check the brake light circuit (see Section 6).
2 The front brake light switch is mounted on the underside of the brake master cylinder. Disconnect the wiring connectors from the switch (see illustration). Using a continuity tester, connect the probes to the terminals on the switch. With the brake lever at rest,

14.2 Front brake light switch wiring connectors (A) and screw (B)

13.8 Rear turn signal wiring connectors (A) and mounting nuts/bolts (B)

there should be no continuity. With the brake lever applied, there should be continuity. If the switch does not behave as described, replace it with a new one.
3 The rear brake light switch is mounted on the top of the rear master cylinder (see illustration). Lift the rubber boot off the switch and disconnect the wiring connector. Using a continuity tester, connect the probes to the terminals on the switch. With the brake pedal at rest, there should be no continuity. With the brake pedal applied, there should be continuity. If the switch does not behave as described, replace it with a new one.
4 If the switches are good, check for voltage at one of the connectors (it could be either one) for the front brake switch, and at the orange/green wire terminal in the connector for the rear brake switch, with the ignition switch ON – there should be battery voltage.

14.3 Rear brake light wiring connector (A) and switch (B)

8•10 Electrical system

14.9 Seal the banjo using a nut and bolt and the sealing washers

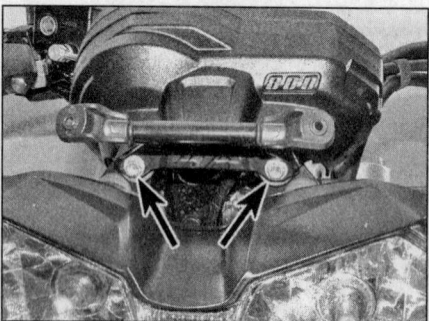

15.5 Unscrew the bolts (arrowed) and remove the bracket

15.6 Pull the cover off...

If there's no voltage present, check the wiring between the switch and the ignition switch (refer to Section 2 at the beginning of this chapter and the *Wiring Diagrams* at the end of it). If there is voltage check the wiring from the switch to the tail light assembly.

Removal and installation

Front brake light switch

5 The switch is mounted on the underside of the brake master cylinder. Disconnect the wiring connectors from the switch **(see illustration 14.2)**.
6 Undo the single screw and remove the switch from the bottom of the master cylinder, noting how it locates.
7 Installation is the reverse of removal. The switch isn't adjustable.

Rear brake light switch

Note: *On models with ABS, before removing the brake light switch, which involves detaching the brake hose from the master cylinder, bear in mind that the system must be bled on completion of work, and although this is done initially in the same way as models without ABS, to complete the procedure effectively the Triumph Diagnostic tool must be used to open and close the solenoids within the ABS modulator, and this can only be carried out by a dealer. The bike should be transported, not ridden, to the dealer.*

8 The rear brake light switch is mounted on the top of the rear master cylinder. Lift the rubber boot off the switch and disconnect the wiring connector **(see illustration 14.3)**.
9 Have some rag handy to catch any fluid spills, then unscrew the brake light switch from the master cylinder. Seal the banjo union and secure the hose upright to minimise fluid loss and prevent air getting in **(see illustration)**. New sealing washers must be fitted on reassembly.
10 Installation is the reverse of removal. Use new sealing washers on each side of the brake hose union and tighten the switch to the torque setting specified at the beginning of the Chapter. Connect the wiring connector, then fit the rubber boot. Bleed the rear brake system as described in Chapter 6.

15 Instrument cluster

Check

1 Specific test data for the instruments is not available. Refer below for access to the wiring connector and check that it is securely connected to the instrument cluster, and also refer to the relevant Section of this Chapter or to other Chapters and check that the other end of the wiring is securely connected to its source (i.e. gear position switch, oil pressure switch, fuel level sensor, coolant temperature sensor etc). Check all wires for continuity from pin to pin, referring to electrical system fault finding (Section 2) and to the wiring diagrams at the end of the Chapter.
2 Check that all earth wires have a good connection. If all the wiring is good, it is possible that there are faults in the switches or sensors or the electronic control module (ECM) of the engine management system, which provide much of the information to the instruments. Refer to Chapter 4 for details. If all checks point at faulty instruments rather than wiring or the engine management system, take the instrument cluster to a Triumph dealer for further assessment.
3 All of the warning and instrument lights are LEDs. If the cause of any problem (i.e. neutral light not coming on) cannot be traced it is possible the LED has failed, in which case a new instrument cluster must be fitted.

Removal and installation

4 Disconnect the battery negative (-) terminal (see Section 3).
5 Remove the windshield (see Chapter 7). Remove the windshield bracket **(see illustration)**.
6 Remove the cover from the back of the instrument cluster – it is a push fit with a peg locating in a grommet **(see illustration)**.
7 Pull the rubber boot back and disconnect the wiring connector **(see illustration)**.
8 Undo the screw, collect the washer, and detach the instrument cluster from the bracket, noting how the pegs locate in the grommets **(see illustration)**.
9 Installation is the reverse of removal. Check the rubber grommets for cracks and deterioration and replace them with new ones if necessary. Make sure the wiring connector is secure. Make sure the cover seats correctly.

16 Headlight relay and starter circuit relay

Note: *Refer to the Wiring Diagrams at the end of the Chapter for relay terminal identification.*
1 The following circuit relays are fitted: headlight relay, starter circuit relay, cooling fan relay (see Chapter 3), engine management

15.7 ...then disconnect the wiring connector

15.8 Instrument cluster screw (arrowed)

Electrical system 8•11

16.1 Cooling fan relay (A), headlight relay (B), EMS relay (C), starter circuit relay (D), fuel pump relay (E)

17.1 Ignition switch wiring connector (arrowed)

system (EMS) relay (see Chapter 4) and fuel pump relay (see Chapter 4) **(see illustration)**. There is also the turn signal relay (see Section 12) and the starter relay (see Section 23). See below to test the headlight and starter circuit relays, and refer to the relevant Section or Chapter as stated for the rest.

Headlight relay

2 Remove the rider's seat (see Chapter 7). Disconnect the battery negative (-) terminal (see Section 3).

3 Disconnect the relay from its connector block **(see illustration 16.1)**. Check the terminals and sockets for damage and corrosion.

4 Referring to the Wiring Diagrams at the end of Chapter 8 for terminal identification, connect a continuity tester or a multimeter set to the ohms x 1 scale between the No. 3 and No. 5 wire terminals on the relay – there should be no continuity or infinite resistance. If there is continuity or zero resistance replace the relay with a new one. Using a fully-charged 12 volt battery and two insulated jumper wires, connect the positive (+) terminal of the battery to the No. 1 wire terminal on the relay, and the negative (–) terminal to the No. 2 wire terminal on the relay. At this point the relay should be heard to click and there should be continuity or zero resistance between No. 3 and No. 5 terminals. If this is the case the relay is proved good. If the relay does not click when battery voltage is applied and the tester or meter indicates no continuity (infinite resistance), the relay is faulty and must be replaced with a new one.

Starter circuit relay

5 The starter circuit relay performs a load relief function for the headlight circuit. In its normal position, the relay completes the power supply circuit to the headlight. When the starter button is pressed, the relay switches its supply from the headlight circuit to the starter motor relay, thus enabling full battery power to be available for operation of the starter motor.

6 Remove the rider's seat (see Chapter 7). Disconnect the battery negative (-) terminal (see Section 3).

7 Disconnect the relay from its connector block **(see illustration 16.1)**. Check the terminals and sockets for damage and corrosion.

8 Referring to the Wiring Diagrams at the end of Chapter 8 for terminal identification, connect a continuity tester or a multimeter set to the ohms x 1 scale between the No. 3 and No. 4 wire terminals on the relay – there should be continuity or zero resistance. If there is no continuity or infinite resistance replace the relay with a new one. Now connect between No. 3 and No. 5 – there should be no continuity or infinite resistance. If there is continuity or zero resistance replace the relay with a new one. Using a fully-charged 12 volt battery and two insulated jumper wires, connect the positive (+) terminal of the battery to the No. 1 wire terminal on the relay, and the negative (–) terminal to the No. 2 wire terminal on the relay. At this point the relay should be heard to click and there should be continuity or zero resistance between No 3. and No. 5, and no continuity between No. 3 and No. 4. If this is the case the relay is proved good. If the relay does not click when battery voltage is applied and the tester or meter does not indicate what it should, the relay is faulty and must be replaced with a new one.

17 Ignition switch

⚠️ **Warning: To prevent the risk of short circuits, remove the seat(s) and disconnect the battery negative (–ve) lead before making any ignition switch checks.**

Check

1 Remove the fuel tank (see Chapter 4). Release and disconnect the switch wiring connector **(see illustration)**. Make the checks on the switch side of the connector.

2 Using an ohmmeter or a continuity tester, check the continuity of the connector terminal pairs (see the *Wiring Diagrams* at the end of this Chapter). Continuity should exist between the terminals connected by a solid line on the diagram when the switch key is turned to the indicated position.

3 If the switch fails any of the tests, replace it with a new one.

Removal

4 Refer to Step 1 and disconnect the switch wiring connector.

5 Undo the switch cover screws **(see illustration)**. Using a screwdriver ease the front of the cover over the steering lock,

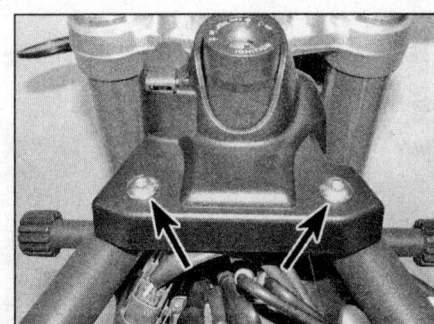

17.5a Undo the screws (arrowed)...

8•12 Electrical system

17.5b ...ease the cover up...

17.5c ...and disconnect the connector (arrowed)

17.6 Ignition switch bolts (arrowed)

then disconnect the auxiliary socket wiring connector **(see illustrations)**.

6 Two shear-head bolts mount the ignition switch to the frame **(see illustration)**. The heads of the bolts must be driven round using a suitable punch or drift, or drilled off, before the switch can be removed. If you drill the heads off remove the studs using a stud removal tool or a good pair of grips. Keep the washers to use with the new bolts. Note the fitting of the spacer plate between the switch and the frame on models from VIN 487166 to 488066.

Installation

7 Obtain new shear-head bolts. Fit the switch onto the frame, with the spacer plate between them on models from VIN 487166 to 488066.

Fit the washers and tighten the bolts until their heads shear off **(see illustration 17.6)**.
8 Route the wiring back to the connector and reconnect it, then fit it onto the bracket **(see illustration 17.1)**.
9 Connect the auxiliary socket connector and fit the cover **(see illustrations 17.5c, b and a)**.
10 Install the fuel tank (see Chapter 4).

18 Handlebar switches

Check

1 Most problems are caused by dirty or corroded contacts, but wear and breakage of

internal parts is a possibility that should not be overlooked. If breakage does occur, the entire switch and related wiring harness will have to be replaced with a new one, as individual parts are not available.
2 The switches can be checked for continuity using an ohmmeter or a continuity test light (see Section 2).
3 Remove the fuel tank (see Chapter 4). Disconnect the switch wiring connector **(see illustration)**. Make the checks on the switch side of the connector.
4 Check for continuity between the relevant terminals of the switch harness with the switch in both positions (i.e. switch off – no continuity, switch on – continuity) – see the *Wiring Diagrams* at the end of this Chapter.
5 If the continuity check indicates a problem, split the switch housing (see Step 9) and spray the switch contacts with electrical contact cleaner. If they are accessible, the contacts can be scraped clean with a knife or polished with crocus cloth. If switch components are damaged or broken, it should be obvious when the switch is disassembled.

Removal and installation

6 If the switch is to be removed from the bike, rather than just displaced from the handlebar, refer to Step 3 and disconnect the wiring connector – feed the wiring back to the switch, freeing it from all guides and ties and noting its correct routing.
7 When displacing or removing the right-hand switch, disconnect the wiring connectors from the front brake light switch **(see illustration 18.2)**.
8 When displacing or removing the left-hand switch first release the clutch switch from the lever bracket – use a small screwdriver to release the clip on the underside of the switch and pull it out **(see illustration)**.
9 Unscrew the handlebar switch screws and free the switch from the handlebar by separating the halves **(see illustrations)**.
10 Installation is the reverse of removal. Locate the pin in the switch housing in the

18.3 Right-hand switch wiring connector (A), left-hand switch wiring connector (B)

18.8 Press in the clip and withdraw the switch

18.9a Right-hand switch housing screws (arrowed)

18.9b Left-hand switch housing screws (arrowed)

Electrical system 8•13

18.10 Locate the pin (A) in the hole (B) – left-hand switch housing shown

19.2 Disconnect the switch wiring connector (arrowed)

19.7 Sidestand switch screws (arrowed)

hole in the handlebar **(see illustration)**. Make sure the wiring connectors are correctly routed and securely connected. Make sure the clutch switch tabs are aligned with the cut-outs in the lever bracket and the retaining clip engages in its hole.

19 Sidestand switch

Check

1 The sidestand switch is mounted on the sidestand bracket. The switch is part of the safety circuit, which stops the engine running if the transmission is put into gear whilst the sidestand is down. Before checking the electrical circuit, check the fuses (see Section 5).
2 Trace the wiring from the switch and disconnect it at the connector **(see illustration)**.
3 Check the operation of the switch using an ohmmeter or continuity test light. Connect the meter probes to the terminals on the switch side of the connector. With the sidestand up there should be continuity (zero resistance) between the terminals, and with the stand down there should be no continuity (infinite resistance).
4 If the switch does not perform as expected replace it with a new one.
5 If the switch is good, check the other components in the starter circuit as described in the relevant sections of this Chapter. If all components are good, check the wiring between the various components, referring to Section 2 at the beginning of this Chapter and to the wiring diagrams at the end of it.

Removal and installation

6 Trace the wiring from the switch and disconnect it at the connector **(see illustration 19.2)**. Feed the wiring to the switch, freeing it from any guides and ties and noting its routing.
7 Undo the screws and remove the switch **(see illustration)** – if you don't have the correct tools to get on the inner screw refer to Chapter 5 and remove the sidestand bracket.
8 Fit the new switch and tighten the screws.
9 Feed the wiring to the connector and reconnect it. Check the operation of the switch.

20 Clutch switch

Check

1 The clutch switch is mounted in the clutch lever bracket. The switch is part of the safety circuit, which prevents or stops the engine running if the transmission is in gear whilst the sidestand is down, and prevents the engine from starting unless the transmission is in neutral, the sidestand is up and the clutch lever is pulled in.
2 To check the switch, refer to Section 18 and disconnect the left-hand switch assembly wiring connector. Connect the probes of an ohmmeter or a continuity tester to the black and black/yellow wire terminals on the switch side of the connector. With the clutch lever pulled in, continuity should be indicated. With the clutch lever out, no continuity (infinite resistance) should be indicated. If this is not the case use a small screwdriver to release the clip on the underside of the switch and pull it out of the clutch lever bracket **(see illustration 18.8)**. Check that the plunger is not broken or seized in the switch **(see illustration)**.
3 If the switch is good, turn the ignition on and check that there is voltage at the black/orange wire terminal on the loom side of the connector, and check that there is continuity to earth (ground) in the black wire. If not, check the wiring. Otherwise, check the other components in the starter circuit as described in the relevant sections of this Chapter, and check the wiring between the various components (see the Wiring Diagrams at the end of this Chapter).

Removal and installation

4 The clutch switch is mounted in the clutch lever bracket. Refer to Section 18 for removal and installation of the handlebar switch.

21 Oil pressure switch

Check

1 The oil pressure warning light should come on when the ignition switch is turned ON and extinguish a few seconds after the engine is started. If the oil pressure warning light comes on whilst the engine is running, stop the engine immediately and carry out an oil level check (see Pre-ride checks), and if the level is correct, then an oil pressure check (see Chapter 2).
2 The oil pressure switch is screwed into the top of the crankcase behind the cylinders. Remove the throttle bodies (see Chapter 4). Disconnect the wiring connector from the switch **(see illustration)**. With the ignition switched ON, and using an auxiliary piece of wire fitted against the connector terminal, earth (ground) the wire on the crankcase and check that the warning light comes on. If the light comes on, the switch is proven defective and must be replaced with a new one.

20.2 Make sure the plunger (arrowed) is not seized or broken

21.2 Oil pressure switch (arrowed)

22.2 Horn wiring connectors (A) and mounting bolt (B)

23.4 Starter motor lead terminal (M), battery lead terminal (B), white/red wire terminal (1), black wire terminal (2)

3 If the light still does not come on, check for voltage at the wire terminal. If there is no voltage present, check the wiring between the switch and the instrument cluster for continuity, referring to Section 2 at the beginning of the Chapter and to the wiring diagrams at the end of it.

4 If the warning light comes on whilst the engine is running, yet the oil pressure is satisfactory, remove the wire from the oil pressure switch. With the wire detached and the ignition switched ON the light should be out. If it is illuminated, the wire between the switch and instrument cluster must be earthed (grounded) at some point. If the wiring is good, the switch must be assumed faulty and be replaced with a new one.

Removal and installation

5 The oil pressure switch is screwed into the top of the crankcase on the right-hand side. Remove the throttle bodies (see Chapter 4).
6 Disconnect the wiring connector from the switch **(see illustration 21.2)**.
7 Unscrew the switch and withdraw it from the crankcase. Discard the sealing washer – a new one should be used.
8 Fit the switch using a new sealing washer and tighten it to the torque setting specified at the beginning of the Chapter. Connect the wiring connector **(see illustration 21.2)**.
9 Install the throttle bodies (see Chapter 4).
10 Run the engine and check that the switch operates correctly.

22 Horn

Check

1 If the horn doesn't work, first check the fuse (see Section 5).
2 The horn is mounted to the front of the frame below the headlight **(see illustration)**.
3 Disconnect the wiring connectors from the horn. Using two jumper wires, apply battery voltage directly to the terminals on the horn. If the horn doesn't sound, replace it with a new one.
4 If the horn sounds, check for voltage at the black/blue wire terminal with the ignition switch on. If there is voltage check for continuity in the violet/black wire to the horn button, then in the black/yellow wire from the horn button to earth, referring to Section 2 at the beginning of this Chapter and to the wiring diagrams at the end of it, and check the horn button itself in the switch housing (see Section 18). If there was no voltage at the black/blue wire terminal check it for continuity between the connector and the fusebox.

Removal and installation

5 The horn is mounted to the front of the frame below the headlight **(see illustrations 22.2)**.
6 Disconnect the wiring connectors, then unscrew the bolt and remove the horn.
7 Fit the horn and securely tighten the bolt. Connect the wiring connectors and check the operation of the horn.

23 Starter relay

Check

1 If the starter circuit is faulty, first check the main and starter circuit fuses (see Section 5) and the starter circuit relay (see Section 16).
2 To access the starter motor relay, remove the battery (see Section 3), and the ECM (see Chapter 4).
3 Disconnect the AP sensor wiring connector, then displace the starter relay, turn it upside down and disconnect the wiring connector **(see illustrations 5.2a and b)**. Remove the plastic cover **(see illustration 5.2c)**.
4 Unscrew the bolt securing the starter motor lead (marked M) to the relay; position the lead away from the terminal **(see illustration)**. Reconnect the relay wiring connector. With the ignition switch ON, the engine kill switch in the RUN position, the transmission in neutral, and the clutch lever pulled in, press the starter button. The relay should be heard to click. If the relay doesn't click, switch the ignition OFF and remove the relay as described below; then test it as follows.
5 Set a multimeter to the ohms x 1 scale and connect it across the relay's starter motor and battery lead terminals **(see illustration 23.4)**. Using a fully-charged 12 volt battery and two insulated jumper wires, connect the battery across the B and M terminals of the relay (there are terminals the white/red and black wires from the loom connect to). At this point the relay should be heard to click and the multimeter read 0 ohms (continuity). If this is the case the relay is proved good. If the relay does not click when battery voltage is applied and indicates no continuity (infinite resistance) across its terminals, it is faulty and must be replaced with a new one.
6 If the relay is good, check for battery voltage at the white/red wire terminal on the loom side of the wiring connector with the ignition switch ON, the engine kill switch in the RUN position, the transmission in neutral, the clutch lever pulled in and the starter button pressed. If no voltage is present, check the other components and their wiring and connectors in the starter circuit from the battery to the relay (see *Wiring Diagrams* at the end of this Chapter).If voltage is present, check the black wire for continuity to earth.

Removal and installation

7 To access the relay, remove the battery (see Section 3), and the ECM (see Chapter 4).
8 Disconnect the AP sensor wiring connector, then displace the starter relay, turn it upside down and disconnect the wiring connector **(see illustrations 5.2a and b)**. Remove the plastic cover **(see illustration 5.2c)**.
9 Unscrew the bolts securing the starter motor and battery leads, noting which fits

Electrical system 8•15

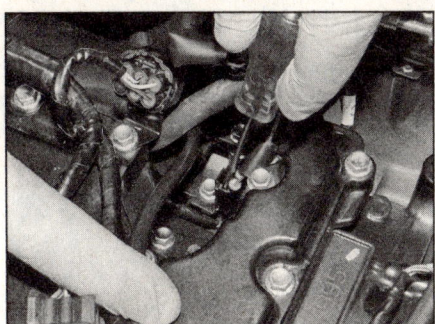

24.3 Release the connector from the bracket

24.4 Lift the rubber cover, then undo the screw (arrowed) and detach the lead

24.5 Starter motor bolts (arrowed)

where **(see illustration 23.4)**. If required remove the main fuse and its spare.

10 Installation is the reverse of removal. The lead from the battery goes on the terminal marked B, the lead to the starter motor goes on the terminal marked M **(see illustration 23.4)**. Make sure the terminal bolts are securely tightened.

24 Starter motor removal and installation

Removal

1 The starter motor is mounted on the crankcase, behind the cylinder block. Disconnect the battery negative (–) lead (see Section 3).
2 Remove the throttle bodies (see Chapter 4).
3 Disconnect the wiring connector from the oil pressure switch **(see illustration 21.2)**. Release the wiring connector from the bracket on the starter motor **(see illustration)**.
4 Peel back the rubber terminal cover and undo the screw securing the lead to the starter motor **(see illustration)**.
5 Unscrew the two bolts securing the starter motor, noting the connector bracket with the rear bolt **(see illustration)**. Draw the starter motor out of the crankcase, using a screwdriver to lever it out if necessary, then remove it.
6 Remove the O-ring from the end of the motor – a new one must be used **(see illustration 24.7)**.

24.7 Fit a new O-ring (arrowed) and smear it with grease

Installation

7 Fit a new O-ring on the end of the starter motor, making sure it is seated in its groove, and smear it with grease **(see illustration)**.
8 Manoeuvre the motor into position and slide it into the crankcase. Make sure that the starter motor teeth mesh correctly with those of the starter idle/reduction gear. Fit the mounting bolts, not forgetting the connector bracket with the rear bolt, and tighten them to the torque setting specified at the beginning of the Chapter.
9 Connect the lead to the starter motor and secure it with the screw **(see illustration 24.3)**. Fit the rubber cover over the terminal.
10 Fit the connector onto the bracket. Connect the oil pressure switch wiring connector.
11 Install the throttle bodies (see Chapter 4).

25.2 Make some alignment marks between the housing and the end covers

12 Connect the battery negative (–) lead (see Section 3).

25 Starter motor overhaul

Disassembly

1 Remove the starter motor (see Section 24).
2 Make some alignment marks between the housing and both end covers **(see illustration)**.
3 Unscrew the two long bolts, then remove the front cover from the motor **(see illustrations)**. Remove the tabbed washer from the cover **(see illustration)**.
4 Slide the shim off the armature shaft (see

25.3a Unscrew the two long bolts (arrowed), noting the O-rings...

25.3b ...and remove the front cover...

25.3c ...and its tabbed washer

8•16 Electrical system

25.4a Slide the shim off the shaft

25.4b Draw the main housing off the armature

25.5 Draw the armature out of the cover

illustration). Hold the armature in place and draw the main housing off, noting that the attraction of the magnets will hold it in place **(see illustration)**.

5 Draw the armature out of the rear cover **(see illustration)**.

Inspection

Note: *No replacement parts are available from Triumph for the starter motor. If the following checks indicate a worn or faulty internal component, seek the advice of a Triumph dealer or auto electrical specialist before buying a new starter motor.*

6 The parts of the starter motor that are most likely to wear are the brushes **(see illustration)**. No specification is given for the minimum length, but anything over 5 mm should be serviceable. Also check the brushes are not cracked, chipped, or otherwise damaged. Make sure each brush is securely connected to its wire, and the wire is securely connected to its terminal. Make sure the springs in the brush housings are good.

7 Inspect the commutator bars for scoring, scratches and discoloration. The bars can be cleaned and polished with crocus cloth – do not use sandpaper or emery paper. After cleaning, wipe away any residue with a cloth soaked in electrical system cleaner or denatured alcohol. Make sure the insulation material (mica) between each of the bars is below the bars themselves **(see illustration)** – if necessary carefully scrape some away.

8 Using an ohmmeter or a continuity test light, check for continuity between the commutator bars **(see illustration)**. Continuity should exist between each bar and all of the others. Also, check for continuity between the commutator bars and the armature shaft **(see illustration)**. There should be no continuity (infinite resistance) between the commutator and the shaft. If the checks indicate otherwise, the armature is defective.

9 Check there is no continuity between the terminal and the rear cover **(see illustration)**. Check for continuity between the terminal and each positive brush **(see illustration)**. Check for continuity between the cover and each negative brush **(see illustration)**.

25.6 Check the brushes (arrowed) for wear and damage

25.8a There should be continuity between the bars...

25.8b ...and no continuity between the bars and the shaft

25.7 Check the commutator bars and make sure the mica (1) is below the bars (2)

25.9a Check there is no continuity between the terminal and the cover...

25.9b ...and there is continuity between the terminal and each positive brush...

25.9c ...and between the cover and each negative brush

Electrical system 8•17

25.10a Check the front cover oil seal (A) and bearing (B)...

25.10b ...the rear cover bush (arrowed)...

10 Check the oil seal and bearing in the front cover (see illustration). Check the bush in the rear cover (see illustration). Inspect the covers for signs of cracks or wear, and make sure the sealing rings are in good condition (see illustration).
11 Inspect the magnets in the main housing and the housing itself for cracks.
12 Check the starter shaft teeth and the idle/reduction gear in the engine for worn, cracked, chipped and broken teeth.

Reassembly

13 Make sure the sealing ring is in place on the rim of each cover (see illustration 25.10c).
14 Using crocodile clips over the brush wire and the rim of the cover, secure each brush so it is held retracted in the housing (see illustration). Fit the armature into the rear cover, seating the shaft in its bush (see illustration). Remove the crocodile clips – check that each brush locates against the commutator.
15 Identify the rear end of the main housing – it has an indented tab that locates between the two posts on the rear cover. Grasp the armature to prevent it being draw out of the rear cover and carefully fit the main housing over it, rear end first, aligning the marks made

25.10c ...and the cover sealing rings (arrowed)

on removal, and making sure the tab locates between the posts (see illustration). Slide the shim onto the shaft (see illustration 25.4a).
16 Fit the tabbed washer into the front cover, locating the tabs between the raised ribs (see illustration 25.3c). Fit the cover over the shaft and onto the housing, aligning the marks made on removal and locating the post between the magnets (see illustration 25.3b).
17 Check the marks made on removal are correctly aligned, then fit the long bolts with their O-rings and tighten them (see illustration).
18 Install the starter motor (see Section 24).

25.14a Secure each brush in its housing using crocodile clips as shown...

26 Charging system testing

1 If the performance of the charging system is suspect, the system as a whole should be checked first, followed by testing of the individual components. **Note:** *Before beginning the checks, make sure the battery is fully charged (using a remote charger – see Section 4), and that all system connections are clean and tight.*

25.14b ...then fit the armature

25.15 Carefully fit the housing over the armature making sure it locates correctly

25.17 Make sure the O-ring (arrowed) is fitted under the head of each bolt

8•18 Electrical system

2 Checking the output of the charging system and the performance of the various components within the charging system requires the use of a multimeter (with voltage, current and resistance checking facilities). If a multimeter is not available, the job of checking the system should be left to a Triumph dealer or specialist.

3 When making the checks, follow the procedures carefully to prevent incorrect connections or short circuits resulting in irreparable damage to electrical system components.

4 Remove the rider's seat (see Chapter 7).

Regulated voltage output test

5 Start the engine, warm it up and allow the engine to idle with the headlight on main beam. Connect a multimeter set to the 0-20 volts DC scale across the terminals of the battery with the positive (+) meter probe to battery positive (+) terminal and the negative (-) meter probe to battery negative (-) terminal (see Section 3) **(see illustration)**.

6 Slowly increase the engine speed to 4000 rpm and note the reading obtained. Compare the result with the Specification at the beginning of this Chapter. If the regulated voltage output is outside the specification, check the alternator and the regulator/rectifier (Sections 27 and 28).

> **HAYNES HiNT** Clues to a faulty regulator are constantly blowing bulbs, with brightness varying considerably with engine speed, and battery overheating.

Leakage test

Caution: *Always connect an ammeter in series, never in parallel with the battery, otherwise it will be damaged. Do not turn the ignition ON or operate the starter motor when the ammeter is connected – a sudden surge in current will blow the meter's fuse.*

7 Make sure the ignition is OFF. Disconnect the negative (–) lead from the battery (see Section 3). Set the multimeter to the Amps function and connect its negative (-) probe to the battery negative (-) terminal, and positive (+)

26.5 Checking the charging system output – connect the voltmeter as shown

probe to the disconnected negative (-) lead **(see illustration)**. Always set the meter to a high amps range initially and then bring it down to the mA (milli Amps) range; if there is a high current flow in the circuit it may blow the meter's fuse.

8 Battery current leakage should not exceed the maximum limit (see Specifications). If a higher leakage rate is shown there is a short circuit in the wiring, although if an after-market immobiliser or alarm is fitted, its current draw should be taken into account. Disconnect the meter and reconnect the battery negative (-) lead.

9 If leakage is indicated, refer to the Wiring Diagrams at the end of this Chapter to systematically disconnect individual electrical components and repeat the test until the source is identified.

27 Alternator

1 The alternator rotor is mounted on the left-hand end of the crankshaft and the stator is located inside the alternator engine cover. Disconnect the battery negative (-) lead (see Section 3).

Testing

2 Refer to Section 28, Step 1 for access, and disconnect the grey wiring connector from the regulator/rectifier **(see illustration 28.3)**. Check for loose wires and bent terminals.

3 Using a multimeter set to the ohms scale,

26.7 Checking the charging system leakage rate – connect the ammeter as shown

connect the meter probes to one pair of terminals at a time on the alternator side of the wiring connector and measure the resistance between the terminals. Make a note of the three readings obtained. Now check for continuity between each terminal and ground (earth).

4 If the stator coil windings are in good condition the three readings should be within the range specified at the beginning of the Chapter, and there should be no continuity (infinite resistance) between any of the terminals and ground (earth). If not, the alternator stator coil assembly is probably faulty and should be taken to a Triumph dealer or specialist for further assessment. **Note:** *Before condemning the stator, check the fault is not due to a loose wire in the connector or damaged wiring between the connector and coils. In some cases stators can be rewound.*

Removal

5 Displace the radiator (see Section 28, Step 1, and Chapter 3), and remove the starter motor (see Section 24). Displace the ignition switch wiring connector from its bracket **(see illustration 17.1)**. On models with ABS also displace the front wheel speed sensor connector **(see illustration)**. Unscrew the left-hand bolt securing the immobiliser ECM **(see illustration)**. Disconnect the grey wiring connector from the regulator/rectifier **(see illustration 28.3)**. Draw the wiring connect back past the immobiliser ECM **(see illustration)**. On models with engine No. 612714-on, but excluding 613308 to 613370, disconnect the CKP sensor wiring connector

27.5a Displace the wheel sensor wiring connector (arrowed)

27.5b Unscrew the bolt (arrowed)…

27.5c …and draw the connector back

Electrical system 8•19

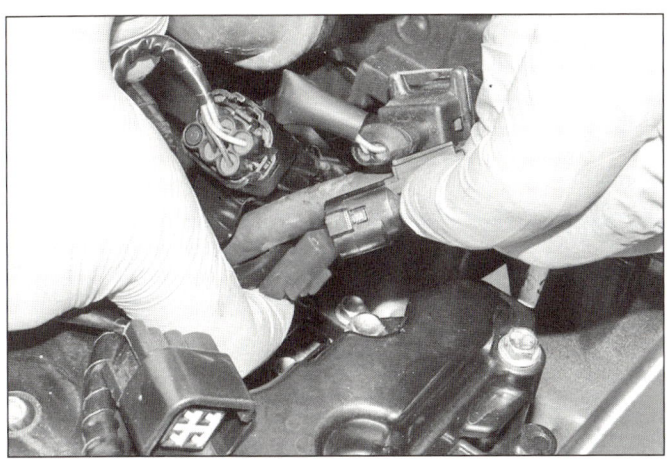

27.5d Disconnect the CKP sensor connector

27.7 Alternator cover bolts (arrowed)

(see illustration). Feed the connector(s) down to the alternator cover, releasing any ties and guides and noting the routing.

6 If the bike is on its sidestand drain the engine oil (see Chapter 1).

7 Working in a criss-cross pattern, evenly slacken then remove the alternator cover bolts, noting how two of them secure the coolant hose guide (see illustration). Also note the positions of the two longer bolts.

8 Draw the cover off, noting that it will be held by the attraction of the magnets, and be prepared to catch any residual oil. Remove the gasket – a new one must be used. Note the two locating dowels and remove them for safekeeping if loose (see illustration 27.19a). On models up to engine No. 612713 remove the O-ring from the alternator oil spray bar – a new one must be used.

9 Withdraw the shaft from the idle/reduction gear and remove the gear (see illustration).

10 To remove the rotor bolt it is necessary to stop the crankshaft from turning. Triumph produces a Service Tool (Part No. T3880375) to do this, or alternatively a number of different rotor straps are commercially available (make sure you select the correct type), one type of which is shown (see illustration). First clean the rotor with solvent to remove all traces of

27.9 Withdraw the shaft and remove the gear

oil. Fit the strap, making sure it is clear of the crankshaft position (CKP) sensor triggers. Unscrew the bolt and remove the washer.

11 To remove the rotor from the crankshaft taper it is necessary to use a rotor puller. Triumph produces a service tool (Part No. T3880365) to do this, or alternatively a number of rotor pullers are commercially available (make sure you select the correct type), one type of which is shown (see illustration). The Triumph puller should come with two thrust pads, of which you need the larger one – fit the pad spigot into the crankshaft so the pad seats over the end of the shaft, inside

27.10 Using a rotor holder while unscrewing the bolt

the inner rim of the rotor, to protect the end of the shaft. If you are using an after-market tool protect the end of the crankshaft using a nut or similar that sits against the end of the shaft, but not against the rim of the rotor – the idea is to stop the hollow end of the shaft spreading when the puller bolt is tightened against it. Fit the pad, then thread the puller body onto the rotor and tighten the centre bolt against the pad. Hold the rotor as before to prevent it turning, or use a spanner on any flats provided on the puller body, and turn the centrebolt clockwise until the rotor is displaced (see illustration).

27.11a Fit the puller onto the rotor...

27.11b ...then hold the rotor and tighten the puller bolt

8•20 Electrical system

27.12 Remove the key (arrowed) from its slot if loose

27.13 Alternator stator, CKP sensor and wiring clamp bolts (arrowed)

27.15a Clean the tapered section (A) and lubricate the bearing (B)

27.15b Fit the driven gear into the starter clutch

27.16 Slide the rotor onto the shaft, locating its cut-out over the key

12 Draw off the rotor, bringing the starter driven gear with it, or if it stays in place slide it off afterwards. Note the location of the Woodruff key in the crankshaft – remove it for safekeeping if it is loose **(see illustration)**. Take care not to damage the CKP sensor triggers on the rotor.

13 To remove the stator assembly, unscrew the bolts securing it, and on models with engine No. 612714-on, but excluding 613308 to 613370, the bolts securing the CKP sensor, and the bolt(s) securing the wiring guide(s), then remove the assembly, noting how the wiring grommet fits **(see illustration)**.

Installation

14 Apply a suitable sealant to the stator wiring grommet, then fit the stator assembly into the cover, aligning the grommet with the cut-out **(see illustration 27.13)**. Clean the stator, CKP sensor (where fitted) and wiring guide bolt(s) and apply threadlock, then tighten them to the torque settings specified at the beginning of the Chapter.

15 Clean the tapered end of the crankshaft and the corresponding mating surface on the inside of the rotor with a suitable solvent **(see illustration)**. Lubricate the needle bearing on the crankshaft with clean oil, making sure none gets on the tapered end. If removed, fit the Woodruff key in its slot in the crankshaft **(see illustration 27.12)**. If not already in place, lubricate the outside of the starter driven gear hub, then fit it into the starter clutch on the back of the rotor, turning it anti-clockwise as you do to ease its entry **(see illustration)**.

16 Make sure that no metal objects have attached themselves to the magnet on the inside of the rotor, then align the slot on the inside of the rotor boss with the Woodruff key and slide the rotor onto the shaft **(see illustration)**.

17 Fit the rotor bolt with its washer and tighten it to the torque setting specified at the beginning of this Chapter, holding the rotor as on removal to prevent it turning **(see illustrations)**.

18 Lubricate the idle/reduction gear shaft, then locate the gear and fit the shaft through **(see illustration 27.9)**.

19 If removed, fit the cover locating dowels into the crankcase, then seat the new gasket onto them **(see illustration)**. On models up to engine No. 612713 fit a new O-ring onto the alternator oil spray bar. Carefully fit the cover, noting that it will be forcibly drawn on by the magnets – make sure it locates correctly onto the dowels. Clean the threads of the two longer bolts and apply some threadlock. Fit

27.17a Fit the bolt and washer...

27.17b ...and tighten the bolt to the specified torque

Electrical system 8•21

27.19a Fit the gasket onto the dowels (arrowed)

27.19b Alternator cover bolt tightening sequence

the bolts, securing the coolant hose guide, and fitting the two longer bolts where the dowels are fitted. Tighten the bolts evenly in the sequence shown to the specified torque setting, then go round the bolts again to the same torque **(see illustration)**.

20 Refer to Step 5 and feed the wiring back to its connector(s), making sure it is correctly routed and secured by any clips or ties, and reconnect it/them. Refit all components displaced or removed as required according to model.

21 Replenish the engine oil if drained (see Chapter 1).

22 Connect the battery negative (–) lead and install the seat.

28 Regulator/rectifier

1 The regulator/rectifier is mounted to the frame, below the steering head. Displace the radiator from its mounts to access it (see Chapter 3) – there is no need to drain the cooling system or disconnect any hoses, but you do need to disconnect the fan wiring connector. The radiator supports itself, held by the hoses **(see illustration)**.

2 The internal circuitry of the regulator/rectifier consists of three diodes and three field-effect transistors (FET) – these can be tested using a multimeter set to the diode test function.

3 Disconnect the wiring connectors from the regulator/rectifier **(see illustration)**.

4 To test the diodes connect the positive (+) lead of the meter to the left-hand terminal in the black socket (as viewed from the front of the bike with the regulator/rectifier installed), then connect the negative (-) lead to each of the three pins in the grey socket in turn, thereby taking three readings. In each case there should be a reading of 0.4 to 0.7 volts – if not, replace the regulator/rectifier with a new one. Now reverse the meter leads, so the negative is connected to the left-hand black socket terminal and the positive connects to the grey socket terminals in turn. In each case there should be a reading of more than 1.4 volts, or OL (open loop) should be displayed (according to meter type) – if not, replace the regulator/rectifier with a new one.

5 To test the FETs connect the negative (-) lead of the meter to the right-hand terminal in the black socket (as viewed from the front of the bike with the regulator/rectifier installed), then connect the positive (+) lead to each of the three pins in the grey socket in turn, thereby taking three readings. In each case there should be a reading of 0.1 to 0.3 volts – if not, replace the regulator/rectifier with a new one. Now reverse the meter leads, so the positive is connected to the right-hand black socket terminal and the negative connects to the grey socket terminals in turn. In each case there should be a reading of more than 1.4 volts, or OL (open loop) should be displayed (according to meter type) – if not, replace the regulator/rectifier with a new one.

6 If all appears to be good check the power supply to the regulator/rectifier – there should be a constant battery voltage (i.e. voltage present with ignition switch on or off) at the brown wire terminal in the loom side of the black connector. If there is none check for continuity in the wire to the main fuse in the starter motor relay, referring to the wiring diagrams at the end of the chapter. If there is voltage, check for continuity to earth in the black wire.

7 Refer to Step 1 for access. Disconnect the wiring connectors from the regulator/rectifier **(see illustration 28.3)**.

8 Unscrew the two bolts and remove the regulator/rectifier.

9 Installation is the reverse of removal.

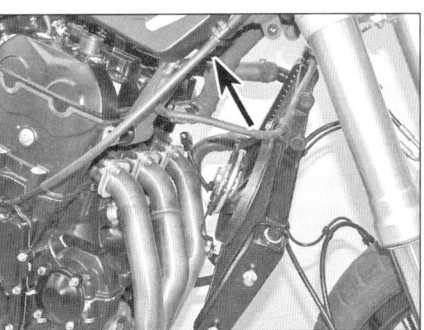

28.1 Radiator displaced for access to the regulator/rectifier (arrowed)

28.3 Regulator/rectifier wiring connectors (A) and mounting bolts (B)

Wiring diagrams 8•23

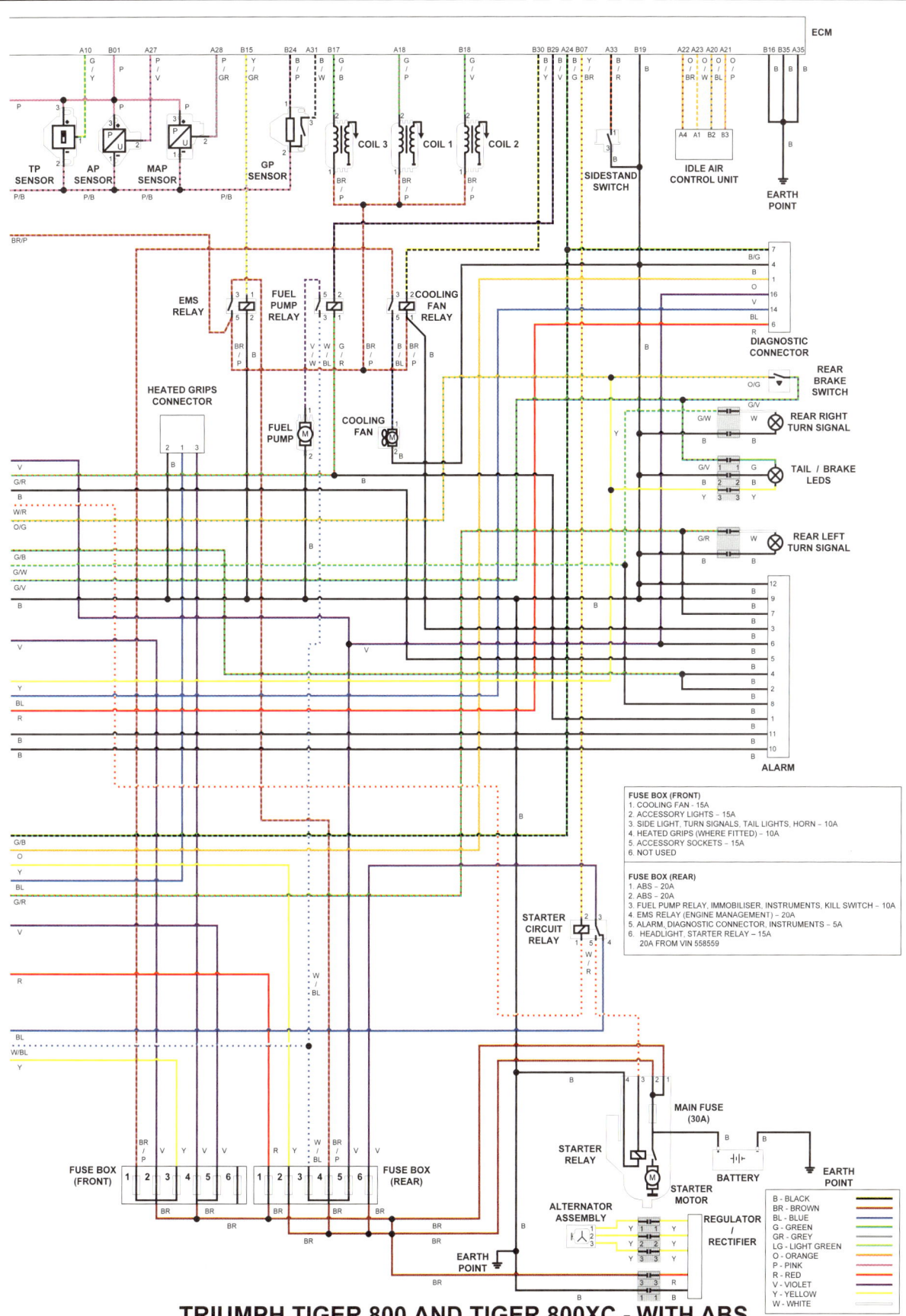

TRIUMPH TIGER 800 AND TIGER 800XC - WITH ABS

Notes

Reference REF•1

Reference

Tools and Workshop Tips REF•2

- Building up a tool kit and equipping your workshop ● Using tools
- Understanding bearing, seal, fastener and chain sizes and markings
- Repair techniques

Security REF•20

- Locks and chains
- U-locks ● Disc locks
- Alarms and immobilisers
- Security marking systems ● Tips on how to prevent bike theft

Lubricants and fluids REF•23

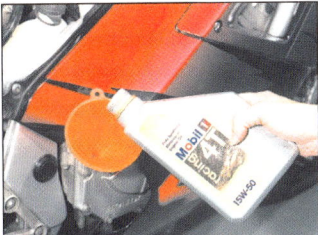

- Engine oils
- Transmission (gear) oils
- Coolant/anti-freeze
- Fork oils and suspension fluids ● Brake/clutch fluids
- Spray lubes, degreasers and solvents

MOT Test Checks REF•26

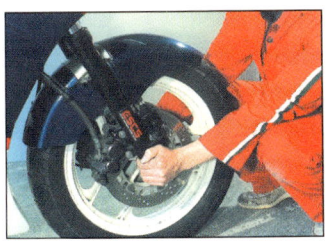

- A guide to the UK MOT test ● Which items are tested ● How to prepare your motorcycle for the test and perform a pre-test check

Storage REF•31

- How to prepare your motorcycle for going into storage and protect essential systems ● How to get the motorcycle back on the road

Conversion Factors REF•34

- Formulae for conversion of the metric (SI) units used throughout the manual into Imperial measures

Fault Finding REF•35

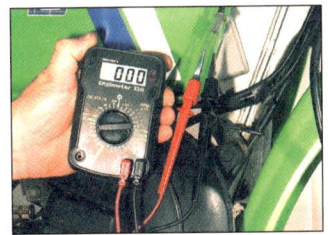

- Common faults and their likely causes ● Links to main chapters for testing and repair procedures

Technical Terms Explained REF•47

- Component names, technical terms and common abbreviations explained

Index REF•51

REF•2 Tools and Workshop Tips

Buying tools

A toolkit is a fundamental requirement for servicing and repairing a motorcycle. Although there will be an initial expense in building up enough tools for servicing, this will soon be offset by the savings made by doing the job yourself. As experience and confidence grow, additional tools can be added to enable the repair and overhaul of the motorcycle. Many of the specialist tools are expensive and not often used so it may be preferable to hire them, or for a group of friends or motorcycle club to join in the purchase.

As a rule, it is better to buy more expensive, good quality tools. Cheaper tools are likely to wear out faster and need to be renewed more often, nullifying the original saving.

Warning: To avoid the risk of a poor quality tool breaking in use, causing injury or damage to the component being worked on, always aim to purchase tools which meet the relevant national safety standards.

The following lists of tools do not represent the manufacturer's service tools, but serve as a guide to help the owner decide which tools are needed for this level of work. In addition, items such as an electric drill, hacksaw, files, soldering iron and a workbench equipped with a vice, may be needed. Although not classed as tools, a selection of bolts, screws, nuts, washers and pieces of tubing always come in useful.

For more information about tools, refer to the Haynes *Motorcycle Workshop Practice Techbook* (Bk. No. 3470).

Manufacturer's service tools

Inevitably certain tasks require the use of a service tool. Where possible an alternative tool or method of approach is recommended, but sometimes there is no option if personal injury or damage to the component is to be avoided. Where required, service tools are referred to in the relevant procedure.

Service tools can usually only be purchased from a motorcycle dealer and are identified by a part number. Some of the commonly-used tools, such as rotor pullers, are available in aftermarket form from mail-order motorcycle tool and accessory suppliers.

Maintenance and minor repair tools

1. Set of flat-bladed screwdrivers
2. Set of Phillips head screwdrivers
3. Combination open-end and ring spanners
4. Socket set (3/8 inch or 1/2 inch drive)
5. Set of Allen keys or bits
6. Set of Torx keys or bits
7. Pliers, cutters and self-locking grips (Mole grips)
8. Adjustable spanners
9. C-spanners
10. Tread depth gauge and tyre pressure gauge
11. Cable oiler clamp
12. Feeler gauges
13. Spark plug gap measuring tool
14. Spark plug spanner or deep plug sockets
15. Wire brush and emery paper
16. Calibrated syringe, measuring vessel and funnel
17. Oil filter adapters
18. Oil drainer can or tray
19. Pump type oil can
20. Grease gun
21. Straight-edge and steel rule
22. Continuity tester
23. Battery charger
24. Hydrometer (for battery specific gravity check)
25. Anti-freeze tester (for liquid-cooled engines)

Tools and Workshop Tips   REF•3

Repair and overhaul tools

1 Torque wrench (small and mid-ranges)
2 Conventional, plastic or soft-faced hammers
3 Impact driver set
4 Vernier gauge
5 Circlip pliers (internal and external, or combination)
6 Set of cold chisels and punches
7 Selection of pullers
8 Breaker bars
9 Chain breaking/riveting tool set
10 Wire stripper and crimper tool
11 Multimeter (measures amps, volts and ohms)
12 Stroboscope (for dynamic timing checks)
13 Hose clamp (wingnut type shown)
14 Clutch holding tool
15 One-man brake/clutch bleeder kit

Specialist tools

1 Micrometers (external type)
2 Telescoping gauges
3 Dial gauge
4 Cylinder compression gauge
5 Vacuum gauges (left) or manometer (right)
6 Oil pressure gauge
7 Plastigauge kit
8 Valve spring compressor (4-stroke engines)
9 Piston pin drawbolt tool
10 Piston ring removal and installation tool
11 Piston ring clamp
12 Cylinder bore hone (stone type shown)
13 Stud extractor
14 Screw extractor set
15 Bearing driver set

REF•4 Tools and Workshop Tips

1 Workshop equipment and facilities

The workbench

● Work is made much easier by raising the bike up on a ramp - components are much more accessible if raised to waist level. The hydraulic or pneumatic types seen in the dealer's workshop are a sound investment if you undertake a lot of repairs or overhauls **(see illustration 1.1)**.

1.1 Hydraulic motorcycle ramp

● If raised off ground level, the bike must be supported on the ramp to avoid it falling. Most ramps incorporate a front wheel locating clamp which can be adjusted to suit different diameter wheels. When tightening the clamp, take care not to mark the wheel rim or damage the tyre - use wood blocks on each side to prevent this.

● Secure the bike to the ramp using tie-downs **(see illustration 1.2)**. If the bike has only a sidestand, and hence leans at a dangerous angle when raised, support the bike on an auxiliary stand.

1.2 Tie-downs are used around the passenger footrests to secure the bike

● Auxiliary (paddock) stands are widely available from mail order companies or motorcycle dealers and attach either to the wheel axle or swingarm pivot **(see illustration 1.3)**. If the motorcycle has a centrestand, you can support it under the crankcase to prevent it toppling whilst either wheel is removed **(see illustration 1.4)**.

1.3 This auxiliary stand attaches to the swingarm pivot

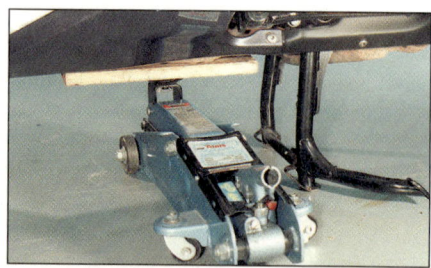

1.4 Always use a block of wood between the engine and jack head when supporting the engine in this way

Fumes and fire

● Refer to the Safety first! page at the beginning of the manual for full details. Make sure your workshop is equipped with a fire extinguisher suitable for fuel-related fires (Class B fire - flammable liquids) - it is not sufficient to have a water-filled extinguisher.

● Always ensure adequate ventilation is available. Unless an exhaust gas extraction system is available for use, ensure that the engine is run outside of the workshop.

● If working on the fuel system, make sure the workshop is ventilated to avoid a build-up of fumes. This applies equally to fume build-up when charging a battery. Do not smoke or allow anyone else to smoke in the workshop.

Fluids

● If you need to drain fuel from the tank, store it in an approved container marked as suitable for the storage of petrol (gasoline) **(see illustration 1.5)**. Do not store fuel in glass jars or bottles.

1.5 Use an approved can only for storing petrol (gasoline)

● Use proprietary engine degreasers or solvents which have a high flash-point, such as paraffin (kerosene), for cleaning off oil, grease and dirt - never use petrol (gasoline) for cleaning. Wear rubber gloves when handling solvent and engine degreaser. The fumes from certain solvents can be dangerous - always work in a well-ventilated area.

Dust, eye and hand protection

● Protect your lungs from inhalation of dust particles by wearing a filtering mask over the nose and mouth. Many frictional materials still contain asbestos which is dangerous to your health. Protect your eyes from spouts of liquid and sprung components by wearing a pair of protective goggles **(see illustration 1.6)**.

1.6 A fire extinguisher, goggles, mask and protective gloves should be at hand in the workshop

● Protect your hands from contact with solvents, fuel and oils by wearing rubber gloves. Alternatively apply a barrier cream to your hands before starting work. If handling hot components or fluids, wear suitable gloves to protect your hands from scalding and burns.

What to do with old fluids

● Old cleaning solvent, fuel, coolant and oils should not be poured down domestic drains or onto the ground. Package the fluid up in old oil containers, label it accordingly, and take it to a garage or disposal facility. Contact your local authority for location of such sites or ring the oil care hotline.

Note: It is antisocial and illegal to dump oil down the drain. To find the location of your local oil recycling bank in the UK, call 03708 506 506 or visit www.oilbankline.org.uk

In the USA, note that any oil supplier must accept used oil for recycling.

2 Fasteners - screws, bolts and nuts

Fastener types and applications

Bolts and screws

● Fastener head types are either of hexagonal, Torx or splined design, with internal and external versions of each type **(see illustrations 2.1 and 2.2)**; splined head fasteners are not in common use on motorcycles. The conventional slotted or Phillips head design is used for certain screws. Bolt or screw length is always measured from the underside of the head to the end of the item **(see illustration 2.11)**.

2.1 Internal hexagon/Allen (A), Torx (B) and splined (C) fasteners, with corresponding bits

2.2 External Torx (A), splined (B) and hexagon (C) fasteners, with corresponding sockets

● Certain fasteners on the motorcycle have a tensile marking on their heads, the higher the marking the stronger the fastener. High tensile fasteners generally carry a 10 or higher marking. Never replace a high tensile fastener with one of a lower tensile strength.

Washers (see illustration 2.3)

● Plain washers are used between a fastener head and a component to prevent damage to the component or to spread the load when torque is applied. Plain washers can also be used as spacers or shims in certain assemblies. Copper or aluminium plain washers are often used as sealing washers on drain plugs.

2.3 Plain washer (A), penny washer (B), spring washer (C) and serrated washer (D)

● The split-ring spring washer works by applying axial tension between the fastener head and component. If flattened, it is fatigued and must be renewed. If a plain (flat) washer is used on the fastener, position the spring washer between the fastener and the plain washer.
● Serrated star type washers dig into the fastener and component faces, preventing loosening. They are often used on electrical earth (ground) connections to the frame.
● Cone type washers (sometimes called Belleville) are conical and when tightened apply axial tension between the fastener head and component. They must be installed with the dished side against the component and often carry an OUTSIDE marking on their outer face. If flattened, they are fatigued and must be renewed.
● Tab washers are used to lock plain nuts or bolts on a shaft. A portion of the tab washer is bent up hard against one flat of the nut or bolt to prevent it loosening. Due to the tab washer being deformed in use, a new tab washer should be used every time it is disturbed.
● Wave washers are used to take up endfloat on a shaft. They provide light springing and prevent excessive side-to-side play of a component. Can be found on rocker arm shafts.

Nuts and split pins

● Conventional plain nuts are usually six-sided **(see illustration 2.4)**. They are sized by thread diameter and pitch. High tensile nuts carry a number on one end to denote their tensile strength.

2.4 Plain nut (A), shouldered locknut (B), nylon insert nut (C) and castellated nut (D)

● Self-locking nuts either have a nylon insert, or two spring metal tabs, or a shoulder which is staked into a groove in the shaft - their advantage over conventional plain nuts is a resistance to loosening due to vibration. The nylon insert type can be used a number of times, but must be renewed when the friction of the nylon insert is reduced, ie when the nut spins freely on the shaft. The spring tab type can be reused unless the tabs are damaged. The shouldered type must be renewed every time it is disturbed.
● Split pins (cotter pins) are used to lock a castellated nut to a shaft or to prevent slackening of a plain nut. Common applications are wheel axles and brake torque arms. Because the split pin arms are deformed to lock around the nut a new split pin must always be used on installation - always fit the correct size split pin which will fit snugly in the shaft hole. Make sure the split pin arms are correctly located around the nut **(see illustrations 2.5 and 2.6)**.

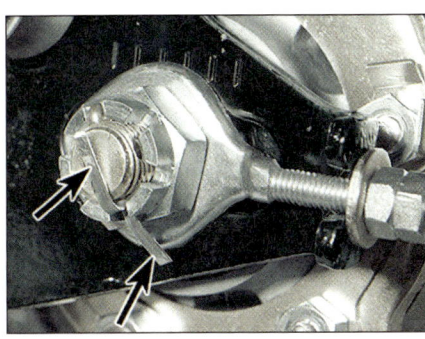

2.5 Bend split pin (cotter pin) arms as shown (arrows) to secure a castellated nut

2.6 Bend split pin (cotter pin) arms as shown to secure a plain nut

Caution: *If the castellated nut slots do not align with the shaft hole after tightening to the torque setting, tighten the nut until the next slot aligns with the hole - never slacken the nut to align its slot.*

● R-pins (shaped like the letter R), or slip pins as they are sometimes called, are sprung and can be reused if they are otherwise in good condition. Always install R-pins with their closed end facing forwards **(see illustration 2.7)**.

REF•6 Tools and Workshop Tips

2.7 Correct fitting of R-pin. Arrow indicates forward direction

Circlips (see illustration 2.8)

● Circlips (sometimes called snap-rings) are used to retain components on a shaft or in a housing and have corresponding external or internal ears to permit removal. Parallel-sided (machined) circlips can be installed either way round in their groove, whereas stamped circlips (which have a chamfered edge on one face) must be installed with the chamfer facing away from the direction of thrust load **(see illustration 2.9)**.

2.8 External stamped circlip (A), internal stamped circlip (B), machined circlip (C) and wire circlip (D)

● Always use circlip pliers to remove and install circlips; expand or compress them just enough to remove them. After installation, rotate the circlip in its groove to ensure it is securely seated. If installing a circlip on a splined shaft, always align its opening with a shaft channel to ensure the circlip ends are well supported and unlikely to catch **(see illustration 2.10)**.

2.9 Correct fitting of a stamped circlip

2.10 Align circlip opening with shaft channel

● Circlips can wear due to the thrust of components and become loose in their grooves, with the subsequent danger of becoming dislodged in operation. For this reason, renewal is advised every time a circlip is disturbed.

● Wire circlips are commonly used as piston pin retaining clips. If a removal tang is provided, long-nosed pliers can be used to dislodge them, otherwise careful use of a small flat-bladed screwdriver is necessary. Wire circlips should be renewed every time they are disturbed.

Thread diameter and pitch

● Diameter of a male thread (screw, bolt or stud) is the outside diameter of the threaded portion **(see illustration 2.11)**. Most motorcycle manufacturers use the ISO (International Standards Organisation) metric system expressed in millimetres, eg M6 refers to a 6 mm diameter thread. Sizing is the same for nuts, except that the thread diameter is measured across the valleys of the nut.

● Pitch is the distance between the peaks of the thread **(see illustration 2.11)**. It is expressed in millimetres, thus a common bolt size may be expressed as 6.0 x 1.0 mm (6 mm thread diameter and 1 mm pitch). Generally pitch increases in proportion to thread diameter, although there are always exceptions.

● Thread diameter and pitch are related for conventional fastener applications and the accompanying table can be used as a guide. Additionally, the AF (Across Flats), spanner or socket size dimension of the bolt or nut **(see illustration 2.11)** is linked to thread and pitch specification. Thread pitch can be measured with a thread gauge **(see illustration 2.12)**.

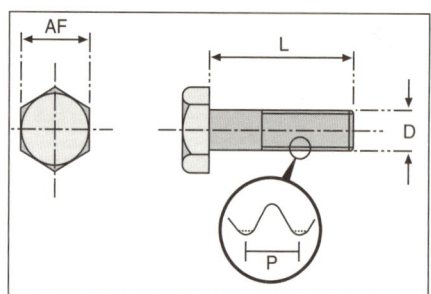

2.11 Fastener length (L), thread diameter (D), thread pitch (P) and head size (AF)

2.12 Using a thread gauge to measure pitch

AF size	Thread diameter x pitch (mm)
8 mm	M5 x 0.8
8 mm	M6 x 1.0
10 mm	M6 x 1.0
12 mm	M8 x 1.25
14 mm	M10 x 1.25
17 mm	M12 x 1.25

● The threads of most fasteners are of the right-hand type, ie they are turned clockwise to tighten and anti-clockwise to loosen. The reverse situation applies to left-hand thread fasteners, which are turned anti-clockwise to tighten and clockwise to loosen. Left-hand threads are used where rotation of a component might loosen a conventional right-hand thread fastener.

Seized fasteners

● Corrosion of external fasteners due to water or reaction between two dissimilar metals can occur over a period of time. It will build up sooner in wet conditions or in countries where salt is used on the roads during the winter. If a fastener is severely corroded it is likely that normal methods of removal will fail and result in its head being ruined. When you attempt removal, the fastener thread should be heard to crack free and unscrew easily - if it doesn't, stop there before damaging something.

● A smart tap on the head of the fastener will often succeed in breaking free corrosion which has occurred in the threads **(see illustration 2.13)**.

● An aerosol penetrating fluid (such as WD-40) applied the night beforehand may work its way down into the thread and ease removal. Depending on the location, you may be able to make up a Plasticine well around the fastener head and fill it with penetrating fluid.

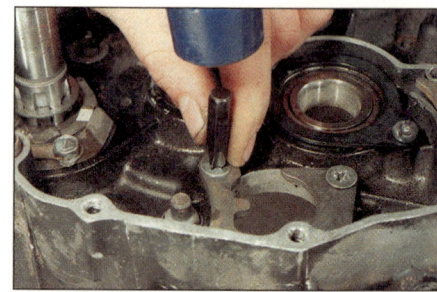

2.13 A sharp tap on the head of a fastener will often break free a corroded thread

Tools and Workshop Tips

● If you are working on an engine internal component, corrosion will most likely not be a problem due to the well lubricated environment. However, components can be very tight and an impact driver is a useful tool in freeing them **(see illustration 2.14)**.

2.14 Using an impact driver to free a fastener

● Where corrosion has occurred between dissimilar metals (eg steel and aluminium alloy), the application of heat to the fastener head will create a disproportionate expansion rate between the two metals and break the seizure caused by the corrosion. Whether heat can be applied depends on the location of the fastener - any surrounding components likely to be damaged must first be removed **(see illustration 2.15)**. Heat can be applied using a paint stripper heat gun or clothes iron, or by immersing the component in boiling water - wear protective gloves to prevent scalding or burns to the hands.

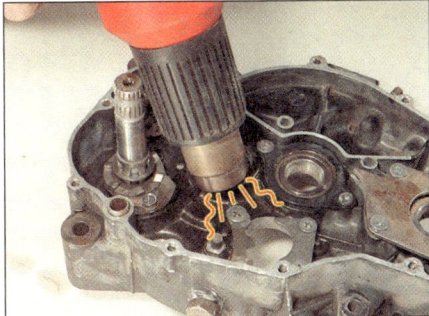

2.15 Using heat to free a seized fastener

● As a last resort, it is possible to use a hammer and cold chisel to work the fastener head unscrewed **(see illustration 2.16)**. This will damage the fastener, but more importantly extreme care must be taken not to damage the surrounding component.

Caution: Remember that the component being secured is generally of more value than the bolt, nut or screw - when the fastener is freed, do not unscrew it with force, instead work the fastener back and forth when resistance is felt to prevent thread damage.

2.16 Using a hammer and chisel to free a seized fastener

Broken fasteners and damaged heads

● If the shank of a broken bolt or screw is accessible you can grip it with self-locking grips. The knurled wheel type stud extractor tool or self-gripping stud puller tool is particularly useful for removing the long studs which screw into the cylinder mouth surface of the crankcase or bolts and screws from which the head has broken off **(see illustration 2.17)**. Studs can also be removed by locking two nuts together on the threaded end of the stud and using a spanner on the lower nut **(see illustration 2.18)**.

2.17 Using a stud extractor tool to remove a broken crankcase stud

2.18 Two nuts can be locked together to unscrew a stud from a component

● A bolt or screw which has broken off below or level with the casing must be extracted using a screw extractor set. Centre punch the fastener to centralise the drill bit, then drill a hole in the fastener **(see illustration 2.19)**. Select a drill bit which is approximately half to three-quarters the diameter of the fastener

2.19 When using a screw extractor, first drill a hole in the fastener . . .

and drill to a depth which will accommodate the extractor. Use the largest size extractor possible, but avoid leaving too small a wall thickness otherwise the extractor will merely force the fastener walls outwards wedging it in the casing thread.

● If a spiral type extractor is used, thread it anti-clockwise into the fastener. As it is screwed in, it will grip the fastener and unscrew it from the casing **(see illustration 2.20)**.

2.20 . . . then thread the extractor anti-clockwise into the fastener

● If a taper type extractor is used, tap it into the fastener so that it is firmly wedged in place. Unscrew the extractor (anti-clockwise) to draw the fastener out.

 Warning: Stud extractors are very hard and may break off in the fastener if care is not taken - ask an engineer about spark erosion if this happens.

● Alternatively, the broken bolt/screw can be drilled out and the hole retapped for an oversize bolt/screw or a diamond-section thread insert. It is essential that the drilling is carried out squarely and to the correct depth, otherwise the casing may be ruined - if in doubt, entrust the work to an engineer.

● Bolts and nuts with rounded corners cause the correct size spanner or socket to slip when force is applied. Of the types of spanner/socket available always use a six-point type rather than an eight or twelve-point type - better grip

REF•8 Tools and Workshop Tips

2.21 Comparison of surface drive ring spanner (left) with 12-point type (right)

is obtained. Surface drive spanners grip the middle of the hex flats, rather than the corners, and are thus good in cases of damaged heads **(see illustration 2.21)**.

● Slotted-head or Phillips-head screws are often damaged by the use of the wrong size screwdriver. Allen-head and Torx-head screws are much less likely to sustain damage. If enough of the screw head is exposed you can use a hacksaw to cut a slot in its head and then use a conventional flat-bladed screwdriver to remove it. Alternatively use a hammer and cold chisel to tap the head of the fastener around to slacken it. Always replace damaged fasteners with new ones, preferably Torx or Allen-head type.

> **HAYNES HiNT**
>
> A dab of valve grinding compound between the screw head and screwdriver tip will often give a good grip.

Thread repair

● Threads (particularly those in aluminium alloy components) can be damaged by overtightening, being assembled with dirt in the threads, or from a component working loose and vibrating. Eventually the thread will fail completely, and it will be impossible to tighten the fastener.

● If a thread is damaged or clogged with old locking compound it can be renovated with a thread repair tool (thread chaser) **(see illustrations 2.22 and 2.23)**; special thread

2.22 A thread repair tool being used to correct an internal thread

2.23 A thread repair tool being used to correct an external thread

chasers are available for spark plug hole threads. The tool will not cut a new thread, but clean and true the original thread. Make sure that you use the correct diameter and pitch tool. Similarly, external threads can be cleaned up with a die or a thread restorer file **(see illustration 2.24)**.

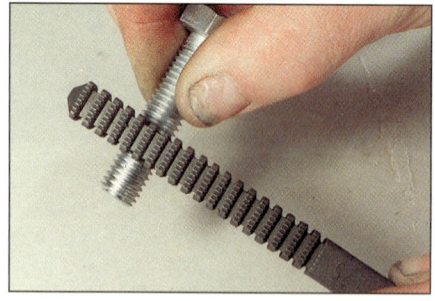

2.24 Using a thread restorer file

● It is possible to drill out the old thread and retap the component to the next thread size. This will work where there is enough surrounding material and a new bolt or screw can be obtained. Sometimes, however, this is not possible - such as where the bolt/screw passes through another component which must also be suitably modified, also in cases where a spark plug or oil drain plug cannot be obtained in a larger diameter thread size.

● The diamond-section thread insert (often known by its popular trade name of Heli-Coil) is a simple and effective method of renewing the thread and retaining the original size. A kit can be purchased which contains the tap, insert and installing tool **(see illustration 2.25)**. Drill out the damaged thread with the size drill specified **(see illustration 2.26)**. Carefully retap the thread **(see illustration 2.27)**. Install the

2.25 Obtain a thread insert kit to suit the thread diameter and pitch required

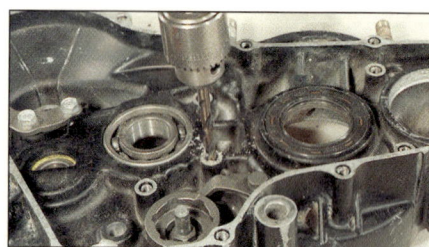

2.26 To install a thread insert, first drill out the original thread . . .

2.27 . . . tap a new thread . . .

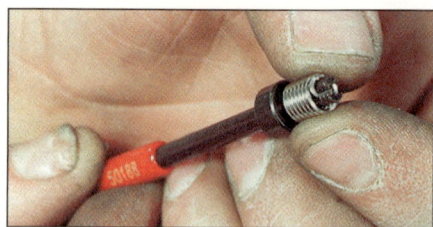

2.28 . . . fit insert on the installing tool . . .

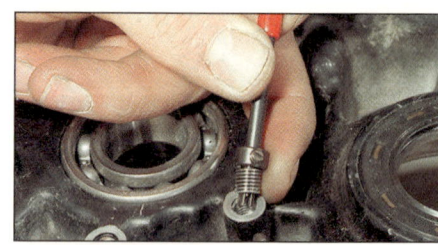

2.29 . . . and thread into the component . . .

2.30 . . . break off the tang when complete

insert on the installing tool and thread it slowly into place using a light downward pressure **(see illustrations 2.28 and 2.29)**. When positioned between a 1/4 and 1/2 turn below the surface withdraw the installing tool and use the break-off tool to press down on the tang, breaking it off **(see illustration 2.30)**.

● There are epoxy thread repair kits on the market which can rebuild stripped internal threads, although this repair should not be used on high load-bearing components.

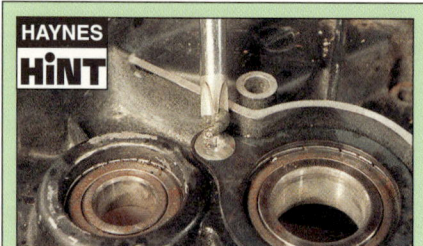

Tools and Workshop Tips

Thread locking and sealing compounds

● Locking compounds are used in locations where the fastener is prone to loosening due to vibration or on important safety-related items which might cause loss of control of the motorcycle if they fail. It is also used where important fasteners cannot be secured by other means such as lockwashers or split pins.

● Before applying locking compound, make sure that the threads (internal and external) are clean and dry with all old compound removed. Select a compound to suit the component being secured - a non-permanent general locking and sealing type is suitable for most applications, but a high strength type is needed for permanent fixing of studs in castings. Apply a drop or two of the compound to the first few threads of the fastener, then thread it into place and tighten to the specified torque. Do not apply excessive thread locking compound otherwise the thread may be damaged on subsequent removal.

● Certain fasteners are impregnated with a dry film type coating of locking compound on their threads. Always renew this type of fastener if disturbed.

● Anti-seize compounds, such as copper-based greases, can be applied to protect threads from seizure due to extreme heat and corrosion. A common instance is spark plug threads and exhaust system fasteners.

3 Measuring tools and gauges

Feeler gauges

● Feeler gauges (or blades) are used for measuring small gaps and clearances **(see illustration 3.1)**. They can also be used to measure endfloat (sideplay) of a component on a shaft where access is not possible with a dial gauge.

● Feeler gauge sets should be treated with care and not bent or damaged. They are etched with their size on one face. Keep them clean and very lightly oiled to prevent corrosion build-up.

3.1 Feeler gauges are used for measuring small gaps and clearances - thickness is marked on one face of gauge

● When measuring a clearance, select a gauge which is a light sliding fit between the two components. You may need to use two gauges together to measure the clearance accurately.

Micrometers

● A micrometer is a precision tool capable of measuring to 0.01 or 0.001 of a millimetre. It should always be stored in its case and not in the general toolbox. It must be kept clean and never dropped, otherwise its frame or measuring anvils could be distorted resulting in inaccurate readings.

● External micrometers are used for measuring outside diameters of components and have many more applications than internal micrometers. Micrometers are available in different size ranges, eg 0 to 25 mm, 25 to 50 mm, and upwards in 25 mm steps; some large micrometers have interchangeable anvils to allow a range of measurements to be taken. Generally the largest precision measurement you are likely to take on a motorcycle is the piston diameter.

● Internal micrometers (or bore micrometers) are used for measuring inside diameters, such as valve guides and cylinder bores. Telescoping gauges and small hole gauges are used in conjunction with an external micrometer, whereas the more expensive internal micrometers have their own measuring device.

External micrometer

Note: *The conventional analogue type instrument is described. Although much easier to read, digital micrometers are considerably more expensive.*

● Always check the calibration of the micrometer before use. With the anvils closed (0 to 25 mm type) or set over a test gauge

3.2 Check micrometer calibration before use

(for the larger types) the scale should read zero **(see illustration 3.2)**; make sure that the anvils (and test piece) are clean first. Any discrepancy can be adjusted by referring to the instructions supplied with the tool. Remember that the micrometer is a precision measuring tool - don't force the anvils closed, use the ratchet (4) on the end of the micrometer to close it. In this way, a measured force is always applied.

● To use, first make sure that the item being measured is clean. Place the anvil of the micrometer (1) against the item and use the thimble (2) to bring the spindle (3) lightly into contact with the other side of the item **(see illustration 3.3)**. Don't tighten the thimble down because this will damage the micrometer - instead use the ratchet (4) on the end of the micrometer. The ratchet mechanism applies a measured force preventing damage to the instrument.

● The micrometer is read by referring to the linear scale on the sleeve and the annular scale on the thimble. Read off the sleeve first to obtain the base measurement, then add the fine measurement from the thimble to obtain the overall reading. The linear scale on the sleeve represents the measuring range of the micrometer (eg 0 to 25 mm). The annular scale

3.3 Micrometer component parts

1 Anvil
2 Thimble
3 Spindle
4 Ratchet
5 Frame
6 Locking lever

REF•10 Tools and Workshop Tips

on the thimble will be in graduations of 0.01 mm (or as marked on the frame) - one full revolution of the thimble will move 0.5 mm on the linear scale. Take the reading where the datum line on the sleeve intersects the thimble's scale. Always position the eye directly above the scale otherwise an inaccurate reading will result.

In the example shown the item measures 2.95 mm (see illustration 3.4):

Linear scale	2.00 mm
Linear scale	0.50 mm
Annular scale	0.45 mm
Total figure	2.95 mm

3.5 Micrometer reading of 46.99 mm on linear and annular scales . . .

3.7 Expand the telescoping gauge in the bore, lock its position . . .

3.4 Micrometer reading of 2.95 mm

3.6 . . . and 0.004 mm on vernier scale

3.8 . . . then measure the gauge with a micrometer

Most micrometers have a locking lever (6) on the frame to hold the setting in place, allowing the item to be removed from the micrometer.
● Some micrometers have a vernier scale on their sleeve, providing an even finer measurement to be taken, in 0.001 increments of a millimetre. Take the sleeve and thimble measurement as described above, then check which graduation on the vernier scale aligns with that of the annular scale on the thimble. Note: *The eye must be perpendicular to the scale when taking the vernier reading - if necessary rotate the body of the micrometer to ensure this.* Multiply the vernier scale figure by 0.001 and add it to the base and fine measurement figures.

In the example shown the item measures 46.994 mm (see illustrations 3.5 and 3.6):

Linear scale (base)	46.000 mm
Linear scale (base)	00.500 mm
Annular scale (fine)	00.490 mm
Vernier scale	00.004 mm
Total figure	46.994 mm

Internal micrometer

● Internal micrometers are available for measuring bore diameters, but are expensive and unlikely to be available for home use. It is suggested that a set of telescoping gauges and small hole gauges, both of which must be used with an external micrometer, will suffice for taking internal measurements on a motorcycle.
● Telescoping gauges can be used to measure internal diameters of components. Select a gauge with the correct size range, make sure its ends are clean and insert it into the bore. Expand the gauge, then lock its position and withdraw it from the bore (see illustration 3.7). Measure across the gauge ends with a micrometer (see illustration 3.8).
● Very small diameter bores (such as valve guides) are measured with a small hole gauge. Once adjusted to a slip-fit inside the component, its position is locked and the gauge withdrawn for measurement with a micrometer (see illustrations 3.9 and 3.10).

Vernier caliper

Note: *The conventional linear and dial gauge type instruments are described. Digital types are easier to read, but are far more expensive.*
● The vernier caliper does not provide the precision of a micrometer, but is versatile in being able to measure internal and external diameters. Some types also incorporate a depth gauge. It is ideal for measuring clutch plate friction material and spring free lengths.
● To use the conventional linear scale vernier, slacken off the vernier clamp screws (1) and set its jaws over (2), or inside (3), the item to be measured (see illustration 3.11). Slide the jaw into contact, using the thumbwheel (4) for fine movement of the sliding scale (5) then tighten the clamp screws (1). Read off the main scale (6) where the zero on the sliding scale (5) intersects it, taking the whole number to the left of the zero; this provides the base measurement. View along the sliding scale and select the division which

3.9 Expand the small hole gauge in the bore, lock its position . . .

3.10 . . . then measure the gauge with a micrometer

lines up exactly with any of the divisions on the main scale, noting that the divisions usually represents 0.02 of a millimetre. Add this fine measurement to the base measurement to obtain the total reading.

Tools and Workshop Tips REF•11

3.11 Vernier component parts (linear gauge)

1 Clamp screws
2 External jaws
3 Internal jaws
4 Thumbwheel
5 Sliding scale
6 Main scale
7 Depth gauge

In the example shown the item measures 55.92 mm (see illustration 3.12):

Base measurement	55.00 mm
Fine measurement	00.92 mm
Total figure	55.92 mm

3.12 Vernier gauge reading of 55.92 mm

3.13 Vernier component parts (dial gauge)

1 Clamp screw
2 External jaws
3 Internal jaws
4 Thumbwheel
5 Main scale
6 Sliding scale
7 Dial gauge

● Some vernier calipers are equipped with a dial gauge for fine measurement. Before use, check that the jaws are clean, then close them fully and check that the dial gauge reads zero. If necessary adjust the gauge ring accordingly. Slacken the vernier clamp screw (1) and set its jaws over (2), or inside (3), the item to be measured (see illustration 3.13). Slide the jaws into contact, using the thumbwheel (4) for fine movement. Read off the main scale (5) where the edge of the sliding scale (6) intersects it, taking the whole number to the left of the zero; this provides the base measurement. Read off the needle position on the dial gauge (7) scale to provide the fine measurement; each division represents 0.05 of a millimetre. Add this fine measurement to the base measurement to obtain the total reading.

In the example shown the item measures 55.95 mm (see illustration 3.14):

Base measurement	55.00 mm
Fine measurement	00.95 mm
Total figure	55.95 mm

3.14 Vernier gauge reading of 55.95 mm

Plastigauge

● Plastigauge is a plastic material which can be compressed between two surfaces to measure the oil clearance between them. The width of the compressed Plastigauge is measured against a calibrated scale to determine the clearance.

● Common uses of Plastigauge are for measuring the clearance between crankshaft journal and main bearing inserts, between crankshaft journal and big-end bearing inserts, and between camshaft and bearing surfaces. The following example describes big-end oil clearance measurement.

● Handle the Plastigauge material carefully to prevent distortion. Using a sharp knife, cut a length which corresponds with the width of the bearing being measured and place it carefully across the journal so that it is parallel with the shaft (see illustration 3.15). Carefully install both bearing shells and the connecting rod. Without rotating the rod on the journal tighten its bolts or nuts (as applicable) to the specified torque. The connecting rod and bearings are then disassembled and the crushed Plastigauge examined.

3.15 Plastigauge placed across shaft journal

● Using the scale provided in the Plastigauge kit, measure the width of the material to determine the oil clearance (see illustration 3.16). Always remove all traces of Plastigauge after use using your fingernails.

Caution: Arriving at the correct clearance demands that the assembly is torqued correctly, according to the settings and sequence (where applicable) provided by the motorcycle manufacturer.

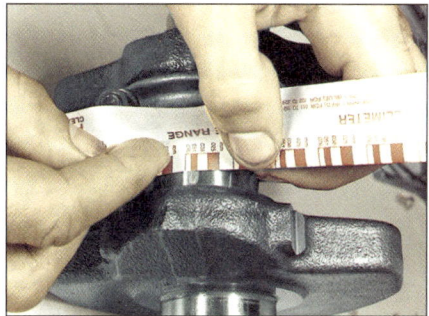

3.16 Measuring the width of the crushed Plastigauge

Tools and Workshop Tips

Dial gauge or DTI (Dial Test Indicator)

● A dial gauge can be used to accurately measure small amounts of movement. Typical uses are measuring shaft runout or shaft endfloat (sideplay) and setting piston position for ignition timing on two-strokes. A dial gauge set usually comes with a range of different probes and adapters and mounting equipment.

● The gauge needle must point to zero when at rest. Rotate the ring around its periphery to zero the gauge.

● Check that the gauge is capable of reading the extent of movement in the work. Most gauges have a small dial set in the face which records whole millimetres of movement as well as the fine scale around the face periphery which is calibrated in 0.01 mm divisions. Read off the small dial first to obtain the base measurement, then add the measurement from the fine scale to obtain the total reading.

In the example shown the gauge reads 1.48 mm (see illustration 3.17):

Base measurement	1.00 mm
Fine measurement	0.48 mm
Total figure	1.48 mm

3.17 Dial gauge reading of 1.48 mm

● If measuring shaft runout, the shaft must be supported in vee-blocks and the gauge mounted on a stand perpendicular to the shaft. Rest the tip of the gauge against the centre of the shaft and rotate the shaft slowly whilst watching the gauge reading (see illustration 3.18). Take several measurements along the length of the shaft and record the maximum gauge reading as the amount of runout in the shaft. Note: *The reading obtained will be total runout at that point - some manufacturers specify that the runout figure is halved to compare with their specified runout limit.*

● Endfloat (sideplay) measurement requires that the gauge is mounted securely to the surrounding component with its probe touching the end of the shaft. Using hand pressure, push and pull on the shaft noting the maximum endfloat recorded on the gauge (see illustration 3.19).

3.19 Using a dial gauge to measure shaft endfloat

● A dial gauge with suitable adapters can be used to determine piston position BTDC on two-stroke engines for the purposes of ignition timing. The gauge, adapter and suitable length probe are installed in the place of the spark plug and the gauge zeroed at TDC. If the piston position is specified as 1.14 mm BTDC, rotate the engine back to 2.00 mm BTDC, then slowly forwards to 1.14 mm BTDC.

Cylinder compression gauges

● A compression gauge is used for measuring cylinder compression. Either the rubber-cone type or the threaded adapter type can be used. The latter is preferred to ensure a perfect seal against the cylinder head. A 0 to 300 psi (0 to 20 Bar) type gauge (for petrol/gasoline engines) will be suitable for motorcycles.

● The spark plug is removed and the gauge either held hard against the cylinder head (cone type) or the gauge adapter screwed into the cylinder head (threaded type) (see illustration 3.20). Cylinder compression is measured with the engine turning over, but not running. The gauge will hold the reading until manually released.

Oil pressure gauge

● An oil pressure gauge is used for measuring engine oil pressure. Most gauges come with a set of adapters to fit the thread of the take-off point (see illustration 3.21). If the take-off point specified by the motorcycle manufacturer is an external oil pipe union, make sure that the specified replacement union is used to prevent oil starvation.

3.21 Oil pressure gauge and take-off point adapter (arrow)

● Oil pressure is measured with the engine running (at a specific rpm) and often the manufacturer will specify pressure limits for a cold and hot engine.

Straight-edge and surface plate

● If checking the gasket face of a component for warpage, place a steel rule or precision straight-edge across the gasket face and measure any gap between the straight-edge and component with feeler gauges (see illustration 3.22). Check diagonally across the component and between mounting holes (see illustration 3.23).

3.22 Use a straight-edge and feeler gauges to check for warpage

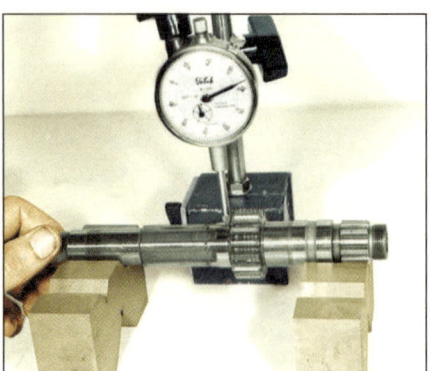

3.18 Using a dial gauge to measure shaft runout

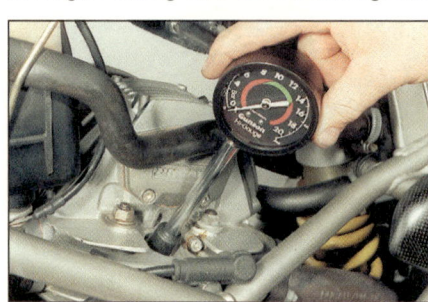

3.20 Using a rubber-cone type cylinder compression gauge

3.23 Check for warpage in these directions

Tools and Workshop Tips

● Checking individual components for warpage, such as clutch plain (metal) plates, requires a perfectly flat plate or piece or plate glass and feeler gauges.

4 Torque and leverage

What is torque?

● Torque describes the twisting force about a shaft. The amount of torque applied is determined by the distance from the centre of the shaft to the end of the lever and the amount of force being applied to the end of the lever; distance multiplied by force equals torque.

● The manufacturer applies a measured torque to a bolt or nut to ensure that it will not slacken in use and to hold two components securely together without movement in the joint. The actual torque setting depends on the thread size, bolt or nut material and the composition of the components being held.

● Too little torque may cause the fastener to loosen due to vibration, whereas too much torque will distort the joint faces of the component or cause the fastener to shear off. Always stick to the specified torque setting.

Using a torque wrench

● Check the calibration of the torque wrench and make sure it has a suitable range for the job. Torque wrenches are available in Nm (Newton-metres), kgf m (kilograms-force metre), lbf ft (pounds-feet), lbf in (inch-pounds). Do not confuse lbf ft with lbf in.

● Adjust the tool to the desired torque on the scale **(see illustration 4.1)**. If your torque wrench is not calibrated in the units specified, carefully convert the figure (see Conversion Factors). A manufacturer sometimes gives a torque setting as a range (8 to 10 Nm) rather than a single figure - in this case set the tool midway between the two settings. The same torque may be expressed as 9 Nm ± 1 Nm. Some torque wrenches have a method of locking the setting so that it isn't inadvertently altered during use.

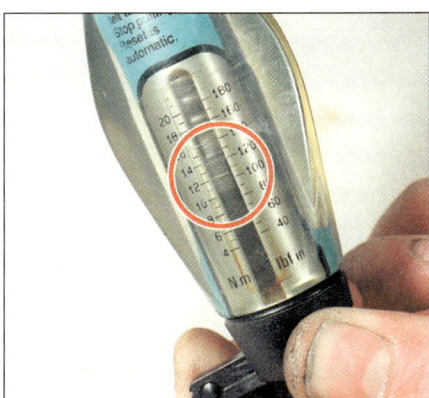

4.1 Set the torque wrench index mark to the setting required, in this case 12 Nm

● Install the bolts/nuts in their correct location and secure them lightly. Their threads must be clean and free of any old locking compound. Unless specified the threads and flange should be dry - oiled threads are necessary in certain circumstances and the manufacturer will take this into account in the specified torque figure. Similarly, the manufacturer may also specify the application of thread-locking compound.

● Tighten the fasteners in the specified sequence until the torque wrench clicks, indicating that the torque setting has been reached. Apply the torque again to double-check the setting. Where different thread diameter fasteners secure the component, as a rule tighten the larger diameter ones first.

● When the torque wrench has been finished with, release the lock (where applicable) and fully back off its setting to zero - do not leave the torque wrench tensioned. Also, do not use a torque wrench for slackening a fastener.

Angle-tightening

● Manufacturers often specify a figure in degrees for final tightening of a fastener. This usually follows tightening to a specific torque setting.

● A degree disc can be set and attached to the socket **(see illustration 4.2)** or a protractor can be used to mark the angle of movement on the bolt/nut head and the surrounding casting **(see illustration 4.3)**.

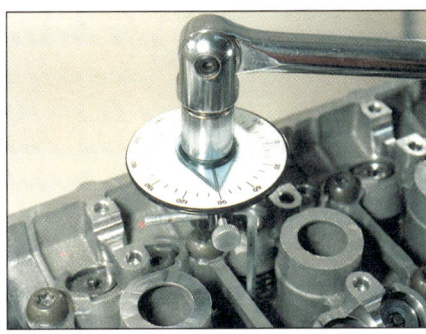

4.2 Angle tightening can be accomplished with a torque-angle gauge . . .

4.3 . . . or by marking the angle on the surrounding component

Loosening sequences

● Where more than one bolt/nut secures a component, loosen each fastener evenly a little at a time. In this way, not all the stress of the joint is held by one fastener and the components are not likely to distort.

● If a tightening sequence is provided, work in the REVERSE of this, but if not, work from the outside in, in a criss-cross sequence **(see illustration 4.4)**.

4.4 When slackening, work from the outside inwards

Tightening sequences

● If a component is held by more than one fastener it is important that the retaining bolts/nuts are tightened evenly to prevent uneven stress build-up and distortion of sealing faces. This is especially important on high-compression joints such as the cylinder head.

● A sequence is usually provided by the manufacturer, either in a diagram or actually marked in the casting. If not, always start in the centre and work outwards in a criss-cross pattern **(see illustration 4.5)**. Start off by securing all bolts/nuts finger-tight, then set the torque wrench and tighten each fastener by a small amount in sequence until the final torque is reached. By following this practice,

4.5 When tightening, work from the inside outwards

REF•14 Tools and Workshop Tips

the joint will be held evenly and will not be distorted. Important joints, such as the cylinder head and big-end fasteners often have two- or three-stage torque settings.

Applying leverage

● Use tools at the correct angle. Position a socket wrench or spanner on the bolt/nut so that you pull it towards you when loosening. If this can't be done, push the spanner without curling your fingers around it **(see illustration 4.6)** - the spanner may slip or the fastener loosen suddenly, resulting in your fingers being crushed against a component.

4.6 If you can't pull on the spanner to loosen a fastener, push with your hand open

● Additional leverage is gained by extending the length of the lever. The best way to do this is to use a breaker bar instead of the regular length tool, or to slip a length of tubing over the end of the spanner or socket wrench.
● If additional leverage will not work, the fastener head is either damaged or firmly corroded in place (see Fasteners).

5 Bearings

Bearing removal and installation

Drivers and sockets

● Before removing a bearing, always inspect the casing to see which way it must be driven out - some casings will have retaining plates or a cast step. Also check for any identifying markings on the bearing and if installed to a certain depth, measure this at this stage. Some roller bearings are sealed on one side - take note of the original fitted position.
● Bearings can be driven out of a casing using a bearing driver tool (with the correct size head) or a socket of the correct diameter. Select the driver head or socket so that it contacts the outer race of the bearing, not the balls/rollers or inner race. Always support the casing around the bearing housing with wood blocks, otherwise there is a risk of fracture. The bearing is driven out with a few blows on the driver or socket from a heavy mallet. Unless access is severely restricted (as with wheel bearings), a pin-punch is not recommended unless it is moved around the bearing to keep it square in its housing.

● The same equipment can be used to install bearings. Make sure the bearing housing is supported on wood blocks and line up the bearing in its housing. Fit the bearing as noted on removal - generally they are installed with their marked side facing outwards. Tap the bearing squarely into its housing using a driver or socket which bears only on the bearing's outer race - contact with the bearing balls/rollers or inner race will destroy it **(see illustrations 5.1 and 5.2)**.
● Check that the bearing inner race and balls/rollers rotate freely.

5.1 Using a bearing driver against the bearing's outer race

5.2 Using a large socket against the bearing's outer race

Pullers and slide-hammers

● Where a bearing is pressed on a shaft a puller will be required to extract it **(see illustration 5.3)**. Make sure that the puller clamp or legs fit securely behind the bearing and are unlikely to slip out. If pulling a bearing

5.3 This bearing puller clamps behind the bearing and pressure is applied to the shaft end to draw the bearing off

off a gear shaft for example, you may have to locate the puller behind a gear pinion if there is no access to the race and draw the gear pinion off the shaft as well **(see illustration 5.4)**.

Caution: Ensure that the puller's centre bolt locates securely against the end of the shaft and will not slip when pressure is applied. Also ensure that puller does not damage the shaft end.

5.4 Where no access is available to the rear of the bearing, it is sometimes possible to draw off the adjacent component

● Operate the puller so that its centre bolt exerts pressure on the shaft end and draws the bearing off the shaft.
● When installing the bearing on the shaft, tap only on the bearing's inner race - contact with the balls/rollers or outer race with destroy the bearing. Use a socket or length of tubing as a drift which fits over the shaft end **(see illustration 5.5)**.

5.5 When installing a bearing on a shaft use a piece of tubing which bears only on the bearing's inner race

● Where a bearing locates in a blind hole in a casing, it cannot be driven or pulled out as described above. A slide-hammer with knife-edged bearing puller attachment will be required. The puller attachment passes through the bearing and when tightened expands to fit firmly behind the bearing **(see illustration 5.6)**. By operating the slide-hammer part of the tool the bearing is jarred out of its housing **(see illustration 5.7)**.
● It is possible, if the bearing is of reasonable weight, for it to drop out of its housing if the casing is heated as described opposite.

Tools and Workshop Tips REF•15

5.6 Expand the bearing puller so that it locks behind the bearing . . .

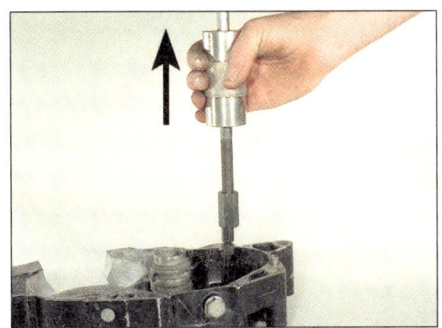

5.7 . . . attach the slide hammer to the bearing puller

If this method is attempted, first prepare a work surface which will enable the casing to be tapped face down to help dislodge the bearing - a wood surface is ideal since it will not damage the casing's gasket surface. Wearing protective gloves, tap the heated casing several times against the work surface to dislodge the bearing under its own weight **(see illustration 5.8)**.

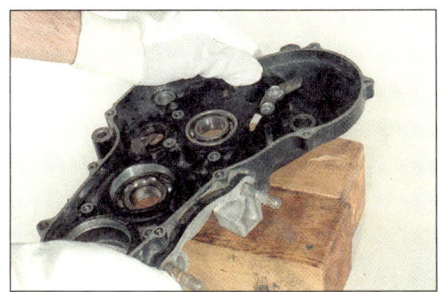

5.8 Tapping a casing face down on wood blocks can often dislodge a bearing

● Bearings can be installed in blind holes using the driver or socket method described above.

Drawbolts
● Where a bearing or bush is set in the eye of a component, such as a suspension linkage arm or connecting rod small-end, removal by drift may damage the component. Furthermore, a rubber bushing in a shock absorber eye cannot successfully be driven out of position. If access is available to a engineering press, the task is straightforward. If not, a drawbolt can be fabricated to extract the bearing or bush.

5.9 Drawbolt component parts assembled on a suspension arm

1 Bolt or length of threaded bar
2 Nuts
3 Washer (external diameter greater than tubing internal diameter)
4 Tubing (internal diameter sufficient to accommodate bearing)
5 Suspension arm with bearing
6 Tubing (external diameter slightly smaller than bearing)
7 Washer (external diameter slightly smaller than bearing)

5.10 Drawing the bearing out of the suspension arm

● To extract the bearing/bush you will need a long bolt with nut (or piece of threaded bar with two nuts), a piece of tubing which has an internal diameter larger than the bearing/bush, another piece of tubing which has an external diameter slightly smaller than the bearing/bush, and a selection of washers **(see illustrations 5.9 and 5.10)**. Note that the pieces of tubing must be of the same length, or longer, than the bearing/bush.
● The same kit (without the pieces of tubing) can be used to draw the new bearing/bush back into place **(see illustration 5.11)**.

5.11 Installing a new bearing (1) in the suspension arm

Temperature change
● If the bearing's outer race is a tight fit in the casing, the aluminium casing can be heated to release its grip on the bearing. Aluminium will expand at a greater rate than the steel bearing outer race. There are several ways to do this, but avoid any localised extreme heat (such as a blow torch) - aluminium alloy has a low melting point.
● Approved methods of heating a casing are using a domestic oven (heated to 100°C) or immersing the casing in boiling water **(see illustration 5.12)**. Low temperature range localised heat sources such as a paint stripper heat gun or clothes iron can also be used **(see illustration 5.13)**. Alternatively, soak a rag in boiling water, wring it out and wrap it around the bearing housing.

> ⚠ **Warning: All of these methods require care in use to prevent scalding and burns to the hands. Wear protective gloves when handling hot components.**

5.12 A casing can be immersed in a sink of boiling water to aid bearing removal

5.13 Using a localised heat source to aid bearing removal

● If heating the whole casing note that plastic components, such as the neutral switch, may suffer - remove them beforehand.
● After heating, remove the bearing as described above. You may find that the expansion is sufficient for the bearing to fall out of the casing under its own weight or with a light tap on the driver or socket.
● If necessary, the casing can be heated to aid bearing installation, and this is sometimes the recommended procedure if the motorcycle manufacturer has designed the housing and bearing fit with this intention.

Tools and Workshop Tips

● Installation of bearings can be eased by placing them in a freezer the night before installation. The steel bearing will contract slightly, allowing easy insertion in its housing. This is often useful when installing steering head outer races in the frame.

Bearing types and markings

● Plain shell bearings, ball bearings, needle roller bearings and tapered roller bearings will all be found on motorcycles **(see illustrations 5.14 and 5.15)**. The ball and roller types are usually caged between an inner and outer race, but uncaged variations may be found.

5.14 Shell bearings are either plain or grooved. They are usually identified by colour code (arrow)

5.15 Tapered roller bearing (A), needle roller bearing (B) and ball journal bearing (C)

● Shell bearings (often called inserts) are usually found at the crankshaft main and connecting rod big-end where they are good at coping with high loads. They are made of a phosphor-bronze material and are impregnated with self-lubricating properties.
● Ball bearings and needle roller bearings consist of a steel inner and outer race with the balls or rollers between the races. They require constant lubrication by oil or grease and are good at coping with axial loads. Taper roller bearings consist of rollers set in a tapered cage set on the inner race; the outer race is separate. They are good at coping with axial loads and prevent movement along the shaft - a typical application is in the steering head.
● Bearing manufacturers produce bearings to ISO size standards and stamp one face of the bearing to indicate its internal and external diameter, load capacity and type **(see illustration 5.16)**.
● Metal bushes are usually of phosphor-bronze material. Rubber bushes are used in suspension mounting eyes. Fibre bushes have also been used in suspension pivots.

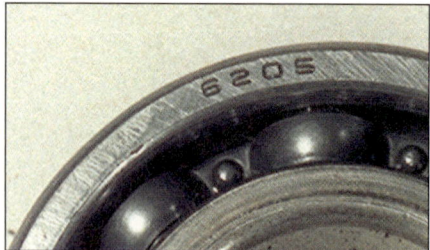

5.16 Typical bearing marking

Bearing fault finding

● If a bearing outer race has spun in its housing, the housing material will be damaged. You can use a bearing locking compound to bond the outer race in place if damage is not too severe.
● Shell bearings will fail due to damage of their working surface, as a result of lack of lubrication, corrosion or abrasive particles in the oil **(see illustration 5.17)**. Small particles of dirt in the oil may embed in the bearing material whereas larger particles will score the bearing and shaft journal. If a number of short journeys are made, insufficient heat will be generated to drive off condensation which has built up on the bearings.

5.17 Typical bearing failures

● Ball and roller bearings will fail due to lack of lubrication or damage to the balls or rollers. Tapered-roller bearings can be damaged by overloading them. Unless the bearing is sealed on both sides, wash it in paraffin (kerosene) to remove all old grease then allow it to dry. Make a visual inspection looking to dented balls or rollers, damaged cages and worn or pitted races **(see illustration 5.18)**.
● A ball bearing can be checked for wear by listening to it when spun. Apply a film of light oil to the bearing and hold it close to the ear - hold the outer race with one hand and spin the inner race with the other hand **(see illustration 5.19)**. The bearing should be almost silent when spun; if it grates or rattles it is worn.

5.18 Example of ball journal bearing with damaged balls and cages

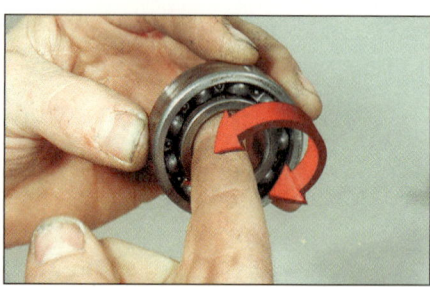

5.19 Hold outer race and listen to inner race when spun

6 Oil seals

Oil seal removal and installation

● Oil seals should be renewed every time a component is dismantled. This is because the seal lips will become set to the sealing surface and will not necessarily reseal.
● Oil seals can be prised out of position using a large flat-bladed screwdriver **(see illustration 6.1)**. In the case of crankcase seals, check first that the seal is not lipped on the inside, preventing its removal with the crankcases joined.

6.1 Prise out oil seals with a large flat-bladed screwdriver

● New seals are usually installed with their marked face (containing the seal reference code) outwards and the spring side towards the fluid being retained. In certain cases, such as a two-stroke engine crankshaft seal, a double lipped seal may be used due to there being fluid or gas on each side of the joint.

Tools and Workshop Tips

● Use a bearing driver or socket which bears only on the outer hard edge of the seal to install it in the casing - tapping on the inner edge will damage the sealing lip.

Oil seal types and markings

● Oil seals are usually of the single-lipped type. Double-lipped seals are found where a liquid or gas is on both sides of the joint.
● Oil seals can harden and lose their sealing ability if the motorcycle has been in storage for a long period - renewal is the only solution.
● Oil seal manufacturers also conform to the ISO markings for seal size - these are moulded into the outer face of the seal **(see illustration 6.2)**.

6.2 These oil seal markings indicate inside diameter, outside diameter and seal thickness

7 Gaskets and sealants

Types of gasket and sealant

● Gaskets are used to seal the mating surfaces between components and keep lubricants, fluids, vacuum or pressure contained within the assembly. Aluminium gaskets are sometimes found at the cylinder joints, but most gaskets are paper-based. If the mating surfaces of the components being joined are undamaged the gasket can be installed dry, although a dab of sealant or grease will be useful to hold it in place during assembly.
● RTV (Room Temperature Vulcanising) silicone rubber sealants cure when exposed to moisture in the atmosphere. These sealants are good at filling pits or irregular gasket faces, but will tend to be forced out of the joint under very high torque. They can be used to replace a paper gasket, but first make sure that the width of the paper gasket is not essential to the shimming of internal components. RTV sealants should not be used on components containing petrol (gasoline).
● Non-hardening, semi-hardening and hard setting liquid gasket compounds can be used with a gasket or between a metal-to-metal joint. Select the sealant to suit the application: universal non-hardening sealant can be used on virtually all joints; semi-hardening on joint faces which are rough or damaged; hard setting sealant on joints which require a permanent bond and are subjected to high temperature and pressure. **Note:** *Check first if the paper gasket has a bead of sealant impregnated in its surface before applying additional sealant.*
● When choosing a sealant, make sure it is suitable for the application, particularly if being applied in a high-temperature area or in the vicinity of fuel. Certain manufacturers produce sealants in either clear, silver or black colours to match the finish of the engine. This has a particular application on motorcycles where much of the engine is exposed.
● Do not over-apply sealant. That which is squeezed out on the outside of the joint can be wiped off, whereas an excess of sealant on the inside can break off and clog oilways.

Breaking a sealed joint

● Age, heat, pressure and the use of hard setting sealant can cause two components to stick together so tightly that they are difficult to separate using finger pressure alone. Do not resort to using levers unless there is a pry point provided for this purpose **(see illustration 7.1)** or else the gasket surfaces will be damaged.
● Use a soft-faced hammer **(see illustration 7.2)** or a wood block and conventional hammer to strike the component near the mating surface. Avoid hammering against cast extremities since they may break off. If this method fails, try using a wood wedge between the two components.

Caution: If the joint will not separate, double-check that you have removed all the fasteners.

7.1 If a pry point is provided, apply gently pressure with a flat-bladed screwdriver

7.2 Tap around the joint with a soft-faced mallet if necessary - don't strike cooling fins

Removal of old gasket and sealant

● Paper gaskets will most likely come away complete, leaving only a few traces stuck

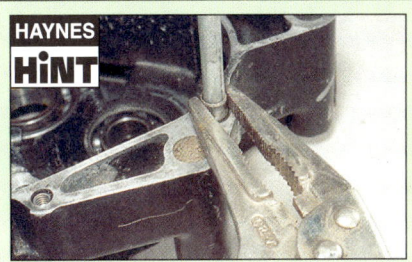

Most components have one or two hollow locating dowels between the two gasket faces. If a dowel cannot be removed, do not resort to gripping it with pliers - it will almost certainly be distorted. Install a close-fitting socket or Phillips screwdriver into the dowel and then grip the outer edge of the dowel to free it.

on the sealing faces of the components. It is imperative that all traces are removed to ensure correct sealing of the new gasket.
● Very carefully scrape all traces of gasket away making sure that the sealing surfaces are not gouged or scored by the scraper **(see illustrations 7.3, 7.4 and 7.5)**. Stubborn deposits can be removed by spraying with an aerosol gasket remover. Final preparation of

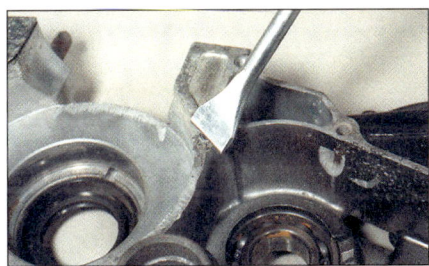

7.3 Paper gaskets can be scraped off with a gasket scraper tool . . .

7.4 . . . a knife blade . . .

7.5 . . . or a household scraper

REF•18 Tools and Workshop Tips

7.6 Fine abrasive paper is wrapped around a flat file to clean up the gasket face

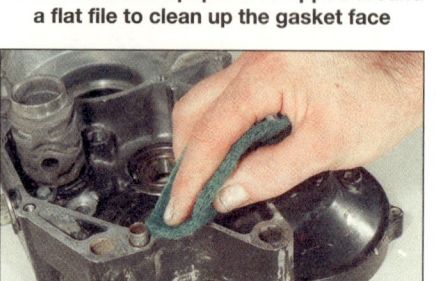

7.7 A kitchen scourer can be used on stubborn deposits

8.1 Tighten the chain breaker to push the pin out of the link . . .

8.2 . . . withdraw the pin, remove the tool . . .

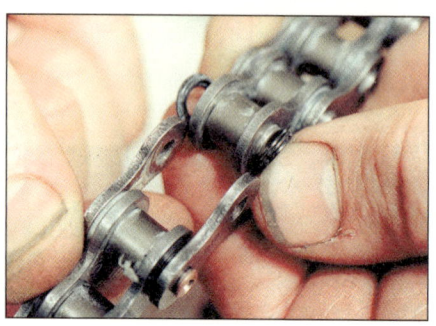

8.3 . . . and separate the chain link

8.4 Insert the new soft link, with O-rings, through the chain ends . . .

8.5 . . . install the O-rings over the pin ends . . .

8.6 . . . followed by the sideplate

the gasket surface can be made with very fine abrasive paper or a plastic kitchen scourer **(see illustrations 7.6 and 7.7)**.

● Old sealant can be scraped or peeled off components, depending on the type originally used. Note that gasket removal compounds are available to avoid scraping the components clean; make sure the gasket remover suits the type of sealant used.

8 Chains

Breaking and joining final drive chains

● Drive chains for all but small bikes are continuous and do not have a clip-type connecting link. The chain must be broken using a chain breaker tool and the new chain securely riveted together using a new soft rivet-type link. Never use a clip-type connecting link instead of a rivet-type link, except in an emergency. Various chain breaking and riveting tools are available, either as separate tools or combined as illustrated in the accompanying photographs - read the instructions supplied with the tool carefully.

> **Warning:** *The need to rivet the new link pins correctly cannot be overstressed - loss of control of the motorcycle is very likely to result if the chain breaks in use.*

● Rotate the chain and look for the soft link. The soft link pins look like they have been deeply centre-punched instead of peened over like all the other pins **(see illustration 8.9)** and its sideplate may be a different colour. Position the soft link midway between the sprockets and assemble the chain breaker tool over one of the soft link pins **(see illustration 8.1)**. Operate the tool to push the pin out through the chain **(see illustration 8.2)**. On an O-ring chain, remove the O-rings **(see illustration 8.3)**. Carry out the same procedure on the other soft link pin.

> **Caution:** *Certain soft link pins (particularly on the larger chains) may require their ends to be filed or ground off before they can be pressed out using the tool.*

● Check that you have the correct size and strength (standard or heavy duty) new soft link - do not reuse the old link. Look for the size marking on the chain sideplates **(see illustration 8.10)**.

● Position the chain ends so that they are engaged over the rear sprocket. On an O-ring chain, install a new O-ring over each pin of the link and insert the link through the two chain ends **(see illustration 8.4)**. Install a new O-ring over the end of each pin, followed by the sideplate (with the chain manufacturer's marking facing outwards) **(see illustrations 8.5 and 8.6)**. On an unsealed chain, insert the link through the two chain ends, then install the sideplate with the chain manufacturer's marking facing outwards.

● Note that it may not be possible to install the sideplate using finger pressure alone. If using a joining tool, assemble it so that the plates of the tool clamp the link and press the sideplate over the pins **(see illustration 8.7)**. Otherwise, use two small sockets placed over

8.7 Push the sideplate into position using a clamp

Tools and Workshop Tips   REF•19

8.8 Assemble the chain riveting tool over one pin at a time and tighten it fully

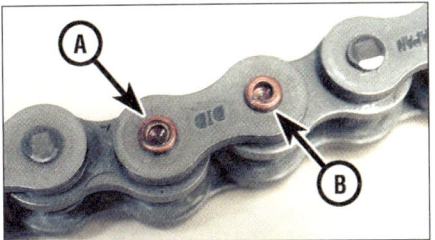

8.9 Pin end correctly riveted (A), pin end unriveted (B)

the rivet ends and two pieces of the wood between a G-clamp. Operate the clamp to press the sideplate over the pins.
● Assemble the joining tool over one pin (following the maker's instructions) and tighten the tool down to spread the pin end securely **(see illustrations 8.8 and 8.9)**. Do the same on the other pin.

> ⚠ **Warning:** Check that the pin ends are secure and that there is no danger of the sideplate coming loose. If the pin ends are cracked the soft link must be renewed.

Final drive chain sizing

● Chains are sized using a three digit number, followed by a suffix to denote the chain type **(see illustration 8.10)**. Chain type is either standard or heavy duty (thicker sideplates), and also unsealed or O-ring/X-ring type.
● The first digit of the number relates to the pitch of the chain, ie the distance from the centre of one pin to the centre of the next pin **(see illustration 8.11)**. Pitch is expressed in eighths of an inch, as follows:

8.10 Typical chain size and type marking

8.11 Chain dimensions

Sizes commencing with a 4 (eg 428) have a pitch of 1/2 inch (12.7 mm)

Sizes commencing with a 5 (eg 520) have a pitch of 5/8 inch (15.9 mm)

Sizes commencing with a 6 (eg 630) have a pitch of 3/4 inch (19.1 mm)

● The second and third digits of the chain size relate to the width of the rollers, again in imperial units, eg the 525 shown has 5/16 inch (7.94 mm) rollers **(see illustration 8.11)**.

9 Hoses

Clamping to prevent flow

● Small-bore flexible hoses can be clamped to prevent fluid flow whilst a component is worked on. Whichever method is used, ensure that the hose material is not permanently distorted or damaged by the clamp.
a) A brake hose clamp available from auto accessory shops **(see illustration 9.1)**.
b) A wingnut type hose clamp **(see illustration 9.2)**.

9.1 Hoses can be clamped with an automotive brake hose clamp . . .

9.2 . . . a wingnut type hose clamp . . .

c) Two sockets placed each side of the hose and held with straight-jawed self-locking grips **(see illustration 9.3)**.
d) Thick card each side of the hose held between straight-jawed self-locking grips **(see illustration 9.4)**.

9.3 . . . two sockets and a pair of self-locking grips . . .

9.4 . . . or thick card and self-locking grips

Freeing and fitting hoses

● Always make sure the hose clamp is moved well clear of the hose end. Grip the hose with your hand and rotate it whilst pulling it off the union. If the hose has hardened due to age and will not move, slit it with a sharp knife and peel its ends off the union **(see illustration 9.5)**.
● Resist the temptation to use grease or soap on the unions to aid installation; although it helps the hose slip over the union it will equally aid the escape of fluid from the joint. It is preferable to soften the hose ends in hot water and wet the inside surface of the hose with water or a fluid which will evaporate.

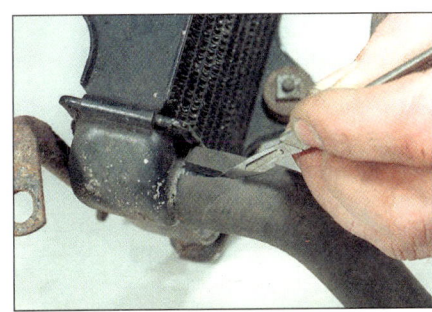

9.5 Cutting a coolant hose free with a sharp knife

Security

Introduction

In less time than it takes to read this introduction, a thief could steal your motorcycle. Returning only to find your bike has gone is one of the worst feelings in the world. Even if the motorcycle is insured against theft, once you've got over the initial shock, you will have the inconvenience of dealing with the police and your insurance company.

The motorcycle is an easy target for the professional thief and the joyrider alike and the official figures on motorcycle theft make for depressing reading; on average a motor-cycle is stolen every 16 minutes in the UK!

Motorcycle thefts fall into two categories, those stolen 'to order' and those taken by opportunists. The thief stealing to order will be on the look out for a specific make and model and will go to extraordinary lengths to obtain that motorcycle. The opportunist thief on the other hand will look for easy targets which can be stolen with the minimum of effort and risk.

Whilst it is never going to be possible to make your machine 100% secure, it is estimated that around half of all stolen motorcycles are taken by opportunist thieves. Remember that the opportunist thief is always on the look out for the easy option: if there are two similar motorcycles parked side-by-side, they will target the one with the lowest level of security. By taking a few precautions, you can reduce the chances of your motorcycle being stolen.

Security equipment

There are many specialised motorcycle security devices available and the following text summarises their applications and their good and bad points.

Once you have decided on the type of security equipment which best suits your needs, we recommended that you read one of the many equipment tests regularly carried out by the motorcycle press. These tests compare the products from all the major manufacturers and give impartial ratings on their effectiveness, value-for-money and ease of use.

No one item of security equipment can provide complete protection. It is highly recommended that two or more of the items described below are combined to increase the security of your motorcycle (a lock and chain plus an alarm system is just about ideal). The more security measures fitted to the bike, the less likely it is to be stolen.

Lock and chain

Ensure the lock and chain you buy is of good quality and long enough to shackle your bike to a solid object

Pros: *Very flexible to use; can be used to secure the motorcycle to almost any immovable object. On some locks and chains, the lock can be used on its own as a disc lock (see below).*

Cons: *Can be very heavy and awkward to carry on the motorcycle, although some types will be supplied with a carry bag which can be strapped to the pillion seat.*

● Heavy-duty chains and locks are an excellent security measure **(see illustration 1).** Whenever the motorcycle is parked, use the lock and chain to secure the machine to a solid, immovable object such as a post or railings. This will prevent the machine from being ridden away or being lifted into the back of a van.

● When fitting the chain, always ensure the chain is routed around the motorcycle frame or swingarm **(see illustrations 2 and 3)**. Never merely pass the chain around one of the wheel rims; a thief may unbolt the wheel and lift the rest of the machine into a van, leaving you with just the wheel! Try to avoid having excess chain free, thus making it difficult to use cutting tools, and keep the chain and lock off the ground to prevent thieves attacking it with a cold chisel. Position the lock so that its lock barrel is facing downwards; this will make it harder for the thief to attack the lock mechanism.

Pass the chain through the bike's frame, rather than just through a wheel . . .

. . . and loop it around a solid object

Security

U-locks

Pros: *Highly effective deterrent which can be used to secure the bike to a post or railings. Most U-locks come with a carrier which allows the lock to be easily carried on the bike.*

Cons: *Not as flexible to use as a lock and chain.*

- These are solid locks which are similar in use to a lock and chain. U-locks are lighter than a lock and chain but not so flexible to use. The length and shape of the lock shackle limit the objects to which the bike can be secured **(see illustration 4)**.

Disc locks

Pros: *Small, light and very easy to carry; most can be stored underneath the seat.*

Cons: *Does not prevent the motorcycle being lifted into a van. Can be very embarrassing if you forget to remove the lock before attempting to ride off!*

- Disc locks are designed to be attached to the front brake disc. The lock passes through one of the holes in the disc and prevents the wheel rotating by jamming against the fork/brake caliper **(see illustration 5)**. Some are equipped with an alarm siren which sounds if the disc lock is moved; this not only acts as a theft deterrent but also as a handy reminder if you try to move the bike with the lock still fitted.

- Combining the disc lock with a length of cable which can be looped around a post or railings provides an additional measure of security **(see illustration 6)**.

Alarms and immobilisers

Pros: *Once installed it is completely hassle-free to use. If the system is 'Thatcham' or 'Sold Secure-approved', insurance companies may give you a discount.*

Cons: *Can be expensive to buy and complex to install. No system will prevent the motorcycle from being lifted into a van and taken away.*

- Electronic alarms and immobilisers are available to suit a variety of budgets. There are three different types of system available: pure alarms, pure immobilisers, and the more expensive systems which are combined alarm/immobilisers **(see illustration 7)**.
- An alarm system is designed to emit an audible warning if the motorcycle is being tampered with.
- An immobiliser prevents the motorcycle being started and ridden away by disabling its electrical systems.
- When purchasing an alarm/immobiliser system, check the cost of installing the system unless you are able to do it yourself. If the motorcycle is not used regularly, another consideration is the current drain of the system. All alarm/immobiliser systems are powered by the motorcycle's battery; purchasing a system with a very low current drain could prevent the battery losing its charge whilst the motorcycle is not being used.

U-locks can be used to secure the bike to a solid object – ensure you purchase one which is long enough

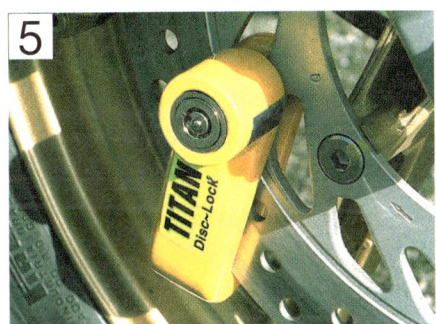

A typical disc lock attached through one of the holes in the disc

A disc lock combined with a security cable provides additional protection

A typical alarm/immobiliser system

REF•22 Security

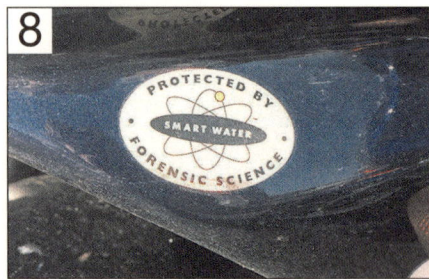

Indelible markings can be applied to most areas of the bike – always apply the manufacturer's sticker to warn off thieves

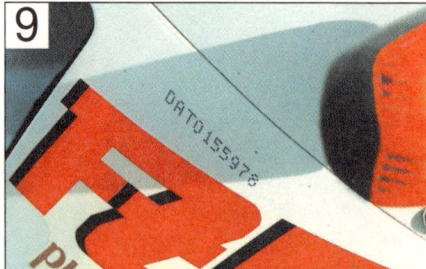

Chemically-etched code numbers can be applied to main body panels . . .

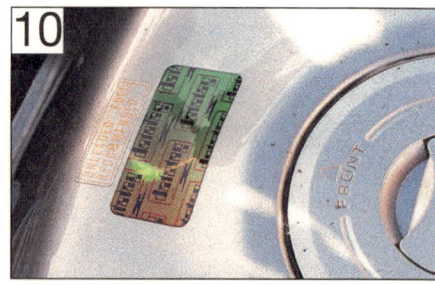

. . . again, always ensure that the kit manufacturer's sticker is applied in a prominent position

Security marking kits

Pros: *Very cheap and effective deterrent. Many insurance companies will give you a discount on your insurance premium if a recognised security marking kit is used on your motorcycle.*

Cons: *Does not prevent the motorcycle being stolen by joyriders.*

● There are many different types of security marking kits available. The idea is to mark as many parts of the motorcycle as possible with a unique security number **(see illustrations 8, 9 and 10)**. A form will be included with the kit to register your personal details and those of the motorcycle with the kit manufacturer. This register is made available to the police to help them trace the rightful owner of any motorcycle or components which they recover should all other forms of identification have been removed. Always apply the warning stickers provided with the kit to deter thieves.

Ground anchors, wheel clamps and security posts

Pros: *An excellent form of security which will deter all but the most determined of thieves.*

Cons: *Awkward to install and can be expensive.*

● Whilst the motorcycle is at home, it is a good idea to attach it securely to the floor or a solid wall, even if it is kept in a securely locked garage. Various types of ground anchors, security posts and wheel clamps are available for this purpose **(see illustration 11)**. These security devices are either bolted to a solid concrete or brick structure or can be cemented into the ground.

Permanent ground anchors provide an excellent level of security when the bike is at home

Security at home

A high percentage of motorcycle thefts are from the owner's home. Here are some things to consider whenever your motorcycle is at home:
● Where possible, always keep the motorcycle in a securely locked garage. Never rely solely on the standard lock on the garage door, these are usual hopelessly inadequate. Fit an additional locking mechanism to the door and consider having the garage alarmed. A security light, activated by a movement sensor, is also a good investment.
● Always secure the motorcycle to the ground or a wall, even if it is inside a securely locked garage.
● Do not regularly leave the motorcycle outside your home, try to keep it out of sight wherever possible. If a garage is not available, fit a motorcycle cover over the bike to disguise its true identity.
● It is not uncommon for thieves to follow a motorcyclist home to find out where the bike is kept. They will then return at a later date. Be aware of this whenever you are returning home on your motorcycle. If you suspect you are being followed, do not return home, instead ride to a garage or shop and stop as a precaution.
● When selling a motorcycle, do not provide your home address or the location where the bike is normally kept. Arrange to meet the buyer at a location away from your home. Thieves have been known to pose as potential buyers to find out where motorcycles are kept and then return later to steal them.

Security away from the home

As well as fitting security equipment to your motorcycle here are a few general rules to follow whenever you park your motorcycle.
● Park in a busy, public place.
● Use car parks which incorporate security features, such as CCTV.
● At night, park in a well-lit area, preferably directly underneath a street light.
● Engage the steering lock.
● Secure the motorcycle to a solid, immovable object such as a post or railings with an additional lock. If this is not possible, secure the bike to a friend's motorcycle. Some public parking places provide security loops for motorcycles.
● Never leave your helmet or luggage attached to the motorcycle. Take them with you at all times.

Lubricants and fluids

A wide range of lubricants, fluids and cleaning agents is available for motor-cycles. This is a guide as to what is available, its applications and properties.

Four-stroke engine oil

● Engine oil is without doubt the most important component of any four-stroke engine. Modern motorcycle engines place a lot of demands on their oil and choosing the right type is essential. Using an unsuitable oil will lead to an increased rate of engine wear and could result in serious engine damage. Before purchasing oil, always check the recommended oil specification given by the manufacturer. The manufacturer will state a recommended 'type or classification' and also a specific 'viscosity' range for engine oil.

● The oil 'type or classification' is identified by its API (American Petroleum Institute) rating. The API rating will be in the form of two letters, e.g. SG. The S identifies the oil as being suitable for use in a petrol (gasoline) engine (S stands for spark ignition) and the second letter, ranging from A to J, identifies the oil's performance rating. The later this letter, the higher the specification of the oil; for example API SG oil exceeds the requirements of API SF oil. **Note:** *On some oils there may also be a second rating consisting of another two letters, the first letter being C, e.g. API SF/CD. This rating indicates the oil is also suitable for use in a diesel engines (the C stands for compression ignition) and is thus of no relevance for motorcycle use.*

● The 'viscosity' of the oil is identified by its SAE (Society of Automotive Engineers) rating. All modern engines require multigrade oils and the SAE rating will consist of two numbers, the first followed by a W, e.g. 10W/40. The first number indicates the viscosity rating of the oil at low temperatures (W stands for winter – tested at –20°C) and the second number represents the viscosity of the oil at high temperatures (tested at 100°C). The lower the number, the thinner the oil. For example an oil with an SAE 10W/40 rating will give better cold starting and running than an SAE 15W/40 oil.

● As well as ensuring the 'type' and 'viscosity' of the oil match the recommendations, another consideration to make when buying engine oil is whether to purchase a standard mineral-based oil, a semi-synthetic oil (also known as a synthetic blend or synthetic-based oil) or a fully-synthetic oil. Although all oils will have a similar rating and viscosity, their cost will vary considerably; mineral-based oils are the cheapest, the fully-synthetic oils the most expensive with the semi-synthetic oils falling somewhere in-between. This decision is very much up to the owner, but it should be noted that modern synthetic oils have far better lubricating and cleaning qualities than traditional mineral-based oils and tend to retain these properties for far longer. Bearing in mind the operating conditions inside a modern, high-revving motorcycle engine it is highly recommended that a fully synthetic oil is used. The extra expense at each service could save you money in the long term by preventing premature engine wear.

● As a final note always ensure that the oil is specifically designed for use in motorcycle engines. Engine oils designed primarily for use in car engines sometimes contain additives or friction modifiers which could cause clutch slip on a motorcycle fitted with a wet-clutch.

Two-stroke engine oil

● Modern two-stroke engines, with their high power outputs, place high demands on their oil. If engine seizure is to be avoided it is essential that a high-quality oil is used. Two-stroke oils differ hugely from four-stroke oils. The oil lubricates only the crankshaft and piston(s) (the transmission has its own lubricating oil) and is used on a total-loss basis where it is burnt completely during the combustion process.

● The Japanese have recently introduced a classification system for two-stroke oils, the JASO rating. This rating is in the form of two letters, either FA, FB or FC – FA is the lowest classification and FC the highest. Ensure the oil being used meets or exceeds the recommended rating specified by the manufacturer.

● As well as ensuring the oil rating matches the recommendation, another consideration to make when buying engine oil is whether to purchase a standard mineral-based oil, a semi-synthetic oil (also known as a synthetic blend or synthetic-based oil) or a fully-synthetic oil. The cost of each type of oil varies considerably; mineral-based oils are the cheapest, the fully-synthetic oils the most expensive with the semi-synthetic oils falling somewhere in-between. This decision is very much up to the owner, but it should be noted that modern synthetic oils have far better lubricating properties and burn cleaner than traditional mineral-based oils. It is therefore recommended that a fully synthetic oil is used. The extra expense could save you money in the long term by preventing premature engine wear, engine performance will be improved, carbon deposits and exhaust smoke will be reduced.

- Always ensure that the oil is specifically designed for use in an injector system. Many high quality two-stroke oils are designed for competition use and need to be pre-mixed with fuel. These oils are of a much higher viscosity and are not designed to flow through the injector pumps used on road-going two-stroke motorcycles.

Transmission (gear) oil

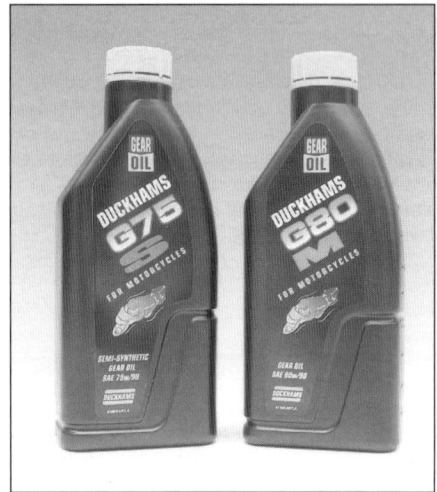

- On a two-stroke engine, the transmission and clutch are lubricated by their own separate oil bath which must be changed in accordance with the Maintenance Schedule.
- Although the engine and transmission units of most four-strokes use a common lubrication supply, there are some exceptions where the engine and gearbox have separate oil reservoirs and a dry clutch is used.
- Motorcycle manufacturers will either recommend a monograde transmission oil or a four-stroke multigrade engine oil to lubricate the transmission.
- Transmission oils, or gear oils as they are often called, are designed specifically for use in transmission systems. The viscosity of these oils is represented by an SAE number, but the scale of measurement applied is different to that used to grade engine oils. As a rough guide a SAE90 gear oil will be of the same viscosity as an SAE50 engine oil.

Shaft drive oil

- On models equipped with shaft final drive, the shaft drive gears are will have their own oil supply. The manufacturer will state a recommended 'type or classification' and also a specific 'viscosity' range in the same manner as for four-stroke engine oil.
- Gear oil classification is given by the number which follows the API GL (GL standing for gear lubricant) rating, the higher the number, the higher the specification of the oil, e.g. API GL5 oil is a higher specification than API GL4 oil. Ensure the oil meets or exceeds the classification specified and is of the correct viscosity. The viscosity of gear oils is also represented by an SAE number but the scale of measurement used is different to that used to grade engine oils. As a rough guide an SAE90 gear oil will be of the same viscosity as an SAE50 engine oil.
- If the use of an EP (Extreme Pressure) gear oil is specified, ensure the oil purchased is suitable.

Fork oil and suspension fluid

- Conventional telescopic front forks are hydraulic and require fork oil to work. To ensure the forks function correctly, the fork oil must be changed in accordance with the Maintenance Schedule.
- Fork oil is available in a variety of viscosities, identified by their SAE rating; fork oil ratings vary from light (SAE 5) to heavy (SAE 30). When purchasing fork oil, ensure the viscosity rating matches that specified by the manufacturer.
- Some lubricant manufacturers also produce a range of high-quality suspension fluids which are very similar to fork oil but are designed mainly for competition use. These fluids may have a different viscosity rating system which is not to be confused with the SAE rating of normal fork oil. Refer to the manufacturer's instructions if in any doubt.

Brake and clutch fluid

- All disc brake systems and some clutch systems are hydraulically operated. To ensure correct operation, the hydraulic fluid must be changed in accordance with the Maintenance Schedule.
- Brake and clutch fluid is classified by its DOT rating with most motorcycle manufacturers specifying DOT 3 or 4 fluid. Both fluid types are glycol-based and can be mixed together without adverse effect; DOT 4 fluid exceeds the requirements of DOT 3 fluid. Although it is safe to use DOT 4 fluid in a system designed for use with DOT 3 fluid, never use DOT 3 fluid in a system which specifies the use of DOT 4 as this will adversely affect the system's performance. The type required for the system will be marked on the fluid reservoir cap.
- Some manufacturers also produce a DOT 5 hydraulic fluid. DOT 5 hydraulic fluid is silicone-based and is not compatible with the glycol-based DOT 3 and 4 fluids. Never mix DOT 5 fluid with DOT 3 or 4 fluid as this will seriously affect the performance of the hydraulic system.

Coolant/antifreeze

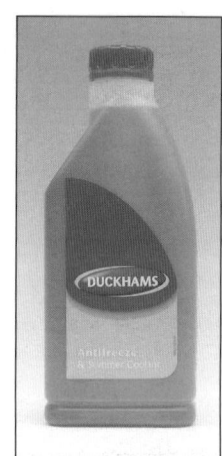

- When purchasing coolant/antifreeze, always ensure it is suitable for use in an aluminium engine and contains corrosion inhibitors to prevent possible blockages of the internal coolant passages of the system. As a general rule, most coolants are designed to be used neat and should not be diluted whereas antifreeze can be mixed with distilled water to provide a coolant solution of the required strength. Refer to the manufacturer's instructions on the bottle.
- Ensure the coolant is changed in accordance with the Maintenance Schedule.

Chain lube

- Chain lube is an aerosol-type spray lubricant specifically designed for use on motorcycle final drive chains. Chain lube has two functions, to minimise friction between the final drive chain and sprockets and to prevent corrosion of the chain. Regular use of a good-quality chain lube will extend the life of the drive chain and sprockets and thus maximise the power being transmitted from the transmission to the rear wheel.
- When using chain lube, always allow some time for the solvents in the lube to evaporate before riding the motorcycle. This will minimise the amount of lube which will

Lubricants and fluids

'fling' off from the chain when the motorcycle is used. If the motorcycle is equipped with an 'O-ring' chain, ensure the chain lube is labelled as being suitable for use on 'O-ring' chains.

Degreasers and solvents

● There are many different types of solvents and degreasers available to remove the grime and grease which accumulate around the motorcycle during normal use. Degreasers and solvents are usually available as an aerosol-type spray or as a liquid which you apply with a brush. Always closely follow the manufacturer's instructions and wear eye protection during use. Be aware that many solvents are flammable and may give off noxious fumes; take adequate precautions when using them (see Safety First!).

● For general cleaning, use one of the many solvents or degreasers available from most motorcycle accessory shops. These solvents are usually applied then left for a certain time before being washed off with water.

Brake cleaner is a solvent specifically designed to remove all traces of oil, grease and dust from braking system components. Brake cleaner is designed to evaporate quickly and leaves behind no residue.

Carburettor cleaner is an aerosol-type solvent specifically designed to clear carburettor blockages and break down the hard deposits and gum often found inside carburettors during overhaul.

Contact cleaner is an aerosol-type solvent designed for cleaning electrical components. The cleaner will remove all traces of oil and dirt from components such as switch contacts or fouled spark plugs and then dry, leaving behind no residue.

Gasket remover is an aerosol-type solvent designed for removing stubborn gaskets from engine components during overhaul. Gasket remover will minimise the amount of scraping required to remove the gasket and therefore reduce the risk of damage to the mating surface.

Spray lubricants

● Aerosol-based spray lubricants are widely available and are excellent for lubricating lever pivots and exposed cables and switches. Try to use a lubricant which is of the dry-film type as the fluid evaporates, leaving behind a dry-film of lubricant. Lubricants which leave behind an oily residue will attract dust and dirt which will increase the rate of wear of the cable/lever.

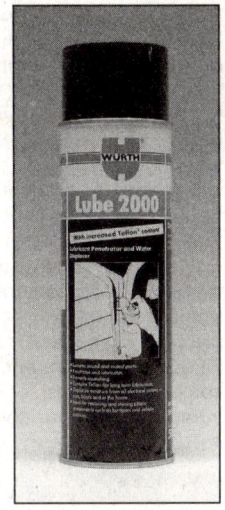

● Most lubricants also act as a moisture dispersant and a penetrating fluid. This means they can also be used to 'dry out' electrical components such as wiring connectors or switches as well as helping to free seized fasteners.

Greases

● Grease is used to lubricate many of the pivot-points. A good-quality multi-purpose grease is suitable for most applications but some manufacturers will specify the use of specialist greases for use on components such as swingarm and suspension linkage bushes. These specialist greases can be purchased from most motorcycle (or car) accessory shops; commonly specified types include molybdenum disulphide grease, lithium-based grease, graphite-based grease, silicone-based grease and high-temperature copper-based grease.

Gasket sealing compounds

● Gasket sealing compounds can be used in conjunction with gaskets, to improve their sealing capabilities, or on their own to seal metal-to-metal joints. Depending on their type, sealing compounds either set hard or stay relatively soft and pliable.

● When purchasing a gasket sealing compound, ensure that it is designed specifically for use on an internal combustion engine. General multi-purpose sealants available from DIY stores may appear visibly similar but they are not designed to withstand the extreme heat or contact with fuel and oil encountered when used on an engine (see 'Tools and Workshop Tips' for further information).

Thread locking compound

● Thread locking compounds are used to secure certain threaded fasteners in position to prevent them from loosening due to vibration. Thread locking compounds can be purchased from most motorcycle (and car) accessory shops. Ensure the threads of the both components are completely clean and dry before sparingly applying the locking compound (see 'Tools and Workshop Tips' for further information).

Fuel additives

● Fuel additives which protect and clean the fuel system components are widely available. These additives are designed to remove all traces of deposits that build up on the carburettors/injectors and prevent wear, helping the fuel system to operate more efficiently. If a fuel additive is being used, check that it is suitable for use with your motorcycle, especially if your motorcycle is equipped with a catalytic converter.

● Octane boosters are also available. These additives are designed to improve the performance of highly-tuned engines being run on normal pump-fuel and are of no real use on standard motorcycles.

REF•26 MOT Test Checks

About the MOT Test

In the UK, all vehicles more than three years old are subject to an annual test to ensure that they meet minimum safety requirements. A current test certificate must be issued before a machine can be used on public roads, and is required before a road fund licence can be issued. Riding without a current test certificate will also invalidate your insurance.

For most owners, the MOT test is an annual cause for anxiety, and this is largely due to owners not being sure what needs to be checked prior to submitting the motorcycle for testing. The simple answer is that a fully roadworthy motorcycle will have no difficulty in passing the test.

This is a guide to getting your motorcycle through the MOT test. Obviously it will not be possible to examine the motorcycle to the same standard as the professional MOT tester, particularly in view of the equipment required for some of the checks. However, working through the following procedures will enable you to identify any problem areas before submitting the motorcycle for the test.

It has only been possible to summarise the test requirements here, based on the regulations in force at the time of printing. Test standards are becoming increasingly stringent, although there are some exemptions for older vehicles. More information about the MOT test can be obtained from the TSO publications, *How Safe is your Motorcycle* and *The MOT Inspection Manual for Motorcycle Testing*.

Many of the checks require that one of the wheels is raised off the ground. If the motorcycle doesn't have a centre stand, note that an auxiliary stand will be required. Additionally, the help of an assistant may prove useful.

Certain exceptions apply to machines under 50 cc, machines without a lighting system, and Classic bikes - if in doubt about any of the requirements listed below seek confirmation from an MOT tester prior to submitting the motorcycle for the test.

Check that the frame number is clearly visible.

Electrical System

Lights, turn signals, horn and reflector

- With the ignition on, check the operation of the following electrical components. **Note:** *The electrical components on certain small-capacity machines are powered by the generator, requiring that the engine is run for this check.*
  a) *Headlight and tail light. Check that both illuminate in the low and high beam switch positions.*
  b) *Position lights. Check that the front position (or sidelight) and tail light illuminate in this switch position.*
  c) *Turn signals. Check that all flash at the correct rate, and that the warning light(s) function correctly. Check that the turn signal switch works correctly.*
  d) *Hazard warning system (where fitted). Check that all four turn signals flash in this switch position.*
  e) *Brake stop light. Check that the light comes on when the front and rear brakes are independently applied. Models first used on or after 1st April 1986 must have a brake light switch on each brake.*
  f) *Horn. Check that the sound is continuous and of reasonable volume.*
- Check that there is a red reflector on the rear of the machine, either mounted separately or as part of the tail light lens.
- Check the condition of the headlight, tail light and turn signal lenses.

Headlight beam height

- The MOT tester will perform a headlight beam height check using specialised beam setting equipment **(see illustration 1)**. This equipment will not be available to the home mechanic, but if you suspect that the headlight is incorrectly set or may have been maladjusted in the past, you can perform a rough test as follows.
- Position the bike in a straight line facing a brick wall. The bike must be off its stand, upright and with a rider seated. Measure the height from the ground to the centre of the headlight and mark a horizontal line on the wall at this height. Position the motorcycle 3.8 metres from the wall and draw a vertical line up the wall central to the centreline of the motorcycle. Switch to dipped beam and check that the beam pattern falls slightly lower than the horizontal line and to the left of the vertical line **(see illustration 2)**.

Headlight beam height checking equipment

Home workshop beam alignment check

MOT Test Checks REF•27

Exhaust System and Final Drive

Exhaust

● Check that the exhaust mountings are secure and that the system does not foul any of the rear suspension components.
● Start the motorcycle. When the revs are increased, check that the exhaust is neither holed nor leaking from any of its joints. On a linked system, check that the collector box is not leaking due to corrosion.
● Note that the exhaust decibel level ("loudness" of the exhaust) is assessed at the discretion of the tester. If the motorcycle was first used on or after 1st January 1985 the silencer must carry the BSAU 193 stamp, or a marking relating to its make and model, or be of OE (original equipment) manufacture. If the silencer is marked NOT FOR ROAD USE, RACING USE ONLY or similar, it will fail the MOT.

Final drive

● On chain or belt drive machines, check that the chain/belt is in good condition and does not have excessive slack. Also check that the sprocket is securely mounted on the rear wheel hub. Check that the chain/belt guard is in place.
● On shaft drive bikes, check for oil leaking from the drive unit and fouling the rear tyre.

Steering and Suspension

Steering

● With the front wheel raised off the ground, rotate the steering from lock to lock. The handlebar or switches must not contact the fuel tank or be close enough to trap the rider's hand. Problems can be caused by damaged lock stops on the lower yoke and frame, or by the fitting of non-standard handlebars.
● When performing the lock to lock check, also ensure that the steering moves freely without drag or notchiness. Steering movement can be impaired by poorly routed cables, or by overtight head bearings or worn bvearings. The tester will perform a check of the steering head bearing lower race by mounting the front wheel on a surface plate, then performing a lock to lock check with the weight of the machine on the lower bearing **(see illustration 3)**.
● Grasp the fork sliders (lower legs) and attempt to push and pull on the forks

Front wheel mounted on a surface plate for steering head bearing lower race check

(see illustration 4). Any play in the steering head bearings will be felt. Note that in extreme cases, wear of the front fork bushes can be misinterpreted for head bearing play.
● Check that the handlebars are securely mounted.
● Check that the handlebar grip rubbers are secure. They should by bonded to the bar left end and to the throttle cable pulley on the right end.

Front suspension

● With the motorcycle off the stand, hold the front brake on and pump the front forks up and down **(see illustration 5)**. Check that they are adequately damped.

Checking the steering head bearings for freeplay

Hold the front brake on and pump the front forks up and down to check operation

MOT Test Checks

Inspect the area around the fork dust seal for oil leakage (arrow)

Bounce the rear of the motorcycle to check rear suspension operation

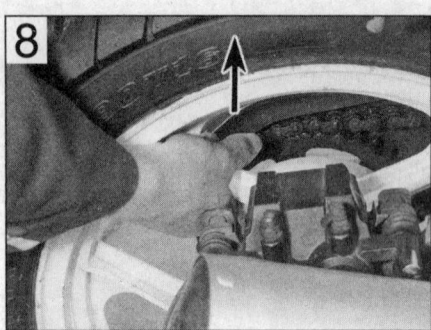

Checking for rear suspension linkage play

● Inspect the area above and around the front fork oil seals **(see illustration 6)**. There should be no sign of oil on the fork tube (stanchion) nor leaking down the slider (lower leg). On models so equipped, check that there is no oil leaking from the anti-dive units.
● On models with swingarm front suspension, check that there is no freeplay in the linkage when moved from side to side.

Rear suspension

● With the motorcycle off the stand and an assistant supporting the motorcycle by its handlebars, bounce the rear suspension **(see illustration 7)**. Check that the suspension components do not foul on any of the cycle parts and check that the shock absorber(s) provide adequate damping.
● Visually inspect the shock absorber(s) and check that there is no sign of oil leakage from its damper. This is somewhat restricted on certain single shock models due to the location of the shock absorber.
● With the rear wheel raised off the ground, grasp the wheel at the highest point and attempt to pull it up **(see illustration 8)**. Any play in the swingarm pivot or suspension linkage bearings will be felt as movement.
Note: *Do not confuse play with actual suspension movement. Failure to lubricate suspension linkage bearings can lead to bearing failure* **(see illustration 9)**.
● With the rear wheel raised off the ground, grasp the swingarm ends and attempt to move the swingarm from side to side and forwards and backwards - any play indicates wear of the swingarm pivot bearings **(see illustration 10)**.

Worn suspension linkage pivots (arrows) are usually the cause of play in the rear suspension

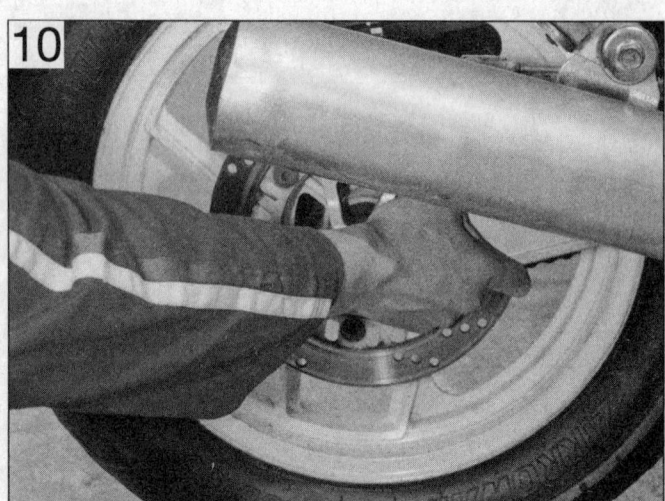

Grasp the swingarm at the ends to check for play in its pivot bearings

MOT Test Checks REF•29

Brake pad wear can usually be viewed without removing the caliper. Most pads have wear indicator grooves (arrowed) and some also have indicator tangs or cut-outs.

On drum brakes, check the angle of the operating lever with the brake fully applied. Most drum brakes have a wear indicator pointer or scale.

Brakes, Wheels and Tyres

Brakes

- With the wheel raised off the ground, apply the brake then free it off, and check that the wheel is about to revolve freely without brake drag.
- On disc brakes, examine the disc itself. Check that it is securely mounted and not cracked.
- On disc brakes, view the pad material through the caliper mouth and check that the pads are not worn down beyond the limit **(see illustration 11)**.
- On drum brakes, check that when the brake is applied the angle between the operating lever and cable or rod is not too great **(see illustration 12)**. Check also that the operating lever doesn't foul any other components.
- On disc brakes, examine the flexible hoses from top to bottom. Have an assistant hold the brake on so that the fluid in the hose is under pressure, and check that there is no sign of fluid leakage, bulges or cracking. If there are any metal brake pipes or unions, check that these are free from corrosion and damage. Where a brake-linked anti-dive system is fitted, check the hoses to the anti-dive in a similar manner.
- Check that the rear brake torque arm is secure and that its fasteners are secured by self-locking nuts or castellated nuts with split-pins or R-pins **(see illustration 13)**.
- On models with ABS, check that the self-check warning light in the instrument panel works.
- The MOT tester will perform a test of the motorcycle's braking efficiency based on a calculation of rider and motorcycle weight. Although this cannot be carried out at home, you can at least ensure that the braking systems are properly maintained. For hydraulic disc brakes, check the fluid level, lever/pedal feel (bleed of air if its spongy) and pad material. For drum brakes, check adjustment, cable or rod operation and shoe lining thickness.

Wheels and tyres

- Check the wheel condition. Cast wheels should be free from cracks and if of the built-up design, all fasteners should be secure. Spoked wheels should be checked for broken, corroded, loose or bent spokes.
- With the wheel raised off the ground, spin the wheel and visually check that the tyre and wheel run true. Check that the tyre does not foul the suspension or mudguards.
- With the wheel raised off the ground, grasp the wheel and attempt to move it about the axle (spindle) **(see illustration 14)**. Any play felt here indicates wheel bearing failure.

Brake torque arm must be properly secured at both ends

Check for wheel bearing play by trying to move the wheel about the axle (spindle)

REF•30 MOT Test Checks

Checking the tyre tread depth

Tyre direction of rotation arrow can be found on tyre sidewall

Castellated type wheel axle (spindle) nut must be secured by a split pin or R-pin

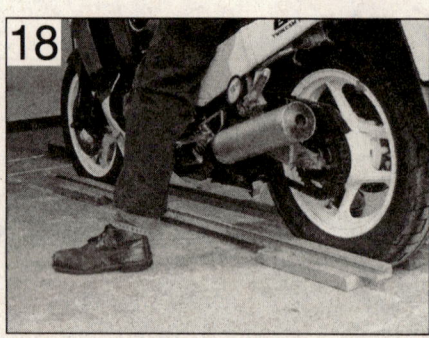
Two straightedges are used to check wheel alignment

- Check the tyre tread depth, tread condition and sidewall condition **(see illustration 15)**.
- Check the tyre type. Front and rear tyre types must be compatible and be suitable for road use. Tyres marked NOT FOR ROAD USE, COMPETITION USE ONLY or similar, will fail the MOT.
- If the tyre sidewall carries a direction of rotation arrow, this must be pointing in the direction of normal wheel rotation **(see illustration 16)**.
- Check that the wheel axle (spindle) nuts (where applicable) are properly secured. A self-locking nut or castellated nut with a split-pin or R-pin can be used **(see illustration 17)**.
- Wheel alignment is checked with the motorcycle off the stand and a rider seated. With the front wheel pointing straight ahead, two perfectly straight lengths of metal or wood and placed against the sidewalls of both tyres **(see illustration 18)**. The gap each side of the front tyre must be equidistant on both sides. Incorrect wheel alignment may be due to a cocked rear wheel (often as the result of poor chain adjustment) or in extreme cases, a bent frame.

General checks and condition

- Check the security of all major fasteners, bodypanels, seat, fairings (where fitted) and mudguards.
- Check that the rider and pillion footrests, handlebar levers and brake pedal are securely mounted.
- Check for corrosion on the frame or any load-bearing components. If severe, this may affect the structure, particularly under stress.

Sidecars

A motorcycle fitted with a sidecar requires additional checks relating to the stability of the machine and security of attachment and swivel joints, plus specific wheel alignment (toe-in) requirements. Additionally, tyre and lighting requirements differ from conventional motorcycle use. Owners are advised to check MOT test requirements with an official test centre.

Storage REF•31

Preparing for storage

Before you start

If repairs or an overhaul is needed, see that this is carried out now rather than left until you want to ride the bike again.

Give the bike a good wash and scrub all dirt from its underside. Make sure the bike dries completely before preparing for storage.

Engine

● Remove the spark plug(s) and lubricate the cylinder bores with approximately a teaspoon of motor oil using a spout-type oil can **(see illustration 1)**. Reinstall the spark plug(s). Crank the engine over a couple of times to coat the piston rings and bores with oil. If the bike has a kickstart, use this to turn the engine over. If not, flick the kill switch to the OFF position and crank the engine over on the starter **(see illustration 2)**. If the nature on the ignition system prevents the starter operating with the kill switch in the OFF position, remove the spark plugs and fit them back in their caps; ensure that the plugs are earthed (grounded) against the cylinder head when the starter is operated **(see illustration 3)**.

⚠️ **Warning: It is important that the plugs are earthed (grounded) away from the spark plug holes otherwise there is a risk of atomised fuel from the cylinders igniting.**

HAYNES HiNT *On a single cylinder four-stroke engine, you can seal the combustion chamber completely by positioning the piston at TDC on the compression stroke.*

● Drain the carburettor(s) otherwise there is a risk of jets becoming blocked by gum deposits from the fuel **(see illustration 4)**.

● If the bike is going into long-term storage, consider adding a fuel stabiliser to the fuel in the tank. If the tank is drained completely, corrosion of its internal surfaces may occur if left unprotected for a long period. The tank can be treated with a rust preventative especially for this purpose. Alternatively, remove the tank and pour half a litre of motor oil into it, install the filler cap and shake the tank to coat its internals with oil before draining off the excess. The same effect can also be achieved by spraying WD40 or a similar water-dispersant around the inside of the tank via its flexible nozzle.

● Make sure the cooling system contains the correct mix of antifreeze. Antifreeze also contains important corrosion inhibitors.

● The air intakes and exhaust can be sealed off by covering or plugging the openings. Ensure that you do not seal in any condensation; run the engine until it is hot,

Squirt a drop of motor oil into each cylinder

Flick the kill switch to OFF . . .

. . . and ensure that the metal bodies of the plugs (arrows) are earthed against the cylinder head

Connect a hose to the carburettor float chamber drain stub (arrow) and unscrew the drain screw

REF•32 Storage

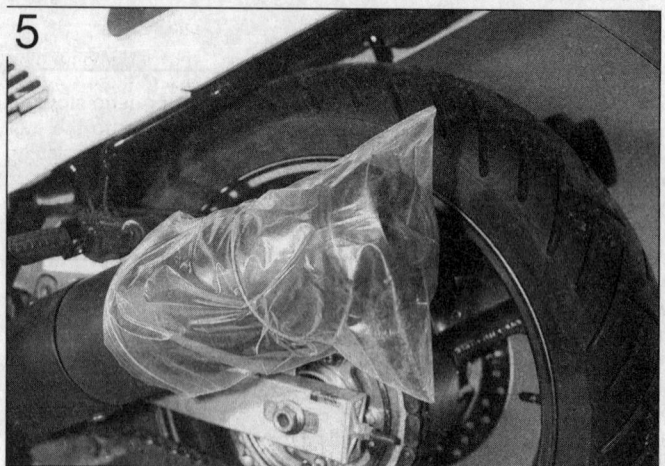

Exhausts can be sealed off with a plastic bag

Disconnect the negative lead (A) first, followed by the positive lead (B)

Use a suitable battery charger - this kit also assess battery condition

then switch off and allow to cool. Tape a piece of thick plastic over the silencer end(s) **(see illustration 5)**. Note that some advocate pouring a tablespoon of motor oil into the silencer(s) before sealing them off.

Battery

- Remove it from the bike - in extreme cases of cold the battery may freeze and crack its case **(see illustration 6)**.
- Check the electrolyte level and top up if necessary (conventional refillable batteries). Clean the terminals.
- Store the battery off the motorcycle and away from any sources of fire. Position a wooden block under the battery if it is to sit on the ground.
- Give the battery a trickle charge for a few hours every month **(see illustration 7)**.

Tyres

- Place the bike on its centrestand or an auxiliary stand which will support the motorcycle in an upright position. Position wood blocks under the tyres to keep them off the ground and to provide insulation from damp. If the bike is being put into long-term storage, ideally both tyres should be off the ground; not only will this protect the tyres, but will also ensure that no load is placed on the steering head or wheel bearings.
- Deflate each tyre by 5 to 10 psi, no more or the beads may unseat from the rim, making subsequent inflation difficult on tubeless tyres.

Pivots and controls

- Lubricate all lever, pedal, stand and footrest pivot points. If grease nipples are fitted to the rear suspension components, apply lubricant to the pivots.
- Lubricate all control cables.

Cycle components

- Apply a wax protectant to all painted and plastic components. Wipe off any excess, but don't polish to a shine. Where fitted, clean the screen with soap and water.
- Coat metal parts with Vaseline (petroleum jelly). When applying this to the fork tubes, do not compress the forks otherwise the seals will rot from contact with the Vaseline.
- Apply a vinyl cleaner to the seat.

Storage conditions

- Aim to store the bike in a shed or garage which does not leak and is free from damp.
- Drape an old blanket or bedspread over the bike to protect it from dust and direct contact with sunlight (which will fade paint). This also hides the bike from prying eyes. Beware of tight-fitting plastic covers which may allow condensation to form and settle on the bike.

Getting back on the road

Engine and transmission

- Change the oil and replace the oil filter. If this was done prior to storage, check that the oil hasn't emulsified - a thick whitish substance which occurs through condensation.
- Remove the spark plugs. Using a spout-type oil can, squirt a few drops of oil into the cylinder(s). This will provide initial lubrication as the piston rings and bores comes back into contact. Service the spark plugs, or fit new ones, and install them in the engine.
- Check that the clutch isn't stuck on. The plates can stick together if left standing for some time, preventing clutch operation. Engage a gear and try rocking the bike back and forth with the clutch lever held against the handlebar. If this doesn't work on cable-operated clutches, hold the clutch lever back against the handlebar with a strong elastic band or cable tie for a couple of hours **(see illustration 8)**.
- If the air intakes or silencer end(s) were blocked off, remove the bung or cover used.
- If the fuel tank was coated with a rust

Hold clutch lever back against the handlebar with elastic bands or a cable tie

Storage REF•33

preventative, oil or a stabiliser added to the fuel, drain and flush the tank and dispose of the fuel sensibly. If no action was taken with the fuel tank prior to storage, it is advised that the old fuel is disposed of since it will go off over a period of time. Refill the fuel tank with fresh fuel.

Frame and running gear

● Oil all pivot points and cables.
● Check the tyre pressures. They will definitely need inflating if pressures were reduced for storage.
● Lubricate the final drive chain (where applicable).
● Remove any protective coating applied to the fork tubes (stanchions) since this may well destroy the fork seals. If the fork tubes weren't protected and have picked up rust spots, remove them with very fine abrasive paper and refinish with metal polish.
● Check that both brakes operate correctly. Apply each brake hard and check that it's not possible to move the motorcycle forwards, then check that the brake frees off again once released. Brake caliper pistons can stick due to corrosion around the piston head, or on the sliding caliper types, due to corrosion of the slider pins. If the brake doesn't free off after repeated operation, take the caliper off for examination. Similarly drum brakes can stick due to a seized operating cam, cable or rod linkage.
● If the motorcycle has been in long-term storage, renew the brake fluid and clutch fluid (where applicable).
● Depending on where the bike has been stored, the wiring, cables and hoses may have been nibbled by rodents. Make a visual check and investigate disturbed wiring loom tape.

Battery

● If the battery has been previously removal and given top up charges it can simply be reconnected. Remember to connect the positive cable first and the negative cable last.
● On conventional refillable batteries, if the battery has not received any attention, remove it from the motorcycle and check its electrolyte level. Top up if necessary then charge the battery. If the battery fails to hold a charge and a visual checks show heavy white sulphation of the plates, the battery is probably defective and must be renewed. This is particularly likely if the battery is old. Confirm battery condition with a specific gravity check.
● On sealed (MF) batteries, if the battery has not received any attention, remove it from the motorcycle and charge it according to the information on the battery case - if the battery fails to hold a charge it must be renewed.

Starting procedure

● If a kickstart is fitted, turn the engine over a couple of times with the ignition OFF to distribute oil around the engine. If no kickstart is fitted, flick the engine kill switch OFF and the ignition ON and crank the engine over a couple of times to work oil around the upper cylinder components. If the nature of the ignition system is such that the starter won't work with the kill switch OFF, remove the spark plugs, fit them back into their caps and earth (ground) their bodies on the cylinder head. Reinstall the spark plugs afterwards.
● Switch the kill switch to RUN, operate the choke and start the engine. If the engine won't start don't continue cranking the engine - not only will this flatten the battery, but the starter motor will overheat. Switch the ignition off and try again later. If the engine refuses to start, go through the fault finding procedures in this manual. **Note:** *If the bike has been in storage for a long time, old fuel or a carburettor blockage may be the problem. Gum deposits in carburettors can block jets - if a carburettor cleaner doesn't prove successful the carburettors must be dismantled for cleaning.*
● Once the engine has started, check that the lights, turn signals and horn work properly.
● Treat the bike gently for the first ride and check all fluid levels on completion. Settle the bike back into the maintenance schedule.

Conversion factors

Length (distance)
Inches (in)	x 25.4	= Millimetres (mm)	x 0.0394	=	Inches (in)
Feet (ft)	x 0.305	= Metres (m)	x 3.281	=	Feet (ft)
Miles	x 1.609	= Kilometres (km)	x 0.621	=	Miles

Volume (capacity)
Cubic inches (cu in; in^3)	x 16.387	= Cubic centimetres (cc; cm^3)	x 0.061	=	Cubic inches (cu in; in^3)
Imperial pints (Imp pt)	x 0.568	= Litres (l)	x 1.76	=	Imperial pints (Imp pt)
Imperial quarts (Imp qt)	x 1.137	= Litres (l)	x 0.88	=	Imperial quarts (Imp qt)
Imperial quarts (Imp qt)	x 1.201	= US quarts (US qt)	x 0.833	=	Imperial quarts (Imp qt)
US quarts (US qt)	x 0.946	= Litres (l)	x 1.057	=	US quarts (US qt)
Imperial gallons (Imp gal)	x 4.546	= Litres (l)	x 0.22	=	Imperial gallons (Imp gal)
Imperial gallons (Imp gal)	x 1.201	= US gallons (US gal)	x 0.833	=	Imperial gallons (Imp gal)
US gallons (US gal)	x 3.785	= Litres (l)	x 0.264	=	US gallons (US gal)

Mass (weight)
Ounces (oz)	x 28.35	= Grams (g)	x 0.035	=	Ounces (oz)
Pounds (lb)	x 0.454	= Kilograms (kg)	x 2.205	=	Pounds (lb)

Force
Ounces-force (ozf; oz)	x 0.278	= Newtons (N)	x 3.6	=	Ounces-force (ozf; oz)
Pounds-force (lbf; lb)	x 4.448	= Newtons (N)	x 0.225	=	Pounds-force (lbf; lb)
Newtons (N)	x 0.1	= Kilograms-force (kgf; kg)	x 9.81	=	Newtons (N)

Pressure
Pounds-force per square inch (psi; lbf/in^2; lb/in^2)	x 0.070	= Kilograms-force per square centimetre (kgf/cm^2; kg/cm^2)	x 14.223	=	Pounds-force per square inch (psi; lbf/in^2; lb/in^2)
Pounds-force per square inch (psi; lbf/in^2; lb/in^2)	x 0.068	= Atmospheres (atm)	x 14.696	=	Pounds-force per square inch (psi; lbf/in^2; lb/in^2)
Pounds-force per square inch (psi; lbf/in^2; lb/in^2)	x 0.069	= Bars	x 14.5	=	Pounds-force per square inch (psi; lbf/in^2; lb/in^2)
Pounds-force per square inch (psi; lbf/in^2; lb/in^2)	x 6.895	= Kilopascals (kPa)	x 0.145	=	Pounds-force per square inch (psi; lbf/in^2; lb/in^2)
Kilopascals (kPa)	x 0.01	= Kilograms-force per square centimetre (kgf/cm^2; kg/cm^2)	x 98.1	=	Kilopascals (kPa)
Millibar (mbar)	x 100	= Pascals (Pa)	x 0.01	=	Millibar (mbar)
Millibar (mbar)	x 0.0145	= Pounds-force per square inch (psi; lbf/in^2; lb/in^2)	x 68.947	=	Millibar (mbar)
Millibar (mbar)	x 0.75	= Millimetres of mercury (mmHg)	x 1.333	=	Millibar (mbar)
Millibar (mbar)	x 0.401	= Inches of water (inH$_2$O)	x 2.491	=	Millibar (mbar)
Millimetres of mercury (mmHg)	x 0.535	= Inches of water (inH$_2$O)	x 1.868	=	Millimetres of mercury (mmHg)
Inches of water (inH$_2$O)	x 0.036	= Pounds-force per square inch (psi; lbf/in^2; lb/in^2)	x 27.68	=	Inches of water (inH$_2$O)

Torque (moment of force)
Pounds-force inches (lbf in; lb in)	x 1.152	= Kilograms-force centimetre (kgf cm; kg cm)	x 0.868	=	Pounds-force inches (lbf in; lb in)
Pounds-force inches (lbf in; lb in)	x 0.113	= Newton metres (Nm)	x 8.85	=	Pounds-force inches (lbf in; lb in)
Pounds-force inches (lbf in; lb in)	x 0.083	= Pounds-force feet (lbf ft; lb ft)	x 12	=	Pounds-force inches (lbf in; lb in)
Pounds-force feet (lbf ft; lb ft)	x 0.138	= Kilograms-force metres (kgf m; kg m)	x 7.233	=	Pounds-force feet (lbf ft; lb ft)
Pounds-force feet (lbf ft; lb ft)	x 1.356	= Newton metres (Nm)	x 0.738	=	Pounds-force feet (lbf ft; lb ft)
Newton metres (Nm)	x 0.102	= Kilograms-force metres (kgf m; kg m)	x 9.804	=	Newton metres (Nm)

Power
Horsepower (hp)	x 745.7	= Watts (W)	x 0.0013	=	Horsepower (hp)

Velocity (speed)
Miles per hour (miles/hr; mph)	x 1.609	= Kilometres per hour (km/hr; kph)	x 0.621	=	Miles per hour (miles/hr; mph)

Fuel consumption*
Miles per gallon, Imperial (mpg)	x 0.354	= Kilometres per litre (km/l)	x 2.825	=	Miles per gallon, Imperial (mpg)
Miles per gallon, US (mpg)	x 0.425	= Kilometres per litre (km/l)	x 2.352	=	Miles per gallon, US (mpg)

Temperature

Degrees Fahrenheit = (°C x 1.8) + 32   Degrees Celsius (Degrees Centigrade; °C) = (°F - 32) x 0.56

*It is common practice to convert from miles per gallon (mpg) to litres/100 kilometres (l/100km), where mpg x l/100 km = 282

Fault Finding   REF•35

This Section provides an easy reference-guide to the more common faults that are likely to afflict your machine. Obviously, the opportunities are almost limitless for faults to occur as a result of obscure failures, and to try and cover all eventualities would require a book. Indeed, a number have been written on the subject.

Successful troubleshooting is not a mysterious 'black art' but the application of a bit of knowledge combined with a systematic and logical approach to the problem. Approach any troubleshooting by first accurately identifying the symptom and then checking through the list of possible causes, starting with the simplest or most obvious and progressing in stages to the most complex.

Take nothing for granted, but above all apply liberal quantities of common sense.

The main symptom of a fault is given in the text as a major heading below which are listed the various systems or areas which may contain the fault. Details of each possible cause for a fault and the remedial action to be taken are given, in brief, in the paragraphs below each heading. Further information should be sought in the relevant Chapter.

1 Engine doesn't start or is difficult to start
- [ ] Starter motor doesn't rotate
- [ ] Starter motor rotates but engine does not turn over
- [ ] Starter works but engine won't turn over (seized)
- [ ] No fuel flow
- [ ] Engine flooded
- [ ] No spark or weak spark
- [ ] Compression low
- [ ] Stalls after starting
- [ ] Rough idle

2 Poor running at low speed
- [ ] Spark weak
- [ ] Fuel/air mixture incorrect
- [ ] Compression low
- [ ] Poor acceleration

3 Poor running or no power at high speed
- [ ] Firing incorrect
- [ ] Fuel/air mixture incorrect
- [ ] Compression low
- [ ] Knocking or pinking
- [ ] Miscellaneous causes

4 Overheating
- [ ] Engine overheats
- [ ] Firing incorrect
- [ ] Fuel/air mixture incorrect
- [ ] Compression too high
- [ ] Engine load excessive
- [ ] Lubrication inadequate
- [ ] Miscellaneous causes

5 Clutch problems
- [ ] Clutch slipping
- [ ] Clutch not disengaging completely

6 Gearchanging problems
- [ ] Doesn't go into gear, or lever doesn't return
- [ ] Jumps out of gear
- [ ] Overselects

7 Abnormal engine noise
- [ ] Knocking or pinking
- [ ] Piston slap or rattling
- [ ] Valve noise
- [ ] Other noise

8 Abnormal driveline noise
- [ ] Clutch noise
- [ ] Transmission noise
- [ ] Final drive noise

9 Abnormal frame and suspension noise
- [ ] Front end noise
- [ ] Shock absorber noise
- [ ] Brake noise

10 Oil pressure low
- [ ] Engine lubrication system

11 Excessive exhaust smoke
- [ ] White smoke
- [ ] Black smoke
- [ ] Brown smoke

12 Poor handling or stability
- [ ] Handlebar hard to turn
- [ ] Handlebar shakes or vibrates excessively
- [ ] Handlebar pulls to one side
- [ ] Poor shock absorbing qualities

13 Braking problems
- [ ] Brakes are spongy, don't hold
- [ ] Brake lever or pedal pulsates
- [ ] Brakes drag

14 Electrical problems
- [ ] Battery dead or weak
- [ ] Battery overcharged

Fault Finding

1 Engine doesn't start or is difficult to start

Starter motor doesn't rotate
- [ ] Engine kill switch OFF.
- [ ] Clutch lever not pulled in.
- [ ] Fuse blown. Check main fuse and EMS fuse (Chapter 8).
- [ ] Battery voltage low. Check battery condition and recharge or replace battery (Chapter 8).
- [ ] Loose or corroded battery connections/terminals. Tighten or clean connections.
- [ ] Starter motor defective. Make sure the wiring to the starter is secure and free of corrosion. Replace or repair the motor if defective (Chapter 8).
- [ ] Starter motor relay defective. Make sure the wiring to relay is secure and free of corrosion. Test the operation of the relay, internal corrosion or arcing can cause the relay to not pass sufficient current to the starter motor even if it clicks when the start button is operated (Chapter 8).
- [ ] Starter switch not contacting. The contacts could be wet, corroded or dirty. Disassemble and clean the switch (Chapter 8).
- [ ] Wiring open or shorted. Check all wiring connections and harnesses to make sure that they are dry, tight and not corroded. Also check for broken or frayed wires that can cause a short to ground (earth) (see *Wiring diagrams*, Chapter 8).
- [ ] Ignition or kill switch defective. This is usually caused by water, corrosion, damage or excessive wear. The switches can be disassembled and cleaned with electrical contact cleaner. If cleaning does not help, replace the switches (Chapter 8).
- [ ] Faulty gear position sensor (neutral switch), sidestand switch or clutch switch. Check the wiring to each switch and the switch itself (Chapter 8).
- [ ] Faulty starter circuit relay (Chapter 8).
- [ ] Engine management system shutdown due to system fault (Chapter 4).

Starter motor rotates but engine does not turn over
- [ ] Starter clutch defective. Inspect and repair or replace with a new one (Chapter 2).
- [ ] Damaged idler or starter gears. Inspect and replace the damaged parts (Chapter 2).

Starter works but engine won't turn over (seized)
- [ ] Seized engine caused by one or more internally damaged components. Failure due to wear, abuse or lack of lubrication. Damage can include seized valves, followers, camshafts, pistons, crankshaft, connecting rod bearings, or transmission gears or bearings. Refer to Chapter 2 for engine disassembly.

No fuel flow
- [ ] No fuel in tank.
- [ ] Fuel tank breather hose obstructed.
- [ ] Faulty fuel pump relay. Check the relay (Chapter 4).
- [ ] Fuel pump faulty or blocked fuel pump filter. Replace the pump (Chapter 4).
- [ ] Electronic control module (ECM) defective (Chapter 4).
- [ ] Ignition key not recognised by immobiliser system.
- [ ] Fuel hose kinked. Replace the fuel hose.
- [ ] Fuel injector clogged. For all the injectors to be clogged, either a very bad batch of fuel with an unusual additive has been used, or some other foreign material has entered the tank. In some cases, if a machine has been unused for several months, the fuel turns to a varnish-like liquid, which can cause an injector needle to stick to its seat. Drain the tank and fuel system, ultrasonically clean or replace fuel injectors (Chapter 4).

Engine flooded
- [ ] Injector needle valve worn or stuck open causing excess fuel to be admitted to the throttle body. In this case, the injectors should be renewed.
- [ ] Starting technique incorrect. Under normal circumstances (i.e. if all the components of the fuel injection system are good) the machine should start with the throttle closed.

No spark or weak spark
- [ ] Ignition switch OFF.
- [ ] Engine kill switch turned to the OFF position.
- [ ] Ignition or kill switch shorted. This is usually caused by water, corrosion, damage or excessive wear. The switches can be disassembled and cleaned with electrical contact cleaner. If cleaning does not help, replace the switches (Chapter 8).
- [ ] Battery voltage low. Check battery condition and recharge or replace battery (Chapter 8).
- [ ] Spark plug contact in bottom of ignition coil not making good contact. Make sure that the coils are pushed fully onto the spark plugs.
- [ ] Spark plugs dirty, defective or worn out. Locate reason for fouled plugs using spark plug condition chart on the inside back cover and follow the plug maintenance procedures (Chapter 1).
- [ ] Incorrect spark plugs. Wrong type or heat range. Check and install correct plugs (Chapter 1).
- [ ] Ignition coil defective. Test and replace if necessary (Chapter 4).
- [ ] Engine management system shutdown due to system fault (Chapter 4).
- [ ] Crankshaft position (CKP) sensor defective (Chapter 4).
- [ ] Faulty engine management system relay or tip-over sensor (Chapter 4).

1 Engine doesn't start or is difficult to start (continued)

No spark or weak spark (continued)

- [ ] Electronic control module (ECM) defective (Chapter 4).
- [ ] Faulty sidestand switch (Chapter 8).
- [ ] Ignition key not recognised by immobiliser system.
- [ ] Wiring shorted or broken between:
    a) *Ignition switch and engine kill switch (or blown fuse)*
    b) *ECM and engine kill switch*
    c) *ECM and ignition coils*
    d) *ECM and CKP sensor*
- [ ] Make sure that all wiring connections are clean, dry and tight. Look for chafed and broken wires (Chapters 4 and 8).

Compression low

- [ ] Spark plug loose. Remove the plugs and inspect their threads. Reinstall and tighten securely (Chapter 1).
- [ ] Improper valve clearance. This means that the valve is not closing completely and compression pressure is leaking past the valve. Check and adjust the valve clearances (Chapter 1).
- [ ] Cylinder and/or piston worn. Excessive wear will cause compression pressure to leak past the rings. This is usually accompanied by worn rings as well. A top-end overhaul is necessary (Chapter 2).
- [ ] Piston rings worn, weak, broken, or sticking. Broken or sticking piston rings usually indicate a lubrication or fuelling problem that causes excess carbon deposits to form on the pistons and rings. Top-end overhaul is necessary (Chapter 2).
- [ ] Piston ring-to-groove clearance excessive. This is caused by excessive wear of the piston ring lands. Piston renewal is necessary (Chapter 2).
- [ ] Cylinder head gasket damaged. If a head is allowed to become loose, or if excessive carbon build-up on the piston crown and combustion chamber causes extremely high compression, the head gasket may leak. Retorquing the head is not always sufficient to restore the seal, so a new gasket is necessary (Chapter 2).
- [ ] Cylinder head warped. This is caused by overheating or improperly tightened head bolts. Machine shop resurfacing or head renewal is necessary (Chapter 2).
- [ ] Valve spring broken or weak. Caused by component failure or wear; the springs must be renewed (Chapter 2).
- [ ] Valve not seating properly. This is caused by a bent valve (from over-revving or improper valve adjustment), burned valve or seat (improper fuelling) or an accumulation of carbon deposits on the seat. The valves must be cleaned and/or renewed and the seats serviced (Chapter 2).

Stalls after starting

- [ ] Engine idle speed incorrect. Faulty idle speed control system (Chapter 4).
- [ ] Ignition malfunction (Chapter 4).
- [ ] Fuel injection system malfunction (Chapter 4).
- [ ] Fuel contaminated. The fuel can be contaminated with either dirt or water, or can change chemically if the machine has been unused for several months. Drain the tank and fuel system (Chapter 4).
- [ ] Intake air leak. Check for loose throttle body-to-intake duct connections or a loose or damaged vacuum hose (Chapter 4).

Rough idle

- [ ] Idle speed incorrect (Chapter 4).
- [ ] Throttle bodies not synchronised (Chapter 1).
- [ ] Vacuum take off plug missing. Vacuum hose damaged.
- [ ] Ignition fault (Chapter 4).
- [ ] Fuel injection system malfunction (Chapter 4).
- [ ] Fuel contaminated. The fuel can be contaminated with either dirt or water, or can change chemically if the machine has been unused for several months. Drain the tank and the fuel system (Chapter 4).
- [ ] Intake air leak. Check for loose throttle body-to-intake duct connections (Chapter 4).
- [ ] Air filter clogged. Replace it with a new one (Chapter 1).

2 Poor running at low speeds

Spark weak
- [ ] Battery voltage low. Check battery condition and recharge or replace battery (Chapter 8).
- [ ] Spark plug contact in bottom of ignition coil not making good contact. Make sure that the coils are pushed fully onto the spark plugs.
- [ ] Spark plugs dirty, defective or worn out. Locate reason for fouled plugs using spark plug condition chart on the inside back cover and follow the plug maintenance procedures (Chapter 1).
- [ ] Incorrect spark plugs. Wrong type or heat range. Check and install correct plugs (Chapter 1).
- [ ] Ignition coil defective. Test and replace if necessary (Chapter 4).
- [ ] Loose or corroded connections on coil. Check security and clean connections.

Fuel/air mixture incorrect
- [ ] Fuel tank breather hose obstructed.
- [ ] Fuel pump faulty or blocked fuel pump filter. Replace the pump (Chapter 4).
- [ ] Fuel hose kinked. Replace the fuel hose.
- [ ] Fuel injector clogged. For all the injectors to be clogged, either a very bad batch of fuel with an unusual additive has been used, or some other foreign material has entered the tank. In some cases, if a machine has been unused for several months, the fuel turns to a varnish-like liquid which can cause an injector needle to stick to its seat. Drain the tank and fuel system, ultrasonically clean or replace fuel injectors (Chapter 4).
- [ ] Intake air leak. Check for loose throttle body-to-intake duct connections, loose or damaged vacuum hoses and missing vacuum take-off plug (Chapter 4).
- [ ] Air filter clogged. Replace it with a new one (Chapter 1).

Compression low
- [ ] Spark plug loose. Remove the plugs and inspect their threads. Reinstall and tighten securely (Chapter 1).
- [ ] Improper valve clearance. This means that the valve is not closing completely and compression pressure is leaking past the valve. Check and adjust the valve clearances (Chapter 1).
- [ ] Cylinder and/or piston worn. Excessive wear will cause compression pressure to leak past the rings. This is usually accompanied by worn rings as well. A top-end overhaul is necessary (Chapter 2).
- [ ] Piston rings worn, weak, broken, or sticking. Broken or sticking piston rings usually indicate a lubrication or fuelling problem that causes excess carbon deposits to form on the pistons and rings. Top-end overhaul is necessary (Chapter 2).
- [ ] Piston ring-to-groove clearance excessive. This is caused by excessive wear of the piston ring lands. Piston renewal is necessary (Chapter 2).
- [ ] Cylinder head gasket damaged. If the head is allowed to become loose, or if excessive carbon build-up on the piston crown and combustion chamber causes extremely high compression, the head gasket may leak. Retorquing the head is not always sufficient to restore the seal, so a new gasket is necessary (Chapter 2).
- [ ] Cylinder head warped. This is caused by overheating or improperly tightened head bolts. Machine shop resurfacing or head renewal is necessary (Chapter 2).
- [ ] Valve spring broken or weak. Caused by component failure or wear; the springs must be renewed (Chapter 2).
- [ ] Valve not seating properly. This is caused by a bent valve (from over-revving or improper valve adjustment), burned valve or seat (improper fuelling) or an accumulation of carbon deposits on the seat (from fuelling or lubrication problems). The valves must be cleaned and/or renewed and the seats serviced (Chapter 2).

Poor acceleration
- [ ] Timing not advancing. The crankshaft position sensor (CKP) or the electronic control module (ECM) may be defective (Chapter 4). If so, they must be renewed.
- [ ] Engine oil viscosity too high. Using a heavier oil than that recommended in Chapter 1 can damage the oil pump or lubrication system and cause drag on the engine.
- [ ] Brakes dragging. Usually caused by corrosion behind dust seals, ingestion of dirt past a deteriorated seal or from a warped disc or bent axle (Chapter 6).

Fault Finding REF•39

3 Poor running or no power at high speed

Firing incorrect
- [ ] Spark plug contact in bottom of ignition coil not making good contact. Make sure that the coils are pushed fully onto the spark plugs.
- [ ] Spark plugs dirty, defective or worn out. Locate reason for fouled plugs using spark plug condition chart on the inside back cover and follow the plug maintenance procedures (Chapter 1).
- [ ] Wrongly connected ignition coil wiring.
- [ ] Incorrect spark plugs. Wrong type or heat range. Check and install correct plugs (Chapter 1).
- [ ] Ignition coil defective. Test and replace if necessary (Chapter 4).
- [ ] Faulty ECM (electronic control module) (Chapter 4).

Fuel/air mixture incorrect
- [ ] Fuel tank breather hose obstructed.
- [ ] Fuel pump faulty or blocked fuel pump filter. Replace the pump (Chapter 4).
- [ ] Fuel hose kinked. Replace the fuel hose.
- [ ] Fuel injector clogged. For all the injectors to be clogged, either a very bad batch of fuel with an unusual additive has been used, or some other foreign material has entered the tank. In some cases, if a machine has been unused for several months, the fuel turns to a varnish-like liquid, which can cause an injector needle to stick to its seat. Drain the tank and fuel system, ultrasonically clean or replace fuel injectors (Chapter 4).
- [ ] Intake air leak. Check for loose throttle body-to-intake duct connections, loose or damaged vacuum hoses and missing vacuum take-off plug (Chapter 4).
- [ ] Air filter clogged. Replace it with a new one (Chapter 1).

Compression low
- [ ] Spark plug loose. Remove the plugs and inspect their threads. Reinstall and tighten securely (Chapter 1).
- [ ] Improper valve clearance. This means that the valve is not closing completely and compression pressure is leaking past the valve. Check and adjust the valve clearances (Chapter 1).
- [ ] Cylinder and/or piston worn. Excessive wear will cause compression pressure to leak past the rings. This is usually accompanied by worn rings as well. A top-end overhaul is necessary (Chapter 2).
- [ ] Piston rings worn, weak, broken, or sticking. Broken or sticking piston rings usually indicate a lubrication or fuelling problem that causes excess carbon deposits to form on the pistons and rings. Top-end overhaul is necessary (Chapter 2).
- [ ] Piston ring-to-groove clearance excessive. This is caused by excessive wear of the piston ring lands. Piston renewal is necessary (Chapter 2).
- [ ] Cylinder head gasket damaged. If a head is allowed to become loose, or if excessive carbon build-up on the piston crown and combustion chamber causes extremely high compression, the head gasket may leak. Retorquing the head is not always sufficient to restore the seal, so a new gasket is necessary (Chapter 2).
- [ ] Cylinder head warped. This is caused by overheating or improperly tightened head bolts. Machine shop resurfacing or head renewal is necessary (Chapter 2).
- [ ] Valve spring broken or weak. Caused by component failure or wear; the springs must be replaced with new ones (Chapter 2).
- [ ] Valve not seating properly. This is caused by a bent valve (from over-revving or improper valve adjustment), burned valve or seat (improper fuelling) or an accumulation of carbon deposits on the seat (from fuelling or lubrication problems). The valves must be cleaned and/or renewed and the seats serviced (Chapter 2).

Knocking or pinking
- [ ] Carbon build-up in combustion chamber. Use of a fuel additive that will dissolve the adhesive bonding the carbon particles to the piston crown and chamber is the easiest way to remove the build-up. Otherwise, the cylinder head will have to be removed and decarbonised (Chapter 2).
- [ ] Incorrect or poor quality fuel. Old or improper grades of fuel can cause detonation. This causes the piston to rattle, thus the knocking or pinking sound. Drain old fuel and always use the recommended fuel grade.
- [ ] Spark plug heat range incorrect. Uncontrolled detonation indicates the plug heat range is too hot. The plug in effect becomes a glow plug, raising cylinder temperatures. Install the proper heat range plug (Chapter 1).
- [ ] Improper air/fuel mixture. This will cause the cylinders to run hot, which leads to detonation. A blockage in the fuel system or an air leak can cause this imbalance (Chapter 4).

Miscellaneous causes
- [ ] Throttle valve doesn't open fully. Adjust the throttle twistgrip freeplay (Chapter 1).
- [ ] Clutch slipping due to loose or worn clutch components (Chapter 2).
- [ ] Timing not advancing. The crankshaft position sensor (CKP) or the electronic control module (ECM) may be defective (Chapter 4). If so, they must be replaced with new ones.
- [ ] Engine oil viscosity too high. Using a heavier oil than the one recommended in Chapter 1 can damage the oil pump or lubrication system and cause drag on the engine.
- [ ] Brakes dragging. Usually caused by corrosion behind dust seals, ingestion of dirt past a deteriorated seal or from a warped disc or bent axle (Chapter 6).

4 Overheating

Engine overheats
- ☐ Coolant level low. Check the level and add coolant (see *Pre-ride checks*).
- ☐ Leak in cooling system. Check cooling system hoses and radiator for leaks and other damage. Repair or renew parts as necessary (Chapter 3).
- ☐ Faulty thermostat. Check and renew as described in Chapter 3.
- ☐ Faulty radiator pressure cap. Remove the cap and have it pressure tested.
- ☐ Coolant passages clogged. Have the entire system drained and flushed, then refill with fresh coolant.
- ☐ Water pump defective. Remove the pump and check the components (Chapter 3).
- ☐ Clogged or damaged radiator fins (Chapter 3).
- ☐ Faulty cooling fan, relay or ECT sensor (Chapters 3 and 4).

Firing incorrect
- ☐ Spark plugs dirty, defective or worn out. Locate reason for fouled plugs using spark plug condition chart on the inside back cover and follow the plug maintenance procedures (Chapter 1).
- ☐ Incorrect spark plugs. Wrong type or heat range. Check and install correct plugs (Chapter 1).
- ☐ Ignition coil defective. Test and replace with a new one if necessary (Chapter 4).
- ☐ Faulty ECM (electronic control module) or CKP sensor (Chapter 4).

Fuel/air mixture incorrect
- ☐ Fuel tank breather hose obstructed.
- ☐ Fuel pump faulty or blocked fuel pump filter. Replace the pump (Chapter 4).
- ☐ Fuel hose kinked. Replace the fuel hose.
- ☐ Fuel injector clogged. For all the injectors to be clogged, either a very bad batch of fuel with an unusual additive has been used, or some other foreign material has entered the tank. In some cases, if a machine has been unused for several months, the fuel turns to a varnish-like liquid, which can cause an injector needle to stick to its seat. Drain the tank and fuel system, ultrasonically clean or replace fuel injectors (Chapter 4).
- ☐ Intake air leak. Check for loose throttle body-to-intake duct connections, loose or damaged vacuum hoses and missing vacuum take-off plug (Chapter 4).
- ☐ Air filter clogged. Replace it with a new one (Chapter 1).

Compression too high
- ☐ Carbon build-up in combustion chamber. Use of a fuel additive that will dissolve the adhesive bonding the carbon particles to the piston crown and chamber is the easiest way to remove the build-up. Otherwise, the cylinder head will have to be removed and decarbonised (Chapter 2).
- ☐ Improperly machined head surface or installation of incorrect gasket during engine assembly.

Engine load excessive
- ☐ Clutch slipping due to loose or worn clutch components (Chapter 2).
- ☐ Engine oil level too high. Too much oil will cause pressurisation of the crankcase and inefficient engine operation. Check Specifications and drain to proper level (Chapter 1 and *Pre-ride checks*).
- ☐ Engine oil viscosity too high. Using a heavier oil than the one recommended in Chapter 1 can damage the oil pump or lubrication system as well as cause drag on the engine.
- ☐ Brakes dragging. Usually caused by corrosion behind dust seals, ingestion of dirt past deteriorated seal or from a warped disc or bent axle (Chapter 6).

Lubrication inadequate
- ☐ Engine oil level too low. Friction caused by intermittent lack of lubrication or from oil that is overworked can cause overheating. The oil provides a definite cooling function in the engine. Check the oil level (see *Pre-ride checks*).
- ☐ Low engine oil pressure. Check the pressure (Chapter 2).
- ☐ Blocked oil filter or oil cooler (Chapters 1 and 2).
- ☐ Poor quality engine oil or incorrect viscosity or type. Oil is rated not only according to viscosity but also according to type. Some oils are not rated high enough for use in this engine. Check the Specifications section and change to the correct oil (Chapter 1).

Miscellaneous causes
- ☐ Modification to exhaust system. Most aftermarket exhaust systems cause the engine to run leaner, which make them run hotter. When installing an accessory exhaust system, always check with the manufacturer/supplier as to whether the ECM requires re-mapping.

Fault Finding REF•41

5 Clutch problems

Clutch slipping

- ☐ Clutch plates worn or warped. Overhaul the clutch assembly (see Chapter 2).
- ☐ Clutch spring broken or weak. Old or heat-damaged (from slipping clutch) springs should be replaced with new ones (Chapter 2).
- ☐ Clutch centre or housing unevenly worn. This causes improper engagement of the plates. Replace the damaged or worn parts (see Chapter 2).
- ☐ Clutch release mechanism fault or clutch cable wrongly adjusted (see Chapters 1 and 2).
- ☐ Incorrect type of oil. Use of oils designed for car engines that include friction modifiers can cause clutch slip in a wet clutch application.

Clutch not disengaging completely

- ☐ Clutch release mechanism fault or clutch cable wrongly adjusted (see Chapters 1 and 2).
- ☐ Clutch plates warped or damaged. This will cause clutch drag, which in turn will cause the machine to creep. Overhaul the clutch assembly (see Chapter 2).
- ☐ Clutch springs fatigued or broken. Check and replace the springs with new ones (see Chapter 2).
- ☐ Engine oil deteriorated. Old, thin oil will not provide proper lubrication for the plates, causing the clutch to drag. Renew the oil and filter (see Chapter 1).
- ☐ Engine oil viscosity too high. Using a heavier oil than recommended in Chapter 1 can cause the plates to stick together. Change to the correct weight oil.

6 Gear changing problems

Doesn't go into gear or lever doesn't return

- ☐ Clutch not disengaging (above).
- ☐ Gearchange mechanism stopper arm spring weak or broken, or arm roller broken or worn. Replace the spring or arm with a new one (Chapter 2).
- ☐ Selector fork(s) bent, worn or seized. Overhaul the transmission (Chapter 2).
- ☐ Selector drum binding. Caused by lubrication failure or excessive wear. Replace the drum and/or its bearing with a new one (Chapter 2).
- ☐ Gearchange shaft centralising spring weak or broken (Chapter 2).
- ☐ Gearchange lever or linkage broken. Splines stripped out of arm or shaft, caused by a loose linkage arm pinch bolt or from dropping the machine (Chapter 2).

Jumps out of gear

- ☐ Selector fork(s) worn (Chapter 2).
- ☐ Selector fork groove(s) in selector drum worn (Chapter 2).
- ☐ Gear pinion dogs or dog slots worn or damaged. The gear pinions should be inspected and renewed. No attempt should be made to repair the worn parts.

Overselects

- ☐ Gearchange mechanism stopper arm spring weak or broken, or arm roller broken or worn. Replace the spring or arm with a new one (Chapter 2).
- ☐ Gearchange shaft centralising spring weak or broken (Chapter•2).

7 Abnormal engine noise

Knocking or pinking
- [ ] Carbon build-up in combustion chamber. Use of a fuel additive that will dissolve the adhesive bonding the carbon particles to the piston crown and chamber is the easiest way to remove the build-up. Otherwise, the cylinder head will have to be removed and decarbonised (Chapter 2).
- [ ] Incorrect or poor quality fuel. Old or improper grades of fuel can cause detonation. This causes the pistons to rattle, thus the knocking or pinking sound. Drain old fuel and always use the recommended fuel grade.
- [ ] Spark plug heat range incorrect. Uncontrolled detonation indicates the plug heat range is too hot. The plug in effect becomes a glow plug, raising cylinder temperatures. Install the proper heat range plug (Chapter 1).
- [ ] Improper air/fuel mixture. This will cause the cylinders to run hot, which leads to detonation. A blockage in the fuel system or an intake air leak can cause this imbalance (Chapter 4). Check for loose throttle body-to-intake duct connections, loose or damaged vacuum hoses and missing vacuum take-off plug (Chapter 4).

Piston slap or rattling
- [ ] Cylinder-to-piston clearance excessive. Cylinder and/or piston worn, usually accompanied by worn rings as well. A top-end overhaul is necessary (Chapter 2).
- [ ] Piston ring(s) worn, broken or sticking. Overhaul the top-end (Chapter 2).
- [ ] Piston pin, piston pin bore or connecting rod small-end worn from high mileage or seized due to lack of lubrication (Chapter 2).
- [ ] Piston seizure damage. Usually from lack of lubrication or overheating. Replace the pistons and liners, as necessary (Chapter 2).
- [ ] Connecting rod big-end clearance excessive. Caused by excessive wear or lack of lubrication. Replace worn parts.
- [ ] Connecting rod bent. Caused by over-revving, trying to start a badly flooded engine or from ingesting a foreign object into the combustion chamber. Replace the damaged parts (Chapter 2).

Valve noise
- [ ] Incorrect valve clearances – check and adjust (Chapter 1).
- [ ] Valve spring broken or weak. Check and replace weak valve springs with new ones (Chapter 2).
- [ ] Camshaft or camshaft journals in the cylinder head worn or damaged. Lubrication failure at high rpm is usually the cause of damage due to insufficient oil or failure to change the oil at the recommended intervals. Since there are no replaceable bearings in the head, the head itself will have to be replaced with a new one (Chapter 2).

Other noise
- [ ] Cylinder head gasket leaking. Check around the joint for blowing with the engine running.
- [ ] Exhaust pipe leaking at cylinder head connection. Caused by incorrect fit of pipe(s), loose exhaust flange or damaged gasket. All exhaust system fasteners should be tightened evenly and carefully to avoid leaks (Chapter 4).
- [ ] Crankshaft runout excessive. Caused by a bent crankshaft (from over-revving) or damage from an upper cylinder component failure. Can also be attributed to dropping the machine on either of the crankshaft ends.
- [ ] Engine mounting bolts loose – ensure all the bolts are tightened to the specified torque settings (Chapter 2).
- [ ] Crankshaft bearings worn (Chapter 2).
- [ ] Cam chain rattle, due to worn chain or defective tensioner. Also worn chain tensioner/guide blades (Chapter 2).

8 Abnormal driveline noise

Clutch noise
- [ ] Clutch housing/friction plate clearance excessive (Chapter 2).
- [ ] Wear between the clutch housing splines and input shaft splines (Chapter 2).
- [ ] Worn release bearing (Chapter 2).

Transmission noise
- [ ] Bearings worn. Also includes the possibility that the shafts are worn. Overhaul the transmission (Chapter 2).
- [ ] Gears worn or chipped (Chapter 2).
- [ ] Engine oil level too low. Causes a howl from transmission. Also affects engine power and clutch operation (see *Pre-ride checks*).

Final drive noise
- [ ] Drive chain excessively loose or worn, or drive sprockets excessively worn. Check and adjust chain, or replace chain and sprockets with a new set (Chapters 1 and 6).
- [ ] Front or rear sprocket loose. Tighten fasteners (Chapter 6).
- [ ] Rear sprocket warped. Fit a new sprocket (Chapter 6).
- [ ] Rubber dampers in rear sprocket coupling worn (Chapter 6).
- [ ] Rear sprocket coupling bearing worn or damaged (Chapter 6).

Fault Finding REF•43

9 Abnormal frame and suspension noise

Front end noise

- [ ] Low fluid level or improper viscosity oil in forks. This can sound like spurting and is usually accompanied by irregular fork action (Chapter 5).
- [ ] Spring weak or broken. Makes a clicking or scraping sound. Fork oil, when drained, will have a lot of metal particles in it (Chapter 5).
- [ ] Steering head bearings loose or damaged. Clicks when braking. Check and adjust or replace with new ones as necessary (Chapters 1 and 5).
- [ ] Fork yoke clamp bolts loose – ensure all the bolts are tightened to the specified torque (Chapter 6).
- [ ] Forks bent or twisted in yokes. Good possibility if machine has been dropped. Check, and if necessary replace the inner and outer tubes with new ones as required (Chapter 5).
- [ ] Front axle or axle pinch bolts loose. Tighten them to the specified torque (Chapter 6).
- [ ] Loose or worn wheel bearings. Check and replace with new ones as needed (Chapters 1 and 6).

Rear end noise

- [ ] Shock absorber fluid level incorrect. Indicates a leak caused by defective seal. Shock will be covered with oil. Replace shock with a new one or seek advice on repair from a suspension specialist (Chapter 5).
- [ ] Defective shock absorber with internal damage. This is in the body of the shock and can't be remedied. The shock must be replaced with a new one or rebuilt (Chapter 5).
- [ ] Bent or damaged shock body. Replace the shock with a new one (Chapter 5).
- [ ] Loose or worn swingarm bearings. Check and replace with new ones as necessary (Chapter 5).
- [ ] Loose or worn suspension linkage bearings. Check and replace with new ones as necessary (Chapter 5).
- [ ] Loose or worn wheel bearings/sprocket coupling bearing. Check and replace with new ones as needed (Chapters 1 and 6).

Brake noise

- [ ] Squeal caused by pad shim not installed or positioned incorrectly (where fitted) (Chapter 6).
- [ ] Squeal caused by dust on brake pads. Usually found in combination with glazed pads. Clean using brake cleaning solvent (Chapter 6).
- [ ] Pads glazed. Caused by excessive heat from prolonged hard use or from contamination. DO NOT use sandpaper, emery cloth, carborundum cloth or any other abrasive to roughen the pad surfaces as abrasives will stay in the pad material and damage the disc. A very fine flat file can be used, but new pads is the best remedy (Chapter 6).
- [ ] Contamination of brake pads. Oil or brake fluid can cause the brake pads to chatter or squeal. Fit new pads. Identify the cause of the contamination, especially check the caliper piston seals for leaking fluid. Clean disc thoroughly with brake system cleaner (Chapter 6).
- [ ] Disc warped. Can cause a chattering, clicking or intermittent squeal. Usually accompanied by a pulsating lever and uneven braking. Replace the disc with new one (Chapter 6).
- [ ] Loose or worn wheel bearings. Check and replace with new ones as needed (Chapters 1 and 6).

10 Oil pressure low

Engine lubrication system

- [ ] Engine oil level low. Inspect for leak or other problem causing low oil level and add recommended oil (see *Pre-ride checks*).
- [ ] Engine oil pump defective, blocked oil strainer gauze or failed pressure relief valve. Carry out an oil pressure check (Chapter 2).
- [ ] Engine oil viscosity too low. Very old, thin oil or an improper weight of oil used in the engine. Change to correct oil (Chapter 1).
- [ ] Camshaft or crankshaft journals worn. Excessive wear causing drop in oil pressure. Abnormal wear could be caused by oil starvation at high rpm from low oil level or improper weight or type of oil (Chapter 1).

11 Excessive exhaust smoke

White smoke
- [ ] Piston rings worn or broken, causing oil from the crankcase to be pulled past the piston into the combustion chamber. Replace the rings with new ones (Chapter 2).
- [ ] Plating on cylinder liners worn or scored. Caused by overheating or oil starvation. Renew the liners and pistons (Chapter 2).
- [ ] Valve stem oil seal damaged or worn. Replace the oil seals with new ones (Chapter 2).
- [ ] Valve guide worn. Perform a complete valve job (Chapter 2).
- [ ] Engine oil level too high, which causes the oil to be forced past the rings. Drain oil to the proper level (see *Pre-ride checks*).
- [ ] Head gasket broken between oil return and cylinder. Causes oil to be pulled into the combustion chamber. Replace the head gasket with a new ones and check the head for warpage (Chapter 2).
- [ ] Abnormal crankcase pressurisation which forces oil past the rings, usually caused by a clogged breather.

Black smoke
- [ ] Air filter clogged. Replace it with a new one (Chapter 1).
- [ ] Fuel injection system malfunction (Chapter 4).

Brown smoke
- [ ] Air filter poorly sealed or not installed (Chapter 1).
- [ ] Fuel injection system malfunction (Chapter 4).

12 Poor handling or stability

Handlebar hard to turn
- [ ] Steering head bearing adjuster nut too tight. Check adjustment as described in Chapter 1.
- [ ] Bearings damaged. Roughness can be felt as the bars are turned from side-to-side. Replace the bearings with new ones (Chapter 5).
- [ ] Races dented or worn. Denting results from wear in only one position (e.g., straight ahead), from a collision or hitting a pothole. Replace the bearings with new ones (Chapter 5).
- [ ] Steering stem lubrication inadequate. Causes are grease getting hard from age or being washed out by high pressure car washes. Disassemble steering head and repack bearings (Chapter 5).
- [ ] Steering stem bent. Caused by a collision, hitting a pothole. Replace damaged part. Don't try to straighten the steering stem (Chapter 5).
- [ ] Front tyre air pressure too low (see *Pre-ride checks*).

Handlebar shakes or vibrates excessively
- [ ] Tyres worn or out of balance (Chapter 6).
- [ ] Swingarm bearings worn. Replace the bearings with new ones (Chapter 5).
- [ ] Wheel rim(s) warped or damaged. Inspect wheels for runout (Chapter 6).
- [ ] Wheel bearings worn. Worn front or rear wheel bearings can cause poor tracking. Worn front bearings will cause wobble (Chapters 1 and 6).
- [ ] Fork yoke clamp bolts or handlebar clamp bolts loose. Tighten them to the specified torque (Chapter 5).
- [ ] Engine mounting bolts loose. Will cause excessive vibration with increased engine rpm – ensure all the bolts are tightened to the specified torque settings (Chapter 2).

Machine pulls to one side
- [ ] Frame bent. Definitely suspect this if the machine has been dropped. May or may not be accompanied by cracking near the steering head, swingarm mountings or engine mountings. Replace the frame with a new one (Chapter 5).
- [ ] Wheels out of alignment. Caused by poor chain adjustment, improper location of axle spacers or from bent steering stem or frame (Chapters 1 and 5).
- [ ] Forks bent. Disassemble the forks and replace the damaged parts (Chapter 5).
- [ ] Swingarm bent or twisted. Replace the arm with a new one (Chapter 5).
- [ ] Fork oil level uneven. Check and add or drain as necessary (Chapter 5).

Poor shock absorbing qualities
- [ ] Too hard:
   a) *Rear suspension adjustment incorrect.*
   b) *Fork oil level excessive (Chapter 5).*
   c) *Fork oil viscosity too high. Use a lighter oil (see the Specifications in Chapter 5).*
   d) *Fork tube bent. Causes a harsh, sticking feeling (Chapter 5).*
   e) *Fork internal damage (Chapter 5).*
   f) *Shock shaft or body bent or damaged (Chapter 5).*
   g) *Shock internal damage.*
   h) *Swingarm bearings or suspension linkage bearings seized (Chapter 5).*
   i) *Tyre pressure too high (see Pre-ride checks).*
- [ ] Too soft:
   a) *Rear suspension adjustment incorrect.*
   b) *Fork oil level too low (Chapter 5).*
   c) *Fork oil viscosity too light (Chapter 5).*
   d) *Fork springs weak or broken (Chapter 5).*
   e) *Fork or shock oil leaking (Chapter 5).*
   f) *Shock internal damage (Chapter 5).*

Fault Finding REF•45

13 Braking problems

Brakes are spongy, don't hold

- [ ] Low brake fluid level (see *Pre-ride checks*).
- [ ] Air in hydraulic system. Caused by inattention to master cylinder fluid level or by leakage. Locate problem and bleed brakes (Chapter 6).
- [ ] Pad or disc worn (Chapters 1 and 6).
- [ ] Contaminated pads. Caused by contamination with oil, grease, brake fluid, etc. Fit new pads. Identify the cause of the contamination, especially check the caliper piston seals for leaking fluid. Clean disc thoroughly with brake system cleaner (Chapter 6).
- [ ] Brake fluid deteriorated. Fluid is old or contaminated. Drain system, replenish with new fluid and bleed the system (Chapter 6).
- [ ] Master cylinder internal seals worn or damaged causing fluid to bypass (Chapter 6).
- [ ] Master cylinder bore scratched by foreign material or broken spring. Fit a new master cylinder (Chapter 6).
- [ ] Disc warped. Replace disc with new one (Chapter 6)
- [ ] ABS system faulty (where fitted, Chapter 6).

Brake lever or pedal pulsates

- [ ] Disc warped. Replace disc with new one (Chapter 6).
- [ ] Axle bent. Replace axle with new one (Chapter 6).
- [ ] Brake caliper bolts loose – tighten the bolts to the specified torque (Chapter 6).
- [ ] Wheel warped or otherwise damaged (Chapter 6).
- [ ] Wheel bearings damaged or worn (Chapters 1 and 6).
- [ ] ABS system faulty (where fitted, Chapter 6).

Brakes drag

- [ ] Master cylinder piston seized. Caused by wear or damage to piston or cylinder bore (Chapter 6).
- [ ] Lever balky or stuck. Check pivot and lubricate (Chapter 6).
- [ ] Brake caliper piston seized in bore. Caused by corrosion behind dust seals or ingestion of dirt past deteriorated seal (Chapter 6).
- [ ] Brake caliper slider pins sticking or corroded, preventing full movement of caliper (Chapter 6).
- [ ] Brake pad damaged. Pad material separated from backing plate. Usually caused by faulty manufacturing process or from contact with chemicals. Fit new pads (Chapter 6).
- [ ] Pads improperly installed (Chapter 6).
- [ ] Brake caliper incorrectly installed (Chapter 6).
- [ ] ABS system faulty (where fitted, Chapter 6).

14 Electrical problems

Battery dead or weak

- [ ] Battery faulty. Caused by sulphated plates which are shorted through sedimentation. Confirm with battery condition check (Chapter 8).
- [ ] Broken battery terminal making only occasional contact.
- [ ] Battery leads making poor contact (Chapter 8).
- [ ] Load excessive. Caused by addition of high wattage lights or other electrical accessories.
- [ ] Ignition switch defective. Switch either grounds (earths) internally or fails to shut off system. Renew the switch (Chapter 8).
- [ ] Regulator/rectifier defective (Chapter 8).
- [ ] Alternator stator coil open or shorted (Chapter 8).
- [ ] Charging system fault. Check for excessive current leakage (Chapter 8).
- [ ] Wiring faulty. Wiring grounded (earthed) or connections loose in ignition, charging or lighting circuits (Chapter 8).

Battery overcharged

- [ ] Regulator/rectifier defective. Overcharging is noticed when battery gets excessively warm (Chapter 8).
- [ ] Battery faulty. Confirm with battery condition check (Chapter 8).
- [ ] Battery amperage too low, wrong type or size of battery. Install manufacturer's specified amp-hour battery to handle charging load (Chapter 8).

REF•46 Notes

Technical Terms Explained

A

ABS (Anti-lock braking system) A system, usually electronically controlled, that senses incipient wheel lockup during braking and relieves hydraulic pressure at wheel which is about to skid.
Aftermarket Components suitable for the motorcycle, but not produced by the motorcycle manufacturer.
Allen key A hexagonal wrench which fits into a recessed hexagonal hole.
Alternating current (ac) Current produced by an alternator. Requires converting to direct current by a rectifier for charging purposes.
Alternator Converts mechanical energy from the engine into electrical energy to charge the battery and power the electrical system.
Ampere (amp) A unit of measurement for the flow of electrical current. Current = Volts ÷ Ohms.
Ampere-hour (Ah) Measure of battery capacity.
Angle-tightening A torque expressed in degrees. Often follows a conventional tightening torque for cylinder head or main bearing fasteners **(see illustration)**.

Angle-tightening con-rod bolts

Antifreeze A substance (usually ethylene glycol) mixed with water, and added to the cooling system, to prevent freezing of the coolant in winter. Antifreeze also contains chemicals to inhibit corrosion and the formation of rust and other deposits that would tend to clog the radiator and coolant passages and reduce cooling efficiency.
Anti-dive System attached to the fork lower leg (slider) to prevent fork dive when braking hard.
Anti-seize compound A coating that reduces the risk of seizing on fasteners that are subjected to high temperatures, such as exhaust clamp bolts and nuts.
API American Petroleum Institute. A quality standard for 4-stroke motor oils.
Asbestos A natural fibrous mineral with great heat resistance, commonly used in the composition of brake friction materials. Asbestos is a health hazard and the dust created by brake systems should never be inhaled or ingested.
ATF Automatic Transmission Fluid. Often used in front forks.
ATU Automatic Timing Unit. Mechanical device for advancing the ignition timing on early engines.
ATV All Terrain Vehicle. Often called a Quad.
Axial play Side-to-side movement.
Axle A shaft on which a wheel revolves. Also known as a spindle.

B

Backlash The amount of movement between meshed components when one component is held still. Usually applies to gear teeth.
Ball bearing A bearing consisting of a hardened inner and outer race with hardened steel balls between the two races.
Bearings Used between two working surfaces to prevent wear of the components and a build-up of heat. Four types of bearing are commonly used on motorcycles: plain shell bearings, ball bearings, tapered roller bearings and needle roller bearings.
Bevel gears Used to turn the drive through 90°. Typical applications are shaft final drive and camshaft drive **(see illustration)**.

Bevel gears are used to turn the drive through 90°

BHP Brake Horsepower. The British measurement for engine power output. Power output is now usually expressed in kilowatts (kW).
Bias-belted tyre Similar construction to radial tyre, but with outer belt running at an angle to the wheel rim.
Big-end bearing The bearing in the end of the connecting rod that's attached to the crankshaft.
Bleeding The process of removing air from an hydraulic system via a bleed nipple or bleed screw.
Bottom-end A description of an engine's crankcase components and all components contained there-in.
BTDC Before Top Dead Centre in terms of piston position. Ignition timing is often expressed in terms of degrees or millimetres BTDC.
Bush A cylindrical metal or rubber component used between two moving parts.
Burr Rough edge left on a component after machining or as a result of excessive wear.

C

Cam chain The chain which takes drive from the crankshaft to the camshaft(s).
Canister The main component in an evaporative emission control system (California market only); contains activated charcoal granules to trap vapours from the fuel system rather than allowing them to vent to the atmosphere.
Castellated Resembling the parapets along the top of a castle wall. For example, a castellated wheel axle or spindle nut.
Catalytic converter A device in the exhaust system of some machines which converts certain pollutants in the exhaust gases into less harmful substances.
Charging system Description of the components which charge the battery, ie the alternator, rectifer and regulator.
Circlip A ring-shaped clip used to prevent endwise movement of cylindrical parts and shafts. An internal circlip is installed in a groove in a housing; an external circlip fits into a groove on the outside of a cylindrical piece such as a shaft. Also known as a snap-ring.
Clearance The amount of space between two parts. For example, between a piston and a cylinder, between a bearing and a journal, etc.
Coil spring A spiral of elastic steel found in various sizes throughout a vehicle, for example as a springing medium in the suspension and in the valve train.
Compression Reduction in volume, and increase in pressure and temperature, of a gas, caused by squeezing it into a smaller space.
Compression damping Controls the speed the suspension compresses when hitting a bump.
Compression ratio The relationship between cylinder volume when the piston is at top dead centre and cylinder volume when the piston is at bottom dead centre.
Continuity The uninterrupted path in the flow of electricity. Little or no measurable resistance.
Continuity tester Self-powered bleeper or test light which indicates continuity.
Cp Candlepower. Bulb rating commonly found on US motorcycles.
Crossply tyre Tyre plies arranged in a criss-cross pattern. Usually four or six plies used, hence 4PR or 6PR in tyre size codes.
Cush drive Rubber damper segments fitted between the rear wheel and final drive sprocket to absorb transmission shocks **(see illustration)**.

Cush drive rubbers dampen out transmission shocks

D

Decarbonisation The process of removing carbon deposits - typically from the combustion chamber, valves and exhaust port/system.
Degree disc Calibrated disc for measuring piston position. Expressed in degrees.
Detonation Destructive and damaging explosion of fuel/air mixture in combustion chamber instead of controlled burning.
Dial gauge Clock-type gauge with adapters for measuring runout and piston position. Expressed in mm or inches.

Technical Terms Explained

Diaphragm The rubber membrane in a master cylinder or carburettor which seals the upper chamber.
Diaphragm spring A single sprung plate often used in clutches.
Direct current (dc) Current produced by a dc generator.
Diode An electrical valve which only allows current to flow in one direction. Commonly used in rectifiers and starter interlock systems.
Disc valve (or rotary valve) A induction system used on some two-stroke engines.
Double-overhead camshaft (DOHC) An engine that uses two overhead camshafts, one for the intake valves and one for the exhaust valves.
Drivebelt A toothed belt used to transmit drive to the rear wheel on some motorcycles. A drivebelt has also been used to drive the camshafts. Drivebelts are usually made of Kevlar.
Driveshaft Any shaft used to transmit motion. Commonly used when referring to the final driveshaft on shaft drive motorcycles.

E

Earth return The return path of an electrical circuit, utilising the motorcycle's frame.
ECU (Electronic Control Unit) A computer which controls (for instance) an ignition system, or an anti-lock braking system.
EGO Exhaust Gas Oxygen sensor. Sometimes called a Lambda sensor.
Electrolyte The fluid in a lead-acid battery.
EMS (Engine Management System) A computer controlled system which manages the fuel injection and the ignition systems in an integrated fashion.
Endfloat The amount of lengthways movement between two parts. As applied to a crankshaft, the distance that the crankshaft can move side-to-side in the crankcase.
Endless chain A chain having no joining link. Common use for cam chains and final drive chains.
EP (Extreme Pressure) Oil type used in locations where high loads are applied, such as between gear teeth.
Evaporative emission control system Describes a charcoal filled canister which stores fuel vapours from the tank rather than allowing them to vent to the atmosphere. Usually only fitted to California models and referred to as an EVAP system.
Expansion chamber Section of two-stroke engine exhaust system so designed to improve engine efficiency and boost power.

F

Feeler blade or gauge A thin strip or blade of hardened steel, ground to an exact thickness, used to check or measure clearances between parts.
Final drive Description of the drive from the transmission to the rear wheel. Usually by chain or shaft, but sometimes by belt.
Firing order The order in which the engine cylinders fire, or deliver their power strokes, beginning with the number one cylinder.
Flooding Term used to describe a high fuel level in the carburettor float chambers, leading to fuel overflow. Also refers to excess fuel in the combustion chamber due to incorrect starting technique.
Free length The no-load state of a component when measured. Clutch, valve and fork spring lengths are measured at rest, without any preload.
Freeplay The amount of travel before any action takes place. The looseness in a linkage, or an assembly of parts, between the initial application of force and actual movement. For example, the distance the rear brake pedal moves before the rear brake is actuated.
Fuel injection The fuel/air mixture is metered electronically and directed into the engine intake ports (indirect injection) or into the cylinders (direct injection). Sensors supply information on engine speed and conditions.
Fuel/air mixture The charge of fuel and air going into the engine. See Stoichiometric ratio.
Fuse An electrical device which protects a circuit against accidental overload. The typical fuse contains a soft piece of metal which is calibrated to melt at a predetermined current flow (expressed as amps) and break the circuit.

G

Gap The distance the spark must travel in jumping from the centre electrode to the side electrode in a spark plug. Also refers to the distance between the ignition rotor and the pickup coil in an electronic ignition system.
Gasket Any thin, soft material - usually cork, cardboard, asbestos or soft metal - installed between two metal surfaces to ensure a good seal. For instance, the cylinder head gasket seals the joint between the block and the cylinder head.
Gauge An instrument panel display used to monitor engine conditions. A gauge with a movable pointer on a dial or a fixed scale is an analogue gauge. A gauge with a numerical readout is called a digital gauge.
Gear ratios The drive ratio of a pair of gears in a gearbox, calculated on their number of teeth.
Glaze-busting see Honing
Grinding Process for renovating the valve face and valve seat contact area in the cylinder head.
Gudgeon pin The shaft which connects the connecting rod small-end with the piston. Often called a piston pin or wrist pin.

H

Helical gears Gear teeth are slightly curved and produce less gear noise that straight-cut gears. Often used for primary drives.
Helicoil A thread insert repair system. Commonly used as a repair for stripped spark plug threads **(see illustration)**.

Installing a Helicoil thread insert

Honing A process used to break down the glaze on a cylinder bore (also called glaze-busting). Can also be carried out to roughen a rebored cylinder to aid ring bedding-in.
HT (High Tension) Description of the electrical circuit from the secondary winding of the ignition coil to the spark plug.
Hydraulic A liquid filled system used to transmit pressure from one component to another. Common uses on motorcycles are brakes and clutches.
Hydrometer An instrument for measuring the specific gravity of a lead-acid battery.
Hygroscopic Water absorbing. In motorcycle applications, braking efficiency will be reduced if DOT 3 or 4 hydraulic fluid absorbs water from the air - care must be taken to keep new brake fluid in tightly sealed containers.

I

lbf ft Pounds-force feet. An imperial unit of torque. Sometimes written as ft-lbs.
lbf in Pound-force inch. An imperial unit of torque, applied to components where a very low torque is required. Sometimes written as in-lbs.
IC Abbreviation for Integrated Circuit.
Ignition advance Means of increasing the timing of the spark at higher engine speeds. Done by mechanical means (ATU) on early engines or electronically by the ignition control unit on later engines.
Ignition timing The moment at which the spark plug fires, expressed in the number of crankshaft degrees before the piston reaches the top of its stroke, or in the number of millimetres before the piston reaches the top of its stroke.
Infinity (∞) Description of an open-circuit electrical state, where no continuity exists.
Inverted forks (upside down forks) The sliders or lower legs are held in the yokes and the fork tubes or stanchions are connected to the wheel axle (spindle). Less unsprung weight and stiffer construction than conventional forks.

J

JASO Quality standard for 2-stroke oils.
Joule The unit of electrical energy.
Journal The bearing surface of a shaft.

K

Kickstart Mechanical means of turning the engine over for starting purposes. Only usually fitted to mopeds, small capacity motorcycles and off-road motorcycles.
Kill switch Handebar-mounted switch for emergency ignition cut-out. Cuts the ignition circuit on all models, and additionally prevent starter motor operation on others.
km Symbol for kilometre.
kmh Abbreviation for kilometres per hour.

L

Lambda (λ) sensor A sensor fitted in the exhaust system to measure the exhaust gas oxygen content (excess air factor).

Technical Terms Explained

Lapping see Grinding.
LCD Abbreviation for Liquid Crystal Display.
LED Abbreviation for Light Emitting Diode.
Liner A steel cylinder liner inserted in a aluminium alloy cylinder block.
Locknut A nut used to lock an adjustment nut, or other threaded component, in place.
Lockstops The lugs on the lower triple clamp (yoke) which abut those on the frame, preventing handlebar-to-fuel tank contact.
Lockwasher A form of washer designed to prevent an attaching nut from working loose.
LT Low Tension Description of the electrical circuit from the power supply to the primary winding of the ignition coil.

M

Main bearings The bearings between the crankshaft and crankcase.
Maintenance-free (MF) battery A sealed battery which cannot be topped up.
Manometer Mercury-filled calibrated tubes used to measure intake tract vacuum. Used to synchronise carburettors on multi-cylinder engines.
Micrometer A precision measuring instrument that measures component outside diameters **(see illustration)**.

Tappet shims are measured with a micrometer

MON (Motor Octane Number) A measure of a fuel's resistance to knock.
Monograde oil An oil with a single viscosity, eg SAE80W.
Monoshock A single suspension unit linking the swingarm or suspension linkage to the frame.
mph Abbreviation for miles per hour.
Multigrade oil Having a wide viscosity range (eg 10W40). The W stands for Winter, thus the viscosity ranges from SAE10 when cold to SAE40 when hot.
Multimeter An electrical test instrument with the capability to measure voltage, current and resistance. Some meters also incorporate a continuity tester and buzzer.

N

Needle roller bearing Inner race of caged needle rollers and hardened outer race. Examples of uncaged needle rollers can be found on some engines. Commonly used in rear suspension applications and in two-stroke engines.
Nm Newton metres.
NOx Oxides of Nitrogen. A common toxic pollutant emitted by petrol engines at higher temperatures.

O

Octane The measure of a fuel's resistance to knock.
OE (Original Equipment) Relates to components fitted to a motorcycle as standard or replacement parts supplied by the motorcycle manufacturer.
Ohm The unit of electrical resistance. Ohms = Volts ÷ Current.
Ohmmeter An instrument for measuring electrical resistance.
Oil cooler System for diverting engine oil outside of the engine to a radiator for cooling purposes.
Oil injection A system of two-stroke engine lubrication where oil is pump-fed to the engine in accordance with throttle position.
Open-circuit An electrical condition where there is a break in the flow of electricity - no continuity (high resistance).
O-ring A type of sealing ring made of a special rubber-like material; in use, the O-ring is compressed into a groove to provide the sealing action.
Oversize (OS) Term used for piston and ring size options fitted to a rebored cylinder.
Overhead cam (sohc) engine An engine with single camshaft located on top of the cylinder head.
Overhead valve (ohv) engine An engine with the valves located in the cylinder head, but with the camshaft located in the engine block or crankcase.
Oxygen sensor A device installed in the exhaust system which senses the oxygen content in the exhaust and converts this information into an electric current. Also called a Lambda sensor.

P

Plastigauge A thin strip of plastic thread, available in different sizes, used for measuring clearances. For example, a strip of Plastigauge is laid across a bearing journal. The parts are assembled and dismantled; the width of the crushed strip indicates the clearance between journal and bearing.
Polarity Either negative or positive earth (ground), determined by which battery lead is connected to the frame (earth return). Modern motorcycles are usually negative earth.
Pre-ignition A situation where the fuel/air mixture ignites before the spark plug fires. Often due to a hot spot in the combustion chamber caused by carbon build-up. Engine has a tendency to 'run-on'.
Pre-load (suspension) The amount a spring is compressed when in the unloaded state. Preload can be applied by gas, spacer or mechanical adjuster.
Premix The method of engine lubrication on older two-stroke engines. Engine oil is mixed with the petrol in the fuel tank in a specific ratio. The fuel/oil mix is sometimes referred to as "petroil".
Primary drive Description of the drive from the crankshaft to the clutch. Usually by gear or chain.
PS Pfedestärke - a German interpretation of BHP.
PSI Pounds-force per square inch. Imperial measurement of tyre pressure and cylinder pressure measurement.
PTFE Polytetrafluroethylene. A low friction substance.
Pulse secondary air injection system A process of promoting the burning of excess fuel present in the exhaust gases by routing fresh air into the exhaust ports.

Q

Quartz halogen bulb Tungsten filament surrounded by a halogen gas. Typically used for the headlight **(see illustration)**.

Quartz halogen headlight bulb construction

R

Rack-and-pinion A pinion gear on the end of a shaft that mates with a rack (think of a geared wheel opened up and laid flat). Sometimes used in clutch operating systems.
Radial play Up and down movement about a shaft.
Radial ply tyres Tyre plies run across the tyre (from bead to bead) and around the circumference of the tyre. Less resistant to tread distortion than other tyre types.
Radiator A liquid-to-air heat transfer device designed to reduce the temperature of the coolant in a liquid cooled engine.
Rake A feature of steering geometry - the angle of the steering head in relation to the vertical **(see illustration)**.

Steering geometry

Technical Terms Explained

Rebore Providing a new working surface to the cylinder bore by boring out the old surface. Necessitates the use of oversize piston and rings.

Rebound damping A means of controlling the oscillation of a suspension unit spring after it has been compressed. Resists the spring's natural tendency to bounce back after being compressed.

Rectifier Device for converting the ac output of an alternator into dc for battery charging.

Reed valve An induction system commonly used on two-stroke engines.

Regulator Device for maintaining the charging voltage from the generator or alternator within a specified range.

Relay A electrical device used to switch heavy current on and off by using a low current auxiliary circuit.

Resistance Measured in ohms. An electrical component's ability to pass electrical current.

RON (Research Octane Number) A measure of a fuel's resistance to knock.

rpm revolutions per minute.

Runout The amount of wobble (in-and-out movement) of a wheel or shaft as it's rotated. The amount a shaft rotates 'out-of-true'. The out-of-round condition of a rotating part.

S

SAE (Society of Automotive Engineers) A standard for the viscosity of a fluid.

Sealant A liquid or paste used to prevent leakage at a joint. Sometimes used in conjunction with a gasket.

Service limit Term for the point where a component is no longer useable and must be renewed.

Shaft drive A method of transmitting drive from the transmission to the rear wheel.

Shell bearings Plain bearings consisting of two shell halves. Most often used as big-end and main bearings in a four-stroke engine. Often called bearing inserts.

Shim Thin spacer, commonly used to adjust the clearance or relative positions between two parts. For example, shims inserted into or under tappets or followers to control valve clearances. Clearance is adjusted by changing the thickness of the shim.

Short-circuit An electrical condition where current shorts to earth (ground) bypassing the circuit components.

Skimming Process to correct warpage or repair a damaged surface, eg on brake discs or drums.

Slide-hammer A special puller that screws into or hooks onto a component such as a shaft or bearing; a heavy sliding handle on the shaft bottoms against the end of the shaft to knock the component free.

Small-end bearing The bearing in the upper end of the connecting rod at its joint with the gudgeon pin.

Spalling Damage to camshaft lobes or bearing journals shown as pitting of the working surface.

Specific gravity (SG) The state of charge of the electrolyte in a lead-acid battery. A measure of the electrolyte's density compared with water.

Straight-cut gears Common type gear used on gearbox shafts and for oil pump and water pump drives.

Stanchion The inner sliding part of the front forks, held by the yokes. Often called a fork tube.

Stoichiometric ratio The optimum chemical air/fuel ratio for a petrol engine, said to be 14.7 parts of air to 1 part of fuel.

Sulphuric acid The liquid (electrolyte) used in a lead-acid battery. Poisonous and extremely corrosive.

Surface grinding (lapping) Process to correct a warped gasket face, commonly used on cylinder heads.

T

Tapered-roller bearing Tapered inner race of caged needle rollers and separate tapered outer race. Examples of taper roller bearings can be found on steering heads.

Tappet A cylindrical component which transmits motion from the cam to the valve stem, either directly or via a pushrod and rocker arm. Also called a cam follower.

TCS Traction Control System. An electronically-controlled system which senses wheel spin and reduces engine speed accordingly.

TDC Top Dead Centre denotes that the piston is at its highest point in the cylinder.

Thread-locking compound Solution applied to fastener threads to prevent slackening. Select type to suit application.

Thrust washer A washer positioned between two moving components on a shaft. For example, between gear pinions on gearshaft.

Timing chain See **Cam Chain**.

Timing light Stroboscopic lamp for carrying out ignition timing checks with the engine running.

Top-end A description of an engine's cylinder block, head and valve gear components.

Torque Turning or twisting force about a shaft.

Torque setting A prescribed tightness specified by the motorcycle manufacturer to ensure that the bolt or nut is secured correctly. Undertightening can result in the bolt or nut coming loose or a surface not being sealed. Overtightening can result in stripped threads, distortion or damage to the component being retained.

Torx key A six-point wrench.

Tracer A stripe of a second colour applied to a wire insulator to distinguish that wire from another one with the same colour insulator. For example, Br/W is often used to denote a brown insulator with a white tracer.

Trail A feature of steering geometry. Distance from the steering head axis to the tyre's central contact point.

Triple clamps The cast components which extend from the steering head and support the fork stanchions or tubes. Often called fork yokes.

Turbocharger A centrifugal device, driven by exhaust gases, that pressurises the intake air. Normally used to increase the power output from a given engine displacement.

TWI Abbreviation for Tyre Wear Indicator. Indicates the location of the tread depth indicator bars on tyres.

U

Universal joint or U-joint (UJ) A double-pivoted connection for transmitting power from a driving to a driven shaft through an angle. Typically found in shaft drive assemblies.

Unsprung weight Anything not supported by the bike's suspension (ie the wheel, tyres, brakes, final drive and bottom (moving) part of the suspension).

V

Vacuum gauges Clock-type gauges for measuring intake tract vacuum. Used for carburettor synchronisation on multi-cylinder engines.

Valve A device through which the flow of liquid, gas or vacuum may be stopped, started or regulated by a moveable part that opens, shuts or partially obstructs one or more ports or passageways. The intake and exhaust valves in the cylinder head are of the poppet type.

Valve clearance The clearance between the valve tip (the end of the valve stem) and the rocker arm or tappet/follower. The valve clearance is measured when the valve is closed. The correct clearance is important - if too small the valve won't close fully and will burn out, whereas if too large noisy operation will result.

Valve lift The amount a valve is lifted off its seat by the camshaft lobe.

Valve timing The exact setting for the opening and closing of the valves in relation to piston position.

Vernier caliper A precision measuring instrument that measures inside and outside dimensions. Not quite as accurate as a micrometer, but more convenient.

Wet liner arrangement

VIN Vehicle Identification Number. Term for the bike's engine and frame numbers.

Viscosity The thickness of a liquid or its resistance to flow.

Volt A unit for expressing electrical "pressure" in a circuit. Volts = current x ohms.

W

Water pump A mechanically-driven device for moving coolant around the engine.

Watt A unit for expressing electrical power. Watts = volts x current.

Wear limit see **Service limit**

Wet liner A liquid-cooled engine design where the pistons run in liners which are directly surrounded by coolant **(see illustration)**.

Wheelbase Distance from the centre of the front wheel to the centre of the rear wheel.

Wiring harness or loom Describes the electrical wires running the length of the motorcycle and enclosed in tape or plastic sheathing. Wiring coming off the main harness is usually referred to as a sub harness.

Woodruff key A key of semi-circular or square section used to locate a gear to a shaft. Often used to locate the alternator rotor on the crankshaft.

Wrist pin Another name for gudgeon or piston pin.

Index

Note: *References throughout this index are in the form - "Chapter number" • "Page number"*

A

ABS – 6•1, 6•18
Airbox – 4•5
Air filter – 1•26
Alternator – 8•1, 8•18
Atmospheric pressure sensor – 4•17

B

Balancer shaft – 2•49
Battery – 1•29, 8•1, 8•4, 8•5
Bodywork – 7•1 *et seq*
Brake light – 8•8
   circuit check – 8•6
   switches – 8•9
Brakes – 6•1 *et seq*
   ABS – 6•18
   bleeding – 6•15
   calipers – 6•5, 6•10
   check – 1•18
   discs – 6•7, 6•11
   fluid change – 1•18, 6•18
   fluid level checks – 0•14
   fluid type – 1•2
   hoses – 1•18, 6•14
   lever – 5•5
   master cylinder – 6•8, 6•12
   pads – 1•2, 1•17, 6•3
   pedal – 5•2
   specifications – 6•1
Braking problems – REF•45
Bulbs – 8•2

C

Cables
   clutch – 1•19, 2•35
   freeplay – 1•2
   lubricant – 1•2
   lubrication – 1•29
   throttle – 1•11, 4•11
Cam chain – 2•2, 2•17
Cam chain blades – 2•17
Cam chain tensioner – 2•11
Camshafts – 2•2, 2•14
Catalytic converter – 4•21
Chain (cam) – 3•2, 2•17
Chain (drive) – 6•28
   checks – 0•13, 1•6
   lubrication – 1•2, 1•7
   size/links – 6•2
   slack – 1•2, 1•6, 1•7
   slider – 1•7
   stretch limit – 1•2,
Charging system – 8•1, 8•17
Clutch – 2•3, 2•29
Clutch cable – 1•2, 1•19, 2•35
Clutch lever – 5•5
   span adjuster – 1•20
Clutch problems – REF•41
Clutch switch – 8•13
Cockpit panel – 7•5
Coils (ignition) – 4•13
Connecting rods – 2•3, 2•45
Coolant – 1•2, 3•1
   change – 1•13
   fluid level check – 0•15
   reservoir – 3•2
   temperature sensor – 4•17
Cooling system – 3•1 *et seq*
   check – 1•12
   fan – 3•1, 3•3
   hoses, pipes and unions – 3•6
   radiator – 3•4
   radiator pressure cap – 3•2
   thermostat – 3•4
   water pump – 2•38, 3•5
Conversion factors – REF•34
Crankcases – 2•42, 2•45
Crankshaft – 2•3, 2•47
Crankshaft position sensor – 4•17
Cylinder compression – 2•2, 2•5
Cylinder head – 2•19
Cylinder liners – 2•2, 2•24

D

Dimensions (model) – 0•10
Drive chain – 6•28
   checks – 0•13, 1•6
   lubrication – 1•2, 1•7
   size/links – 6•2
   slack – 1•2, 1•6, 1•7
   slider – 1•7
   stretch limit – 1•2,

Index

Note: References throughout this index are in the form - "Chapter number" • "Page number"

E

ECM – 4•16
EMS relay – 4•16
Electrical system – 8•1 et seq
    battery – 8•1, 8•4, 8•5
    bulbs – 8•2
    fault finding – 8•2, REF•45
    fuses – 8•2, 8•5
    wiring diagrams – 8•22
Engine
    balancer shaft – 2•49
    bearings – 2•45
    cam chain blades – 2•17
    cam chain tensioner – 2•11
    camshafts and followers – 2•14
    connecting rods – 2•45
    crankcases – 2•42, 2•45
    crankshaft – 2•47
    cylinder head – 2•19
    cylinder liners – 2•24
    fault finding – REF•36
    oil – 1•2
    oil and water pump – 2•38
    oil cooler – 2•9
    oil level – 0•13
    oil pressure relief valve – 2•36
    oil strainer – 2•36
    overhaul information – 2•9
    pistons and rings – 2•26
    removal and installation – 2•6
    running-in – 2•59
    specifications – 0•11, 2•1
    sprocket – 6•28
    starter clutch – 2•18
    sump – 2•36
    valve clearances – 1•2, 1•27
    valve cover – 2•10
    valves – 2•20
    wear assessment – 2•5
Engine coolant temperature sensor – 4•17
Engine management – 4•1 et seq
    checks – 1•11
    EMS relay – 4•16
    fault codes – 4•15
    sensors – 4•17
    specifications – 4•1
Engine number – 0•12
Engine protection bars – 7•7
EVAP system – 4•21
Exhaust system – 4•12

F

Fan – 3•1, 3•3
Fault codes – 4•15
Fault finding – REF•35 et seq
    electrical system – 8•2
Filter
    air – 1•26
    fuel – 1•15
    oil – 1•9
Firing order – 2•1
Footrests – 5•2
Frame – 5•2
    specifications – 0•11
Frame number – 0•12
Front brake
    caliper – 6•5
    discs – 6•7
    fluid level check – 0•14
    lever – 5•5
    master cylinder – 6•8
    pads – 1•17, 6•3
Front forks – 5•5, 5•7
    checks – 1•16
    oil – 5•1
    oil change – 5•6
    specifications – 0•11, 5•1
Front mudguard – 7•7
Front wheel – 6•22
Front wheel bearings – 6•24
Fuel – 4•1
Fuel system (injection)
    check – 1•15
    filter – 1•15
    hoses – 1•15
    level sensor – 4•8
    pressure – 4•7
    pump and relay – 4•6
    rail and injectors – 4•10
    specifications – 4•1
    tank – 4•3
    throttle body – 1•22, 4•8
Fuel tank – 4•3
Fuel tank trim panels – 7•5
Fuses – 8•2, 8•5

G

Gear position sensor – 4•18
Gearbox shafts – 2•51, 2•52
Gearchange lever and linkage – 5•3
Gearchange mechanism – 2•40
Gearchange problems – REF•41
Grab-rails – 7•7

Index

Note: *References throughout this index are in the form - "Chapter number" • "Page number"*

H

Hand guards – 7•7
Handlebar switches – 8•12
Handlebars – 5•4
Handling and stability problems – REF•44
Headlight – 8•7
  aim – 8•8
  bulb – 8•2, 8•7
  circuit check – 8•6
  relay – 8•11
History – 0•4, 0•11
Horn – 8•14

I

Idle air control unit – 4•20
Idle speed – 1•2, 1•22
Ignition switch – 8•11
Ignition system
  coils – 4•13
  crankshaft position sensor – 4•17
  ECM – 4•16
  spark plugs – 1•20
  specifications – 4•2
Immobiliser – 4•21
Injectors – 4•10
Instruments – 8•10
Intake air temperature sensor – 4•18

L

Legal checks – 0•16
Lighting system – 8•6
Lubricants – 1•2, REF•23
Lubrication
  drive chain – 1•7
  engine – 0•13, 1•2, 1•9, 2•3, 2•36, 2•38
  pivot points and cables – 1•29
  rear suspension linkage bearings – 1•17, 5•15
  steering head bearings – 1•26, 5•11
  swingarm bearings – 1•17, 5•17
Luggage rack – 7•7

M

Main bearings – 2•47
Manifold absolute temperature sensor – 4•18
Master cylinder – 6•8, 6•12
Mirrors – 7•7
Model development – 0•11
MOT Test Checks – REF•26
Mudguard (front) – 7•7

O

Oil (engine) – 1•2
  change – 1•9
  level check – 0•13
Oil (front forks) – 5•1, 5•6
Oil cooler – 2•9
Oil filter – 1•9
Oil pressure – 2•3, 2•6, REF•43
Oil pressure relief valve – 2•36
Oil pressure switch – 8•13
Oil pump – 2•3, 2•38
Oxygen sensor – 4•18

P

Piston rings – 2•3, 2•26
Pistons – 2•2, 2•26
Pre-ride checks – 0•13 *et seq*
Pressure relief valve – 2•36
Pump
  fuel – 4•6
  oil – 2•3, 2•38
  water – 3•5

R

Radiator – 3•4
Radiator cap – 3•1, 3•2
Radiator covers – 7•2
Rear brake
  caliper – 6•10
  disc – 6•11
  fluid level check – 0•15
  master cylinder – 6•12
  pads – 1•17, 6•4
  pedal – 5•2
Rear sprocket – 6•29
Rear suspension
  checks – 1•16
  linkage – 1•17, 5•15
  shock absorber – 5•13, 5•18
Rear wheel – 6•23
Rear wheel bearings – 6•24
Regulator/rectifier – 8•21
Relay
  cooling fan – 3•4
  EMS – 4•16
  fuel pump – 4•7
  headlight – 8•11
  starter – 8•14
  starter circuit – 8•11
  turn signal – 8•8
Routine maintenance – 1•1 *et seq*

Index

Note: *References throughout this index are in the form - "Chapter number" • "Page number"*

S

Safety – 0•9, 0•16
Seat(s) – 7•2
Security – REF•20
Service schedule – 1•3
Servicing – 1•1 *et seq*
Selector drum and forks – 2•4, 2•58
Side panels – 7•3
Sidelight – 8•7
   circuit check – 8•6
Sidestand – 1•17, 5•3
Sidestand switch – 8•13
Spare parts – 0•12
Spark plugs – 1•2, 1•20
Speed sensor
   ABS – 6•19
   non-ABS – 4•18
Sprocket coupling bearing – 6•25
Sprocket coupling rubber dampers – 6•29
Sprockets – 6•28
   check – 1•7
Starter circuit relay – 8•11
Starter clutch – 2•18
Starter motor – 8•15
Starter relay – 8•14
Starter safety circuit – 1•17
Steering head bearings – 1•24, 5•12
Steering stem – 5•10
Storage – REF•31
Sump – 2•36
Sump guard and bracket – 7•5
Suspension
   checks – 0•13, 1•16
   front forks – 5•5, 5•6, 5•7
   rear linkage – 5•15
   rear shock – 5•13, 5•18
   specifications – 0•11
Swingarm – 5•16
   bearings – 1•17, 5•17

T

Tail light – 8•8
   circuit check – 8•6
Tank (fuel) – 4•3
Thermostat – 3•1, 3•4
Throttle body – 4•8
   synchronisation – 1•22
Throttle cables – 1•2, 1•11, 4•11
Throttle position sensor – 4•18
Tip-over sensor – 4•18
Tools and Workshop Tips – REF•2
Torque settings – 1•2, 2•4, 3•1, 4•2, 5•1, 6•2, 8•2
Transmission
   ratios – 2•3
   shafts – 2•51, 2•52
Turn signals – 8•9
   bulbs – 8•2, 8•9
   relay – 8•8
Tyre pressure monitoring system – 6•27
Tyres – 6•26
   pressures and tread depth – 0•16
   sizes – 0•11, 6•2
   valves – 1•19

V

Valve clearances – 1•2, 1•27
Valve cover – 2•10
Valves – 2•2, 2•20

W

Water pump – 2•38, 3•5
Weights (model) – 0•10
Wheel bearings – 1•19,
Wheels – 6•22, 6•23
   alignment – 6•21
   check – 1•19
   runout – 6•2, 6•21
   specifications – 0•11
Windshield – 7•7
Wiring diagrams – 8•22

Haynes Motorcycle Manuals – The Complete List

Title	Book No
APRILIA RS50 (99 – 06) & RS125 (93 – 06)	4298
Aprilia RSV1000 Mille (98 – 03) ♦	4255
Aprilia SR50	4755
BMW 2-valve Twins (70 – 96) ♦	0249
BMW F650 ♦	4761
BMW K100 & 75 2-valve models (83 – 96)	1373
BMW F800 (F650) Twins (06 – 10) ♦	4872
BMW R850, 1100 & 1150 4-valve Twins (93 – 06) ♦	3466
BMW R1200 (04 – 09) ♦	4598
BMW R1200 dohc Twins (10 – 12) ♦	4925
BSA Bantam (48 – 71)	0117
BSA Unit Singles (58 – 72)	0127
BSA Pre-unit Singles (54 – 61)	0326
BSA A7 & A10 Twins (47 – 62)	0121
BSA A50 & A65 Twins (62 – 73)	0155
CHINESE, Taiwanese & Korean Scooters	4768
Chinese, Taiwanese & Korean 125cc motorcycles	4781
DUCATI 600, 620, 750 & 900 2-valve V-twins (91 – 05) ♦	3290
Ducati Mk III & Desmo singles (69 – 76) ◊	0445
Ducati 748, 916 & 996 4-valve V-twins (94 – 01) ♦	3756
GILERA Runner, DNA, Ice & SKP/Stalker (97 – 11)	4163
HARLEY-DAVIDSON Sportsters (70 – 10) ♦	2534
Harley-Davidson Shovelhead & Evolution Big Twins (70 -99) ♦	2536
Harley-Davidson Twin Cam 88, 96 & 103 models (99 – 10) ♦	2478
HONDA NB, ND, NP & NS50 Melody (81 -85) ◊	0622
Honda NE/NB50 Vision & SA50 Vision Met-in (85-95) ◊	1278
Honda MB, MBX, MT & MTX50 (80 – 93)	0731
Honda C50, C70 & C90 (67 – 03)	0324
Honda XR50/70/80/100R & CRF50/70/80/100F (85 – 07)	2218
Honda XL/XR 80, 100, 125, 185 & 200 2-valve models (78 – 87)	0566
Honda H100 & H100S Singles (80 – 92)	0734
Honda 125 Scooters (00 – 09)	4873
Honda ANF125 Innova Scooters (03 -12) ♦	4926
Honda CB/CD125T & CM125C Twins (77 – 88) ◊	0571
Honda CBF125 (09 – 12)	5540
Honda CG125 (76 – 07) ◊	0433
Honda NS125 (86 – 93)	3056
Honda CBR125R (04 – 10)	4620
Honda MBX/MTX125 & MTX200 (83 – 93) ◊	1132
Honda XL125V & VT125C (99 – 11)	4899
Honda CD/CM185 200T & CM250C 2-valve Twins (77 – 85)	0572
Honda CMX250 Rebel & CB250 Nighthawk Twins (85 – 09) ♦	2756
Honda XL/XR 250 & 500 (78 – 84)	0567
Honda XR250L, XR250R & XR400R (86 – 03)	2219
Honda CB250 & CB400N Super Dreams (78 – 84) ♦	0540
Honda CR Motocross Bikes (86 – 07)	2222
Honda CRF250 & CRF450 (02 – 06)	2630
Honda CBR400RR Fours (88 – 99) ◊♦	3552
Honda VFR400 (NC30) & RVF400 (NC35) V-Fours (89 – 98) ◊♦	3496
Honda CB500 (93 – 02) & CBF500 (03 – 08) ♦	3753
Honda CB400 & CB550 Fours (73 – 77)	0262
Honda CX/GL500 & 650 V-Twins (78 – 86)	0442
Honda CBX550 Four (82 – 86) ♦	0940
Honda XL600R & XR600R (83 – 08) ♦	2183
Honda XL600/650V Transalp & XRV750 Africa Twin (87 – 07) ♦	3919
Honda CB600 Hornet, CBF600 & CBR600F (07 – 12) ♦	5572
Honda CBR600F1 & 1000F Fours (87 – 96) ♦	1730
Honda CBR600F2 & F3 Fours (91 – 98) ♦	2070
Honda CBR600F4 (99 – 06) ♦	3911
Honda CBR600F Hornet & CBF600 (98 – 06) ◊♦	3915
Honda CBR600RR (03 – 06) ♦	4590
Honda CBR600RR (07 -12) ♦	4795
Honda CB650 sohc Fours (78 – 84)	0665
Honda NTV600 Revere, NTV650 & NT650V Deauville (88 – 05) ◊♦	3243
Honda Shadow VT600 & 750 (USA) (88 – 09)	2312
Honda NT700V Deauville & XL700V Transalp (06 -13) ♦	5541
Honda CB750 sohc Four (69 – 79)	0131
Honda V45/65 Sabre & Magna (82 – 88)	0820
Honda VFR750 & 700 V-Fours (86 – 97) ♦	2101
Honda VFR800 V-Fours (97 – 01) ♦	3703
Honda VFR800 V-Tec V-Fours (02 – 09) ♦	4196
Honda CB750 & CB900 dohc Fours (78 – 84)	0535
Honda CBF1000 (06 -10) & CB1000R (08 – 11) ♦	4927
Honda VTR1000 Firestorm, Super Hawk & XL1000V Varadero (97 – 08) ♦	3744
Honda CBR900RR Fireblade (92 – 99) ♦	2161
Honda CBR900RR Fireblade (00 – 03) ♦	4060
Honda CBR1000RR Fireblade (04 – 07) ♦	4604
Honda CBR1100XX Super Blackbird (97 – 07) ♦	3901
Honda ST1100 Pan European V-Fours (90 – 02) ♦	3384
Honda ST1300 Pan European (02 -11) ♦	4908

Title	Book No
Honda Shadow VT1100 (USA) (85 – 07)	2313
Honda GL1000 Gold Wing (75 – 79)	0309
Honda GL1100 Gold Wing (79 – 81)	0669
Honda Gold Wing 1200 (USA) (84 – 87)	2199
Honda Gold Wing 1500 (USA) (88 – 00)	2225
Honda Goldwing GL1800 ♦	2787
KAWASAKI AE/AR 50 & 80 (81 – 95)	1007
Kawasaki KC, KE & KH100 (75 – 99)	1371
Kawasaki KMX125 & 200 (86 – 02) ◊	3046
Kawasaki 250, 350 & 400 Triples (72 – 79)	0134
Kawasaki 400 & 440 Twins (74 – 81)	0281
Kawasaki 400, 500 & 550 Fours (79 – 91)	0910
Kawasaki EN450 & 500 Twins (Ltd/Vulcan) (85 – 07)	2053
Kawasaki ER-6F & ER-6N (06 -10) ♦	4874
Kawasaki EX500 (GPZ500S) & ER500 (ER-5) (87 – 08) ♦	2052
Kawasaki ZX600 (ZZ-R600 & Ninja ZX-6) (90 – 06) ♦	2146
Kawasaki ZX-6R Ninja Fours (95 – 02) ♦	3451
Kawasaki ZX-6R (03 – 06) ♦	4742
Kawasaki ZX600 (GPZ600R, GPX600R, Ninja 600R & RX) & ZX750 (GPX750R, Ninja 750R) (85 – 97)	1780
Kawasaki 650 Four (76 – 78)	0373
Kawasaki Vulcan 700/750 & 800 (85 – 04)	2457
Kawasaki Vulcan 1500 & 1600 (87 – 08)	4913
Kawasaki 750 Air-cooled Fours	0574
Kawasaki ZR550 & 750 Zephyr Fours (90 – 97)	3382
Kawasaki Z750 & Z1000 (03 – 08) ♦	4762
Kawasaki ZX750 (Ninja ZX-7 & ZXR750) Fours (89 – 96) ♦	2054
Kawasaki Ninja ZX-7R & ZX-9R (94 – 04) ♦	3721
Kawasaki 900 & 1000 Fours (73 – 77)	0222
Kawasaki ZX900, 1000 & 1100 Liquid-cooled Fours (83 – 97) ♦	1681
KTM EXC Enduro & SX Motocross (00 – 07) ♦	4629
LAMBRETTA Scooters (58 – 00)	5573
MOTO GUZZI 750, 850 & 1000 V-Twins (74 – 78) ♦	0339
MZ ETZ models (81 – 95)	1680
NORTON 500, 600, 650 & 750 Twins (57 – 70)	0187
Norton Commando (68 – 77)	0125
PEUGEOT Speedfight, Trekker & Vivacity Scooters (96 – 08) ◊	3920
PIAGGIO (Vespa) Scooters (91 – 09)	3492
SUZUKI GT, ZR & TS50 (77 – 90) ◊	0799
Suzuki TS50X (84 – 00) ◊	1599
Suzuki 100, 125, 185 & 250 Air-cooled Trail bikes (79 – 89)	0797
Suzuki GP100 & 125 Singles (78 – 93)	0576
Suzuki GS, GN, GZ & DR125 Singles (82 – 05) ◊	0888
Suzuki Burgman 250 & 400 (98 – 11) ♦	4909
Suzuki GSX-R600/750 (06 – 09) ♦	4790
Suzuki 250 & 350 Twins (68 – 78)	0120
Suzuki GT250X7, GT200X5 & SB200 Twins (78 – 83)	0469
Suzuki DR-Z400 (00 – 10) ♦	2933
Suzuki GS/GSX250, 400 & 450 Twins (79 – 85)	0736
Suzuki GS500 Twin (89 – 08) ♦	3238
Suzuki GS550 (77 – 82) & GS750 Fours (76 – 79)	0363
Suzuki GS/GSX550 4-valve Fours (83 – 88)	1133
Suzuki SV650 & SV650S (99 – 08) ♦	3912
Suzuki GSX-R600 & 750 (96 – 00) ♦	3553
Suzuki GSX-R600 (01 – 03), GSX-R750 (00 – 03) & GSX-R1000 (01 – 02) ♦	3986
Suzuki GSX-R600/750 (04 – 05) & GSX-R1000 (03 – 06) ♦	4382
Suzuki GSF600, 650 & 1200 Bandit Fours (95 – 06) ♦	3367
Suzuki Intruder, Marauder, Volusia & Boulevard (85 – 09) ♦	2618
Suzuki GS850 Fours (78 – 88)	0536
Suzuki GS1000 Four (77 – 79)	0484
Suzuki GSX-R750, GSX-R1100 (85 – 92) GSX600F, GSX750F, GSX1100F (Katana) Fours (88 – 96)	2055
Suzuki GSX600/750F & GSX750 (98 – 02) ♦	3987
Suzuki GS/GSX1000, 1100 & 1150 4-valve Fours (79 – 88)	0737
Suzuki TL1000S/R & DL V-Strom (97 – 04) ♦	4083
Suzuki GSF650/1250 (07 – 09) ♦	4798
Suzuki GSX1300R Hayabusa (99 – 04) ♦	4184
Suzuki GSX1400 (02 – 08) ♦	4758
TRIUMPH Tiger Cub & Terrier (52 – 68)	0414
Triumph 350 & 500 Unit Twins (58 – 73)	0137
Triumph Pre-Unit Twins (47 – 62)	0251
Triumph 650 & 750 2-valve Unit Twins (63 – 83)	0122
Triumph 675 (06 – 10) ♦	4876
Triumph 1050 Sprint, Speed Triple & Tiger (05 -13) ♦	4796
Triumph Trident & BSA Rocket 3 (69 – 75)	0136
Triumph Bonneville (01 – 12) ♦	4364
Triumph Daytona, Speed Triple, Sprint & Tiger (97 – 05) ♦	3755
Triumph Triples & Fours (carburetor engines) (91 – 04) ♦	2162
VESPA P/PX125, 150 & 200 Scooters (78 – 12)	0707
Vespa GTS125, 250 & 300 (05 – 10)	4898

Title	Book No
Vespa Scooters (59 – 78)	0126
YAMAHA DT50 & 80 Trail Bikes (78 – 95) ◊	0800
Yamaha T50 & 80 Townmate (83 – 95) ◊	1247
Yamaha YB100 Singles (73 – 91) ◊	0474
Yamaha RS/RXS 100 & 125 Singles (74 – 95)	0331
Yamaha RD & DT125LC (82 – 87) ◊	0887
Yamaha TZR125 (87 – 93) & DT125R (88 – 07) ◊	1655
Yamaha TY50, 80, 125 & 175 (74 – 84) ◊	0464
Yamaha XT & SR125 (82 – 03) ◊	1021
Yamaha YBR125 & XT125R/X (05 – 13)	4797
Yamaha YZF-R125 (08 – 11) ♦	5543
Yamaha Trail Bikes (81 – 00)	2350
Yamaha 2-stroke Motocross Bikes (86 – 06)	2662
Yamaha YZ & WR 4-stroke Motocross Bikes (98 – 08)	2689
Yamaha 250 & 350 Twins (70 – 79)	0040
Yamaha XS250, 360 & 400 sohc Twins (75 – 84)	0378
Yamaha RD250 & 350LC Twins (80 – 82)	0803
Yamaha RD350 YPVS Twins (83 – 95)	1158
Yamaha RD400 Twin (75 – 79)	0333
Yamaha XT, TT & SR500 Singles (75 – 83)	0342
Yamaha XZ550 Vision V-Twins (82 – 85)	0821
Yamaha FJ, FX, XY & YX600 Radian (84 – 92)	2100
Yamaha XT660 & MT-03 (04 – 11) ♦	4910
Yamaha XJ600S (Diversion, Seca II) & XJ600N Fours (92 – 03) ♦	2145
Yamaha YZF600R Thundercat & FZS600 Fazer (96 – 03) ♦	3702
Yamaha FZ-6 Fazer (04 – 07) ♦	4751
Yamaha YZF-R6 (99 – 02) ♦	3900
Yamaha YZF-R6 (03 – 05) ♦	4601
Yamaha YZF-R6 (06 – 13) ♦	5544
Yamaha 650 Twins (70 – 83)	0341
Yamaha XJ650 & 750 Fours (80 – 84)	0738
Yamaha XS750 & 850 Triples (76 – 85)	0340
Yamaha TDM850, TRX850 & XTZ750 (89 – 99) ◊♦	3450
Yamaha YZF750R & YZF1000R Thunderace (93 – 00) ♦	3720
Yamaha FZR600, 750 & 1000 Fours (87 – 96) ♦	2056
Yamaha XV (Virago) V-Twins (81 – 03) ♦	0802
Yamaha XVS650 & 1100 Drag Star/V-Star (97 – 05) ♦	4195
Yamaha XJ900F Fours (83 – 94) ♦	3239
Yamaha XJ900S Diversion (94 – 01) ♦	3739
Yamaha YZF-R1 (98 – 03) ♦	3754
Yamaha YZF-R1 (04 – 06) ♦	4605
Yamaha FZS1000 Fazer (01 – 05) ♦	4287
Yamaha FJ1100 & 1200 Fours (84 – 96) ♦	2057
Yamaha XJR1200 & 1300 (95 – 06) ♦	3981
Yamaha V-Max (85 – 03) ♦	4072
ATV's	
Honda ATC 70, 90, 110, 185 & 200 (71 – on)	0565
Honda Rancher, Recon & TRX250EX ATVs	2553
Honda TRX300 Shaft Drive ATVs (88 – 00)	2125
Honda Foreman (95 – 11)	2465
Honda TRX300EX, TRX400EX & TRX450ER/ER ATVs (93 – 06)	2318
Kawasaki Bayou 220/250/300 & Prairie 300 ATVs (86 – 03)	2351
Polaris ATVs (85 – 97)	2302
Polaris ATVs (98 – 07)	2508
Suzuki/Kawasaki/Artic Cat ATVs (03 – 09)	2910
Yamaha YFS200 Blaster ATV (88 – 06)	2317
Yamaha YFM350 & YFM400 (ER & Big Bear) ATVs (87 – 09)	2126
Yamaha YFZ450 & YFZ450R (04 – 10)	2899
Yamaha Banshee and Warrior ATVs (87 – 10)	2314
Yamaha Kodiak and Grizzly ATVs (93 – 05)	2567
ATV Basics	10450
TECHBOOK SERIES	
Twist and Go (automatic transmission) Scooters Service and Repair Manual	4082
Motorcycle Basics Techbook (2nd edition)	3515
Motorcycle Electrical Techbook (3rd edition)	3471
Motorcycle Fuel Systems Techbook	3514
Motorcycle Maintenance Techbook	4071
Motorcycle Modifying	4272
Motorcycle Workshop Practice Techbook (2nd edition)	3470

◊ = not available in the USA ♦ = Superbike

The manuals on this page are available through good motorcycle dealers and accessory shops.
In case of difficulty, contact: **Haynes Publishing**
(UK) +44 1963 442030   (USA) +1 805 498 6703
(SV) +46 18 124016
(Australia/New Zealand) +61 2 8713 1400

MCL 30.09.13

Preserving Our Motoring Heritage

The Model J Duesenberg Derham Tourster. Only eight of these magnificent cars were ever built – this is the only example to be found outside the United States of America

Almost every car you've ever loved, loathed or desired is gathered under one roof at the Haynes Motor Museum. Over 300 immaculately presented cars and motorbikes represent every aspect of our motoring heritage, from elegant reminders of bygone days, such as the superb Model J Duesenberg to curiosities like the bug-eyed BMW Isetta. There are also many old friends and flames. Perhaps you remember the 1959 Ford Popular that you did your courting in? The magnificent 'Red Collection' is a spectacle of classic sports cars including AC, Alfa Romeo, Austin Healey, Ferrari, Lamborghini, Maserati, MG, Riley, Porsche and Triumph.

A Perfect Day Out

Each and every vehicle at the Haynes Motor Museum has played its part in the history and culture of Motoring. Today, they make a wonderful spectacle and a great day out for all the family. Bring the kids, bring Mum and Dad, but above all bring your camera to capture those golden memories for ever. You will also find an impressive array of motoring memorabilia, a comfortable 70 seat video cinema and one of the most extensive transport book shops in Britain. The Pit Stop Cafe serves everything from a cup of tea to wholesome, home-made meals or, if you prefer, you can enjoy the large picnic area nestled in the beautiful rural surroundings of Somerset.

John Haynes O.B.E., Founder and Chairman of the museum at the wheel of a Haynes Light 12.

The 1936 490cc sohc-engined International Norton – well known for its racing success

The Museum is situated on the A359 Yeovil to Frome road at Sparkford, just off the A303 in Somerset. It is about 40 miles south of Bristol, and 25 minutes drive from the M5 intersection at Taunton.
Open 9.30am - 5.30pm (10.00am - 4.00pm Winter) 7 days a week, *except Christmas Day, Boxing Day and New Years Day*
Special rates available for schools, coach parties and outings Charitable Trust No. 292048